# Beckett's Theaters

# Beckett's Theaters

*Interpretations for Performance*

## Sidney Homan

*Lewisburg*
*Bucknell University Press*
*London and Toronto: Associated University Presses*

© 1984 by Associated University Presses, Inc.


Associated University Presses
440 Forsgate Drive
Cranbury, NJ 08512


Associated University Presses
25 Sicilian Avenue
London WC1A 2QH, England


Associated University Presses
2133 Royal Windsor Drive
Unit 1
Mississauga, Ontario
Canada L5J 1K5


**Library of Congress Cataloging in Publication Data**

Homan, Sidney, 1938–
   Beckett's theaters.

   Includes bibliographical references and index.
   1. Beckett, Samuel, 1906–   —Dramatic production.
2. Beckett, Samuel, 1906–   —Criticism and interpretation.  I. Title.
PR6003.E282Z684  1984     848'.91409     83-45918
ISBN 0-8387-5064-8


Printed in the United States of America

To
Christopher, artist of the book jacket
Elizabeth of the theater
David and Daniel, who will take the stage in good time
And to Norma, as always and ever, my own beloved Maddy Rooney

# Contents

# Preface    Beckett's Aesthetics:
# Theories and Practice

I knew it, on a rock, lashed to a rock, in the midst of silence, its great swell rears towards me, I'm streaming with it, it's an image, those are words, it's a body, it's not I, I knew it wouldn't be I, I'm not outside, I'm inside, I'm in something, I'm shut up, the silence is outside, outside, inside, there is nothing but here, and the silence outside, nothing but this voice and the silence all round, no need of walls, yes, we must have walls, I need walls, good and thick, I need a prison, I was right, for me alone, I'll go there now, I'll put me in it, I'm there already, I'll start looking for me now, I'm there somewhere, it won't be I, no matter, I'll say it's I, perhaps it will be I, perhaps that's all they're waiting for, there they are again, to give me quittance, waiting for me to say I'm someone, to say I'm somewhere, to put me out, into the silence, I see nothing, it's because there is nothing, or it's because I have no eyes, or both, that makes three possibilities, to choose from, but do I really see nothing, it's not the moment to tell a lie. . . .[1]

One could almost pick at random any passage from *The Unnamable* and come up with an aesthetic statement—on the character's part, if not Beckett's—as thorough as the passage above. Indeed, there is nothing obscure about Beckett's aesthetic principles. *The Unnamable*'s nonstop prose, however convoluted and neurotic, is also cleanly divided into sections that, taken as a whole, stand as a sort of impassioned *apologia* for what has properly been called Beckett's "art of the microcosm": the moment of revelation; the narrator's silence against the counterpart of the sea's swell (a moment also recorded by Krapp on his tape); the scorn of language for being at once the only vehicle and therefore the only inadequate vehicle for revealing this microcosm (not of the public man, it should be noted, but rather of the "inner man"); the inside-outside dichotomy that Beckett inherits from pessimistic medieval philosophers as well as from Descartes; the obsession with the silence of both the discredited external world and one's own incomprehensible inner world; the contradictory need for form ("walls") to contain what is mysterious, formless, and ultimately unfathomable; the narrator's self-consciousness or the narrator/narrated ("I'll put me in it"); the goal of self-knowledge coupled with the powerful qualification that such self-knowledge may be nothing more than a self-portrait, with all the fraudulence, both actual and psychological, implied by the word *portrait;* the relapse into habit and well-worn concepts as a ways of making sense of the external world, or—more accurately—pumping it with meaning (the Unnamable's "three possibilities" link him with other systems-analysts in Beckett, such as Moran and Watt); and, finally, the second revelation, in the form of a question, that there is nothing to see, along with the insistence on telling the truth, on not wanting to act as if there were, absolutely, something there.

Again, there seems nothing particularly obscure about Beckett's aesthetic principles, no matter how idiosyncratic, perhaps even crabbed, unworkable, or even displeasing they may appear to some. Beckett announces his aesthetics all the time, both in fiction and nonfiction; he almost seems evangelical about the issue. If there *is* obscurity in Beckett, it is thematic, I think, not aesthetic. As the Unnamable says, "No, all is not clear. But the discourse must go on. So one invents obscurities."[2] If we think of Beckett's announced aesthetics as a clean, efficient knife, as No's knife, if you will, still the object of the artist's search, that inside world, is itself obscure, contradictory, comprehensible enough on the surface of society, habit, time, and concepts (even metaphysics, for which Beckett has little taste), but incomprehensible and, therefore, "unsayable" below the surface, within the world's most celebrated microcosm, man himself. And it is man that alone interests Beckett: no Wordsworthian nature for him, except to mock it in short stories such as "Love and Lethe"; no mania to untangle the complex threads of the public world as there was for his friend Joyce; no sociological or political interests. When a few years ago Beckett, along with two prominent Frenchmen, sent a congratulatory telegram to a chess player who had defected from the Soviet Union, the potential political overtones of that telegram seemed strangely out of place for the playwright, and one suspects it was the chess game itself, and not politics, that prompted the correspondence.

The stories themselves may be so complex in meaning, or potential meanings, that we would wish for a little more guidance. Beckett's well-known response to the question "Who is Godot?" ought to suffice here to demonstrate the enormity of the problem, of the problem, that is, when we try to impose a thematic schema on his works.

And if it is not the actual stories, it is the language itself, the double-edged inheritance from the external world of concepts and time, that presents problems, chained as language is to the "assumption"—the title of one of Beckett's first short stories as well—that the external world exists, that it has "real" objects, principles of organization that are somehow "caught" in words. Thus as early as "Poetry is Vertical," the manifesto to which Beckett put his signature in 1932, we find him calling for a "revolutionary attitude toward word and syntax," and for a "hermetic language" to replace an impossible existing language.[3]

But, again, the aesthetic principles—at least as they exist independently from the works—are clear, and we will find them announced and re-phrased and qualified in a variety of sources: Beckett's direct writings on aesthetic issues, such as "Poetry is Vertical" or conversations on the subject recorded by Beckett scholars and now assembled in Deirdre Bair's biography of the artist;[4] critical essays and book reviews, such as the "Three Dialogues with Georges Duthuit" or the reviews of work by Rilke, O'Casey, MacGreevy, Pound, Denis Devlin, and, especially, Jack Yeats; "indirect" writings, such as Beckett's book on Proust (at once a fine scholarly study of Proust and, at the same time, an announcement, subject to change of course, of things to come in Beckett); and the works themselves, as evidenced by the passage quoted above from *The Unnamable.*

Yet even these principles are somewhat clouded by the diverse sources of Beckett's aesthetics. For Beckett seems eclectic, if nothing else, when we examine the springs of his discontent with the external world as well as the resulting aesthetics of an art designed at once to defy that world and at the same time to "excavate"[5] the buried "world" with what Frederick Hoffman has rightly called the "Language of Self."[6] Along with the general debt to the existentialists, Beckett seems especially influenced by: Descartes, of course, whose coldly deterministic world as delineated by mathematics sprang from his distrust of the senses' ability to verify reality; Vico, a "mystic that rejects the transcendental in every shape and form,"[7] thereby disputing any notion that the individual, even if he be alone, an island unto himself, is still watched and therefore ratified by an all-seeing God; Geulincx, who championed what we might call today "self-actualization," the cultivation of one's private self regardless of, indeed in defiance of the world outside; Malebranche, who could not accept the basic premise that the physical world exists; Bishop Berkeley, whose idea that one's reality was dependent on one's being perceived attracted Beckett, but whose complementary notion that a benevolent God was doing the perceiving proved unacceptable; and Schopenhauer, who advocated silencing the individual will, and whose irrationalist approach to philosophy and more specific attack on Augustine were compatible with what might be called Beckett's pessimism or, better yet, realism.[8] To these varied sources, which often tend to contradict each other or from which Beckett extracts principles even while disagreeing with what are often their more significant tenets, one must add numerous other thinkers and artists, many of whom Beckett met while in his early scholarly career. There are also numerous literary influences, with Dante and Shakespeare at the top of the list.

As much as schemas for Beckett's aesthetics smack of both the abstractionism and categorization that he himself at once employs and despises, perhaps there is a balanced position or "calm" (to use a favorite word) between exclusive ordering and terrifyingly inclusive chaos. It might be well, then, to put down in logical order the components, as I see them, of Beckett's aesthetics, though one must remember that his is not an aesthetics formulated in any standard way.

**i**

Beckett starts with a clear rejection of the external world, doubting that it has substantiality, let alone meaning. In this regard he follows the existentialists, who had eroded that world fashioned by the rational positivists and, earlier, by the empiricists. Rejecting that external world, he also rejects any notion of a divinity, dismissing the reader in "Text 12" as one who alone might "need" a god, "unwitnessed witness of witnesses."[9] The small comfort is that as he rejects the external world and is subsequently exposed to both the "threat" and the "beauty" of its opposite,[10] that internal world, Beckett finds a weak justification for faith in the "nature outside" in that it may be "compensating for the nature inside."[11] Still, that nature outside is rejected not only because of his lack of faith, but also because of Beckett's own assessment of what passes as everyday reality, especially everyday reality for an Irishman who, in the tradition of Joyce and other countrymen, faults the world for imposing its system on him. One of Beckett's first social essays is a diatribe against Ireland for censoring both the physical life (through stringent regulations against birth control) and the artistic life (through its censorship).[12] Society only satisfies needs it defines, needs that evaporate once the notion of society and the concomitant outside world is rejected. Art at least brings one into confrontation with real needs, even though these needs cannot be satisfied. The dichotomy asserts itself: outside, false needs are defined and satisfied; inside, real needs are confronted yet remain unsatisfied. In "Imagination Dead Imagine" the dichotomy is put in a way reminiscent of Robert Frost: there is "the stress of that storm, or of a worse [interior] storm."[13]

The internal world, the inner macrocosm, is the alternative to this discredited outer world, and this deeper world asserts itself whenever we feel an "obscure internal tension."[14] Below the surface there is a "mystery,"[15] a world where things "don't exist, or only exist elsewhere."[16] If the world so established in the imagination resembles the external world, it is only an illusion: the sky is not a normal sky but rather a "strange sky." More often, the world is that of "a strange room,"[17] the tomb-womb-room of the mind. "We are alone. We cannot know and we cannot be known"[18]—here is the dilemma stated most graphically. It is a sad reality, one particularly akin to suffering, and Beckett observes in *Proust* that suffering "opens a window on the real and is the main condition of the artistic experience."[19] Here is the realm of true Being; Beckett's art, therefore, is an attempt "to let Being into art."[20] Against the noise of the external world is the *silent noise* of this internal world; only the oxymoron can capture the paradox of thinking of the interior world with the vocabulary and concepts of the discredited external world. In Beckett's early short story "Assumption" the would-be artist fails precisely because he can't "whisper the turmoil down" in others;[21] nor can he avoid that interior turmoil in himself. Stuck with the internal world as our only reality, we are all alone, individuals, not members of any collective, or any society; we exist "between two parting dreams, knowing none, known of none."[22] Love, friendship—these bind us to the outside reality and are, as Murphy demonstrates, incompatible with the artistic or self-reflective temperament.

There is a fairly specific "geography" of this interior world, and it is perhaps best described in the early novel *Murphy*. Not even deigning to describe any reality outside the mind, Murphy divides his own mind into three zones—or Beckett does it for him.[23] The "light" zone of the mind contains "forms with parallel" in the real world: the physical dog implies a conceptual "dog" in the mind. Here one indulges in illusory physical equivalents of reality: in this light zone Murphy can imagine Ticklepenny raping Miss Carridge. Here the "physical fiasco" of reality is witnessed and is recreated as a "howling success." In the "half-light" zone parallels with reality fall away; this is the realm of abstraction, contemplation, a self-indulgent world without any obligation to the exterior. But the true realm, the third and the only "real" realm, is the "dark." Composed neither of elements nor of states, this dark zone is one of endlessly shifting forms, the shifting itself having no ethical, let alone philosophical consequence. Here is the point of calm, stillness, and, yes, silence, where Murphy is a "mote in the dark of absolute freedom." This is the core of all cores—nothingness. Mr. Endon is nothing but this third, dark zone, and when Murphy gazes into the schizophrenic's eyes he finds himself but a "speck" in Endon's "unseen."[24] Endon himself is perceived but does not himself perceive—that is, does not acknowledge any world outside himself. In "Text 13" the trinity of zones is restated as: "how things were before"; "a moment free in dream of days and nights"; "here, all memory gone."[25]

In our normal sense of the word, this is a world that cannot be understood, for all concepts we possess are derived from an external world that has nothing in common with the third, dark zone. In this realm beyond logic we are caught between two absolute realities, though the external one is merely the illusion of a reality, propped up, as it is, by all people given to abstractions, by all those who insist there be some correspondence and, beyond correspondence, some "trade-off" between perceiving and being, between the physical and some Platonic "real." "But [there is] nothing to signify"[26]; and when Beckett says his work is "noises signifying nothing"[27] he means that it signifies everything of consequence, even though the quest for this everything is ultimately futile. There is *something,* though the signification cannot be translated outside the individual realm. In this third zone, where all is "nothing" (as long as we defined "something" by the external reality in which Pozzo and Watt, for example, put their trust), *"Nothing is more real than nothing."*[28] Little wonder that Beckett distrusts, indeed scorns philosophers, metaphysicians, and perhaps literary critics devising schemas for his work and finding in the plays a simple point-by-point allegory for their own reality. Beckett warns, "no symbols where none intended."[29] Lawrence Harvey offers an interesting list, a sort of capsule holding the issues and areas of human inquiry that Beckett finds irrelevant or beneath the dignity of a real artist: national and more generally public matters; the love of women and, perhaps, that inspiration stemming from the literary tradition; social causes; the problem of evil and suffering innocence; questions of sexuality and sterility; other human beings; the things of time; and finally, the search itself.[30] We "need" the external world, but it cannot satisfy that need. Illusions cannot be "actualized"—to use the jargon of planners—though as Hamlet knows when speaking to Rosencrantz and Guildenstern, they ("dreams" in Hamlet's terms) can be the object of a lifetime search.

However, balance is everywhere in Beckett. If the artist moves toward the third zone and, at the same time, toward the silence and ultimate negation, that ablation of desire it promises, toward the rejection (escape, exile, expulsion from—to echo the titles of the short stories) of the external world, he also never reaches that "dark" zone. In trying to speak of nothing "as though it were something,"[31] the artist only confirms the external world by using its vocabulary or—to put it another way—by his inability to abandon what he knows must be abandoned. He can never escape from a would-be abandoned work, and, conversely, all his own work, his art, is "abandoned" in the sense of being unfulfilled, incomplete—inauthentic. Metaphysics, any attempt to bridge the seen with the unseen (let alone with the ultimately unknowable), is rejected in this equation. Trying to make that bridge, compelled to make that impossible bridge because it is his only option, the artist is something of an absurd figure. The Unnamable thus describes himself: "I who am on my way, words bellying out my sails, am also that unthinkable ancestor of whom nothing can be said."[32] What frustration! And to complicate matters, there is no audience; this is the very problem for the Unnamable, who worries if he is even being heard or seen, or both. Giving form and the subsequent witness to the third zone is a purely individual effort. With the audience at best a "peripheral" concern,[33] the only possible audience is the narrator himself.

Again, words are the problem here, and Beckett, as John Pilling points out, seems particularly indebted to the German philosopher Mauthner, whose call for a criticism of language is based on the argument that there is " 'no thinking without speaking,' and since, when we speak, there is no distinguishing between the report and that which it is supposed to be a report of . . . we are continually uttering meaningless statements."[34] In this sense, is Watt's destruction of syntax at the end of his novel any less or any more meaningful than his rigid attempts earlier to make sense of Knott's world? Given the problem with words, to be an artist "is to fail, as no other dare fail:"[35] "The expression that there is nothing to express, nothing with which to express, nothing from which to express, no power to express, no desire to express, together with the obligation to express."[36] Little wonder that the artists in Beckett—and they are legion—get "very tired of one's toil, very tired of one's quill."[37]

The most competent way—though all ways are, ultimately, futile—of conveying this inner world, stretching from the logical mind through the half-light zone to that of absolute freedom, is through the "involuntary memory," a device best defined in Beckett's study of Proust. This involuntary memory, it should be noted, is not to be confused with "voluntary memory,"[38] that function of the intellect which acts like a concordance to the Old Testament, making connections between past and present for the purposes of historicity or philosophy. Here is a memory, in effect, that is nothing more than the servant of time and of the concepts of time. This lower function is ultimately a memory chained to consciousness, and is therefore exclusive.

The involuntary memory, on the other hand, has nothing to do with the logic or time-sequences of reality. It is unconscious, immediate, unplanned; it not only recreates the past object or experience, but also encompasses the whole "mystery" of the past, informing the present with that mystery. Even as the past and the future are not separate entities for Hamlet, even as for him alone *The Murder of Gonzago* is at once the present-tense recreation of a past event (the regicide) and also a present-tense creation of the future (Claudius's own execution), so for Beckett, I believe, the involuntary memory, by overriding time, by refusing any categorical imperatives, by being mysterious, inclusive, is "explosive," capable of being "possessive," that is, of allowing for complete identification of object and subject.[39] Caught in the moment, we cannot understand the moment's full ramifications. Nor can we understand that the moment—the experience, the house, the person who holds our hand, the tragedy, or the comedy—is only an illusion, triply so since it happens in the external world, is not perceived in the same fashion by any two people, and—no less important—is caught in time. It comes and goes, and there can be no "truth" in such impermanence. "Memories are killing"[40] in the historical novel, or the naturalistic novel, in any art form that pretends to embody the past. Such recreation only cements time's hold on us.

However, when the involuntary memory is properly exercised, when the artist, relaxed, *calm*, contemplates the inner, dark zone both of his present state and of that present state in the matrix of experiences from times remembered, then we have the chance—Beckett says there are roughly a dozen such moments in Proust—for the "identification of immediate with past experience, the recurrence of past action or reaction in the present." And this "amounts to a participation between the ideal and real, imagination and direction apprehension, symbol and substance."[41] This moment frees the artist and, by implication, the reader from the unreality of both the contemplative (zone two) and the active life (zone one, as it impinges on the external world). The art work so resulting offers us an experience that "is at once imaginative and empirical, at once an evocation and a direct perception, real without being merely actual, ideal wihout being merely abstract, the ideal real, the essential, the extratemporal."[42]

Time, therefore, is both "destructive" and "creative,"[43] though it is destructive only if the artist—such as metaphysical poets, satirists, or social commentators disguised as poets—conceives of his work as documenting or "capturing" time, or as speaking of the present in those conceptual terms wrested from the past. How far this notion is from Sir Philip Sidney's praise of the poet as the ideal historian! Style for Beckett beomes not only inseparable from substance (the point he made in "Dante . . . Bruno. Vico. . Joyce"[44]) but is, properly, to be equated with vision: how one goes about the work of art is its meaning. The method and not the medium is the message—albeit here a sobering message for anyone trusting in the substantiality of that world ruled by time.

Again, the villain here, as well as the savior, is time, and Beckett offers two ways to "deal" with time. One is through that "involuntary memory"; the other is through "habit," an all-purpose word for Beckett that includes habits both physical and mental. Through habit we try to fill up our days with routines, paradigms, scenarios so that we can implant order, perhaps even meaning on existence. The problem, of course, is that all such attempts are based on illusion, on a fallacy. Corporate order is even more heinous than individual efforts, since even one extra person in the social contract only increases that illusory "content." To avoid the trap of this reality where "every instant / spills in the void the ignorance of having been,"[45] one abandons habit in all its forms, and cultivates, not so surprisingly, "simple feeling"[46] geared to the "mood of the moment."[47] One consciously avoids systems, prerequisites, thereby ablating the desire for the external world. The period of transition in moving from one world to the other is, to be sure, "perilous," but also "mysterious and fertile."[48]

Proust was the optimist, believing that through the exercise of involuntary memory one could—artist and spectator alike—*reinvest* a time-tormented present with greater meaning, as past events in their essence, their deepest reality, informed and thereby invigorated the moment. With such optimism Beckett parts company. For him the journey through involuntary memory and the subsequently negative context it provides for the physical, visible reality do not lead to a brave new world where essence is no less manifest than existence. Rather, for Beckett the search leads to the realization that "there is nothing,"[49] that it is all playing, "cantering" as Vladimir and Estragon would have it, that at the very center of our being is nothing: "Fortunately it's all a dream," as the Unnamable says.[50]

Little wonder that Vico's "negative mysticism" attracted Beckett. Not only do we find this nothingness, but in finding it we also prepare for "The final disintegration of the 'I' in the creative act."[51] Descartes's *cogito ergo sum* becomes *cogito ergo non sum*. This is our "unthinkable end."[52] Still, I find this conclusion heroic, perhaps even romantic, and not pessimistic on Beckett's part: "to know you are beyond knowing anything, that is when peace enters in."[53] Only if this conclusion were a simple one, only if the journey to it were effortless, could we accuse Beckett of despair, cowardice. Vladimir and Estragon don't take suicide lightly, but then the inadequate rope and tree also inhibit them. Even for Beckett's clowns, to reach nonbeing, silence, is at once difficult *and* impossible. The dichotomy reasserts itself once more: on one hand, the uncertainties of physical existence; on the other, the return to calm, before life as we know it, before civilization. Yet we can never reach this state, since it can be conveyed only by words. We can try. We have no choice but to try: none of the Beckett artists can give up on their task, let alone on life. "Ping," the work that moves closest to the ideal, still ends with "ping silence ping over," and I take "over" as "start it over," "begin again."

ii

When we abstract Beckett's aesthetics in this fashion, we must also make several qualifications, especially before we attempt to speak of the aesthetic or—if I may now transpose that word—*metadramatic* principles manifest in his work for the various "theaters." The artist is not, necessarily, an unqualified commentator, either on his own work or on the aesthetic principles underlining that work. I do not mean to propose here an artist of the unconscious but rather only to recognize that he or she is not a disinterested party.

There is an extraordinary moment in *Hamlet* where Claudius, angered by Hamlet's sarcastic response ("You cannot feed capons so") to his formal "How fares our cousin Hamlet?," dismisses the Prince's dialogue with "These words are not mine"—that is, as long as you talk in this fashion, I won't engage in dialogue (3.2.90–95). Hamlet's reply is the cryptic "No, nor mine now," a line I take as meaning: and the words I speak are not mine (they came from the playwright), nor, once I have said them, are they mine since the audience is their newest owner, making of them what it will. Perhaps the same "passing of the ball" occurs among Beckett, his characters, and, at length, his audiences.

In addition, the sources by which we might formulate Beckett's aesthetics are too varied. The *Proust* book is more about Proust and a better book than many would believe, but it is still Proust through Beckett or, if you will, Beckett through Proust. Either way the work cannot be taken as doctrine, or at least as doctrine that will find its way unchanged in the plays. And book reviews of friends' works are by definition suspect: at the very least, Beckett may be pleading his cause through another; at most he may be assimilating another's aesthetic principles in the interests of championing a fellow artist.

Most important, aesthetic principles so abstracted are not the same thing as aesthetic principles operating within a work of art. Nor is my concern here with Beckett's aesthetic theory as a thing in itself. I propose, instead, to look at his plays for the legitimate theater, radio, television, and the cinema from what we may properly call a metadramatic perspective. That is, my focus is on the self-reflective nature of his theater, and the imagery I will be looking at most closely is that based on anything within the gamut of our theatrical experience: the playwright, his craft, the physical theater, the theater itself as a metaphor, actors, the concept of dialogue, metaphor or simile, the audience, and, most important, the energies generated among that trinity of playwright, actor, and audience in sustaining a meaningful illusion on stage. I am concerned ultimately with what is "HERE,"[54] with what happens as the play is being performed. Hence the book's subtitle, "Interpretations for Performance," and since I am writing about such performance before an English-speaking audience, I have confined my study to the English texts of the plays that are readily available, as well as to the scholarship and criticism on Beckett, with a few notable exceptions, in that language. Actually, the original subtitle was to have been "A Metadramatic Approach," but it was a thoughtful reader for Bucknell University Press who showed me that mine was really "performance criticism." Since metadramatic criticism is also concerned with the play as enacted, perhaps it may be said to be a more theoretical expression of such performance criticism. An example from Shakespeare may illustrate how this metadramatic approach can be used.

### iii

There is a scene in *Antony and Cleopatra* that seems to charm even the queen's many detractors, even those critics who see her as some sort of female Vice seducing Antony from his rightful place in Rome.[55] It is Cleopatra's death scene (act 5, sc. 2), and it is literally a "scene" because this is how Cleopatra thinks of it, wearing both her robe and crown to signify the uniqueness of the occasion. The clown, confused as to why a woman would request a basket of asps, has just departed. With his leering rejoinder, "I wish you joy o' th' worm," he may stand for that uncomprehending world, the unimaginative Rome for whom the queen is nothing more than the stimulus for a phallic joke. Then, as Cleopatra takes the asp to her breast something extraordinary happens. By the force of her vision she metamorphoses the disgusting serpent, still dripping the "slime and ooze" (2.7.23) from its bed in the Nile, into a lover. The first bite becomes "a lover's pinch, / Which hurts, and is desired" (5.2.295–96). Fourteen lines later Cleopatra, by her alchemy, changes a second asp into a baby nursed at her breast. Applying another asp to her arm she calls it Antony. In this manner a gruesome occasion is transformed into the rather homey picture of a mother embracing her husband and their sleeping child feeding at her breast. If just for a moment, something base and ugly has become something symbolic and lovely.

There are, of course, thematic reasons for Cleopatra's metaphoric encounter with the asp. Moments later the Roman conquerors come on stage and in an almost obscene clinical detachment notice the "vent" of blood on Cleopatra's chest, after searching for more obvious signs of her death. Then they spot the mud that the unclean serpent has dragged over the "tawny front" (1.1.6) of the Egyptian. For them the manner of death only justifies their assessment of her character.

This encounter, however, also marks a moment when the theater turns to itself. Here Cleopatra triumphs with bad material in a way that parallels Shakespeare's own achievement in suggesting highly sensual femininity with what, on the stage of the Globe, would most probably be enacted by an older boy actor. She is an artist, one given to metamorphosis no less than her playwright. Properly done, the role of Shakespeare's Cleopatra represents the epitome of mature, amoral sexual love. Surely it dwarfs the portrait in the film version of the Cleopatra story starring Claudette Colbert, complete with fans discreetly hiding the lovers during climax and the phallic beating of the ship's oars. Earlier in the play the actor playing the queen has reminded us of the painful reality behind the stage impersonation when Cleopatra fears that, if she compromises with Octavius and follows him to Rome, she will be parodied on stage. Her prediction is that Antony will be reduced to the caricature of a drunkard, while "Some squeaking Cleopatra [will] boy [her] greatness" (5.2.220). Though lacking the thousands of Nubian slaves, special effects, panoramic sweeps of the countryside, pliant actors, and so forth that were available to the De Milles of Hollywood, Shakespeare's modest company worked with the "essence" of splendor, sexuality, and drama, rather than with its physical verification. They did so not with money or scrupulous attention to "historic detail," but only with talent and with what I suggest is a use of the theater itself as metaphor. It is, I believe, the metadramatic approach that is peculiarly sensitive to performance.

### iv

The approach, however, can all too easily be abused, and when this happens, the resulting "play" becomes a warehouse of aesthetic commentary, or a manifesto for the playwright, or at worst a happy hunting ground for the critic alert to every moment when characters deliver a sort of aesthetic in-joke to a too-knowing audience. I am not concerned with the aesthetic dimension, the play's metadramatic nature, as something in itself, but rather as a way of approaching the "world" of play for interpretation, even if that world ultimately be the creation of the individual critic. No harm here: criticism is surely a matter of the marketplace, with the critic offering up his wares and the reader buying or not buying, or buying with qualifications.

Yet this approach does confirm the essential *immediacy* and the *democracy* of these images based on the theatrical experience, for aesthetic metaphors take no prior orientation on the audience's part: they come out of, indeed are born out of (as is Madame Pace in Pirandello's *Six Characters in Search of an Author*) our immediate experience with the play. The play so approached has the least possible distance between style and content: the play is about the artistic experience, but that experience itself is at once a literal and an allegorical imitation of the experiences in life outside the play—or, with a bow to Beckett, an imitation of the inner and real experience of the human psyche, be its zone light, half-light, or dark.

Indeed, this lack of separation between what is said (thematics) and how

it is being said (aesthetics) is precisely the quality that Beckett most celebrates in his essay on Joyce. In addition, the metadramatic approach "goes"
with whatever theatrical metaphors exist in the play; it can come at the
play, I would argue, with a minimum of preconceptions or prerequisites:
the play is not examined to illuminate history, or to ratify contemporary
philosophy, or to find its place in a larger pattern of the playwright's
"major themes." These latter approaches are, of course, no less valid, but
since they consider the play from the outside or at least initially on grounds
other than the immediate theatrical experience, they can be distinguished
from a metadramatic approach. At best, that approach is a loose system
based on the response of the critic playing the dual but complementary
roles of person in the macrocosm (reality) and audience of one of the
microcosm (the theater).[56] Of course the play makes a thematic statement
about the world outside the theater (or in Beckett's case, the unseen world
inside the perceiver) and thereby uses material from that outside world to
sustain a stage illusion. But in the some twenty years since the publication
of Lionel Abel's *Metatheatre: A New View of Dramatic Form,* we know that the
play has its own integrity, and creates its own world of "materials" for
metaphors to assist in sustaining that illusion. Yet this seeming independence from life is, on closer inspection, actually an *imitation,* and indeed a
commentary through the theater's own workings, its metadramatics, no less
substantial than that generated by thematic or historical criticism. Nor were
the existentialists the first to suggest that life itself is a play, that all the
world's a stage.

The metadramatic approach, then, is loose, drawing on metaphors
generated by a variety of elements in the theater; but its object is "tight": a
reading of the play on the very terms by which it operates. Listen to Beckett
himself inveigh against critics, or spectators for that matter, who would
separate form from content, or metadramatics from thematics:

> if you don't understand it, Ladies and Gentlemen, it is because you are
> too decadent to receive it. You are not satisfied unless form is so strictly
> divorced from content that you can comprehend the one without almost
> bothering to read the other. . . . Here form is content, content is form.[57]

This metadramatic method can be applied, I would think, to any playwright since every playwright, consciously or unconsciously, must have
some aesthetic principles, some reason for choosing the medium of the
theater. It is inevitable that one of the most fertile grounds for metaphor is
the play itself. We are "present" for a play in a way that we cannot be
"present" for a poem or a novel. Beckett himself, perhaps even more than
most modern playwrights, seems concerned with this immediate metadramatic dimension: from Hamm's self-conscious theatricality ("Me to
play") to works such as *Cascando* and *Words and Music* that are, in effect,
abstract presentations of the artist at work, not to mention the actor and
audience who must piece those plays together. When the three characters

in *Play* or in *Come and Go* face the audience, we are seeing the ultimate in metadrama: ourselves, an audience observing an audience.

v

Some personal experiences have reinforced this notion that the theater, at the high level practiced by Beckett, *turns to itself*, to that trinity of play-wright, actor, and audience as the basis for its metaphor that imitates and thereby comments on the world outside the playhouse. Over the last eight years I have tried, with the help of my students, to work as an actor and director in Beckett's plays for all four media. The tired dialogue on campus soon became: "Looks like Homan's giving another seminar in playing Beckett?" "You mean to say, he's making his way again through the Beckett canon—thank goodness it isn't Shakespeare." I have also experienced Beckett's plays with two professional theater companies: Bacchus Productions and the Hippodrome Theater.[58]

Several years ago Bacchus Productions received a grant from the Florida Endowment for the Humanities to take a production of *Waiting for Godot* to ten Florida state prisons. By chance we had performed, as sort of a "public service," at Florida State Prison, the state's maximum-security prison. The response from the inmates was extraordinary; they were the most eloquent, passionate, productive audience we had ever known. They shouted up comments and questions to Vladimir and Estragon, asked Pozzo to step forward to explain himself, curiously berated Lucky in his downtrodden state, all the while talking with actors onstage as easily as they talked to each other offstage. With little or no theatrical orientation, not having learned the stultifying etiquette that often characterizes Broadway, the inmates assumed that *Godot* was just another experience, a "happening" in which they had no need to remain passive. In 1957, after *Godot* had failed with polite audiences in Miami and later in New York, the Actor's Workshop took the play to San Quentin Prison and there received the same wonderful reception that almost twenty years later we would experience at all ten Florida state prisons.

One night in particular stands out. We had played at a moderate-security prison on the Gulf Coast. It was two in the morning and we were still excited from the performance as well as from long conversations afterward with the inmates and later with the warden and his staff. Once those con-versations were over, we were led by a phalanx of guards from the au-ditorium and across the gravel-lined prison yard, with cold yellow searchlights glaring down on us. On the opposite side we could just make out the dark outlines of the dormitory-style cell blocks. As we neared the entrance gate a most extraordinary thing happened. In violation of the curfew regulations, the prisoners suddenly flung open their windows and began calling out goodnights from the opposite side of the yard. I heard a familiar voice across the darkness, the heavy Brooklyn accent of one inmate who, because of transfers, had seen our *Godot* in three separate prisons: "Hey, Sid, that Beckett fellow—he wrote a thing called *Endgame,* didn't he?" I shouted back, "Yes, *yes* he did," glad to talk with a true Beckett fan. "Well, listen buddy, you bring that *Endgame* here tomorrow night—you hear?" I knew what he meant: for him the theater was so inseparable from life, so much a part of his own existence as he waited for his personal Godot, just as Didi and Gogo waited for theirs, that of course actors didn't need to rehearse this second Beckett play, and of course we could bring it tomorrow as easily as we could bring ourselves. For my Brooklyn friend, for this unique, precious audience, the theater was nothing more than acting and talking. It didn't matter to him whether one did that on the stage or on the world's stage.

More recently, I have "learned" about Beckett, and about the relation between stage characters and the audience, by directing the playlet *Come and Go* under somewhat unusual circumstances. A few years ago I received a call from a friend who was organizing a conference composed of industrialists and those people associated with industry who deal with physical and emotional problems of employees. The two-day conference in Orlando would consist of practical, serious reports from people involved with employee morale, drinking problems, relations with employers, and programs designed to increase employee stability and hence their productivity. But could I bring something involving the theater to this conference, at very least as a change of pace from the regular agenda? I impulsively volunteered Beckett and the only play I had on hand—*Come and Go.* I also pretentiously titled my presentation: "Finding the Self through a Performance of Beckett's *Come and Go.*" A favor for a friend—that was certain. Yet at worst I was "responsible" for only one hour on the Saturday night of the conference, after which my wife and I could retire to our conference-paid hotel room and there dine on our conference-paid dinner.

That night, as I greeted my "audience," I was panic-stricken with a feeling very much like that experienced when I first saw the inmates, even though this audience, in terms of social and professional success, was at the opposite pole from the residents of Florida State Prison. Again I was a victim of my own ignorance and prejudices. They had just finished a banquet, the culmination of two grueling days of a conference where, as I learned later, there was considerable tension among the participants. As I chatted with them, I thought: these people don't care about such an illusive thing as theater, much less about a playwright like Beckett; my part of the evening is going to be a flop. Putting on an actor's face—one of the most shallow and painfully pleasant expressions I had ever mustered—I asked for three women volunteers from the audience to play the parts of Flo, Vi, and Ru. I was surprised: more than three volunteers raced to the podium and I had a happy choice. We then "did" *Come and Go* three times for the conference participants: first, a straight reading, just to familiarize everyone, actresses included, with the lines; then a rehearsal, complete with

Beckett's exacting stage directions; and at last, a little performance, though
the actresses were allowed to stay on-book. Now came the hard part: audience discussion. I thanked the actresses and then announced to the group:
"I want you to think about the play, about what it means to you. I'm going
to leave this room for ten minutes, and walk about the hotel. When I come
back I would be tremendously interested in what you have to say." I made
my exit, my stomach in a foul mood: would they have anything to say,
especially about a play that even the Beckett scholars have given little
attention? I did have an emergency plan: if, when I reentered the banquet
room, I saw that they would not be up to formal discussion from the tables,
I would announce that we could convene informally over coffee at the rear
of the room. Surely only those who had something to say and wanted to say
it would join me. Yet despite the contingency plan I spent ten wretched
minutes walking about a strange hotel in Orlando, with a large audience
waiting, waiting for me and my "guest," this obscure dramaticule by a
playwright who, it is said, never even stays around to see performances of
his own plays.

The ten minutes were up. Stomach in hand, I returned to the banquet
room. What a fantastic surprise! The moment I entered the door I knew by
the faces (indeed, by the hands that were raised before I said a word) that
this audience would not have to break for coffee, that we would be able to
*talk* about *Come and Go*. And talk they did. The audience worked with that
last line, with the "rings," with the names of the three characters, with the
two-part structure, with the play's conscious violation of the laws of the
theater. They did all this in a very personal way, easily on a level with that
of our inmates. For the inmates *Godot* recreated the very problem of their
existence: what significance does life have, or can it have, when we have no
assurance of goals (no firm notion of Godot) but only the "nongoal" of
waiting without purpose, or at least without apparent purpose? For these
industrialists and for these professionals involved in rehabilitating others,
*Come and Go* raised an equally basic question: how do we square the past
with the present, all those things that haven't happened with all those
things that are still possibilities, however dim? Two hours later, after exchanging many kisses and sharing many variations of "Hope we can see
each other again" with that audience, my wife and I retired to our hotel
room, forgetting to order that free meal, sitting in a silence that reminded
me very much of those silences that occurred upon returning to Gainesville
from the prisons. I like to think that this was not an inappropriate response
for a playwright for whom silence is the end of our existence and for whom
dialogue, no matter how pathetic, is our human and, if I may add, romantic
ways of containing the horrible truth.

I have also tried the play using three elderly women as the characters. As
the opening event for a three-day comparative drama conference held on
this campus, I asked seven senior citizens from Gainvesville to join me on
stage, three playing the parts of Flo, Vi, and Ru, the other four later
forming with them an onstage audience with whom I could discuss *Come*

*and Go.* The "real" audience, on this occasion, were some two hundred scholars and teachers visiting the campus, along with a large number of students, mostly undergraduates. I was—shamelessly—cutting things close: senior citizens talking about a play about senior citizens played by senior citizens. Pirandello revisited! The evening followed the pattern of my experience in Orlando: a reading, a rehearsal, and finally a miniature production. I then began talking with my seven guests, who were fully at home onstage, chatting with me as if no one were staring at them from the audience. After some conversation—very beautiful conversation, I might add, with the onstage audience offering a variety of interpretations about just where the characters "were," about what the linking of hands meant—I invited the offstage audience to join the conversation. They did, and the resulting conversation was equally touching and perceptive. Indeed, as the discussions wore on, a very special friendship developed between those senior citizens and, particularly, the undergraduates in the audience.

Students and inmates—is there a connection here?—and senior citizens and those professionals involved daily with raw human problems, those who have seen or are seeing enough of human "realities"—these were the people in Florida who responded to Beckett, who had much to say, who, in a word, *taught* me. He may not be a playwright of the people in the way Shakespeare is. Still, Beckett, I think, if not of the people generally, *dramatizes* the people generally, in the form of the two tramps of *Godot* and the three old ladies of *Come and Go.*

## vi

If this were a survey or a historical study of Beckett's work in the theater, then some time would be devoted to his youthful adaptation of Corneille's *Le Cid,* and to a larger work such as *Eleutheria,* written in 1947 and an early, if aborted announcement of some major issues in later plays. However, there is, surely, adequate commentary elsewhere on these plays.[60] My intent, again, is to deal with Beckett's work in English that *does exist* in repertory, that is here and now: "For what I tell this evening is passing this evening, at this passing hour."[61]

Because the study springs from a personal encounter with Beckett, I have for the most part talked about the Beckett critics and scholars in the notes, for often they are speaking about another, no less valuable Beckett, or about their own portrait of the playwright, whether placed in a philosophical, biographical, literary, historical, or theatrical context. I have profited much from them. Indeed, I am often embarrassed at my debt.[62]

The organization of the book follows at times chronology, at other times a given medium: separate chapters on *Godot, Endgame,* and *Happy Days;* a chapter on three stage plays, *Krapp's Last Tape, Play,* and *Come and Go;* a chapter on the radio plays, *All That Fall, Embers, Cascando,* and *Words and Music;* a chapter on *Film, Eh Joe,* and the two mimes (in effect, cinema, television, and silent theater); and a chapter examining the plays, with the addition of *Breath,* in a later collection from Beckett, *Ends and Odds.*[63] My dear wife read the final draft—as she always does—and, among many other loving "corrections," suggested that I include a chapter of conclusions. I had been reluctant to do this with a living playwright, and especially with one who seems to deplore abstractions. However, my wife was—again, as always—right, and I have taken the opportunity in chapter 8 ("Beckett's Black Holes") both to summarize and to push my inquiry a bit further. And there was a delightful bonus. While I was working on those conclusions, two excellent studies of Beckett appeared (Ruby Cohn's *Just Play: Beckett's Theater,* and *Frescoes of the Skull: The Later Prose and Drama of Samuel Beckett,* by James Knowlson and John Pilling) and I thus had a chance to incorporate them in my manuscript.[64] In the appendixes, I comment on three recent Beckett plays (*Rockaby, Ohio Impromptu,* and *A Piece of Monologue*), along with . . . *but the clouds* . . ., which appeared first in the Faber and then later in the Grove edition of *Ends and Odds.* By working with such a cooperative Press, I was able to "open up" the manuscript just before production and include some very recent studies of Beckett, especially of the plays in *Ends and Odds* and those discussed in the appendixes. I also had a chance to profit from that very fine collection of essays, *Samuel Beckett Humanistic Perspectives,* edited by Morris Beja, S. E. Gontarski, and Pierre Astier for Ohio State University Press in 1983. Of cross-references there will be plenty, not only from nondramatic to dramatic works, but among the dramatic works for the four media. I hope, when finished, that I can say with Beckett (or with his surrogate Malone): "Aesthetics are therefore on my side,"[65] with the qualification, "at least a certain kind of aesthetics."

# Acknowledgments

Quotations from Beckett's plays, fiction, non-fiction, and poetry are through the kind permission of the Grove Press and, for the plays alone, Faber and Faber Ltd, London.

Lines from "The Tower" are reprinted with permission of Macmillan Publishing Company from *Collected Poems of W. B. Yeats.* Copyright 1928 by Macmillan Publishing Co., Inc., renewed 1956 by Georgie Yeats. The remarks on *Antony and Cleopatra* in the preface are "lifted" from my *When the Theater Turns to Itself: The Aesthetic Metaphor in Shakespeare* (Lewisburg, Pa.: Bucknell University Press, 1981), pp. 9–10. And the account of my stage experience with two of the plays was first published as "Florida and Beckett: *Waiting for Godot* and *Come and Go*," *Vision* 1 (1979): 122–29.

Mills Edgerton, Director of Bucknell University Press, Cynthia Fell, Associate Director, and Julien Yoseloff, Director of Associated University Presses, should know—surely they know already—that my association with them is a joyful one.

I also have a very special debt to Marilyn Gaddis Rose, Professor of Comparative Literature and Director of the Translation Research and Instruction Program at the State University of New York at Binghamton.

My work with the wonderful "kids" of the Hippodrome Theater of Gainesville informs everything I do with the theater, and most certainly this present study.

My colleague and fellow actor in the "Eleventh Hour Players," Barbara Stephenson, worked as my on-campus editor here, though every error that remains is entirely my own. Our conversations, during the writing of her dissertation on Tom Stoppard, a playwright compatible in so many ways with Beckett, made their way in many ways into the manuscript.

With my "Beckett students"—Charles Collingswood, Thomas Duke, Linda Huba, Craig Saper, Gail Shepherd, and Ann Waters—I had wonderful talks, and talks that were later enacted onstage.

I am grateful to my chairman, Melvyn New, and the English Department at the University of Florida for released time, encouragement, and willing ears.

*A Tree for Godot* by Christopher Homan

# Beckett's Theaters

# 1 *Waiting for Godot*: The Art of Playing

Its allegory, or its symbolism, may ultimately be indeterminable, or at best a purely personal matter, with critics seeing in the play what they themselves feel while waiting for their own Godot.[1] Like Watt, we throw a paradigm on the play, a rational schema, because we cannot allow the Knott of the story, its Godot, to remain beyond analysis. Still, there seems no *consensus gentium*, but only a myriad of correspondences, as myriad as the number of available spectators. Yet at the very least *Godot* "is"—it *happens*.

If *Godot* is a happening, it is not, however, like the "happenings" we know from the *avant-garde* theater of New York where, say, spectators might be assembled on a street corner with instructions to wait until the first automobile accident occurs, the director on this occasion surrounding a purely chance event with an audience serving as a witness to elevate that event above the meaninglessness of an accident. In *Godot* what "happens" is that nothing happens; the tantalizing name Godot in the title does not appear, at least not to the level of physical satisfaction demanded in the conventional theater of sight and sound.[2] But like the New York happening, Beckett's fictive nonhappening only suggested here does underscore its present-tense nature and thereby in the process undervalues past and future.

On one side, then, is the physical and immediate, a recognition only of the present, without those "terrors of history"[3] that Eliade defines as contemporary man's enslavement to an evolutionary scheme wherein the past always pales beside the present and the present remains stained and incomplete before the promise of the future. On the other side lies thinking, the intellection that can see the present in no other terms than past and future, as a continuum, and that subsequently values time only for what has been or will be. The play's opening dialogue establishes in Hegelian fashion the dialectic: "nothing to be done" (a positive or negative remark depending on whether the audience hears the line as "there will be a pleasure in doing nothing" or as "there will be the pain of having nothing to do"). This ambiguous statement is then followed by its antithesis, the circle implied by Estragon's "I'm coming round to that opinion myself" (with its sense of agreement through time, even though the opposite is implied, that he is reaffirming a position once held, then denied, and now held again). There is, finally, a synthesis of the two previous statements characterzing both speakers either as victims of time or as men liberated from time by the nothingness of the present when seen only within itself: "We're waiting for

31

Godot" (with the purely present-tense construction of "waiting" also suggesting a god who will liberate those waiting, the Hegelian *Geist* above the dialectic).

Yet what do we do with a projected synthesis that is never shown? So we are back to the present, together "again" with Gogo and Didi, with our surrogates also waiting onstage. And rather than working out an allegory, that is, bringing the god Godot to them, they reverse the process: they wait for Godot, whatever he be, because they have been told to wait. However, that instruction is given before the play proper. Thus it is as difficult for us to envision that a priori event as it is for the two tramps to deal with the past, let alone the future.[4]

Trying to recount the events of the previous day and very brief night—the substance of Act 1—Estragon admits, "I'm not a historian" (42a). The characters will make attempts by memory and its end-product, history, to order a Knott-like world, caught as it is between the immobile tree and the agent of mobility itself, the road passing by that tree. History, as an ordering principle, as a guide to the present and to future possibilities, will not be one of those ways. As the narrator in "Text 8" says: "Yes, my past has thrown me out."[5]

i

The play assaults the basic unities of the conventional theater: time, place, and plot. In doing so *Godot* comments metadramatically on itself and our experience with its "world."

What few accounts of the past there are seem terribly confusing, even misleading. Estragon can tell us only that in his lifetime much water has passed under the bridge, "a million years ago" (p. 76). He and Vladimir refer to a time when their powers were greater, when they were even trusted to climb to the top of the Eiffel Tower, trusted to raise for themselves that question Camus calls most basic to our integrity as humans: do we choose either to take our life or, at whatever meager level, to affirm existence (and possibly a plan and a justification for that existence) by deciding to live? But they have lost those powers and thereby lost their place in human society that measures itself in terms of its past and that, the terrors of history notwithstanding, banks the present on the future.

Even the vague measurement for this glorious past, "a million years ago," is called into doubt by Estragon's qualification that his friend only refers to the "nineties." Does he mean the Gay or 1890s? We learn later that the tramps have been together some fifty years, though when Pozzo estimates their ages at sixty or seventy there is no reply. Is this confirmation, denial—or simply indifference? Both Lucky and Pozzo are said to be over sixty, but Pozzo looks much younger. To complicate matters, Pozzo is now the master (and presumably older), though he was once the student or disciple. When

Pozzo challenges Vladimir and Estragon to estimate Lucky's age, Estragon replies "eleven" (p. 19a).

In any case consciousness of the past is fading, indeed is almost obliterated by the present task of waiting for Godot. The central importance of that task is underscored by comic repetition, both in the neurotically recurrent phrase "We're waiting for Godot" as well as in the companion cry, "Ah!," a nonword with no need for a linguistic history and with no promise of a future with or without Godot. I have heard actors playing Estragon deliver that cry with everything from a soul-deep anguish to the flippancy of an "Oh, yes, I forgot."[6]

Pozzo and Lucky seem to come from a more definite past; as master and student (whatever reversal in the relationship has occurred), they travel from Pozzo's estate, and they are in progress to the fair where Lucky will be sold. Yet perhaps that fair is itself an illusion, like the fair described in "The Expelled," where the farting and shitting of the horses mock the event itself. (The "fun of the fair" is the Unnamable's sarcastic way of describing the external world.[7]) While not known for any conspicuous modesty, Pozzo himself confesses to having a "defective" memory (25b), and though he is given to schedules, calendars, and a discourse on the night and the passing of the hours into twilight, he also loses his watch. That watch is described in some detail as a half-hunter with deadbeat escapement, but, of course, since the object itself is lost, its description, be it specific or general, is irrelevant. One of those men with a definite "agenda,"[8] Pozzo seems threatened by the same problems in measuring reality by time, perhaps even by the same timelessness as are Vladimir and Estragon.[9] Here Pozzo's future dissolves as suddenly as an offstage fall, and such a catastrophic event as his blindness occurs between acts, outside of whatever time-scheme there may be within the play. Pozzo's and Lucky's second fall, no less significant, literally occurs offstage, out of the play proper. We hear a sound and we see Vladimir's miming of the event, but not the event itself. The sense of time seems confined to messengers' reports, onstage parodies of serious acts not acted before us, and nebulous histories flitting over the dialogue. There are other measurements of time. Pozzo's heart beats— Vladimir and Estragon attest to that fact—but the heartbeats are, for Pozzo, a poor substitute for the forward sweep of the minute hand of that watch which cannot be found, though with which Pozzo's own heart is comically confused.

Alternately wise and foolish, Vladimir is surely wise when he characterizes Estragon's condition, and also his own, with: "When I think . . . all these years . . . but for me . . . where would you be . . . (*Decisively.*) You'd be nothing more than a little heap of bones at the present minute, no doubt about it" (p. 7b). The finality of man's brief history, that heap of bones, is itself subject to the instability of the present minute. The truth is so obvious, so indisputable, that Estragon, while normally given to contradicting or at the very least qualifying whatever Vladimir says, can only respond,

"And what of it?" *Bones,* as an image for the sum of our existence, rings true, yet it provides no guide for future action.

Knowing the humiliating end product of time, the characters still persist in the play's grinding presence: they go on, clinging to each other as a hedge against the possibility of time's cruel terminus. Instead of progress there is here only stasis, most evident on those occasions when the clowns cleave to each other as the temporal world, outside the stage set, threatens them, and no less evident at the play's own end when, wishing to move in time from the present set itself to that exit offstage that has so far eluded them, they remain stationary. Perhaps such stasis is both a sign of their human poverty and, in a curious way, their escape from time. Time moves Pozzo and Lucky, from a glorious past (for Lucky, if not for Pozzo) to a present that is only a transition to the goal of selling the servant at the fair, to the future, rudely defined by an offstage fall. Vladimir and Estragon cannot move, even if they wanted to. By the logic extrapolated from the ends of both acts and manifest in Estragon's line "Well, here we are again," they will be back tomorrow, at the same place, at the same time—as if nothing had happened, as if whatever day marks the opening of Act 1 simply recurs and recurs, in violation of any normal calendar.

If past and future are moot points, if the play so revolving around a scheduled nonevent is itself so lacking a definite agenda, there is still one certain thing. All that we, audience and actors, have is the present moment.[10] Exposition, initial incident, rising action, climax, falling action, even an anti-climax—those comforting terms from drama textbooks which find their home in the conventional three- or five-act structure, even that reassuring march of time in the well-made play ("First Act: a garden, that afternoon; Second Act: the garden later that night; Third Act [and resolution]: Mr. Whimple's study the next morning")—all the temporal anchors to the otherwise fictitiously time-informed stage world become irrelevant.[11] Imposing the play structure *("Act I . . . A country road. A tree. Evening.")* on a nonevent that disregards one of the three unities of the drama, perhaps imposing it because the audience, disoriented enough already, can conceive of this world in no other fashion, Beckett is true both to his vision and to the theater as he perceives it: a present-tense collaboration between "us" (offstage) and "them" (onstage). As the clowns say in their punning, we, actors and audience, are tired and tried and yet tied together (p. 14a, b) by an inescapable present defying the logic of time that argues if Act 1 precedes Act 2, then the play imitates real-world time. But as even Pozzo will say later, we have here only an "immediate future" (p. 19b). There is only "is," not "was" or "will be"; Vladimir reminds us that "One is what one is" (p. 14b), and he refers here as much to the pressures of an overwhelming present (unrelieved by history or the promise of a future) as he does to the no-exit of one's inherited character. Even *Godot*'s own touchstone for the world of the absurdist theater—"Nothing happens, nobody comes, nobody goes, it's awful" (p. 27b)—does not put down the present, for the words here are chained to the future, to possibilities that have turned sour. Time requires movement from a discernible past, through, but only *through* the present, and toward the future. Eliminate the first and third parts and you eliminate time. In what else can one find meaning than the present? "Here!" Estragon cries (p. 40a).

If time is stripped of two-thirds of its gamut, place itself is also diminished; in effect, both the abstraction of time and the concreteness of place are denied. The stage is little more than the bare boards on which the action occurs. In the vague terms of the Unnamable, we are "somewhere on a road."[12]

The tree and the road—and the road is nothing more than the stage itself—this is all that is required. The setting is so simple that it is at once literal—the stage is the stage—and symbolic, for the stage is our only metaphor here that is clear and of which we can be sure. Dr. Johnson's retort to conservative proponents of the three unities, that the mind that can imagine Act 1 set in one city can just as easily imagine another location for Act 2, is itself now irrelevant.

Even the scenery, or what little there is, remains unchanged except for a few pathetic leaves pasted on the tree during intermission. In our prison productions of *Godot* a stagehand, clearly seen by an audience forbidden to leave their seats between acts, came on minutes before the start of Act 2 and pasted a few ill-designed green leaves on the tree, all this done in full view of inmates anxious for the "action" to begin again.[13] I like to think that this captive audience thereby contributed to the grinding uniformity and impoverishment of "place" in the play. For them the man pasting on the leaves was simply another member of the company "acting" on our makeshift stage. Instead of an object that approaches implications and therefore meanings beyond its physical self, we confront an object whose "symbolism" is closer to the chaos of those almost infinite possibilities which so frustrate Watt as he tries with his exhausted Cartesianism to determine meaning behind the façade of the physical world:[14] is the tree a symbol of stasis? of paradox (growth and suicide)? the tree of life? or knowledge? or nature? or human nature? or whatever? Beckett's warning at the end of the addendum to *Watt* should be invoked here: "no symbols where none intended."[15]

There is also a possibility, though not confirmed, that someone has substituted a different pair of boots for the ones left by Estragon. Has someone from the time zone of the real world made the substitution? Are there events, not realized within the confines of the two acts, that cross the eternal present of *Godot*? Are there, indeed, individuals who can and do come and go, more secure in their futures than Pozzo and Lucky? Individuals who have worn boots too large and have thereby wisely substituted a pair that fits Estragon for a pair, left from Act 1, that brings him only trouble? Are we in the more optimistic world of Frost's "Tuft of Flowers," where a past action—the mower's saving a tuft of flowers now growing incongruously in the middle of a field otherwise destined for the plow—enriches that present in which we participate as spectators? The comrades quarrel over the color, a possible indication, along with the size, of some change. Are the boots, or are they not, the same color? Are they, or are they not, a different size? There is no certainty about the boots, just as there is no certainty about Godot. New boots may not have come.

Conversely, would it follow that Godot himself cannot come because, like the boots, he has been there all the time? Some spectators would argue that Godot is an abstraction, a projection of the characters' wishes or needs; that, in point of fact, he dwells within them; that he represents what Jung would call their collective unconscious; that Vladimir and Estragon search for him everywhere but the right place, the boards, at the present moment. We can no more solve this problem than the characters can the "problem" of the boots.

Other places are only referred to by the characters, such as the ditch where Estragon spends the night. In *Fizzles* that ditch is said to be "wide enough for one" (as a bed, or as a grave?), and it is in a ditch that Watt experiences the mystery of the frog's sounds, though he reduces, or attempts to reduce such sounds to a formula.[16] Vladimir does go offstage to relieve himself, and in one college production we used the bathroom, complete with a flushing toilet, adjacent to the run-down train-station lobby that served as our theater. While this "indelicate" extension of the nonstage set is fortunately not shown, we found audiences stretching their necks to see beyond the stage. I like to think that it was not voyeurism operating here—as is surely the case for Estragon, who tries to make a running commentary on the act—but rather the audience's own uneasiness—dissatisfaction?—with *Godot*'s deficient treatment of the unity of place.[17] Beckett's play at once refuses to admit a real set and, at the same time, tantalizes us with suggestions of a set—a bathroom, an estate, a fair. However, suggestions are not facts; in similar fashion, we never see Clov's kitchen in *Endgame,* and the one ingredient it holds of significance for Hamm, the painkiller, itself never materializes. I have, however, seen audiences applaud for two minutes for the Ascot Downs set of *My Fair Lady,* forcing the actors to freeze into position for the duration. Estragon insists on being a chorus to Vladimir's offstage activity, but perhaps we ourselves would wish for a more reliable spokesman.

Some places exist only as fictions within fictions, such as the pretty pictures to which Estragon reduces the illustrated Bible of his youth. Maybe even the present waiting place is a fiction within a fiction, for Godot does not come and this causes the clowns to speculate that they are waiting at the wrong place, a fear the Boy neither confirms nor denies. Perhaps the set, based on misdirections, is one of God's "little jokes."[18] But gods don't normally misdirect their followers: the straight and narrow path ought to be certain enough. If the god exists only in the command to wait, in the process of living, if God is not an end (neither in Himself nor of our earthly journey), then what certainty can we have about *place* that certainly seems as infinite as the waiting itself? Appropriately, Pozzo, a man caught in time, thinks concretely of place, and therefore celebrates *terra firma* in a way not shared by his fellow humans, placing his stool resolutely on stage, sitting with equal resolution for a dinner of chicken and wine. His sense of concreteness is taken to an absurd extreme when, minus stool, he falls to the ground, able neither by his own efforts nor those of his servant to remove himself from the boards.

Still, one thing is certain: we, actors and audience, are in the right place of and for illusions, the theater. For, as Genet observes, the theater *is* certain in its fakery.[19] The theater pretends to be nothing more than an illusion; it pretends to nothing more than it is. That place is the boards, the slang word for the stage, be it the literal stage or that figurative stage about which Jaques speaks in *As You Like It*. A fictive god, in the sense that he is invisible or is only a projection of human imagination, and a fictive place— the latter, at least, has the virtue of being "there."

The vague or minimal unities of time and place are "complemented" by the sparseness of the action. No chance here of the "underplot" that Hamm fears in *Endgame*.[20] Even the "story" of Lucky and Pozzo exists only to the degree of their interaction with Vladimir and Estragon. Their alleged story, how Pozzo overcame his teacher, what they have been doing before they stumble on stage, what will happen to them—all this is only a reported past or a never-realized future. Like the night spent in a ditch, the separate lives that Vladimir and Estragon live before and after the stage action proper, like Vladimir's urination just offstage, and, most important, like Godot in his never coming but always coming in the Boy's optimistic message—action as we know it, as Aristotle understood the force of probability connecting separate but related events, does not exist. We are left with a unity of plot that exceeds even the purist's expectations: there is no action, or what little there is cannot qualify for the term *plot*.[21] And in his final moments in Act 2 Pozzo denounces even his own time-oriented plot by arguing that one can be born and live and die in the "same second," thereby compressing the "plot" of life itself to a birth "astride of a grave" (p. 57b), an instant and insignificant light like Macbeth's own brief candle.

We have, then, two sets of characters, with two separate nonstories, if you will. By definition there can be no meaningful interweaving of the plots. The problem, again, is compounded by the confusions or the nonexistence of a meaningful and thereby measurable time—in any normal sense of the word. When we place this, Beckett's longest play in the canon, against his shortest, *Breath*, a strange paradox emerges. The longest play seems, more than any other, to violate the conventions of time. The shortest play, a mere thirty-five seconds or so in production, charts an entire history, from the birth cry, through the garbage of our lives, to the death cry, offering in its brief but temporally conventional stage picture documentation for Pozzo's own picture of that copulation between birth and death.

If the play lacks the normal resolution of and through plot, it does raise a question about action: could we bear an endless wait in a world that offers only the game of waiting and not the endgame, the final hand? Could we endure a world, like that described in *Mercier and Camier,* where life is only a handful of slippery millet grains surrounded before and after by dreams?[22] This is, I think, the question posed, or rather *enacted* by the play. The passing of time for Beckett's clowns is the passing of time for the audience as well. A friend who had directed *Godot* once speculated that in coming to the play as audience, we only do what Vladimir and Estragon do without knowing it;[23] we also participate in a process, and if Godot fails to come for the pathetic specimens of humanity represented onstage, he also fails for the specimens offstage as well. Our own search in life (or in attending the play) for meaning or, barring that, at least for entertainment, is identical with that of the unworthies before us—and around us and behind us, I might add. Like the clowns onstage, we are surrounded by "all humanity" (p. 54a); yet perhaps in our single role as spectator each of us might be all humanity as well. Each struggles alone or with others to find an acceptable allegory for the nontime, nonplace, nonaction of *Godot*.

Estragon at one point screams to his partner, "Don't speak to me! Stay with me" (p. 37b). "Stay"—like "be," the word for the present. There are no alternatives to the present reality, and yet what meaning, above the physical, above carrots, turnips, chicken bones, can there be in this raw existence? The difficulty, I believe, is not within the play itself but in what we *must* bring to it. We cannot abide its purity, its seeming lack of an overall order or purpose. Vladimir's "In an instant all will vanish" (p. 52a) surely speaks to others than those onstage. Our *experience* here supersedes any doctrine, be it Christian, existential, absurdist, fatalistic.[24] For doctrines would impose a "meaning" on a stage world offering no such guarantee, whereas Beckett, in his tantalizingly scant critical commentary, has championed "style" over meaning.[25] Vladimir speaks to this issue near the end, just seconds before the Boy makes his appearance. (Or is it the first appearance of the second boy? Even a physical entrance or exit is not so clear-cut.) He tries to reduce what happened to a single statement packed with meaning, but he fails. All he can do is offer a plot synopsis of the slim happenings of the play: "That with Estragon, my friend, at this place, until the fall of night, I waited for Godot? That Pozzo passed, with his carrier, and that he spoke to us? Probably. But in all that what truth will there be?" (p. 58a). What Vladimir describes, of course, is nothing so grand as a "truth" but rather only an experience totally circumscribed by the moment: "I waited until a certain time, and someone passed by and, while passing by, spoke to us." He realizes that Estragon, no less than he himself, will at best be able to *tell* what happens, at worst will forget. There is nothing shameful about forgetting, since the amount of material to be so forgotten is so small. To forget a god-ordained truth is a different matter and material for a different play.[26] We live only "to grow old" (58a). If there is a god, a greater power ratifying this spectacle by his witness, a god attaching a metaphysic to the grinding physicality of this world, Vladimir shies away from such a possibility: "What have I said?"

I would submit that it is this function of the theater, as a present happening, an experience demarcated by the two acts of the play, shared, indeed *created* and *sustained* by audience and actors that is the ultimate "good" or "goal" or Godot of the play. For our audience of inmates at the ten state prisons the play they watched *was* their reality, and not a transcription for anything beyond itself.[27] Consigned and confined to waiting, they found the experience at one with life in the cell or in the larger macrocosm of the prison, be its walls those actual or imaginary ones that all of us, with varying degrees of "buried lives," experience.[28]

The frantic, physical action of the play underscored this present-tense, nonintellectual, nonallegorical dimension. Consider the hat routine snatched from vaudeville, Estragon's posing as a fighter, the tramps' constant embracings, Pozzo's brutish treatment of Lucky, the assault on Lucky during his monologue, the quartet of falling and writhing bodies in Act 2, the entrances and exits in both acts (and, most especially, the highly visible entrances, the ropes and then the falls, peculiar to Pozzo and Lucky), and the ongoing stage "business" (Estragon with his boots, Vladimir with his hat, and so on). Here is action, and most often action that defies or denies interpretation. One such way of frustrating a single or, at least, clear interpretation is to combine actions that are mutually exclusive, such as pulling on and pulling off one's pants, taking off and replacing a hat on the head.[29]

In trying to charge the play's actions, its overbearing presence, with meaning, the two tramps can only be comic figures. Thus the imposing Old Testament divinity gives way here to a man with a white beard.[30] Similarly, Estragon finds the Bible not a source of revelation but a pleasant book with pictures that are at best pretty. There the Dead Sea is so convincingly drawn that "the very look of it made me thirsty" (p. 8b). The tramps hear the wind and fear it signals Godot's arrival; and we may think of the biblical association of God and the wind, stirring life into the "dry leaves" of human souls.[31] Once the sound "materializes," however, we find only Pozzo; and his opening statement itself challenges the tramps' identification of him with Godot. Perhaps Pozzo is Godot, though if he is he is surely a caricature of the stern biblical figure, an impostor even as the name Pozzo itself implies.

And the Boy tells us not of a god of love, not of a New Testament figure, but of a bearded old man whose benevolent despotism is visited upon mere children, and who offers the meager satisfaction of material wants for the price of an occasional beating. The boy confesses that he is happy, happier perhaps than his brother, but the happiness hardly resembles the evangelical joy of a true disciple. We are here in a horizontal world, a depressed cosmos where God is missing, or is as dead as the dog (God reversed?) in Vladimir's song. Likewise Hamm, possibly a caricature of that missing god, has turned down a man seeking food for his child, and is more cruel than stern. The sole character of *Act Without Words I* is denied the sustenance of the carafe; Mrs. Rooney in *All That Fall* cries out for Christian charity but receives little from that delightful monstrosity of religion, Miss Fitt. And so the tramps yearn for a guiding hand, a providential figure who witnesses them and who justifies their existence.

With the hierarchical structure or meaningful dialectic abolished by the play's eternal presence, the question then becomes: how does one pass the time? How much meaning can existence have if it only "passes" without a certifiable end?[32] Perhaps in this play we have *only* play. Even this function, playing to pass the time, is undercut: "Vladimir: That passed the time./ Estragon: It would have passed in any case"(p. 31b).

The more positive side of Estragon's diagnosis is that if time passes anyway, and yet if time wears away at, indeed is hostile to meaning, then we must judge the "experience" of life without a goal or preexisting standard. The issue, therefore, is one of the quality of an experience that is *sensual*, physical, if not cerebral or intellectual. Talking itself becomes now not a way of conceptualizing existence, but of being conscious of the experience of passing through existence. One must talk anyway, for Estragon observes that he and Vladimir are "incapable of keeping silent" (p. 40a). No less than the theater, life seems to require conversation; there is no other choice. Speechless plays are mimes, not plays in the conventional sense. When humans are stripped of all other powers (and Beckett emphasizes this by incapacitating his characters with bowel disorders, aching feet, blindness, loss of limbs, fatness, impotence), they are reduced to talk—to Hamlet's "words, words, words" (2.2 193).[33]

To start talking is difficult, as Vladimir observes, but that observation is countered by Estragon's "You can start from anything." By conversation we make something (or at least a seeming something) out of nothing, and this is the very accomplishment that angered Puritan opponents of the Renaissance theater who thought the artist mocked God in trying to make something out of nothing, out of shadowy words. In an extraordinary speech near the end of the play Vladimir winds down to this position: "Let us do someting" (p. 51a). Then the dissolution starts: the chance of helping Pozzo and Lucky on the ground before them does not come every day, but then others could aid them just as well, or better. We should seize the opportunity anyway since, for the moment, all humanity is reduced to and is represented by the two clowns. Not to do something is also justified: to stand with folded arms is also to mean something, to "do" something. In Vladimir's words, tigers both come to the aid of comrades and, just as easily, slink off "away into the depth of the thickets" (p. 51b). Such talk threatens to keep them from being good Samaritans. Out of this immense confusion one sure thing emerges: what they can do and therefore can "mean"—but only because they have no other choice or because they are incapable of going away—is to wait "for Godot to come." To this Estragon adds the blessing, his anguished "Ah!"

In this regard the ultimate in playing, talking to pass the time, is Lucky's speech. It is a set piece, a bit of entertainment ultimately not to be elevated above the other entertainments of the play.[34] Yet Lucky's harangue also calls forth memories of glorious older days, when Lucky was Pozzo's teacher.[35] For the actor it is both an extraordinary feat of memorization and, since it is irritating and confusing to the audience, an easy way to spout nonsense syllables and thereby pass the time. Critics who make too much of the speech are probably in as dangerous waters as those who would make too little.

Perhaps taking a stand—is the speech meaningful or not?—is the wrong approach. Viewed as a catholic experience embracing the heights and depths of human achievement, embracing arguments for man as a creature of free will to man as an insignificant mote in a fatalistic universe, man as a champion of time through theories of history to man as the chump of time (as Lucky himself has been), Lucky's speech becomes not a gloss for the present play, nor intimations of a different or alternative world, but the thing itself, a microcosm amidst the macrocosm of the play. It mirrors the surrounding play, but it does not explain it or the unanswered question of the play: will Godot come or, more important, whether he comes or not, who is Godot? Nor does it follow that the play as microcosm explains life outside itself, the macrocosm. The sobering thought—and the reason for our inability to dismiss the play as mere "entertainment" in the limited sense of something to pass the time—is that if this microcosm does not explain the macrocosm, it may, as does Lucky's speech for its "play," *mirror* it. That is, *Godot* may have all the power and hence justification of realistic or, if you will, naturalistic theater. The play has lasted thirty years; it will not go away. In its path are strewn many plays that have not lasted, some full of ideas, some full of entertainment.

## ii

If waiting is the sole choice, then the audience's own waiting is the one activity shared by those off- and onstage. Our style of waiting is thus no less an issue, and audiences for *Godot* have ranged from the impatient Coconut Grove tourists who walked out of the American premier to the New Yorkers who, finding the play an anti-play, also despaired of Beckett, to the inmates at San Quentin and at the ten prisons visited by my troupe who literally took the play to heart, to the countless literary "audiences" of more recent times who, according to my own well-worth edition, have sent the play to its fifty-fourth printing.

It is little wonder, then, that *Godot* is so conscious of its audience. We are the "inspiring prospects" (p. 10a) surrounding one side of its world; the tree frames the rear, and the exits, which prove to be no exits, frame the other two sides. Estragon advances to front-stage, *"halts facing auditorium,"* and, looking at us, sees those "inspiring prospects" (p. 10a), that phrase itself followed by the cynical and deflating "Let's go." Our prison production allowed the actors at times to play literally to the audience as we alternated between actor-to-actor contact and—whenever demanded by the inmates who wanted to be let into the production—actor-to-audience contact. Because actor is linked to audience and audience to actor, we are "tied" together. If the tree denies a way out, figuratively and literally, the same is true for us, that bog on the opposite side. All that we have is the present, the "charming spot" (p. 10a) stripped of hierarchy and meaningful dichotomy, and of any time or space beyond that framed by the audience. Beckett is even conscious of the critics in his audience, professional or self-styled. At the end of the list of curses the Vladimir and Estragon hurl at each other—Moron, Vermin, Abortion, Morphion, Sewer-rat, Curate, Cretin—is "Crritic!" (p. 48b).[36]

Vladimir's greeting to Estragon, "Together again at last!" (p. 7a), thus bursts the confines of the stage and embraces the audience as well. We are all in it together; another curtain has risen. In the words of *How It Is* we are "glued together."[37] Now, for audience and actors, no less than for Vladimir and Estragon, what shall we do? How shall we pass the time as we singly and mutually wait for our personal Godot? Together at last. "We'll have to celebrate this?" (p. 7a). How easy it is to forget that the theater is a place for and of entertainment sustained by both actors and audience.[38] The issue here is: what will be the level of that entertainment? The hat trick, or vaudeville, or Beckett's finer, more profound "hat" trick? Vaudeville or Chaplin or Beckett—this is the order of ascent. To celebrate is half the answer; the other half, which Vladimir quickly supplies, is a second question: "But how?" (p. 7a).

The image of the audience doubles back on the play. Audiences surrounding the stage are balanced with audiences onstage. Vladimir performs for Estragon, Estragon for Vladimir; audiencelike, the clowns watch Pozzo. The real Pozzo, Beckett's parody of a self-conscious actor ("Is everybody looking at me?" [p. 20b]), performs his discourse on the night for Vladimir and Estragon, complete with a request for audience feedback; appropriately, his "How did you find me?" is met with "Tray bong, tray bong" (p. 25b). In our prison production the actor playing Pozzo, more than any other character, played to our audience, giving them his best half with only cursory attention to his "likes" on stage.

At one point, the audience almost degenerates to a collection of voyeurs, including Lucky, Pozzo, Estragon, and—if we so choose—ourselves: we watch characters watch Vladimir offstage going to the bathroom. I have seen members of the audience strain their necks to see if the reference to nature taking its course is faked or real, as Vladimir offstage, but accompanied by an onstage chorus from Estragon, empties his bladder. In a larger sense, many of the play's rhetorical questions—like the intrusive question from the public address system that shatters the illusory world of the movies: "Is there a doctor in the house?"—are addressed as much to the audience as to anyone onstage: "He wants to know if it hurts" (p. 7b). By extension, the line might even be shouted so as to reach the ears of the absent Godot. Indeed, the number of audiences multiplies: Godot, we assume though at our peril, observes his subjects (above or below or all around, to echo Hamlet's incantation of his father's ghost); we face the boards from our side, while the Boy, who has been there unseen for some time, overhears from the wings, even as characters onstage watch other characters onstage and, in the case of Vladimir's emptying his bladder, offstage. As we watch Hamlet and Horatio observe Claudius in attendance at *The Murder of Gonzago,* or as we observe Oberon and Puck observe Thesesus and his court mock Bottom and his rustic actors, we experience the microcosmic-macrocosmic metaphor inherent in the Renaissance theater. In his metatheater Beckett also reminds us by his mirror-audiences and by his allusions to the real audience that we are part of the stage action. Our sense of participation (we validate the play by our witness; the play is itself validated by being a mirror of ourselves as audience) is a vital contribution to that classic goal of any art: *utile et dulce.* What distinguishes *Godot,* I believe, is that rather than being imposed from above or from outside the play proper, that usefulness and pleasure are determined at performance, by those on- and those offstage.

### iii

Beckett, I believe, takes us down a road leading from that incomplete but happy reality we normally perceive, from all that happens outside the play proper, toward a world of waiting, shared by actor and audiences, and most certainly one not defined by any of the "baggage" of time-honored philosophers and theologians. Lucky, who was once a teacher, as Beckett himself was, must put down his baggage, or rather that bag owned by Pozzo. The nihilistic speech, without baggage, is itself cast in the logical framework of a discourse and generates equally nihilistic actions on the part of its onstage audience, as Vladimir and Estragon stifle the implications of the speech with a burst of crude, physical counteractions that soon degenerate to slapstick.

We cannot go alone; as Pozzo comments, "Yes, the road seems long when one journeys all alone" (p. 16b). To travel together is also difficult, just as leaving together is impossible for any two of the three characters onstage in Sartre's *No Exit.* The basic metaphor is ancient: the poet, accompanied by the reader or spectator, sets out on a quest, down a road that, if it does lead him home, will lead him to that home altered. Here, however, the journey is all, for there is no end, and most certainly no god waiting at the end, if there were one.

Such "strange" roads are numerous in Beckett: Molloy watching A and B, unsure if they are leaving or going home; Molloy himself setting out to find his mother; Moran, to find Molloy; O's journey down a New York street, up the stairs, and into the convenient fiction of his mother's room; Woburn's trip to the sea; the trip by the inmates in *Malone Dies;* Murphy's journeys about London, culminating in the one-way road leading to the insane asylum; Watt's train ride to and from Knott's house, and so on. The journey itself leads to somewhere else, often somewhere unexpected; as Estragon observes, "We're not from these parts, Sir" (p. 15b). Yet these new parts, the inspiring prospects, are somewhere that cannot be imagined at the journey's start. One leaves for a specific destination but winds up in another dimension. Therefore we cannot speak logically of a clear goal, of a journey's end known both before and during that journey.

A common observation about Beckett's work, especially his novels, is that if the goal is indeterminable, the one certain thing is that we seem to be witnessing a work in the process of composition, that the ultimate issue is the creation of a fictive world that escapes or refines or is the inevitable next step away from the discredited outer world. Such creation is both difficult and vital when one considers the lack of what T. S. Eliot would call adequate objective correlatives, along with the pressures of habit and of time, and the neuroses of the narrator himself, unsure—as is the Unnamable—that his words are being heard or that he himself exists. For such creation is a way of escaping the self, the step beyond the existential dilemma of splitting the acting from that thinking self necessary to conceive of the real.[39] But Beckett's would-be artists—Moran, the Unnamable, Malone—never do succeed for they confuse their stories with their own lives and are unable to return home after that epiphany of vision when they see the wellspring of their own creative chaos. This dilemma is magnified in the plays where even the most prominent artist-narrators, such as Mr. Rooney or Krapp, are not the whole fiction, not exclusively the creating spirit of their world, not in full control of its dialogue or its narration. As audience we want someone whose voice we can trust, the way we can trust Portia in *The Merchant of Venice*. Here in *Godot* there is no one. The road, the journey, is difficult for audience as well as characters. This difficulty is certainly not the result of formlessness on Beckett's part; the slippery reality is controlled and is, I believe, a "productive" chaos. Still, we encounter the play with no more guideposts than the characters.

If we wind up somewhere, it is, I believe, in an interior world, though not necessarily the psychotic or schizophrenic world suggested by some critics.[39] This shifting, unmeasurable interior is all the "reality" we can have. Appropriately, Hugh Kenner suggests that the set of *Endgame* might be the inside of a head, with the two narrow windows backstage serving as the eyes.[40] Krapp's desk, whose drawers are turned to the audience, may well be a brain, with its compartments or "drawers" of experiences, memories, and information. If not anti-theater in the sense of being formless, Beckett's theater is unconventional if we think of the conventional theater as a mirror reflecting an external or even god-created world. Beckett gives form to what does not have form as we know it, and hence the futility he sees at the core of the artist's "work." How does one hear and see inside the head that, once opened, ceases to be a magical world, indeed that, once opened, literally and figuratively dies? This is the goal: to imagine what cannot be realized in terms of the only reality we have.[41] The frustration comes when one tries to project this interior reality in a conventional form—and drama must surely rank as one of the most conventional of all genres—to spectators already struggling with giving personal, if not public form to their own interior selves. One needs to be sensitive to Beckett, allowing his theater to embark on this "impossible" task, suspending belief in a public world that the drama, so it is argued, should mirror. There are also sensitive characters in the plays themselves, struggling or struggling through the playwright. Hamm can feel something dripping inside his head, and Winnie is aware of a force inside her, a headache, that no routine can totally obscure. Through limited intellectual effort, memory, and inaccurate citations of literature and philosophy, she tries to convey what she does not fully understand within herself.

Action is therefore only an illusion of this interior existence. We need physical existence since no one can be there to experience, let alone to talk about nonexistence. Yet an admission that we only give "the impression we exist" (p. 44b), as Estragon would have it, is to be preferred to the unwarranted confidence that there is a reality eternal to us, or especially that the world is a physical manifestation of some divine plan. With the cooperation of his audience and actors, Beckett gives us an "impression" of existence that is understood as just that. The playwright is the one who consciously makes an impression, and I use that word in the old sense of putting one's stamp or seal on a mold or receiving surface. Coleridge's metaphor of art's being an interaction between wax (the receiving substance) and form (the impression on that wax) may be helpful here.[42] For Beckett that "form" is impressed on some interior landscape, and his art therefore is not an equivalent to any mysterious forces manifest in the everyday world. The form itself is thus no less (or no more) substantial than the "reality" it captures. Little wonder that the form receives so much attention, whether it be a tape recorder, a cassette, an artist's notebook, the consciousness of storytelling—all of this culminating in the focus on form itself in two of Beckett's most abstract plays, *Words and Music* and *Cascando*.

The playwright acknowledges this form-revealed reality, this fictive world, one of waiting without the clear goal of an external reality, this ultimately inner world, through asides and direct theatrical references from the characters themselves.[43] Estragon senses that he is in a play, its plot already set by the previous act, when he confesses that "for me it's over and done with, no matter what happens" (p. 38a). Hamm, of course, will carry such theatrical consciousness, this metadrama, even farther; but there is enough in *Godot*. For though Vladimir and Estragon pale beside Hamm as a self-conscious "theaterician," they are still aware of their audience, of their own game-playing, of Pozzo's theatricality, of the necessity of consciously crafted dialogue (forget the quality) that helps pass time. If anything, the characters weary of the play world: "That's enough about the boots" (p. 45a).[44] Vladimir at one point observes that though they were just about to weaken, they will "see the evening out"—an evening of theater, among other things, I would presume.

The trinity of playwright, actors, and audience is the conscious—and sometimes unconscious—creator of this illusory world on the boards. And that illusory world calls into question preexisting notions of reality. In this regard, Beckett is a radical, even an anarchist. In the eloquent conversations we had after the prison productions of the play, our inmate friends saw exactly this: the paltry reality of that outside world now blocked from them was daily losing its claim to that of the artificial life as defined by the cells. At the same time the inmates were conscious of the "artificial" prison society—indeed, this was an obsession—and this consciousness in turn forced them to think of life outside the walls as no less artificial.

### iv

In establishing its inner world, ratified by the "performance" of actors and audience on any given evening, the theater thereby turns to itself. Though its primary source must be the external world, once that reality is transformed to artifice *Godot* begins to feed on itself. Thus I do not think that Beckett robs us of one reality without giving us something in return. He does not seem to rest content with that bitter knowledge of which Emily Brontë speaks: "Once drinking deep of that divine anguish, / How could I seek the empty world again?"[45] With increasing earnestness Vladimir and Estragon begin devising actions and dialogue born from events earlier in the play. Their unconscious plan seems to be that of creating a private, provincial world not so dependent on the outside reality supposedly governed by Godot. In a way paralleling the movement from the (superficially) external story of Moran to the semi-external world of Malone, caught between the room and the fictions issuing from that room, to the wholly internal story told and lived by the head in the *The Unnamable*, *Godot* turns inward, feeding upon itself, on past actions and conversations, creating an illusory past in a world for which the real past is not relevant.

In much the same way all of us, I suspect, while waiting for a seemingly interminable time to pass, begin fashioning a cosmos, however petty or absurd, out of the immediate process of waiting. As a child I pitched pennies against the curb while waiting for the buses of an inefficient transit system; with my child, waiting in the doctor's office, I play a game of guessing the objects in the room.

A fictive past, an uncertain future, these, the most blatant unrealities in that life outside the theater, become the source for establishing the waiting world within the theater. While waiting for Godot, Estragon plays the absent god, with Vladimir taking the role of the suppliant on hands and knees (p. 13a and b). This mini-scene itself is spun from words, when Vladimir takes literally Estragon's purely figurative phrase "When do we come in?" "On hands and knees" is his direct response. If the Godot from the outer world, the conventional reality of positive thinkers, will not take form, the clowns will for the time being give him one.

Similarly, Estragon imitates Lucky moments after his dance, but the interval for reflection and assimilation is not enough and he *"almost falls"* during the impersonation. Later in Act 2 the clowns play at being Lucky and Pozzo. The second imitation is more sustained, and for a moment the potential horror of the couple, this Hitler and his slave, is mitigated by parody. Yet the imitation, the mini-play, gives only a moment of comic oblivion and then dissolves into the fear that Pozzo and Lucky, in their real persons, are returning. All of Act 2, far from being a mere repetition of Act 1, may be thought of as a creation, a co-equal to the weak history and dim memories generated by Act 1. Like the clown shoveling up skulls and thereby feeding Hamlet's imagination as the Prince reads into each skull the story of a dead man (Alexander, a realtor, or a lawyer), the clowns here feed on words, memories, and objects from the first act as they try to build a little reality, or this fiction within a fiction.

In the medieval sense of an artist's being a dreamer who, on waking, gives form to his dream, Vladimir and Estragon try in Act 2 to recall and then give form to those events of Act 1 which now seem like a dream or the vestiges (particularly in Estragon's case) of a defective memory. Forgetfulness (an issue throughout the play) and the unformed "reality" of the dream appear synonymous. Estragon charges that Vladimir has "dreamt" (p. 39a) the episode about hanging themselves from the tree. When Vladimir claims the diagnosis is due to a loss of memory on the doctor's part—"Is it possible you've forgotten already?"—Estragon offers two alternatives for his inability to see the tree as part of their past: "Either I forget immediately or I never forget." This movement from fading dreams to minimal form and the use of words to give meaning to what happens or happened—"To say him," as the Voice in *Cascando* repeats—is the clowns' achievement. In Act 2 they can give form, by words or actions or both, to their "life" in Act 1. They establish a "history" in a world that begins with the most meager of histories, a night spent alone in a ditch after a thrashing by strangers. In Act 2 they establish a shared history, a civilization.

It takes two. Caught in their self-inflicting worlds, Beckett's solitary characters need, or create, or demand (as does Pozzo) someone else, whether it be an actual person or an alter ego or a mental projection: Hamm and Clov, Winnie and Willie, Joe and the female voice in the television play, O and E, Henry and the voices from his past, Krapp and his cassette, Bolton and his Holloway, the suicide in *Eh Joe* and her higher love. If the more cerebral characters of the novels, short stories, and sketches seek silence and singleness, they never reach that state; they still populate their world with fictive characters, as do Malone and the Unnamable. Or, from our perspective, they are linked, as Molloy is with Moran, with alter egos or earlier stages of their personalities. The simpler, less cerebral characters in the plays, like Vladimir and Estragon, need companions as collaborators in their creations. Even in the mimes, where we see either a single character or a character unaware of another onstage, there is a link made either with oneself (the reflective posture of the sole character of *Act Without Words I*) or with a god (the kneeling figure at the end of *Act Without Words II*).[46]

Together, then, Vladimir and Estragon create; they establish something, however silly. The growth of a few pathetic leaves on the tree marks this achievement. The dream becomes public; events are remembered and a little civilization is constructed without any ratifying divinity and in the absence of a certain goal. As audience we are *witnesses* to this accomplishment.

The alternative movement, away from publication and form and toward a private, singular world, the world of one, is to be avoided. Vladimir cannot let Estragon sleep and, supposedly, dream; nor does he want Estragon's dream experienced in isolation. Everyone—the truism has it—must dream alone; plays, though, are not dreams but waking dreams made public, however private and isolated their origins. Here there is no room for Estragon's "private nightmares" (p. 11a).

The two acts of *Godot* are, then, not the same; the second act has actions and dialogue for which the first act is a prerequisite. Appropriately, Act 2 shows Vladimir and Estragon at once more conscious of the theater and more given to acting. "Will you not play?" Vladimir entreats Lucky (p. 47a). When Pozzo delivers an impassioned line on his lost vision—that "Wonderful, wonderful sight!" (p. 55b)—Estragon encourages him with a similar command to play: "Expand! Expand!" Sometimes fading memory, sometimes artistic vision, provides the stimulus for this playing. The routine where the clowns pretend to be surrounded by an invisible army, or by an invisible Pozzo and Lucky (who, interestingly enough, soon after take form and appear), is described by Vladimir as a "vision" (p. 48a). Basic theatrics pervade the play: the hat business, the imitations of Lucky and Pozzo, the imitation of Lucky's dance, the set routines such as the cursing culminating in the epithet "Crritic!," Vladimir's various calls for more "dialogue," for passing the ball of conversation, and Pozzo's own unabashed theatrics. The Method School of Acting even comes in for a bit of ridicule when Vladimir suggests they "do the tree." We may think of those acting exercises where one tries to feel and hence to become an inanimate object. Here both clowns try being the tree—without much conviction, it should be added. And Estragon wonders if Godot, the ultimate audience, sees them (p. 49a).

To "do" the tree suggests an aesthetic notion of the tree; it is, after all, just a prop, indeed the play's "major" piece of scenery, excluding the mound. Thus aesthetics here seems to dominate any thematic conception, such as taking the tree as a tree of life or as an objective correlative embodying the paradox of the play itself, life and death, growth and sterility. Aesthetics is, after all, what is immediate; whatever the thematic meanings of the play, it is, at its roots, a play. The art, the function of playwright, actors, and audience, comes first; thematics is, in this light, almost an afterthought. If *Godot* has an existence before the play itself, in the history of theology or in Beckett's life, in the skepticism engendered by existentialism, the war, or some other cause, still such precursors are subject to the aesthetic demands of the theater that in turn are the source for the variety of thematic interpretations to which the play has rightly been subjected. Between its past and future, between the thematic boundaries surrounding the stage, is the play itself, its own aesthetic.[47] Little wonder, when pressed to say something about himself and his partner, that Vladimir blurts out, "Tell him . . . *(he hesitates)* . . . tell him you saw us" (p. 34a). "Us"—the word surely includes those on- and those offstage, all those who experienced the play as it was performed, after its emergence from the past and before Godot's arrival. In Act 2 that "us" becomes "me," and the reference to either side of the stage is that much more personal.[48] If the play is in any sense autobiographical, then the "us" or "me" includes the modest play-wright as well. The tree may indeed mean several things; conversely, as a paradox, a sign of meager life and a defective agent for suicide, it may not be capable of being reduced to a single meaning. But when Vladimir and Estragon try being the tree, the action is complete, pure, itself—and immediately experienced by the audience.

We assist in this creation, this present, by coming to the theater.[49] Like the clowns, we work, even if it be waiting in our seats; even the audience members at the Coconut Grove premiere who stalked out in disgust contributed to the waiting by enacting the alternative to those staying in their place. The actors do likewise onstage, held there by convictions as characters (they have been told to wait) or as actors (it is their role). In this dual partnership of actor and audience, both depending on the other for their present existence, we collectively establish an artifice against an imposed Godot-ruled world, against that difficult, at times incomprehensible reality that for them is *"A country road. A tree. Evening,"* and for us is all that lies outside as well as inside the theater. Vladimir boasts:

> We are no longer alone, waiting for the night, waiting for Godot, waiting for . . . waiting. All evening we have struggled, unassisted. Now it's over. It's already to-morrow. (P. 50a)

Like Hamlet at his end, Vladimir talks to the audience onstage, but surely in his "We" he includes the audience offstage as well.

Tragedies, when all other definitions have been offered, are about death; comedies are about life, about the interrelation between mankind and creation. Oberon's artifice in *A Midsummer Night's Dream,* his conscious manipulation of the mortals into a comic play, with happiness replacing the *Romeo and Juliet* ending that threatens the lovers in Act 1, allows Hermia to surmount Theseus's earlier sterile trinity of alternatives: unwanted marriage, confinement in a convent, or physical death. *Godot* itself become a comedy by Act 2. The dark questions of who is Godot and will he come give way to the human instinct for survival, to that creative urge which will fashion something out of nothing, which will snatch from impending defeat (such as the nonappearance of the divinity) a modest victory (passing the time with dialogue, putting the events of Act 1 in some sort of order, albeit minimal). If we are chained to waiting, we will still find a little leverage, a little breathing and creative space in our chains. *Godot* is not a romantic play, but it *is* realistic. It is not about death, not about suicide. To wait or to go on—these are actions, not nonactions; and waiting and going on are the two alternatives to death. Vladimir and Estragon *wait;* they do not go on. Pozzo and Lucky go on, and they disappear, accordingly and appropriately, from the present play. The clowns stay with us, both to and at the end: *"They do not move"* (p. 60b). We are also the clowns, for in our seats we have done no more, nor no less, than Vladimir and Estragon. Like us, they speculate about the meaning of the play. For them, as for us, the play, even in the absence of meaning, is a way of passing time, though time would have passed anyway, as Estragon observes.

We share the same anxieties, though however aware they may be of the audience the tramps cannot know this. If there is no Godot to witness and ratify their actions, *we* are there, the "Godot" for who they have waited. Without us their audience shrinks to one, Estragon for Vladimir, Vladimir for Estragon. The two other spectators are a sorry lot, mute and egotistical. Again, they are not there at the end as we are. Vladimir is right, albeit a bit melodramatic, when he raises the idea that all one can say of his life is "that with Estragon my friend, at this place, until the fall of night, I waited for Godot" (p. 58a). "Waited"—he uses the word as a slur, as if the time spent were nothing but a bag of actor's tricks; and it is, *it is*. In the absence of anything else—and Vladimir cannot imagine that we as audience both ratify and interpret his stage "life"—to have waited is to have lived, for, as I have been arguing, the play is, at bottom line, nothing more. Nor should it be.

Compared with the artists of the trilogy, Vladimir and Estragon may not seem impressive. For there we might devise a scheme in which Moran, the uncreating bureaucrat, finds his deeper, creative self in Molloy. Incoherent as an artist because he represents chaos without form, Molloy leads to Malone, whose attempt to escape from the self through stories is, after several failures and aborted tales, partially successful. At the end of *Malone Dies* he almost succeeds, *almost,* in escaping on the raft drifting rudderless out to sea with its sorry crew of escaped inmates. The Unnamable, like Shakespeare's Richard II, peoples his isolated world with his own creations, though about that creation he is alternately unsure or neurotic. However, Vladimir and Estragon are caught in the public medium of the theater; their voyage to creation cannot have the armchair immunity appropriate to the reading of a novel. Besides, they lack the vocabulary and the mental equipment necessary for profound creation, and they are tied to the cosmos by a command to wait. Still, their world is comic precisely because in place of that command to wait they substitute their own activities, their "theater" of waiting. When measured against the lazy and self-indulgent Murphy, who cannot give up his material world, and the Cartesian rationalist Watt, however, they are surely creators of—well—the third order. If one goal is not realized, that meeting with Godot, then another is, namely, the creative powers of the human imagination that will draw the image of a rose from a dunghill, that, in the absence of roses or of dunghills, will pass the time and avoid the abyss by dialogue.

Again, nature signals its approval of this creation with its own scrawny leaves in Act 2.[50] Vladimir and Estragon, I maintain, are not the same in the second act; nor are we. We will not let ourselves *not* grow. Time passes and with time there is change, be it progressive or cyclical or inevitable. At its roots "growth" implies only change, not necessarily quality. As long as words are imposed on the chronology of seconds and minutes and hours, time is not an abstraction but only a measuring stick for a civilization marked by language. We cling to life; we avoid the abyss by talking. Every syllable uttered, as Henry observes in *Embers,* is a second gained. The frustration of the unending wait is, from another perspective, a sign for limited joy: death is kept at arm's length, as is silence, as is loneliness.[51]

v

If Vladimir and Estragon are creative, however dimly and however pathetic the creation, Pozzo and Lucky stand as their antithesis—especially Pozzo. He wants to be creative; hence his speech on the night. However, that speech is a sterile thing, since Pozzo is nothing but a mass of preconceptions. He is past tense in a play that has nothing more affirmative than present tense to offer. Clearly, Pozzo is chained to a preexisting, hardened order, the master-slave hierarchy, a theory of dominance rooted in the land, in a feudal-agrarian order that contradicts the freedom characterizing the road and those who travel along it searching for Godot. For Pozzo the road only leads somewhere, and he is thus a victim of his own materialism, most grossly expressed in his desire to sell another human being.

Pozzo may be like Godot, like all gods that exist outside the creative boards. Both Godot and Pozzo are masters who beat their servant, and the old man's white hair is mirrored in Pozzo's own white head. Pozzo and Godot: the sounds are close. On Pozzo's first entrance the tramps mistake him for Godot. Alternate theories would hold that Godot is the absent artist, the God of Bishop Berkeley who—here with a vengeance—does not ratify the existence of man by constant surveillance. Godot may be the nineteenth-century God as watchmaker, who sets his creation moving and then retires to the wings. Still, if Pozzo is Godot, or a surrogate, he is also a parody of the idealized god, a petty god given to things of the flesh (chicken, wine, physical force) rather than of the spirit. Ultimately, he is a fallen or dying god.

Most of all, he is a fraudulent actor-artist, a *poseur,* a Pozzo, a clown, a Bozzo—and arrogantly unconscious of the fact. If the tramps are only dimly creative, Pozzo is the negation of that creation. His grave speech— "They gave birth astride of a grave, the light gleams an instant, then it's night once more" (p. 58a)—may be the truth if we will accept it, but it leads only to annihilation, and this is a destination never reached by the play, try as the clowns will with the suicide tree. Like Shakespeare's melancholy Jaques in *As You Like It,* Pozzo would lead us, for all his sophistication and wisdom, to a no-exit. Jaques remains hermetically sealed in the pastoral Arden, while Pozzo, with comic difficulty, just manages to make it off-stage.[52] Plays, however, are creations, steps away from the abyss; the darkness and chaos of existence are not so extreme, not so final that they cannot be put into a form for the contemplation, if not the enjoyment of the audience. Galsworthy with his Victorian plays embodying ideals of right conduct and Artaud with his theater of cruelty—both are, in this sense, optimists. Both are the "gay" poets of which Yeats speaks in "Lapis Lazuli." There is, I would argue, a message in the theatrical medium that coexists with, indeed that sometimes battles with the message, however nihilistic, consciously espoused by the playwright. Form, "style" as Beckett calls it in that early commentary on Joyce, may be all we have, but by definition it opposes chaos.

Under rules of the conventional, well-made play Pozzo would be more acceptable because he brings a story with him and thereby material for a conventional plot, but his old-fashioned, exclusively "story" theater, this art founded on something as opposed to the liberating nothingness of experience itself, this theater of fact sees its birth, brief life, and death in Lucky, in a life as complete and as brief as *Breath* itself. Lucky starts mute, is slowly roused into action both by Pozzo's maltreatment and by his interactions with Vladimir and Estragon. Stage two of his brief, uneventful story is the dance, a primitive theater perhaps, before or without words; and it is followed, as we know, by Lucky's long speech, at once profound and inane, entertaining and irritating, a speech in which words, in Ionesco's fashion, finally double back on themselves, choking in their own ashes. Stage three is the fall, the silence; Lucky ends the play *"dumb"* and his master blind. It *is* a story, and if we attach an allegory to the pair theirs is a meaningful story; yet it also ends incomplete, violating the storyteller's cardinal rule.[53]

Even the tramps are capable of a product less than commendable, less than creative. Both are given to canned stories, like that set in the brothel or the one about the two thieves. Vladimir's song that opens the second act tells a silly, cyclical tale. Such tales may have considerable thematic significance, as commentaries on the state of the *Godot* world, but aesthetically they seem forced, even more forced than the devices employed by Vladimir and Estragon to beguile the time of waiting. These "imported" stories, especially the one about the tailor, are about *something;* they make a point and they have a moral, in the most pretentious sense of that word. Still, they are crudely, if unconsciously grafted by the teller and consciously so by the playwright himself onto an organic play capable of generating its own experience. Some critics see the stories as shortcuts on Beckett's part, formulas from a flagging mind. I do not think so; there seems to be a clear distinction here between the function of the teller and that of the playwright. Hamm, properly, admires the artist who, looking at his work, saw nothing. In a biblical sense, one must give up everything, even hope and, especially here, all stories peripheral to the present action. To face the "unfaceable" is the proper task for the playwright; his so-called "stories" come from that decision but are not prequisite to it. To look out and see nothing, or to wait and receive nothing, and to talk about it, to act on it, to devise a way or ways of being in the horrible presence of nonbeing—this is the artist's high calling.

## vi

A word, dialogue in the larger sense, is nothing substantial, but only words, words, words.[54] Thus words are the perfect, indeed the only correlative for the state that Beckett wishes to convey. They give form without requiring substance, an object. Words are no more or no less effective, or significant, when uttered in a vacuum than in a room teaming with objects. Words are the instrument of both playwright and actor. Like Krapp, who fondles words such as *viduity,* Beckett's tramps, and particularly Vladimir, are involved with language. Vladimir's very nickname, Didi, suggests the French root for talking. He confesses a special fondness for *appalled.* Both know that they can't stop talking, even for a minute. Even when there is no formal dialogue, the pantomime conveys the essence of the word, much as the student in Ionesco's *The Lesson* silently conveys the essence of the word *kill* when she is fatally assaulted by her teacher.[55] When the dialogue threatens to be disrupted, as at the parting between the tramps and Pozzo, a series of fierce and comic "Adieus" conveys the desperate attempt to rekindle words, however banal.

Words are the way, then, of passing the time, and the theater in this light becomes not an allegory for our human condition but the "thing" itself, the sole "condition" we have as audience and actors. We assert that condition, that momentary reality, in dialogue—not in speechlessness, not in isolated reactions, not in overt monologues (such as Pozzo is given to), not in dreams experienced only by the dreamer, but in *dialogue,* the verbal interaction between two people. Excluding *Act Without Words I,* no dramatic work by Beckett, be it for the legitimate theater, cinema, television, or radio, is a one-character play. Even Krapp has his earlier self on the recorder, and the most loquacious characters, such as Winnie or Mouth in *Not I,* need an audience. One might even argue that in *Act Without Words I* the whistle that blows offstage or the unseen hand tempting the Everyman with refreshment, death instruments, and shade is the partner for the otherwise single mime on stage. Dialogue may be concealed in a seeming monologue, and it is possible, from this perspective, to see Vladimir and Estragon as halves of a single personality. But halves they are, and one talks, at the very least, with a projection of oneself. The situation here parallels the dilemma posed by the existentialist: to think about oneself, to affirm one's existence, one must step outside oneself to conceive that one exists. To be is to be perceived, as the Latin motto for *Film* has it, although here the perceiver is not God (his picture is turned facing backward on the wall). One starts with dialogue; as Vladimir observes, the first task is to start. One speaks and is spoken to, by passing the ball, by doing a little canter (p. 42a).

Words also figure in the various human "stages" underscoring the play. In the first stage there is a fear of nothingness that one struggles to escape. "No use struggling" and then "No use wriggling," Estragon observes. The fall is all-encompassing, as evidenced in speeches such as Lucky's or in the characters' own physical degeneration. Lucky's bags, which seemed to contain something of weight, if not of value in Act 1, are revealed in Act 2 to hold only sand. As the fall accelerates, as the abyss looms, the characters lose confidence even in words. Estragon confesses that they have been "blathering" about "nothing in particular" (p. 42b). In their despair both characters try to disappear behind the tree, to become nothing. Vladimir knows that all that they have said, as well as done, is "insignificant" (p. 44a).

With words failing, and the concurrent possibility of losing one's fragile hold on the world, some characters like Pozzo turn in the second stage to the seeming security of objects: his watch, his pipe, wine, the chicken, the table, the rope. Yet when Pozzo, like Hamm, becomes blind, that philosophical riddle of how something can exist if it is not seen takes on grim overtones. Estragon himself clings to objects, such as his boots, but he has pitifully few such possessions, and a defective memory erases most meanings that have attached themselves to the boots. Vladimir takes some solace in facts, but the facts lack a context. His truisms, the conjectures on this and that, seem to lead nowhere.

Both characters, as we have seen earlier, try in a third stage to create an inner play, with material and dialogue spun not out of external things but out of the play itself. This mythmaking, if you will, is also a dead end, if the object be to create something, to establish, hurriedly and perhaps neurotically, a defense against the possibility of nothingness. Again, to hurl oneself on the myth of time, as an ordering factor in human existence, is no less frustrating. One can always bide one's time, of course, but to be efficacious this demands that one believe in something for which the time passed is well spent. There is no such assurance in the play, and the biblical precept of "patience in adversity" takes on a correspondingly hollow meaning.

The fourth stage completes the series leading beyond the sense of nothingness and those attempts to combat it with objects, myths, and time. We come back to where we started; the road of the play is a high road leading nowhere. "Don't let's do anything. It's safer" (p. 12b). The commitment to nothing, to nonmovement and noncommitment, plows under futile attempts to deny its "existence." Such nothingness is larger, more pervasive, and more powerful because more true than the relative and impotent impositions of objectivity, intellection, mythology, and temporality with which mortals try to deny the "dark zone" at the core of their being.

The stages themselves constitute a cycle suggesting that the end is not the end, but only a stage itself—indeed, that it is only the prelude to the next beginning. The play goes nowhere: Vladimir and Estragon are in the same position at the end as at the beginning. Appropriately, Act 1 opens with a line underlining this cycle: "I'm beginning to come round to that opinion." Act 2 opens with Vladimir's cyclical song about the dog, and his first words to Estragon—and the audience as well, I suspect—are "You again." The play abounds with cycles. The pus is never the same pus from second to second, though the word *pus* includes the entire process of discharge. Night follows night, and, as in *Happy Days,* one can only "wait for day to come" (p. 18). Here, surely, are grounds either for cynicism or for comfort, depending on one's perspective.

If at times the cycle seems to constitute a downward spiral—even as the second pipeful, Pozzo comments, is never so good as the first (though it is still "sweet")—at other times it seems to go upward. The boots in Act 2 fit better, and, as we have observed, Act 2 is more creative, building as it does on the materials furnished by its predecessor. Still, vertical movement is here counterbalanced; the cycle reasserts itself as just that, a linear movement to a point and then a return.

In a similar fashion *Play* suggests upward movement when the characters forget their petty stories and consider their condition before the interrogation light. From another perspective *Play's* second half suggests a downward movement when the light becomes the major focus of their attention. Only by the merciful, agreed-upon time limit of the playwright-director, Beckett, is part two, once repeated, not repeated again. It *will* be repeated the next performance, but only *after* Act 1 is performed.

This is our comfort in *Godot,* a comfort similar to that in *Play* when, after the story of husband, wife, and mistress is established, we can relax, physically, intellectually, and aesthetically. If all changes, the change itself is part, and only a part, of a cycle. That the tree sprouts a few leaves in Act 2 may be taken by some critics as an upward swing of hope, the blossoming of that hope once deferred. However, this comfort is minuscule compared to our brave admission that the "leafiness" will by the next performance be reduced to "leaflessness," to be followed by leafiness, and so on. In that infinity, that cycle, is the comfort. All changes, nothing changes; it was so in Arcady and it is so now, as Mrs. Rooney knows. Like Vladimir we peer inside the hat of the play "as if in search of something," to echo Molloy, whose hat is also a factor (p. 95). The round hat, its symmetrical brim, its position as a covering for the head, and its tendency to fall from that head—these are clear signs that the search for meaning is both futile (circularly unending) and eternal.

## vii

In this light the Boy—like the boy in *Endgame,* or the young boy who reports the death of another in *All that Fall*—is both the epitome of the cycle and the symbol of its comfort. If he is *only* Godot's messenger, he is also, literally and figuratively, the closest thing we have to Godot in the play. In a way he is Godot, the one who, almost anagrammatically, "goes to" Vladimir and Estragon.

He suffers, or his brother suffers, from Godot's beatings, and his life— he sleeps on straw—is meager. But he does not fall, and he *can* leave the stage. He can do what none of the characters in the play can do, and what Hamm and Clov, and Nagg and Nell, cannot do—and Winnie and Willie for good measure. He "is"; he is certain. In our prison productions, in most productions of the play, the same actor plays both boys. Pozzo's and Lucky's second entrance, establishing, as do many other elements, the repetitive nature of the plot, also assures us that the Boy will come again. If his message is not hopeful, or profound, it is, at very least, the same message. In a world where everything falls, in a world of the most enervating mutability, the Boy remains constant.

He is pastoral, for he and his brother mind the sheep and goats, respectively. And he carries with him something of the "wise boy" of folk literature. An innocent, he does not know whether he is happy or unhappy, whether Godot is fond or not fond of him, or why Godot chooses to beat his brother rather than himself. He is in Godot's employ; he knows more about Godot—he has seen Godot—than those waiting for him. For example, he confirms Vladimir's inquiry as to the color of Godot's beard. Yet he says nothing profound. His relationship with Godot is generally *calm*— Vladimir's favorite word—and therefore unlike the relation between Pozzo and Lucky, or Vladimir and Estragon, or Vladimir and the theoretical Godot, or Estragon and the theoretical Godot. If others come and go, he confesses that he has been there in the wings for "a good while" (32b). He is the cheerful servant in a play where other servants or past servants are anguished over the purpose of their existence.

The Boy embodies, then, the spirit of going on, going on not because things in themselves are meaningful, or because some superstructure imparts meaning to our existence, or because there is a god who shapes our ends, rough hew them how we will. He goes on the way the play itself goes on. It is about starting and finishing and starting again; the repetition that would bore us in life is not an issue of debate for the actors onstage. Their conscious participation in a play that is performed only to end, and that ends only to be performed again, is a testament to a spirit, embodied unconsciously in the Boy, to live without means necessarily leading to ends, or to live in the absence of actions that, once done, trammel up the consequences. I take the play's title as, among other things, a cry to persevere without props or objects, or facts, or myth, or measurement, or direction. Vladimir sums it up, for audience, actor, and playwright, and for the characters when they are sentient: "That with Estragon my friend, at this place until the fall of night, I waited for Godot" (p. 58a).

As audience, we are asked to consider the meaning of our existence on life's stage. There are revolutionaries galore for whom the theater is a mere trifle or an example of decadent entertainment. For "everyone knows" we must accomplish something in life, or do things, or—acting as if any human motives could be pure—help our comrades whether they want that help or not. In the presence of such challenges to the meaning of our existence, we can only say—and say only—that on any given night of a performance of *Godot* we acted not alone but in concert, not with an excessive trust in physical life, nor, given the physical nature of the stage, with a pseudo-intellectual, let alone spiritual dismissal of physical reality. Together, actors and audience, we waited for Godot: "Tell him . . . *(he hesitates)* . . . tell him you saw me and that . . . *(he hesitates)* . . . that you saw me" (p. 59a). If that be blasphemy in the eyes of religious or political pietists, then the devil make the most of it.[56]

# 2 *Endgame*: The Playwright Completes Himself

A common practice in the theater is to cover the set once the play is over so that it will be the same set, "virginal" if you will, at the next performance, not changed by the dust and dirt that make their way into the playhouse. *Endgame* opens with the figurative "birth" of its playwright as the servant Clov *"goes to Hamm, removes sheet covering him, folds it over his arms"* (p. 1). To use the technical term from the Elizabethan stage, Hamm is "discovered," though for a time he is stationary while Clov holds the stage.

Some critics have seen in Clov's opening lines, "Finished, it's nearly finished, it must be nearly finished," echoes of the creation story, though the lines themselves are ambiguous: is the creation (Hamm?) nearly finished and therefore soon to blossom in its own right? Or is the world about to end, "finished"? Clov then departs for the kitchen, his own orderly offstage world ("Nice dimensions, nice proportions" [p. 2]).

On Clov's departure, Hamm himself completes the discovery, first yawning under the handkerchief that covers his head and then removing it to reveal a *"Very red face. Black glasses."* Hamm's opening line, "Me," may suggest a tremendous ego, though, as we will see, an ego quite appropriate if we think of him as the play's lead actor, its ham or Hamlet, or perhaps the playwright himself, the creative force behind the stage world. A second yawn introduces the next suggestive line, actually a continuation of "Me": "to play" (p. 2). We might take the word *play* either as a verb—meaning "now I will play"—or as a noun, a compression of "to the play": Hamm will now get to his play. We have heard the phrase before in Beckett: Malone speaks of "play" and the Unnamable directs "Worm to play."[1] If, to echo Hamm himself, we would allow "every man his speciality" (p. 10), then I believe that Hamm's *speciality* is creation itself, however bleak the created world of this play may seem.

i

Hamm's creation here seems to be an internal one, that inner world peopled by the imagination of a blind man. Whereas Clov is concerned with the external, with the one physical setting itself—he speculates that "There's nowhere else" (p. 6)—Hamm's concern is that of "Text 2": "Perhaps we're in a head."[2] Deprived of a sense of perspective by his blindness, he can only think of man and, more specifically, of himself as the macrocosm. Appropriately, his speculation is that there is "no one else" (p. 6). For Hamm the external world *is* the illusion, in the most negative sense of that word: "Outside of here it's death" (p. 9).

At the start Hamm is asleep, his power of creation dormant. He may well be dreaming, for several times during the play he makes reference to the pleasures of this state. As in the medieval dream vision, he moves, after Clov's discovery, from sleep to waking, from dreams to the *informing* of his dreams. The source of that informing, as it was for the medievalist, is not ultimately the external world, for the vision, thus formed, is only an approximation of an internal state that, without art, cannot be known.

There is a falling off, a loss of clarity as one moves from the dream vision to the waking reality. If Hamm could continue sleeping he "might make love"; he might "go into the woods . . . and [his] eyes would see . . . the sky, the earth" (p. 18). His vision here is one of absolute freedom, of a world where one can move, "run"—ironic for an invalid confined to a wheelchair. Still, this idyllic world conjured by the dreamer's fancy is irrelevant to the present play, whose concern, as Hamm immediately qualifies the vision, is the "Nature" of his own "head" and "heart." If that idyllic world, where one is free in space and time, *is* reality, it represents an external force that, later made manifest in the figure of the small boy, would intrude on and ultimately destroy the artist's fictive inscape.

This inner space, the single stage set before us, is the artist's domain, the "now" informed by the narrative itself, with a past that is either irrelevant or tragic (sometime in the past Nagg and Nell lost their legs) and a future that is either irrelevant or potentially tragic (the boy who threatens to unravel Hamm's creation). In an extraordinary compression of the body's two most vital organs, Hamm finds his "heart in his head" (the line is repeated by Nagg [p. 18]), thereby reversing the cliché about thinking with one's heart. The playwright's internal process is a rational one: the feelings of the heart, those emotions allowing him to react positively or negatively to life, are given form in the head. By a sort of reverse gravity the juices of the heart flow upward to the head; Hamm confesses that there is something "dripping" in his head.[3]

We have made a quantum leap from *Godot*. There the set, while clearly external, was sparsely populated, and so the impoverished tree and rock only underscored the barren outer world that, given the intellectual and imaginative capacities of Vladimir and Estragon, served as an appropriate stage for their waiting. Here the set is an inner one, a room, but it is heavily populated with ashbins, a ladder, windows, a picture, numerous props, and with the suggestion of a kitchen just offstage. However, this relatively lavish set, if taken literally, seems an inadequate correlative for the world Hamm struggles to define. Clov, who dons a traveler's costume in the play's final moments, may be a holdover from *Godot*. If this is so, then Hamm, while not Godot himself, is a dominant force, a master or godlike figure who, more than the relatively shallow Pozzo, might be a suitable object for the tramps' quest in the earlier play.

Hamm is physically blind,[4] and Clov must serve as his eyes. Still, the inner eye, the "mind's eye" (1.2.185) as Hamlet would have it, works overtime here. That eye sees not objective reality, nor is it subject to the historic materialism that confirmed existence for those eighteenth-century philosophers like Berkeley whom Beckett studied and in part rejected. Instead, Hamm's "eye" views only an "infinite emptiness" that is "all around" (p. 36). The trick in *Endgame* is to "play" on that infinite emptiness, to give it form through words, even though words themselves are ultimately only empty abstractions. The "game," in the sense that word is used in "Enueg I," is to make something—however meager—out of nothing.[5] Hamm's prediction is that Clov will someday experience that same emptiness, seeing, like the painter-engraver, the apparent something of the external world for what it truly is (p. 44).

That engraver, surely, is a surrogate for the central character, because Hamm has no other source of reference than himself and yet finds it too painful, as well as inappropriate by the rules of this endgame, to reveal himself too completely too soon. For the engraver the entire physical world, from rising corn to the sails of the herring fleet, all that "loveliness" as bounded by land and sea, was nothing—"ashes." Even the possibility of an external world subject to the engraver's or—as Hamm alters it— painter's interpretation no longer exists, for that was "way back," during a time "in the land of the living." Clov delivers the benediction to a reality that is no more: "God be with the days" (p. 44). When he complains that today, in contrast, "There are so many terrible things," he errs not so much in the adjective "terrible" as he does in the assumption that there are still "things." Hamm cautiously corrects him: "No, no, there are not so many now." That correction allows for the more proper definition of the present world, a world of theater or play, an artifice created by Hamm: "Do you not think this has gone on long enough?" It is the play world, then, that is "this . . . this . . . thing" (p. 45). Hamm doubts that Clov will be equal to the task of giving form to nothing or this inner world of artifice, doubting that his actor can turn playwright. (As we shall see, the play itself, *Endgame*, partially disproves this gloomy assessment, but then Hamm has an image to protect.)

Hamm's play thereby becomes the informing of his "misery" (p. 2)—of himself, to be more exact.[6] Whereas Clov has "nothing to say," Hamm has a "few words" to "ponder" in his heart (p. 79), the heart that, we know, leads to the head. For him the greater his suffering the "emptier" (p. 3) he must become: the resulting form has an inverse correlation to its origin. Lesser men—if we can stand Hamm's arrogant pronouncement at the opening of the play—can hold a greater portion of their suffering. Hamm's lot, the playwright's lot—and the very condition about which Shakespeare complains in his Sonnets—is to express everything, to prostitute inner emotions before an audience. The artistic fate is analogous, as several contemporary artists have observed, to the act of masturbation, a metaphor Beckett will revisit in *Eh Joe*. It must be complete, not half-hearted; and once started, there is no turning back. The act is intimate and pleasurable—yet sterile in any biological sense. Hence the bleak bomb shelter of Hamm's world is also the hive of great imaginative activity. Once this inner world is "peopled," given form, the tragedy itself is not resolved but rather is made public. The tragedy remains gruesome, yet there is an aesthetic pleasure in the form, and hence we applaud, rather than weep, at its conclusion.[7] This informing is essentially comic, and while parents may die in Beckett's plays and novels (in *Malone Dies*, for example), the lead characters do not. In Beckett the lead characters' informing of their tragedies, whether it be Malone on his deathbed or Winnie in her earthly prison, depends on their own consciousness of their creation. Malone has a pad and a pencil, however much they have deteriorated; and Winnie has props galore, plus half-remembered snatches from songs, proverbs, and poetry. Aesthetic "life" springs from thematic "death," and in *Endgame* death, though ever-present, does not touch Hamm. Similarly, Vladimir and Estragon, though only dim creators when compared with Hamm, cannot die: the suicide tree is inadequate and the belt breaks.

As a creator Hamm craves rain, since its nourishment is necessary for the seeds of his mind; Clov is equally positive that it won't rain (p. 73). Eager for Clov's seeds to sprout, Hamm is distressed when Clov contends that they won't. He then suggests that Clov might do well to scratch about a bit more; perhaps they were planted too early.

If Hamm opens the play by enumerating his miseries, it is still true that he, as opposed to Nagg whom he dismisses as an "accursed progenitor" (p. 9), is the blessed progenitor of *Endgame* and is strangely optimistic, despite those miseries, whereas Clov, the son, is the pessimist.[8] Old-fashioned in such optimism, Hamm is the sometimes benevolent god or the playwright as god to his little world. Positioned at its center, given to surveying the walls defining its circumference, attended by his not always obedient Ariel—who, like his Shakespearean prototype, also yearns for freedom—Hamm is a jealous god, fearful of having any other god raised before him, whether it be in the person of a small boy or a flea. Like Prospero, he is a word-giver, both father and teacher to Clov. And he is egocentric, as gods are wont to be, just as Vladimir and Estragon are ego-deficient, as true subjects are wont to be. The single set of *Endgame*, the shabby room, *is* the world, the theater of the world both literal and figurative that the father, the playwright, offers his adopted son, Clov. "You can't leave us" (p. 37), he explains ruthlessly, for Clov is an inseparable part of Hamm's world.

Again, Kenner's hypothesis, that the set of *Endgame* resembles the inside of a human skull, with the two rear windows serving as eyes, is especially relevant here.[9] For when the generation of the 1970s spoke of "blowing the mind," that phrase only implied a readjustment in the mind's link to external reality. But "outside of here," outside *Endgame*'s set, outside the mind that is being informed through the artistic process, it is clearly "death" (p. 9). Life, in Beckett's definition here, is not a fact but rather a process involving conscious creation through words, and also actions, as in the two mimes. By such creation one gives the "illusion" of existence, a conscious artifice to be set against the misguided assumption of reality held by those outside *Endgame*'s single stage set. I think it is his avoidance of death, of nothingness, an avoidance not studied but inevitable, that makes Beckett, like Shaw's hero in *Arms and the Man,* the "true romantic."[10]

Hamm as god, Hamm as artist—the ascription seems to work both ways. If he is a god, his world is horribly shrunken, yet, however shrunken that world, Hamm guards it jealously against the rival, outside world of earth, water, color, and light that he knows only through his servant's reports. Omniscient on the stage set, his knowledge of this outside "set" is fully dependent on Clov's eyes. In the several drafts of *Endgame,* Beckett pared away at the description of that rival world, particularly as embodied in the young boy. Yet the mere suggestion of its existence terrifies Hamm, even though for us, as audience, the poverty of reality only accents the richness of the ever-present "little room" before us.

Conversely, we may see Hamm as the artist, his world limitless, eternally growing in his head and heart. Waiting for the painkiller may be only a comic bow in the direction of *Godot.* In point of fact, Hamm as artist uses words as productively in informing his suffering as Vladimir and Estragon used words unproductively in waiting for what they imagine will be their savior, rather than their painkiller or terminus.

Given to stories, Hamm is his own story and storyteller, the narrator/narrated, spinning his tales spiderlike from within himself. Beckett's artists, such as Words in *Words and Music,* protest that the stories do not come from inside them, but I think that by such assertions they only call attention to the ultimate end, the informing or "publication" of an inner vision. All begins from within, from "Me" (again, Hamm's first word), from precisely that acute consciousness that Clov for the most part lacks and that Vladimir and Estragon experience only in dream lapses, or when Lucky and Pozzo provide a mirror image of their own condition. As we shall see, the story of the man begging alms for his son is only superficially about someone else. As Hamm says, "There's no one else" (p. 6), and in his way Hamm embodies all people: he is the man seeking bread, and the object of that charity, and the stern judge who denies succor, and Mother Pegg who, like Socrates, seeks truth with her light, as well as Mother Pegg barely existing in her final days with that light extinguished. In a sense the play is one large monologue parading as a four-character drama. Like Shakespeare's Richard II in his cell, Hamm peoples his little world through this union of heart and head—his equivalent for that coupling of mind and soul in his royal counterpart.

Thus constricted, Hamm sets about creating, or "we do what we can" (p. 11); it is "slow" and, I would add, painful "work" (p. 12). For that story actors are required—and hence Clov. The playwright also needs an audience; unlike the theoretical audience for those novels with which Beckett began his career, the audience here is actual. So dependent, the artist's inner vision relies for its informing on the collective abilities and consciousness of a host of people. The play is a public testament to an inner world. Krapp's one book was a failure—*Effie* sold only thirteen copies—whereas his tape recordings are overheard by a real audience.

If such publication of an inner state can "mean something," then perhaps it "won't all have been for nothing" (pp. 32–33). Given this pragmatic, even didactic sense of mission, I find it misguided, though natural, to say that Beckett has nothing to say. Hamm's struggle to make or to mean something, "to say" himself—to borrow a favorite infinitive from Beckett—separates him as playwright light years from writers of the so-called absurdist theater.

## ii

Clov is the actor to Hamm's playwright, and the latter rightly observes that "gone from me you'd be dead." Conversely, Hamm needs Clov or, as at the end, must turn actor himself to preserve the play.[11] If Vladimir and Estragon are halves of a common personality—brains and body, head and feet, speaker and doer—then so are Hamm and Clov, with an added aesthetic dimension. Clov can't sit: he acts, in the broadest sense of that word. And Hamm can't do anything but sit. He is the cerebral half, both in terms of life and the theater. The literal food, the carrots and radishes that Vladimir furnished Estragon, are here symbolic food: the words, the dialogue. It is to this linguistic food that Hamm refers, I believe, when he threatens to give Clov "nothing more to eat" (p. 5). Clov's "Then we'll die" sustains the theme of a joint aesthetic life. If the actor goes, the playwright's mouthpiece goes, and hence the playwright is rendered inoperative. Some compromise is needed; as "Text 1" phrases it, "let them [the body and the head or, if you will, Clov and Hamm] work it out between them."[12] So Hamm continues, "I'll give you just enough to keep you from dying. You'll be hungry all the time." Surely we have here a perfect description of the increasingly sparse dialogue characterizing Beckett's plays. The lips are both the initial "confrontation" for food destined for the body and—as Ionesco describes so graphically in *The Lesson*—the final outpost for words on their way out into the public atmosphere of conversation or stage dialogue.[13]

In this way the physical relationship between the two always has an aesthetic "otherside." Hamm is concerned whether or not he has made Clov suffer too much or too little (pp. 6–7); when Clov replies that he hasn't been forced to suffer unduly, Hamm is ecstatic. By Hamm's own admission in that first speech, his concern is presenting his own misery—read "tragedy" (p. 2). The more of that tragedy Clov as actor can undertake, the more complete will be Hamm's expression of his inner nature. Like his

Shakespearean namesake, Hamm is concerned with the golden mean of expression. Too little suffering, and hence too little to be experienced by the audience, and the play fails to mean enough. Too much suffering to express, and the actor might die onstage. Either way threatens to abort the process. One must fit action to the word, the word to the action.

As with the Unnamable, others' suffereings are "nothing compared" to those of the artist. Yet others, however deficient in the experience of tragedy, must embody the artist's supreme suffering, whether it be in the form of the Unnamable's fictive characters or Hamm's not-completely-pliant actor. In this sense, Winnie is as much actor as artist; properly, she is surrounded by the artifacts of other artists, whether it be the advertising copy on the toothbrush or actual lines from Shakespeare and Browning. The ultimate artist is absent in *Godot,* though, as I have argued, the tramps try their hand at creation in the second act, even if it be an art that passes the time and does little else. Once Hamm has emerged as artist, even as Beckett feels his way in what was still, for him, a relatively new medium, artists will come at us galore: Krapp, Henry, plus assorted Openers, and Voices, and Mouths. The issue in *Endgame* is how to sustain the tragedy until the fruit ripens sufficiently for the final scene. Die too early or die too late—these are the grounds for melodrama, not tragedy.

Though Hamm and Clov complement each other, their relationship is still an uneasy one, and as the play progresses the disciple threatens revolt. Like Shakespeare's Caliban, he would cease to be only a "brute beast" (p. 80). At one point Clov even hurls the dog—the symbol of Hamm's sterile, albeit illusory creation—at his master (p. 76). But then Beckett's couples always fight; the halves of the composite soul, like the warring body and soul in countless Renaissance poems, are necessary, inevitable, but unhappy bedfellows. Vladimir and Estagon are continually threatening separation; Willie, whom Winnie needs as audience, promises either love or murder at the end of *Happy Days;* Molly and Moran may ultimately be the same being, but the latter seeks to capture the former; the head in *The Unnamable* depends on a waitress who is also a torturer; and for the narrator of *How It Is* to speak with Pim he must deliver an anal insult ("stab him simply in the arse that is to speak" [p. 71]) to his counterpart before the dialogue can begin.

This division is inseparable from the complementary qualities. Clov *must* war with Hamm, actor with playwright, because Clov, constitutionally unlike the playwright, can assert his integrity only as a reverse image of his master's. Truman Capote once spoke of actors as being dumb creatures who only mouth the dialogue as directed. Hamlet himself fears that the clowns of the visiting troupe will ignore the lines of that playwright ultimately responsible for *The Murder of Gonzago.* Playwrights, however, speak from personal bias and, important as they are, are not fully responsible for what happens on stage.

Accordingly, Clov, when compared with the hyperimaginative Hamm, is more a creature of "habits" (p. 81), therefore siding with that half of the habit/imagination dichotomy established by Beckett in his book on Proust. Imagination is the road leading to tragedy, and Hamm fully assumes the tragic post of the sufferer at the end. Habit keeps the specter of tragedy distant, and Clov at the end reappears backstage, away from Hamm's tragic center, dressed like some vaudeville comedian: "*Enter Clov, dressed for the road. Panama hat, tweed coat, raincoat over his arm, umbrella, bag*" (p. 82).[14] In place of Hamm's large and often spectacular mental "visions" (Flora, Pomona, a new mental world that replaces the present stinking universe [p. 46], the ocean, the waves, the horizon, the sun), Clov sees only "gray" (p. 31).[15] His real focus is not on the mind but on the audience surrounding the stage. Whereas Hamm, until his last speech, is primarily responsible for his personal visions, Clov as actor gives first priority to us. He sees in his glass "a multitude . . . in transports . . . of joy" (p. 29).

When it comes time for Clov's one original idea, the limits of his mental abilities are clearly contrasted with Hamm's own "prolonged creative effort" (p. 61). Clov decides to set his alarm clock so that if Hamm whistles for him and he fails to come, then it will follow that even though the alarm rings, he is gone. If the alarm doesn't ring, then he is dead. Hamm then proceeds to destroy Clov's logic with the suggestion that the alarm might not work because it is used either too much or too little. The disciple, in his own immediate and highly physical way, then argues with the master by bringing in the alarm clock and letting it chime against Hamm's ear. Clov's practical demonstrations, though, fail to override the fact that the idea of using an alarm to determine spatial presence or absence is a poor one. Hamm's cynicism about Clov's intelligence remains: "This is perhaps not one of my bright days, but frankly—" (p. 47). A direction-taker, not a direction-giver, a deliverer not a visionary, Clov clings for most of the play to habit and its corollary order. The object of his intellection, the alarm clock, betrays the poverty of his own vision, of a mechanistic universe ruled by time, where existence or absence is measured by the sound or nonsound from a mechanical contrivance, this in a play otherwise mocking mechanisms (the dog with three legs) or destroying them (the bicycles). Instead of the imaginative space of Hamm's stage, Clov prefers his own kitchen with its "nice dimensions, nice proportions," for there he can "lean on the table, and look at the wall, and wait for him to whistle me" (p. 2). The irony here is that the realistic, well-ordered kitchen is never seen, while the surrealistic stage, with its implications as an allegory for Hamm's inner life, is all that we have as audience. Clov's place of order and logic is therefore, at very least, as illusory as anything else in the play. His is a space-and-time-bound world,[16] one having little room for process, uncertainties, let alone the imagination. He likes beginnings and endings, the clear extremes of an otherwise often incoherent existence: for him the "end is terrific" (p. 48), whereas Hamm prefers the "middle." At one point Clov would "stop playing" (p. 77); Hamm, on the other hand, must always be playing, must always be part of an imaginative evolution.[17]

Even this dichotomy breaks down. In section v we shall see how at the end Hamm, in Clov's absence, must become actor as well as playwright. (If Hamm and Clov are, in fact, halves of one composite soul, then Hamm has been this actor all along.) In a parallel fashion, Clov rises above the level of a trained puppet as the play itself "gets" to the actor, even as the play "gets" to the audience.

In his last speech—indeed, a speech that is an exception to his usual short lines—Clov becomes positively creative. He responds to Hamm's direction to "articulate," to say "a few words . . from [his] heart" (p. 80). He talks first of the disparity between a theological promise and the reality that he knows. His most imaginative line, that last line with its picture of "they" who are "dying of their wounds," offends Hamm. Clov has overstepped the bounds between actor and playwright, and is promptly silenced by Hamm with a short "Enough!" His insight is too piercing; the servant, like Words and Music, revolts from the master and threatens to run off with the play. This violation of the actor's lower estate threatens Hamm's centralist position. Still Clov continues:

> I say to myself—sometimes, Clov, you must learn to suffer better than that if you want them to weary of punishing you—one day. I say to myself—sometimes, Clov, you must be there better than that if you want them to let you go—one day. But I feel too old, and too far, to form new habits. Good, it'll never end, I'll never go.
> *(Pause.)*
> Then one day, suddenly, it ends, it changes. I don't understand, it dies, or it's me, I don't understand, that either. I ask the words that remain—sleeping, waking, morning, evening. They have nothing to say.
> *(Pause.)*
> I open the door of the cell and go. I am so bowed I only see my feet, if I open my eyes, and between my legs a little trail of black dust. I say to myself that the earth is extinguished, though I never saw it lit.
> *(Pause.)*
> It's easy going.
> *(Pause.)*
> When I fall I'll weep for happiness.

He dares to use one of Hamm's words, "suffer," and he now realizes that there is a limit to "habits," since they can only gloss over the deeper, more terrifying realities of our existence. Now the words flow from Clov's playwright's lips: "sleeping, waking, morning, evening." He knows that words are nothing, "have nothing to say," and in saying that he himself gives form to the nothingness, the very artistic process defined in my closing comments on *Waiting for Godot*. At last a metaphor worthy of a Pozzo or a Vladimir—or a Godot. Life becomes "a little trail of dust," and the speech ends, all passions spent, with a diminuendo of two short phrases: "It's easy going" and "When I fall I'll weep for happiness."

Clov's character, somethat like Gloucester's in *King Lear*, has at last approached that of the central character.[18] For Gloucester moves from a shallow courtier to a concerned patriot to a man suffering physical insult, all of which acts as the subplot correlative for Lear's mental anguish.

Gloucester's "renaissance," even as it moves him closer to the original pattern set by the greater, betrayed father figure, also demands his extinction as a character. Similarly, Clov, a "mere" actor given to symmetry and habit and to following directions, now experiences his own little "renaissance." At his own endgame, even if it be merely leaving the stage rather than life, he waxes poetic and is, despite a surly disposition, clearly imaginative. He turns playwright, momentarily fusing his character with Hamm's. Then *"Exit Clov"* before he can do the last favor of covering Hamm with a sheet.

The alienation between Hamm and Clov, master and slave, king and fool,[19] if you will, has been mitigated for a few moments. The charade of dualism has been momentarily exposed, for the signification of dramatic language is a joint venture of playwright and actor: the writing is not distinct from the saying. In his moment of poetic inspiration, with the ironic dialectic of its negative theme, Clov carries Hamm's monologue toward dialogue and then back toward the brief monologue of one who will remain outside the final "play" of Hamm's tragic ascension. As if to signify metadramatically this aborted but parallel renaissance in himself, Clov refers to the actual condition of the play: "This is what we call making an exit" (p. 81). He sees the play as a creator, if only for a moment; but, no less important, he sees the play now as the creator himself sees it. A few social graces exchanged between master and servant let us down from this veritable Pyrenees of the muse, and then, with the Clov character complete—having run the gamut from actor to audience to playwright and now back to one whose last two actions will be covering Hamm with the sheet and, this done, making an exit—the character, as a speaking character that is, disappears, represented only by the physical shell of his former verbal-physical self. We have seen or shall see such shells elsewhere in Beckett: the silent Lucky, Krapp staring motionless at us in the final moments of his play, Joe, Keaton at the end of *Film*, the garbage in *Breath*, the silent responder in *Not I*, and so on. The play now reverts to its beginning, as Hamm repeats his opening line of "Me to play." What Hamm does will be the subject of a later section; for now, as prelude to that final ascent of the hero, we examine the other characters, Nagg and Nell, and the little boy, who is beyond both dialogue and tableaux.

### iii

In one sense Nagg and Nell represent a horrible extension of Clov's unimaginative mentality.[20] Their demands are not for the food of a playwright, but for their own "pap"; indeed, one of Nagg's first lines is "Me pap!" (p. 9). If Beckett's theater, as I have argued in the *Godot* chapter, thrives on the aesthetics of that present established by actor and audience, then the parents are nothing more than creatures of pressing and present physical desire: to eat, to be scratched, to make love as best they can in the ashbins.

Conversely, they are mired in the past, imaginatively and mentally. In this sense, if Hamm represents the theatrical present, Clov the impossible future (he expends great effort in getting out of his current prison), then Nagg and Nell are Beckett's vision of some perverse Wordsworthian emotion recollected in tranquillity. They speak of adventures in the Ardennes, the road to Sedan (p. 16), and later of Lake Como (p. 21). The bicycle, so often Beckett's symbol of would-be freedom, has also led to the accident that cost both of them their legs. The visions of loving, traveling, rowing on the lake, and getting into such "fits" (sexual?) that the boat capsized—all is past. Such resurrected memories are clearly voluntary, mechanical, and trite, part of a habitual pattern to efface the present. Conversely, when their son, Hamm, tries to imagine parallel adventures—a trip to the South, adrift on a raft, carried far away (p. 34–35)—he is abruptly pulled back to the present, the projected trip canceled amidst neurotic speculations about the dangers of sharks. Past and future seem only theoretical possibilities; the present—in *Godot,* the present waiting—is all Beckett's characters have. The issue appears to be the quality of that existence lived only in the present. On this score Nagg and Nell are even more crippled than their son. Their own adventures capsizing on Lake Como will recall Krapp's one meaningful experience with the lady in the rowboat. However, that moment for Krapp signaled the end of a love affair, and Krapp, as I will suggest in a later chapter, is able to capitalize, as Hamm's parents cannot, on that memory when he frantically tries a fresh recording to link his present state with memories of his youth.

If Hamm moves toward an imaginative reconstruction of some inner reality, for the parents the present is nothing more than a "farce" (p. 14). Their sight, both physical and artistic (visionary), is going; even the sand in the bottom of their ashbins is not the procreative seashore sand of *Cascando,* but only a cheap substitute for the much-preferred sawdust. Despite many arguments, Hamm in his concern for Clov provides his own "son" with the materials for acting and does so, as we have seen, in the moment just before Clov's exit, where the disciple comes into his own as an artist. In contrast, Nagg—"nagging," even as the name Nell suggests, among other things, death's "knell"—has lost his son, both by his anger at Hamm's ingratitude and by Hamm's own incompatability with an unimaginative old man. In this way Nagg and Nell represent a play within the play, the countermovement to what I take as the procreative, romantic relationship (however strained) between Hamm and Clov and—at length—the audience. Nagg and Nell are a couple, one of the few in Beckett, who do "die" as stage characters with dialogue, who have lost even more than their mobility. Hamm has lost his, to be sure, but that loss is only a springboard to the cultivation of an inner vision. Their movement, however, is a constrictive one from a vaguely romantic past, to tales unwanted and unappreciated by Nagg, to a craving for physical comforts that only mocks their imprisonment, to silence, and at length extinction.[21]

The father's seeking food for the son may bear analogy to Hamm's providing theatrical dialogue for Clov; and the mother Pegg's seeking light may at length suggest the inner visions of the central character. Even the tailor, whose product, he boasts, is finer than God's created world, stands as a parody of Hamm's product, the informing of his vision that resists the other creative world, that of the small boy threatening from the outside. Yet Nagg and Nell contradict Hamm's achievement, for the food they want is literally biscuits—and they are fussy as to the brand—and later sugar-plums (p. 49). Clov is also unimaginative for most of the play in his obsession with "putting things in order" and clearing "everything away," but at least this constitutes his "dream" (p. 57), albeit an excessively mechanical, even sterile one when compared with Hamm's own dreams of magical forests (p. 3). Nagg's and Nell's light, in contrast, is literally extinguished each time Clov is told to "Screw down the lids" (p. 24). Nagg's own "product" is a dirty joke, an anecdote, but hardly the "prolonged creative effort" of his son.

Some critics see the silence achieved by Nagg and Nell as Beckett's own wished-for goal, a cessation of the tension between habit and imagination, between the desire to stop and the enervating desire to go on.[22] Thus Nell's line is taken as a momentary vision of a paradise that Beckett rarely grants his characters: "It was deep, deep. And you could see down to the bottom. So white. So clean" (p. 21). Still, Nell's death wish is contrary, I would think, to the painful, inevitable, but creative tension elsewhere in the play. Beckett's dramas—all of them—are about generating motion from meager sources, about—this is the bottom line—going on, about not sinking.

If hers is a genuine vision of the abalation of desire and of the comfort of total silence, of a formless world, like that in "Enough," where the quintessence of noncolor coincides with the quintessence of nonsound, then Nell still cannot inform the present with that vision. It remains only a voluntary memory of happier days, eternally confined by the past-tense "was," ironically contradicted by the present, in which Lake Como has degenerated to a dry ashbin. Only by truly involuntary memory can one achieve endless mobility in the third region of darkness, so dark, so unconnected to the external world that darkness is paradoxically the same as infinite light and whiteness. Even in "Enough" memory turns sour as the lover describes a serene union with the master that is no more. For all Beckett's yearning for silence, that yearning, when expressed through characters, is either no less futile (Henry in *Embers* may pass into silence in the Bolton-Holloway story, but the concluding sound of the sea mocks his achievement) or is hideously parodied as in the present case. Instead of achieving formlessness, the parents are encased in absurdly rigid forms, just as their silence is conveyed either as a past no longer probable or as a condition imposed on them by a frustrated Godot, by their son who ironically commits theatrical "parricide" to silence them.

Hamm's parallel in *Eh Joe* is down on his luck, to say the least, berated by the off-camera voice, possibly reduced to solitary masturbation. Still, the voice may be an inner one, and Joe may, like Hamm, be giving voice to his inner suffering: conscience, to misquote Hamlet, doth make artists of us all. In trying to pass the time for themselves, Vladimir and Estragon also pass the time for us. Try as they may, they cannt die.[23] Even if we reduce the years between birth and death to silence, or to the rubbish strewn horizontally on the stage, the death cry in *Breath* is still indistinguishable from the birth cry, from the "vagitus," as it is called, that opens that play. "I can't go on, I'll go on."[24] Such affirmative voices are missing in Nell's terrifying vision of a downward spiral into white noise, sterile sand, and a silence that would deny the very words that are our one hold on being.

Nagg curiously needs Nell as audience for his stories, though she protests the role. If we think of their forming with us the other half of a theater-in-the-round, then Nagg and Nell are our own reverse images. Like us they are confined to seats, a captive audience, even if that comparison is a bit bizarre. However, in moving from a potentially significant, surely happier past to their own isolated, present physical wants, they may at length alienate us. For surely we watch *Endgame*, this narrative nicely embodying the three unities and centering on the tragic informing and therefore realization of its central character, because the play itself treats, however obliquely, issues above those of physical appetite. It takes a strong purpose, a reading above the epicurean, to "stomach" *Endgame*. Our audience surrogates on stage have copped out in favor of Sprat's Medium and sugarplums, and ambiguous orders for back scratches. Nor do they stay to the end as viable links between stage and audience.

As the parents retreat into themselves, figuratively as well as literally, Clov and Hamm increasingly move out toward us. Clov does this by definition, as an actor warming to his role. Even Hamm, though at first the isolated, self-pitying playwright confined like Marlowe's Faustus to his study, will become at the end both supreme playwright and actor, feeding himself the very dialogue (or monologue) that he has written.

IV

Hamm's emergence, however, is inseparable from the play's own complex, indeed divided attitude toward art and the imagination. His final performance—and it is toward this performance that the present analysis moves—is, I think, not so much comic or tragic—though some critics see the play itself as a tragicomedy[25]—as it is "inevitable" in Aristotle's sense: the complex final performance mirroring an ongoing, equally complex attitude toward art, here defined as a collaboration of playwright and actor (and ratified by the audience).

Again, this emergence of the playwright-actor occurs in a theater of the mind. Beckett's stage is small because our landscape itself has withered, or never was. If the microcosm of the stage reflects the macrocosm of the "real" (in Beckett's sense) world offstage, then it is right that when Clov looks out he sees this very same diminished world: no sails, no fins, no smoke, but only a light that is "sunk," no gulls, nothing on the horizon, only leaden waves, a "zero" sun, neither light nor day but only gray, "GRRAY!" (pp. 30–31).[26] Perhaps this is akin to the "grey incandescence" of which Malone speaks.[27] Here is material, in Clov's mind, for a "farce" (p. 32)—but nothing beyond that.

Only in the radio plays do we have a change of scenery: the road and the station in *All That Fall,* the journey toward the sea in *Cascando.* In these works the scenery, because it has no physical correlative, is surely an interior one. *Film* concerns precisely the abandonment of larger vistas (the street, even the stairway) for the final end, the room/womb of the mind. A later play, *Not I,* gives up the pretense of a recognizable set, reducing the stage to a man and a mouth, to man and his female conscience, or man-audience and mouth-actor. The itinerary of *Murphy* or *Molloy* and the Irish ramblings of *More Pricks than Kicks* are as much a thing of Beckett's past as is his addiction to Joyce.[28] If "nature" means the country or landscape, then there is "no more nature" in *Endgame,* at least not in the "vicinity" (p. 11). The doctor himself, perhaps the god of the created world, is dead. The issue now is not man in relation to nature or environment or society, but man in relation to his soul-sole self, to that society, always within us, which we may deny or defraud by the busy work of habit, and yet the society that at death—recall the saying that everyone must die alone—is our only refuge.[29]

If all of this suggests a diminished arena for art, and for the artist, Hamm observes that it is still better than nothing (p. 59). He would reject the realist's elevation of environment—be it Hardy or Dreiser or Skinner—as a dominant factor and hence the proper subject matter for art. Properly, Beckett celebrates a subjective and therefore impressionistic art. The outer, as Hamm says, is hell. If the rejection of the external world is painful, if we hesitate in taking the inward journey into the informing of our own suffering and aloneness, Hamm's reassurance is that there are not so many terrible things as we imagined. I. A. Richards echoes the sentiment when he argues that the avoidance of fear constitutes the tragedy; properly, fear is a process, not an object.[30]

Clov's practical, cynical question, "What is there to keep me here?," is met by Hamm's straightforward "The dialogue" (p. 58). When Polonius asks Hamlet what he is reading, the Prince's reply, "Words, words, words" (2.2.193), may indeed be cynical on the surface: what else does one read? Or it may mean: all that I have is words. I take the response, however, as a celebration of the theater that is, ultimately, words; and in the world of Denmark, one of deception, of lustful addiction to objects, in that world elevating physical achievement, even activity above introspection and intellection, language and those arts associated with it *are* a precious commodity. Clov sees Hamm's "story" as only a "farce, day after day" (p. 32), the very word used by Nagg; but both confuse limited stories—the anecdotes, the recollections—with a larger story, the entire process of *Endgame* that encircles them and gives them meaning, even if that meaning implies that their social existence is without, or almost without meaning. Even if the situation here is artificial, this union of playwright and actor and audience still denies, through the use of words, that horrible reality in which each of us is alone, most certainly alone in death as our personal endgame approaches.

As the play moves toward the complex portrait of art and of the playwright-actor who conceives of and then delivers that art, Hamm's own sense of the theater, always keen of course, accelerates. Increasingly, he is given to theatrical terms, sharing an inside joke with us even as he draws closer to the offstage audience and away from the mock audience in ashbins behind him. He seems to acknowledge our presence while we, as audience, ratify his story by our being there. Accordingly, he speaks of his "soliloquy" and of an "underplot" (p. 78). Clov himself talks of making an "exit" (p. 81). We thereby may have before us really two stories, or three, if you will: a main plot, that of Hamm and Clov, in which the inner "stage" comes to the surface; a minor plot, that of Nagg and Nell, where the stage shrinks and is at length extinguished; and, as Hamm himself describes it, a second underplot, one promised but one that never materializes in the course of the play, and this involves the small boy whom Clov sees outside the window. More of him later.

I take Hamm's "prayer" (pp. 69–70)—he also forces his father to pray before giving him the promised sugarplum—as his personal celebration and definition of the artist. In the "old shelter," and alone against the silence, he first calls to his father (to his god) and then, reversing roles, becomes the father calling to his son (Christ?). There is no answer from either side. Hamm then retreats inward, but at the moment that he is seemingly alone he is not alone, but rather being "watched"—by a rat perhaps, by someone in the corridor (the "steps"). Surely he is being watched by us; it is inconceivable that an actor onstage can say that line ("I'm being watched" [p. 70]) without the audience's silently affirming the truth, just as Hamlet's "Now I am alone" (which opens his speech contrasting the actor's tears as Hecuba with his own lack of passion to take revenge [2.2.554]) is contradicted by our presence.

Then Beckett's artist begins, leading first with words ("babble, babble") and following with the portrait of the imaginative efforts of a solitary child who turns himself into children, "two, three, so as to be together, and whisper together, in the dark." The effort is procreative, "patterning down, like the millet grains." Too optimistic, too close to an unqualified celebration of art as a public act challenging our solitude, Hamm cuts off the reverie with "Ah let's get it over." The playlet *Come and Go* seems to be anticipated here: the characters, two and then three, babbling together, needing each other, balancing their private fears with communal responses, and achieving a union with each other and with the audience at the end, this double union itself symbolized by the rings ("I can feel the rings"). At issue here is the bonds of language that at once define our separateness and yet are the human way of sharing our common isolation.

This celebration of art is not unqualified, however; the play is catholic in its complexity, in its ability to suspend antitheses without enforcing choice. For one thing, that communality with the audience and the movement from an outer to an inner world emerge only when form is given to decay, or when one "reality" is demolished so that an illusory "reality" of words and vision can be attempted—I stress *attempted*. More literally, we must sacrifice: bicycles to wheelchairs; real dogs to three-legged imitations; Flora and Pompona to a solitary, inner room; ideas and issues (such as raised by Mother Pegg, the Socratic figure, and the father who calls for Christian charity) to process itself; life, even as narrowly defined, to art; and past-oriented intellect to the experience of the immediate stage.

Hamm's inner world is not a comfortable one; indeed, it thrives only on tensions. He cannot shake off the curiosity to go outside his world; he wants to be near the window, to feel, to experience the elements (the light, the wind, the sound and the smell of the sea) of physical reality. Near the end of the play Hamm feels cold and must be covered with a rug. Moreover, Clov leaves without obeying his master's orders. Physical life threatens this artifice at every moment, whether that life be as insignificant as a flea (which Hamm must promptly kill) or as significant as the small boy seen outside the window. Hamm has denied that boy in the past, in a story; he can refuse bread to his father. Yet the boy comes away, "a potential procreator" (p. 78).[31] If the boy does exist outside, Hamm's hope is that he will die there. If he doesn't die, however, "he'll come here," Hamm argues, as his playwright's mind spins in circles of possibilities. If the end of the play is willed by Hamm, as the final ascension of the tragic character, the approach of the boy, conversely, forces that end upon him. As with government officials who "resign," we always wonder if they jumped or were pushed. Similarly, the flea's mere presence drives Hamm to desiring an escape on a raft, abandoning a ship threatened by a otherwise insignificant creature. Unlike the world of *Godot* with its blooming tree, there is even less celebration of meager life in *Endgame*. A father and a mother, however decrepit, are silenced as a new character, a potential procreator who is also an imagined destroyer, appears on the scene.

Like that of the radio plays, Hamm's blind world lacks even that physical verification known but rejected by the painter-engraver who went mad when he saw only ashes in his own three-dimensional creation.[32] Even Clov observes that there are moments when his master hasn't "much conversation all of a sudden" (p. 65). His is an effort, a prolonged creative effort as much burden as achievement, to keep this inner world, this artifice, alive. Unlike Prospero, Hamm does not have the option of giving up his magic island for the reality of Naples,[33] of abandoning his art by breaking his staff and drowning his magic book. If he "makes" an option by informing his suffering, he does so only by closing off the option for life, however ragged that physical existence is in Beckett when we think of all the impotent, maimed, decaying characters who inhabit his canvas. Something is taking its "course" (p. 42), and in this line we have, perhaps, the celebration of the artistic process itself, that unified artifice composed of actor and audience.

Still, "course" sounds too close to "corpse" to leave us comfortable with any unqualified view of Beckett's portrait of the artist.[34]

It cannot be otherwise. Art and life—no less—are at length a process, a fictive title given to what would otherwise be only an accumulation of seconds, of grains of sand. It is never the same pus from second to second, as Vladimir observes. Beckett seems concerned to record—to "chronicle," to use Hamm's word—that process. The issue is not, I think, whether he is being optimistic or pessimistic, or even whether *Endgame* is more "bleak" than *Godot*. Beckett is optimistic about art, *romantic,* as I have used that word, because without the process we would have only time, seconds, grain upon grain. Art, though, is not a thing but only a process; it is an imposition to make a little meaning, and therefore is better than nothing. The process of using words to talk about what is happening, about the way it is, about our days, whether we see them as happy days or as ones filled by lost ones—all is an imposition. Life is about dying—the Renaissance knew this well enough in their *ars moriendi* tradition—and about decaying; it is all downhill from the womb on. Play—child's play or the play of the legitimate theater—dares to give form to this irrefutable fact, thereby imitating the very life process that mocks any attempt at meaning, let alone stability in our existence. *Endgame* is, I think, more bold than bleak. The dead have nothing to say, to themselves or to us. The process of words and the imagination is compatible only with life, and hence the title of a more recent story by Beckett, "Imagination Dead Imagine."

v

These issues of art and the role of the playwright are focused, I believe, in two of Hamm's major speeches: one, the story of the man begging food for his son (a speech broken off and then taken up three times in *Endgame*); the other, Hamm's final speech in the play.

The story itself begins from the "outside" as a memory that has plagued Hamm, rather than as a response to the present action of *Endgame*. Like that of *Cascando*, the story here becomes inseparable from the telling, and Hamm's struggles with that telling echo the situation of *Cascando*'s narrator, whose account of Woburn soon merges partially and then unmistakably with his own struggles as storyteller. It is the situation of the narrator/narrated all over. The "invasion" of the old man is at one with the story's own invasion of Hamm's inner world in *Endgame*. Like the narrator in *Embers,* Hamm struggles for precision, for the right word, for the most accurate description of the surroundings ("a hundred by the anenometer" and then "zero by the hygrometer," and so on [pp. 51–53]).[35] The hyperconscious effort, however, may be only a façade to keep the subject separated from the teller, for we might ask, with Yeats, "How can we know the dancer from the dance?"

Thematically, the story also underscores that life force threatening

Hamm's aesthetic world. The father demands not food for the mind or for an actor's part, but, literally, food for his son's stomach, the issue being not artistic creation but the preservation of basic life. In his refusal of that request, Hamm resembles a Pozzo, the landowner whose bounty goes no farther than himself. The issue is a dichotomy that, as in *Godot*, we know must ultimately dissolve: life (bread) versus art. The story itself is soon linked to events within *Endgame* when Hamm's own father asks for food for himself and Nell. An aesthetic life-bringer, Hamm is, paradoxically, a would-be death-bringer. Still, he cannot shake off the father's request; the story itself returns, like the Bolton-Holloway story in *Embers*. A compromise is offered: Hamm will hire the father as gardener (appropriately, a life-sustaining process).

The story still acts as an irritant to the artist, like the proverbial grain of sand within the oyster. In his responses Hamm mixes disgust with the father (pp. 68–70), pious rationalizations against charity, neurotic outbursts ("Get out of here and love one another! Lick your neighbor as yourself"), a mockery of the father's state ("Perhaps I could throw myself out on the floor"), and at last an identification with both father and son. As we have seen, he is both the father calling the son and the son calling the father. Such identification leads to self-perception, his sense of being watched, and then to his glorious definition of the artist's process that I have examined earlier. Hamm, in effect, "absorbs" that outer story assaulting his inner world as he incorporates the consciences of his characters and thereby abandons the practiced indifference to life outside. Christ-like, he takes onto himself the roles of father and son and, once having done this, transfers a plea for life to a personal aesthetic plea. Hamm now recognizes his own isolation, his own need for mercy, for understanding, as well as the role of the artist in giving form to that request. He peoples his lonely world the way a child does with the imaginary playmates of his fantasy. The details of the story are changed, but its central issue, the dependency of each of us on an audience—literally, on someone to hear our plea or, thematically, someone to hear our words—remains unchanged.

The final appearance of the story (p. 80) demands that Clov, the actor, take the father's role, and this he does with a plaintive "Ah," much like Estragon's pathetic "Ah" in *Godot* when Vladimir reminds him of the object of their waiting. Once shared, the internalized story gives birth to Clov's own brief career as playwright, much to Hamm's displeasure, as we have seen, yet also delivered at Hamm's request. The futility of the art is also its glory, for the stories Hamm tries to divorce from himself, to pass off as external and as bearing no relation to his situation, turn on their outward trajectory and converge on their creator. The resulting art is, from a pessimist's perspective, an exercise in monomania; from a more optimistic reading, it is the painful, inevitable sharing of one's inner life. All along, Hamm was father and son: we have the missing author-character from Pirandello's *Six Characters in Search of an Author,* but here sufficient, not deficient; present, and not absent.

Despite its seeming chaos on the surface, Hamm's last speech, that string of short phrases and snatches of dialogue much like that of Winnie in *Happy Days,* provides the most sustained insight into his playwright's mentality. In the words of the Unnamable, it is the "end of the joke," the aesthetic painkiller, if you will, as handy as that literal painkiller in the cupboard was not.[36] Unseen, except by us, Clov constitutes the onstage audience of one. The speech itself is surely meant to contrast with Hamm's opening dialogue: this time Hamm is not discovered but rather constitutes *all* the stage, at least as far as he knows, and the speech is about endings rather than beginnings. The proper verbal constructions, in terms of his opening lines, would be something akin to "Me to play having played." No fear of mere "reveling" here.[37]

Hamm's speech seems to be madness without matter. As with the scattered fragments in the closing lines of Eliot's *The Waste Land,* however, there is here an order and a depth of reference below the surface. Clov is absent, though he stands impassive upstage. The sheet with which he "discovered" Hamm at the opening is now useless. In a larger sense, Hamm has been revealed, the play itself representing his disclosure as a symbol. The removal of the sheet itself is thereby the stimulus for an aesthetic revelation. He is now moving toward the purely symbolic, and the chess metaphor comes to the fore, chess itself a symbolic enactment of literal battles and armies: "Me to play" and "Old Endgame." Indeed, Hamm is moving toward the same sense of completeness found by Mr. Endon in *Murphy.* The King, the central piece, is now immobile at the center of the board, the word for both the theater and the field of chess pieces.[38] Then "discard" the last life-support; the gaff is thrown away, though the dog, symbol of Hamm's artifice, is retained.

We see the artist now attempting to document the moment before human extinction. It is the process toward that movement, and not the actual event itself, defining the limits of our earthly inquiry.

Like Shakespeare, Beckett does not depict a hereafter. We may speculate on what will happen to Lear—can a pagan go to any sort of heaven?—but the Renaissance playwright, like the modern one, is content to show him approaching the end, promised or otherwise.[39] There is a farewell here to the audience, obscene to be sure, and with that salute an identification with us as Hamm uses the plural possessive "our." The "You" who wants poetry, or the efficacy of prayer, or night to come is also the "you" that, in an absurdist or relative world, must cry in darkness. Again, we all die alone. Hamm's aesthetic consciousness, like that of the narrator in *Cascando,* is now most acute: "Nicely put, that."

If relativity, both in terms of time itself and the mutability of all human things, relentlessly moves on, Hamm, now enveloped in his story, is about to make time run, to echo the Renaissance poet Marvell. The time is "over, reckoning closed and story ended." The wish for extinction, however, cannot hold as the life force, the final reference to the father and his starving son, is sounded. Hamm cannot shake off that memory. An invasion of his world, the story irritates the aesthetic fiber he has so closely woven. It is another world, with a past, with characters, and involving those issues of life and the sustenance of life that Hamm has otherwise so assiduously blocked out in his bomb shelter, in his circumscribed, lonely, inner world. The "Oh I put him before his responsibilities" sounds as much neurotic as convincing. Then with a *calm*—again, one of Beckett's favorite words—returning, Hamm reverses himself in the recognition that he is not alone, that he is part and parcel of all humanity, including us, including the fictive, or seemingly fictive father and his son: "Well, there we are, there I am, that's enough." This is something "truly," though the aesthetic inner world is itself in flux, only a momentary stay against reality, and yet Hamm will now be able to sustain this playwright-actor's posture at least until the end.

He approaches death with the same sense of "knowing" his story that several modern biblical scholars have attributed to Christ, an "actor" who plays the parts of a visitor to earth, prophet, crucified savior, and risen spirit. We approach now the closest thing to transcendence in Beckett, undercut, of course, by the fact that Hamm "*remains motionless*" as the curtain closes (he can no more leave his stage than Vladimir and Estragon can leave theirs). The dog is discarded, the last vestige of his creation; and then in a brilliant gesture he throws the whistle toward us, the audience—the "*auditorium.*" Though the isolation is illusory—again, Clov is backstage, visible to us if not to Hamm—for Hamm it is a convincing illusion. He is approaching the nonbeing sought by Nell in her vision of a silent, white ocean bottom, an empty world where nothingness is a fact, not a conceit, where we can cease to be like those talkative "political" artists who, in giving form to nothing, are bound to fail. In essence, Hamm is trying to give up the last hold on life, even if that "life" be the illusory existence of the stage world.

The transcendence itself is aborted. However much he would later cut away at the time scheme or the plot or the place of his plays (witness *Breath*), Beckett cannot present us with nothing: "nothing" itself can be spoken of but not enacted. A bare stage is only a bare stage and not a play. Here Beckett is like Emily Dickinson in "I heard a fly buzz when I died," as she tries poetically to cross the thin boundary line between life and death and is frustrated in that attempt when a fly intervenes between her eyes and the "light." Beckett is trying to go to the nonstate, if I may put it that way, of nonbeing. That is the way Hamm would "play it," so that he could "speak no more about it." I repeat his wish: "speak no more." He seeks here not the failure of words, the very possibility that unnerves Winnie. Nor will he use words anymore to define nonbeing.[40]

Now, without words and with the major character free of the tension in seeking physical life or death, we move to the level of mime. Our audience surrogate, the silent Clov, now sees Hamm hold the bloodied handkerchief before him and then cover his face. Two phrases act as glosses to the action. One is the descriptive "Old stauncher," lest an audience member fail to identify properly the symbol, Hamm's Greek-like mask that is the physical correlative for his misery, for his suffering than which no one's is greater, as he reminds us early in the play. In effect, Hamm, like the figures in Greek myths, has passed through earthly existence and literally become a star. He has won his right to be a symbol, a symbol sustained by the play, a symbol that now wordlessly compresses all that he means, or has meant. This wretched piece of a costume, in effect, now equals the entire play. In Beckett, truly, the last shall be first. One also thinks of the handkerchief worn by Keaton in *Film,* and that used by Willie in *Happy Days,* though neither was so developed, nor so perfect a symbol of suffering.

The other phrase, a tantalizing one, is the closing "You . . . remain." Initially, it appears simply an appositive for "Old stauncher," but I also take it as a reference to the audience. That is, Hamm has now *realized* his role; he has been elevated to a symbol. Our task has now just begun; we must leave the theater, refreshed by Beckett's mirror world, and must encounter the suffering anew. Outside of here it is hell, as the Beckett characters are fond of saying. We remain; we are the "mutes and audience" of the act to which Hamlet refers (5.2.337).[41]

The play closes beyond words, as Hamm covers his face with the handkerchief and, like the Auditor in *Not I,* lowers his arms and in a mockery of mime and its movements stops on the stage direction to remain "*motionless.*" Initiated by language, the play ends in silence, the "*Brief tableau,*" like that called for by Beckett in *The Unnamable.*[42] *Curtain.* It will also start again; as Winnie observes, even if the glass breaks, it will be there whole tomorrow. Tomorrow the handkerchief will revert to the old sheet covering Hamm, that, with the blood-stained handkerchief, will in turn be removed, discovering another potential tragic hero—or "figure," if "hero" sounds too affirmative for some readers. The uncovering will allow theatrical life to flow again, the act of artistic creation, the long creative process to which Hamm himself refers, the informing of a vision and the production of a symbol—a symbol that, at the end, will remain with us, only to be undone the next day, the next performance. Curtain. . . .

# 3 *Happy Days*: Creation in Spite of Habit

i

Like Hamm, Winnie is *"discovered sleeping"* (p. 7), her own plump arms forming the cover that is in turn uncovered by the sound of a bell that *"rings piercingly, say ten seconds,* [and then] *stops"* (p. 8).[1] True, the atmosphere here is unpromising: a fat, middle-aged woman, imprisoned to her waist in a burial mound, and beneath harsh stage lights. Yet there is a sense of birth in the play's opening moments, the emergence of an artist who, in retrospect, is no less promising than Beckett's other artists: Hamm, blind and confined to a wheelchair; Krapp, disordered, drunk from the start, communicating with the tape recorder in a series of half-mumbled phrases; Malone, incapacitated in his wretched bed; or the Unnamable, not only a head like Winnie but confined even more grotesquely in a glass jar. In a hell, in her prison, still at first like the characters in *Play*, Winnie emerges slowly, mysteriously, like some primordial creature crawling out of the life-giving sea, only to be beached on the arid, almost sterile plain that constitutes the play's single set. At first *"inaudible"* in her morning prayers, like *Play*'s Man, Woman I, and Woman II, she moves from such linguistic chaos toward articulate speech, indeed toward a speech that is, with the exception of a few interruptions from her husband, the longest monologue in all of Beckett.[2]

If she is an artist, a creator, Winnie still is not Hamm; in fact, in many ways she is his opposite. Her world is as glaringly external as Hamm's is internal.[3] We confront in *Happy Days* a surface world quite unlike the strange mental room/womb in *Endgame;* and Winnie's ancestors are to be found in Vladimir and, perhaps more so, in Estragon, rather than in earlier egocentric, introspective artists. As in *Godot,* the set here is an exterior one: the road and tree are replaced by an expanse of scorched grass rising center to a low mound, with a *"Very pompier trompe-l'oeil backcloth to represent unbroken plain and sky receding to meet in far distance"* (p. 7). To be sure, Winnie will hear the same mysterious voice that on occasion haunts Watt, and this she will try to deny in her addiction to the here and now. Still, the world of *Happy Days* is, most immediately, a surface one that the playwright-in-residence, Winnie, tries to maintain against a darker zone, one of exhilarating but also terrifying involuntary memory that cannot be obscured easily or entirely by her cheerful approach to discomfort or even by the garish lighting of the stage itself. Hers is a world of seeing, of objects, and of light in the form of a merciless, burning sun, a vertical equivalent to the horizontal spotlight of *Play,* giving a seeming "reality" or solidness to the play's many objects. In the words of *The Lost Ones,* she is the "greater fixity" chained to her tangible world no matter how absurd it may seem.[4] In fact, the stage directions call for a *"Blazing light"* (p. 7) so powerful that it ignites Winnie's parasol in the second act.

*Happy Days* stands, then, between the artificial light of *Endgame,* symbol of Hamm's interior and artificial-imaginative world, and the twilight of *Godot,* symbol of the intermediate state of the clowns, caught between the demands of that externality represented by Pozzo (also addicted to objects) and their own inner sense (which they too try to suppress by games and gamelike dialogue) of a larger meaning, or nonmeaning, behind the waiting. For the tramps the darkness of sleep and (perchance) its subsequent dreams is the realm to be avoided. To think of Godot is to risk the tragedy of memory; appropriately, their most sustained thinking, unrelieved by the habit of games and dialogue, occurs when the stage lights suddenly dim, signaling the onrush of night.[5] Winnie herself waits for evening to come, for night to put an end to her travail; a creature of the light and of its superficial existence, she knows that even her muted tragedy demands darkness and its silence for her release. We do not see that night come, and here there is no Pozzo to describe the evening for us. Nor is there the artifice of a sudden change from twilight to night as in *Godot.* Instead, we experience only the endless blazing day of the play, focusing our attention on what *is,* on what Winnie can hold and observe, on what we ourselves as audience can see.

The monologue itself is not of the Shakespearean kind, no increasingly profound inquiry stimulated by an initial question ("To be, or not to be" or "Is it not monstrous that this player here"). Instead, it is a collage built of thousands of pieces—bits of songs, lines of poetry, half-accurate quotations, truisms, clichés, dialogue from the past. No one idea is pursued long enough—as in Lucky's speech or Hamm's farewell—to allow for the sort of intellectual or psychological depth we associate with the theatrical convention of monologue. Winnie cannot guide us through thought as Hamlet or Iago can. Moreover, since she talks in fits and starts, and seems unaware even when she repeats a thought or gives vent to an obsession or a fetish, no single section of *Happy Days* can serve as microcosm or as vortex for the play's larger issues. Instead, we, as audience, must make sense of her disordered collage; and that process for us, though not for Winnie, who is comically but also pathetically forgetful, is a continuous one. Her snatches of dialogue themselves have the almost paradoxical function of invoking other works (and the "worlds" of those works) that are relevant in *Happy Days* only by irony or contrast and, at the same time, by serving as brilliant brush strokes in her unconscious self-portrait.

For example, the snatches "ensign crimson" and "pale flag" extrapolate from the situation in *Romeo and Juliet.* There Romeo misreads Juliet's condition in the tomb, concluding that even though she is dead, death itself cannot rob her cheek of its beauty: her cheek has given no military quarters to death's standard (the "pale flag") and, in spite of death, retains the blush, the crimson of beauty. Romeo's allegorical reading of beauty's victory over death is, of course, flawed: in point of fact, Juliet is not dead and we may perhaps fault Romeo for not examining the body closer. His ignorance leads to hyperbole, and yet his lines are at once fatuous, pathetic, and majestic. Cursed with less than complete knowledge of the situation, he still has a vision that elevates a seeming fact. But in Shakespeare's play such hyperbolic expressions of love and death voiced in the earlier balcony scene will within minutes receive a very literal comedown as Juliet wakes, finds Romeo dead, and makes her fatal bargain with the dagger, to which she supplies her own body as sheath. Winnie's half-remembered quote thus complicates an already complicated dramatic situation, removing Romeo's hyperbole from its context, refining the love-death paradox into an unqualified celebration of love and of the romantic poetry that accompanies it. Winnie is, in a way, Romeo observing a Juliet whom she also plays to the almost wordless Romeo behind her. Like Juliet, she is not dead; like Juliet she is immobile. Like Juliet she will become her own monument when in Act 2 the mound encircles her neck and later at the end when, having sung her song, she gazes out at the audience in a silent tableau, stilled like her dead predecessor. This maddeningly accurate and, at the same time, inaccurate use of quotation characterizes every instance when Winnie reaches into her bag of half-remembered passages and sayings as part of her ritual progress through her day.

We observe her, and she herself tries gamely to keep her eyes on the world, visible under that merciless sun. By observing her immediate world she passes the time, and we—if we have any sympathy for her, if we find, curiously, that we cannot wholly separate ourselves from the heroic-pathetic creature before us—we pass that same time with her, through her.

It is therefore the mouth and not the mind, the actor's external instrument and not the internality of the playwright's imagination, that in this play is the means to lift up all those who fall. Thus the toothbrush provides the stimulus for Winnie, as well as the dialogue, since it is the advertising copy promoting its bristles that first takes her attention. The encounter with the toothbrush is followed by dialogue centering on cough syrup, and then lipstick. Indeed, Winnie, in the fashion of an "unliberated woman," moves all around her own face, and her toiletry, for the subjects of her monologue. She is a disproportionate head, a head with a partial torso in Act 1, and a head exclusively in Act 2. Yet it is the head as an object, not as a covering for the imaginative faculties or for the intellect, that is her "cosmos" here.

In a way *Happy Days* celebrates, even as it questions the theater's physical, external half. We are at almost opposite extremes from the world of the radio plays. For only on the most superficial level is *Cascando* about objects, about things not in the head, though its narrator tries, unsuccessfully, to deny that he speaks about things coming from within himself. *Happy Days,* while superficially a comedy, is preeminently about a woman who owes her existence, her life as a stage character and as a human struggling in her chains, to *things,* and as she says later in the play, "things have their life . . . *things* have a life" (p. 54). For Winnie, words literally exist *on* things, such as toothbrushes, or are associated with things, such as the "genuine pure" on the brush that finds its opposite in the "genuine pure filth" (p. 19) she finds in Willie's postcard. Like Estragon, she is given to pictures, on postcards or in Bibles—it is all one—rather than concepts. Poetlike, rather than philosopherlike, she fashions her dialogue from objects, the source of metaphor, rather than concepts, the source of discourse. With literature itself—she cites everything from lines of the Psalter to Franz Lehar to bad poetry to Browning and Shakespeare[6]—she conveys not the inner context or meaning of lines—indeed most often she horribly misquotes such passages—but simply the bare line itself, and even less than the bare line if we take into account missing subjects and verbs and objects. Literature becomes literally a "piece" in a verbal context that is itself stimulated by the objects about her. For Winnie "all comes back" (p. 20), though in the sense of a concrete object, or a line of poetry as a companion piece to that object. For her the "essence" of the line is not relevant.

Like Clov, and the early Moran and Watt, among others, Winnie is given to systems, habits; indeed she far outshines Clov in this regard. Her entire day is part of a set pattern, a series of rituals, almost all of them mechanical, to help her through the day, through that period beween sunrise and sunset. This is her own "bright boy" promising escape or redemption, though the passage from the *Unnamable* refers sarcastically to dependence on routines and concepts to escape a darker reality.[7] She likes order. The parasol goes up in flames at a certain time: too early and the problem arises of what to do during the longer-than-usual intervening time; too late and the full effect of its time-passing ability will be wasted.[8] Her life of order is first signaled by the ringing of a bell, then proceeds with the unveiling of her toilet, follows a schedule repeated without variation—though she is always open to, indeed delighted by any intrusions the unpredictable Willie makes on that schedule—and ends with the singing of her song. Hers is that habit of which Beckett speaks in his book on Proust, seemingly a way of glossing over the deeper, tragic implications of reality, seemingly a way of reducing the otherwise unfathomable to a surface order, to decorum. If the glass is broken, as it must be according to her schedule, "it will be in the bag tomorrow, without a scratch, to help [her] through the day" (p. 39).

The larger, more obvious fact that the play itself can be repeated, with a subsequent replenishing of props that have been expended (the glass, the parasol), is inseparable from Winnie's own reliance on habit that in turn relies on repetition. The glorious thing about Winnie's accomplishment—and it *is* an accomplishment, I believe—is that it occurs under such minimal conditions.[9] Not the rich girl, nor even a mobile one with a variety of toys, people, and artifacts to use in passing over the deeper, more troubled waters of existence, Winnie is reduced to a few scrawny props, and the minimum, or less, of mobility. If she had a mind, an imagination as unfettered as Hamm's, she could then take pleasure in a nutshell, yet given her reliance on habit instead of imagination, routine rather than intellect, object rather than essence, her accomplishment is both all the more pathetic and wondrous.[10] She is quite unlike the eloquent, often poetic Mrs. Rooney; and her interest in words—is the hair on her head properly called "it" or "them"?—is a parody of the semi-scholarly inquiries of Krapp or Malone or the Voice of *Cascando*. Those characters revel in language, in the artistic exactitude of their own speech. For Winnie the mere word itself is enough, as a sound to occupy the time. Her fear is that she will be left before the bell to sleep with "nothing more to say," and that phrase is coupled with "nothing more to do" (p. 35). Words break the "silence of this place" (p. 21). When words themselves fail, she will have "sound," though she confesses that while she sometimes hears sounds, it is "not often" enough. Yet even sounds "are a boon, they help [her] . . . through the day" (p. 53).

Still, she is heroic in a way.[11] If she shares the death wish with the other Beckett characters, that more general desire not to be, she suppresses that wish more than most, and opts instead for life. Her motto, quite simply, is "On, Winnie" (p. 12), that line delivered appropriately before one of Beckett's pregnant *"Long pauses."* From nothing, from a scorched earth no more, indeed even less promising than the barren landscape of *Godot* (since the set of *Happy Days* doesn't even boast a tree, symbolic or not), Winnie goes on. Given her partial and then almost total immobility, as well as the fear that she will lose her sight or hearing or both at the next installment, Winnie persists. The literature she quotes is classical in that it holds out possibilities: for a love-death to enhance the victims of family rivalries, for the expression of woe to be therapeutic, for conditions to ameliorate, for sentience to be the prize dearly won from suffering, for love to blossom, for love to be "true." Her "personal" literature, however, is one not of possibilities but of impossibilities.[12] Still, she goes on. Like Joyce's own Leopold Bloom, she is Beckett's modern hero, or heroine, more properly; and if she is a thousand cuts below a Saint Joan, even as Bloom falls far short of his Homeric prototype, there is a heroism and there is a resemblance, nevertheless.

Whereas Hamm and Dedalus are destructive, albeit impressive artists, Winnie, like Vladimir and Estragon, is constructive, however minimal or fragile her creation. She waits in a fashion more gross and literal than Hamm, for his own immobility only frees his imagination. To alleviate that waiting she must rely on things outside herself: half-remembered lines, postcards, advertisements, a schedule, conversation with a dull and often crude husband who has lost his "jizz" (p. 63), and a neurotic use of the stage and its props that her playwright, her Godot perhaps, has given her. In all of this there is no certainty that the effort will succeed, and yet she remains confident that she is being witnessed, that she is not like those birds who

delight in singing alone, to themselves. She remains confident that whatever fails or breaks today will be in its place tomorrow. The Tantalus factor
here is both maddening and comforting.

## ii

Sexuality, in the broadest sense of the word, is inseparable from Winnie's
creation. Even if they are immobile, or undesirable, Beckett's women all
breath a sexuality, wholesome or otherwise, that is either at one with their
own sense of creativity or with that creativity they inspire in others. One
thinks, first of all, of Mrs. Rooney in *All That Fall,* still eager, albeit somewhat incapacitated because of age and weight, to do the "trick," a creature
lusting after something more than friendly taps on the shoulder. From her
fertile mind spews a torrent of suggestive, symbolic, playful words. In
*Embers,* Ada, however browbeaten by Henry, at length serves as stimulus
for her husband, inspiring him with her description of his own Belacqua-
like father. We might also think of the woman in the boat with Krapp, or
the woman who berates Joe in Beckett's first television play, or the woman
in the photograph examined by O in *Film,* even Sucky Moll in *Malone Dies,*
serving the dying narrator, at the very least, as the subject for a fiction as he
tries to escape his own death room.

As in Shakespeare's own *A Midsummer Night's Dream,* sex and the imagination are one: the poet is also a lover, giving birth to the creatures of his
fictive venture. To love is to have empathy for that creation, for the ability
to "go on." However inferior the shallow Athenians or the rustic Bottom
are to the rationalist Theseus, the five lovers are still given the chance to
experience Shakespeare's expansive, imaginative world, that forest ex-
panding from finite Athens to the infinite dimensions of Oberon's kingdom. And this power, this chance is denied rationalists like Theseus.
Similarly, in *The Taming of the Shrew* Petruchio's imaginative recreation of
Kate from shrew to model wife, or the imaginative capacity they both share
in fashioning a world that denies the surface facts, is at one with their status
as lovers.[13] It is therefore no surprise that Winnie's sexuality, however
faded, is stressed from the opening. We learn early that she is "*well preserved,*" with "*bare*" arms and shoulders, a "*low bodice, big bosom*" (p. 7).
Though no shapely young girl, she is still miles beyond that dried virgin,
Miss Fitt.

If anything, the sexual problem in the play belongs to Willie, the husband, and this point is emphasized by the double entendres. Winnie's juxtaposition of commentary on the toothpaste and addresses to her husband
suggests that, like the toothpaste, he is "running out," that the situation
cannot be helped, and that both he and his sexual organ are "just one of
those old things [which] . . . can't be cured." There is even a coda for this
hymn joining fading toiletry and sexuality: "ah yes . . . poor dear Willie . . .
good Lord" (p. 9).

Holding the butt of the parasol in her hand, a handle of "*surprising length"* (p. 12), Winnie brings Willie into the comparison as she stretches back and to her right, hanging over him with "Willie" and then "wonderful gift." As she strikes her impotent husband with the handle, she cries, "Wish I had it," whereupon the parasol slips from her grasp and falls beneath the mound. After such sexual taunting she finds that her palm is "damp," perhaps as if from passion.

It is true that at times Winnie seems to be part of a large, symbolic travesty of sexuality: the various phallic instruments at her command (the parasol, the toothbrush, the revolver) arrayed against the vaginal hole into which Willie retreats, and the lubricant that she counsels him to "work it well in" (p. 14). The fact remains that it is Willie who seems to have lost his zest, his "jizz." Almost dead in his use of language, confined to a few monosyllabic utterances, some wordless play, and drawing comments not from his imagination but from the newspaper, he is, until the end of the play, almost extinct as a creative force. For Willie takes only a vicarious verbal pleasure from obscene postcards, from wordplay on "suck," or allusions to an old lover of Winnie. Winnie thus tries to lead him, to bring him out, both sexually and imaginatively. Again, sexuality and the imagination are inseparable: one feeds on the other. She reminds him that he once found her lovable, that in the past he had complimented her hair. Now the relationship is failing, despite Winnie's purposeful distortions of the situation: her attempts to dredge up a more romantic past and the fact that her standards for social intercourse have become so minimal that a mere grunt or monosyllable from Willie can move her to conclude that it will be a happy day.

The sterile relationship of the Showers itself suggests the depths, the negative end possible for Winnie and Willie. Mrs. Shower demands of her husband, "what are you meant to mean?," after he callously asks what significance there is in Winnie's being "stuck up to her diddies in the bleeding ground" (pp. 42–43). She then insults his own sexuality: "what's the idea of you . . . what are you meant to mean? Is it because you're still on your two flat feet, with your old ditty full of tinned muck and changes of underwear, dragging me up and down this fornicating wilderness, coarse creature, fit mate—*(with sudden violence)*—let go of my hand and drop for God's sake . . . drop." Their name, Shower, with its associations of fruition, is now replaced with an alternate form, Cooker, dry and sterile like the blazing sun and scorched grass against which Winnie struggles. After such a tirade we may be inclined to agree with Winnie that mobility can be a curse, as the miserable Showers, the lost Adam and Eve, go off, bags in tow, hand in hand, back to whatever passes as their own "paradise."

Sex and creation here are replaced by meaningless sex and death; the Showers, unlike us, are an audience that cannot comprehend, obsessed as the husband is with "what does she mean." Like Pozzo from *Godot,* they come, observe, and then go their way, to their own private fall, their own hell. They are mobile, not confined to a seemingly endless waiting, yet they are also dead, shallow, uncomprehending, like the man and woman who observe O on his way down the street in *Film*, or the people at the station in *All That Fall*. The Beckett heroes are less happy, but also less shallow; and the argument goes full circle: because they are insightful they are less happy. Winnie may pale beside Hamm or Krapp as an insightful character, but that she is troubled, that she struggles against seemingly impossible odds (to mate with a husband, sexually or imaginatively, or both) elevates her above the more mobile Showers or Cookers. The Showers, the mismatched couple of Pozzo and Lucky, pass on by. Winnie is like Vladimir and Estragon, like Hamm with his stauncher, like us, the audience struggling to comprehend what "it means" (life or the play, or both). As Hamm says, referring to both stauncher and audience, "You remain."

The possibility for creation always raises the possibility of failure, and of death.[14] For if that creation is through the involuntary memory, an aspect of memory that Winnie assiduously, albeit unconsciously avoids for most of the play, then the resulting vision is at once exhilarating and terrifying. Beckett speaks elsewhere of such vision as being like a "mysterious furrow that had been carved, as by a thunderbolt, within me, by the inhuman and supernatural blade of Death, or the revelation of Death."[15] It is against this terror, however revelatory, that habit, driven by the will "not to suffer," expends its mundane program.

The memory of her daughter, Milly, is just such an occasion (pp. 54–55). The glaring present tense of *Happy Days* is itself replaced, though only for a few lines, with another present tense, variously charted as "beginning in the womb" or "before she [Milly] dies," or when the daughter is "now four or five already and has recently been given a big waxen dolly." There is a pause, and then Winnie relives the past in the present: Milly, fully clothed, "a little white straw hat with a chin elastic," "a little picture-book with legends in real print to go under her arm when she takes her walk." This sense of another present tense and the idyllic picture is itself broken when the daughter "tiptoed down the silent passage, entered the nursery and began to undress Dolly," only to be terrified by a mouse. The revelation threatens to go too far, and Winnie checks herself with "gently, Winnie," and then calls out to Willie as if for help, desperately trying to spend her passions on him, and the objects behind her, rather than on the involuntary memory that, in her own words, threatens to "bubble up, for some unknown reason," and ill-timed at that (p. 57).

As we shall see later, Willie's emergence at the play's end may be a more literal bubbling up, with Willie representing the dark, almost hidden dimension of Winnie's existence that she wants both to bring out and to suppress. He is always active, even when unseen by the audience, and Beckett, in directing *Happy Days*, goes to great pains to choreograph movements for the actor playing the husband, even though such movement cannot be witnessed by an audience who, in their way, are even more immobile than Winnie. She can at least turn around her torso and, in Act 2, her head; and what she sees there, in that cauldron of idlike violence and sexuality, both excites her and revolts her, like the obscene postcards that

Willie at one point thrusts on his unsuspecting wife: "Heavens what are they up to! . . . . No but this is just genuine pure filth! . . . . Make any nice-minded person want to vomit! . . . . What does that creature in the background think he's doing? . . . Oh no really! . . . Pah! . . . . Take it away!" (though all this time Willie "*continues to relish card, varying angles and distance from his eyes*" [p. 19]).

In Freud's sense, the creative desire and the destructive desire are not only the twin forces in human existence but also manifestations of the same thing, the same inward energy. Bullets from Winnie's revolver and phalluses, however "dead" Willie's may be, both make entries. It was the Elizabethans who understood this relationship when they made the infinitive "to die" refer to both physical death and sexual intercourse. For Cleopatra at her death, the asp is both a death instrument and, by her metaphoric abilities, a surrogate phallus or lover: it "hurts, and is desired" (5.2 295–296) like a lover's kiss, and then becomes—miracle of miracles—a baby that "sucks the nurse asleep" (line 310).

However bad her start or her circumstances, or her materials either human or verbal, a creative person like Winnie fears other creative, life-bringing rivals even as she, more than Hamm, can sympathize with them. When the emmet first appears she recoils in terror and cries out in a shrill voice. Her reaction, at least initially, is like that of Hamm to the flea. Instead of trying to kill the creature with insect powder, as Hamm does, Winnie examines it with a magnifying glass, following its "progress," and as she becomes calm, she can note that it seems to have a "little white ball in its arms" (p. 29). We may think of the sterile black balls (either literal, like the hard stool, or allegorical of death, like the ball brought to Krapp by the little dog) and of the terror that a life-force such as children or insects instills in characters like Krapp or Mr. Rooney. If white is benevolent (recall Godot's white beard, so the Boy claims, or the white sand to which Nell aspires in *Endgame,* or the comforting whiteness in "Enough"), then the ball may be comic, not tragic. Willie obscenely identifies the ball as eggs, and the process that produces them as "Formication" (p. 30). That word in turn triggers off a comic laugh from husband and wife, like the laughter shared by the Rooneys on the road. When the laughter subsides, Winnie comments that until she heard Willie laugh, she was convinced she "never would, you never would" (p. 31). Does she refer here just to a mutual laugh, or its extension in coupling? If they cannot have sex together, given Winnie's immobility and Willie's possible impotency, at least they can laugh together. The emmet, a caricature of the life-force with its little white ball of eggs, may indeed be one of the Almighty's "little jokes" (p. 31), and perhaps the husband and wife, as Winnie qualifies it, may have been "diverted by two quite different things" (p. 31). Still, whatever the motive for the laughter, they did laugh at the sight, or at the word *formication,* whereas we have just seen Mr. Shower use the correct form in a curse, showering sterility on this "fornicating wilderness" (p. 43).

Winnie urges Willie not to "curl up" on her (p. 13); I take the reference both sexually and generally. She needs him, as she needs us, as an audience. Attending the theater, serving as audience, is, in this sense, somewhat analoguous to love: both activities take two. And self-love, whether it be masturbation or talking to oneself, or being an unpublished playwright, or an actor speaking to an empty auditorium, is an unproductive and—when taken to excess—unhealthy thing. Beckett's works are strewn with relationships, from sexual to familial, that fail: Moran and his son, Krapp and the women in his life, Joe and the young woman, the husband and wife and husband and mistress in *Play*, and so on. But *Happy Days*, Beckett's one certain comedy, if only superficially so, is about a woman who works for success with her husband, her onstage audience of one. Whether she, or her playwright, succeeds with us we shall have to decide: I have seen audiences alternately entranced and bored with *Happy Days*. The verdict, as with any relationship, is an individual, not a pluralistic one.[16]

### iii

It is surely a moot point whether Winnie has any success as a creator, as someone who "brings out" her husband and the audience, as someone who, by her externalizing art, makes life bearable despite adversities.[17] She can have a "leveling effect," not invalidating tragedy, yet not succumbing to it either. Indeed, she constantly tries for some sort of equipoise between antithetical possibilities: thus Winnie's "no better, no worse . . . no change" (p. 9). The dichotomies, if faced, may lead to some balance between them; and we have here again Beckett's own method of playwriting observed in the discussion of *Godot*.

However, at one point in *Happy Days* Winnie imagines a moment of equipoise when "no further pains are possible," when one can just "close the eyes," in effect, rising above even the external, visible world of creation, perfectly balanced between the heat of the day, "when flesh melts at so many degrees," and the cold of the night, when the "moon has so many hundred hours" (p. 18). At such a moment Winnie's vision will elevate her above the "brute beasts," a reminder of which is always present in Willie's own crude behavior, his own artless bestiality. Then she can "fear no more the heat o' the sun" or the cold of the moon, or any dichotomies generated by life or by individual thought. Then, with eyes closed, acting totally as an imaginative being, beyond the physical, she "would simply float up into the blue," yielded up to the sky by the earth, the earth on that occasion cracking all around her and thereby releasing her (p. 33). Similarly, other Beckett characters seek such elevation from that "sky, whence cometh our help."[18] The Unnamable wants to rise in the air, "blown . . . up . . . like a balloon."[19] In *How It Is* the narrator sees Part 3, without Pim, as "lighter than air," though also as a time when "an instant flop fallen."[20] The character in "The End" carries a mirror to reflect the sky.[21] The phrase that Winnie uses to underscore the violence of that new life promised by her vision, "sucked up," triggers a double entendre on Willie's part: "*Sucked up?*" (p. 34). Winnie is then brought back rudely to earth. The problem is: granting her achievement with minimal materials and working under exacting circumstances, does this comic artist, as opposed to the tragic one like Hamm or, say, the Voice of *Cascando,* have the ability, is she willing to take the larger step? Can she move inward?

Winnie raises this very question about her art when she plaintively asks, "What *is* the alternative?" (p. 20). She is troubled by the very equipoise she tries to achieve. The superficiality of the play, its clarity, its simplicity, the very certain achievement of Winnie when measured against the complex, doubt-plagued "achievement" of Hamm, only leads to uncertainty—in her, and in us. If the emmet is the walking example of fecundity, the toothbrush that touches and cleans the actor's mouth and that supplies Winnie with dialogue to ward away boredom and nothingness is itself made of hog's setae. In the closing moments of Act 1 Willie reminds his wife that a hog is a "castrated male swine. . . . Reared for slaughter" (p. 47). Winnie is pleased at the response, at any response to what she says, and the happy expression increases on her face. Perhaps it is the mere fact that Willie has conversed with her—six words, three to a sentence—rather than his meaning that she grasps at here and that delights her.

Her own external creativity is at the expense of something deeper. Willie's rude "*sucked* up" pulls her out of "the blue" or "gossamer" of her imaginative vision, and she agrees with him that "natural laws" (of gravity, of her own externality) are the stronger. When she was "young and . . . foolish" those natural laws may have had less effect; the implication is that now they master her, influencing but also limiting her art. As for Vladimir and Estragon, there was a time when she could have ascended to the top of the Eiffel Tower; those happy days are past. She knows that "something seems to have occurred," that there is some larger, some deeper dimension to existence; but her measurements, her present art can tell her only that "nothing has occurred," and she quickly agrees with Willie and his sterile literalism: "nothing at all, you are quite right, Willie" (p. 39). Thereupon she takes refuge in habit, in the repetition of the theater: "The sunshade will be there again tomorrow, beside me on this mound, to help me through the day" (p. 39).

The deeper, subjective dimension persists in the form of headaches, the migraines she experiences. Clinging to the great mercy of not knowing, trying, as she makes an unintentional rhyme, to separate "deep trouble for the mind" from the fact that nothing troubles "mine" (p. 51), Winnie, like Opener of *Cascando,* would deny internal forces: the sounds are not in her head. "No, no. . . . That was just logic. . . . Reason" (pp. 53–54). All is external, yet she is denied even this easy resolution as she begins qualifying her own denial of internal sounds. She argues that the very logic that would suggest such internal sounds can now be used to refute their existence. Though she has lost some of her reason, she is quick to add that "some remains." Then, for a moment, in a lapse of honest conviction, she envisions those internal sounds, much like the drip that Hamm freely confesses is in his head: "Sounds. . . . Like little . . . . sunderings, little falls . . . . apart." At length she pulls herself back to her narrow world with "It's things."

For a moment here Winnie struggles with inner promptings, with the suspicions, also shared by Vladimir and Estragon, that her external world—the mound and scorched grass and skyline of the present play, the public road and single tree of *Godot*—is not all. Whereas Hamm relishes dreams and sleep, and cultivates to his pain what he feels inside, his suffering, Winnie, like the clowns of *Godot,* has little patience with dreams or nightmares. By "great mercies" (p. 52) our headaches will go. The demonic force—an inner spirit, or playwright, or Godot—who makes the mound, who imprisons us, cannot be wished away; yet he can be put aside—and endured. Still her head remains full of "cries" (p. 60), and, as for Henry in *Embers,* no external sounds—cracking rocks together, "voicing over," to use a phrase from the cinema—can fully drown that inner noise. She is assaulted on both sides: on the one hand "sorrow keeps breaking in" (p. 34) despite her efforts; on the other hand her physical, external creation is not exclusive. The emmet is both friend and enemy, even as the bright boy is— to all of Beckett's artists. Her creation, moreover, is here aided by the fact that it is established against such poor competition, the scorched earth and the dull mound of the play's single set.[21]

Still, for a moment Winnie speculates on the possibility as well as the effect of there being other life: "What a blessing nothing grows, imagine if all this stuff were to start growing. . . . Imagine" (p. 34). The great mercies seem to preclude that, for the present play at least. Yet all the stage is a fiction. If a table is not really a table but only a prop in an illusion perpetrated by playwright and actors, then the physical world that Winnie champions is no more certain, no less an illusion than the subjective inner world she fights against and tries to deny.

She thereby uses words to avoid the possibilities of other worlds, external or internal. Though she knows that sometimes even "words fail" (p. 24), Winnie's hope is that she can make it through the day, that she can get to her song in time. However, the brightness, symbolizing her externality, must coexist with the black bag of death, that bag holding her own particular painkiller, the revolver that would deny in one shot the very physical world she has created and sustains. Curiously, that revolver, though the heaviest item in her bag, is ever "uppermost," and in a monstrous parody of her vision of dwelling in blue skies, the revolver itself seems to float to the top, despite its weight, despite the law of gravity. In a wonderful, if over-ingenious wordplay she identifies the revolver, nicknamed Brownie, with the poet Browning (p. 33). Like her Brownie, Browning himself is "uppermost." The Victorian poet of introspective dramatic monologues is at one with a revolver that, to echo Camus again, forces us to ask life's primary question: is it worthwhile sustaining life? is it worthwhile going on? Willie had urged Winnie to "take it away" from herself; indeed, she reminds him that he used to keep "on at [her]" on this score (p. 33). It threatens to take him "out of [his] misery," but she quickly changes his misery—"Your misery"—to her own. The revolver becomes a surrogate husband, as internal (light) as Willie is external (heavy, stuck in his hole). In a revealing gesture she places the revolver beside her with "I'll leave you out, that's what I'll do. . . . There, that's your home from this day out." Though it is now out of the black bag, its presence then leads her to that vision, previously discussed, of escaping physicality or externality, of entering a world where she "would simply float up into the blue" (p. 33).

Just as Winnie avoids her darker self, she also needs an audience, for she cannot "bear to be alone" (p. 20).[23] But there is the possibility that the audience is lured into justifying, as much for Winnie as for itself, the externality she champions. She cannot be alone, in the way Malone or the head of *The Unnamable* or Henry in *Embers* can, or in the way O or Joe is forced to be. Hamm's reminder to Clov of what life will be like when he is alone might well be directed to Winnie. Again, one must die alone and in that process what thoughts, previously disguised or suppressed, may come rushing into the mind? There's the rub. Unlike the thrush, she cannot sing without auditors, with "no thought of benefit, to oneself or anyone else" (p. 40). She wishes she could pour out "from the inmost, like a thrush," and sing a song "from the heart" that no audience would need to ratify. Then she could sing about what she really feels—the fears, the abyss she semiconsciously knows is there. That would be a true song, an artist's song of the first order, because it would be sung purely, with no hope of gain or ratification, without wanting to please on any shallow level.

But the only "song" we get from Winnie is a ditty from the Franz Lehar musical, a piece of comforting, but cheap sentimentality. We sympathize with her: her avoidance of the imaginative abyss through habit and repetition, through talking and stringing together shreds and patches, is an all-too-human effort. We may not so much fault Winnie as love her because she *is* human, because she cannot help trying to avoid what cannot, at length, be avoided.

Willie is literally a captive audience, and a subject for her indoctrination. However, when Winnie speaks of the "strange feeling" that "someone is looking at" her (p. 40)—again: Beckett, we, a god, or gods—she seems to sense that there are other audiences who are more circumspect, more aware of both her achievement and her shortcomings, of what her "art," in a word, includes as well as excludes. There is a trinity of possible audiences watching her. We will recall the double-lens perspectivs that Beckett calls for in *Film* to distinguish E's sharp from O's hazy vision. Winnie is like O in that she looks out from herself and, however infrequently, at herself, and imagines that other eyes see her as "clear, then dim, then gone, then dim again, then clear again, and so on, back and forth, in and out of someone's eyes" (p. 40). "Strange?" she asks Willie, along with us. He gives no answer; theater etiquette asks that we not respond, thereby leaving the answer rhetorical. I submit that we do respond, as interested and perceptive witnesses to her "story." We do what she herself does imperfectly. In the midst of an imaginative rationalization of her existence, in the midst of a comic, yet strangely heroic effort to keep sorrow, the abyss, at arm's length, she also acknowledges, however fleetingly, that inner world—terrifying because it is almost uncharted—that is there, although not subject to any external, let alone rational measurements.

Thus her voice breaks on occasion; her attempts to brush sorrow away become less than convincing as the play goes on. The pauses, if they can serve to connect such antithetical things as sex and toothpaste, can also be lapses into speechless sorrow, or sorrow that talking cannot override. Winnie's speech now becomes confused, as the platitudes and memorized phrases of Act 1 lose their effect, even as Winnie herself acknowledges that it is easy to lose "one's classics" (p. 57). In Act 2 there is the first mention of her daughter, a sad event kept from us in Act 1; and there is a greater awareness of time, the very force that Beckett in his study of Proust sees as both habit-comforter and imagination-destroyer. The whole pace of Act 2—it is literally half the length of the first act—is less leisurely. We ourselves are more attuned; as with *Play* when it is repeated, or *Godot* when Act 2 resembles in many obvious ways Act 1, we are less "taken in" by Winnie in Act 2, more alert to dimensions of her dialogue that she imperfectly or improperly comprehends, or does not comprehend at all. Like Willie, we come out of our hole.

**iv**

In some ways Willie, as a gross counterpoint to Winnie, resembles the *zani* of Italian Renaissance comedy.[24] He is clearly not as verbal, and his reading matter is confined to postcards, newspapers, ads, articles, and dictionaries. But his few comments do serve as stimuli for Winnie's more fertile imagination. If he leers over the ad for a "smart youth," we can still take the phrase in its larger context, linking that youth with the boy mentioned in *Endgame* and actually appearing in *Godot,* and we can look ahead to the boy of *All That Fall.* Willie's reference to the death of Dr. Hunter in his tub initiates Winnie's reverie embracing the "happy memories [voluntary, however]" of childhood, her first ball, and her first sexual encounter in a toolshed with Mr. Johnston (pp. 15–16). For a moment she engages in the same sort of creative reconstruction to which Hamm is given.

In a sense, Willie as *zani* is also an audience who both "highlights" the feature performer and encourages her. If he is below consciously meaningful speech, and if he himself parodies the actor's delivery—besides his monosyllables and curt phrases we have a *"burst of hoarse song"* from him (p. 40)—he still *ratifies* his wife's performance. He is *needed* by her. She spots his role, although apologetically: "Oh I can well imagine what is passing through your mind, it is not enough to have to listen to the woman, now I must look at her as well" (p. 29). Indeed this is so; we are dealing with dialogue plays for the legitimate theater and not with radio dramas, mime, film, or television. The medium here involves a live audience, and Beckett underscores the point, the way Shakespeare does repeatedly (with Claudius and his court in attendance for *The Murder of Gonzago* or with Theseus and the Athenians watching Bottom's rustic troupe perform *Pyramus and Thisby*) by having our own onstage representative unobtrusive but *necessary,* as Winnie well knows. Winnie's role with Willie, Beckett's role with us, is to draw out that audience, to involve it, to join with it in a production that is properly the union of audience and actor. Willie's speechless reactions, his mime, complements Winnie's torrent of words. Perhaps we too want to be "left in peace" (p. 29). Perhaps both groups should not meet. We will recall again Shakespeare's own fear in the Sonnets of prostituting himself on stage by revealing his emotions to the public.

Through Winnie, Beckett asks a rhetorical question when she says, "One does not appear to be asking a great deal, indeed, at times it would hardly seem possible . . . to ask less—of a fellow creature—to put it mildly . . . look into your heart—see the other—what he needs—peace—to be left in peace—then perhaps the moon—all this time—asking for the moon" (p. 29). Here are audience and actors, reverse mirrors of each other, mirrors for our common and "combined" nature. It is a mutual wooing: we are drawn out of our hole, our constrictive reality, while the actor, conversely, is summoned by our presence. As in *Play,* we are the light evoking the characters. Like that proverbial tree falling the desert, they, the actors, can come into being only when we are present, to hear and to see them. The long-coming union of wife and husband, of this Sucky Moll and her lover, is most intense and, paradoxically, most puzzling when near the end of the play Willie at last emerges from his hole. Beckett seems to be asking here: what happens when the audience and actor break the barrier between them? What are the consequences when the fiction of the stage seems no more so, or no less so, than the fiction at the base of life? In Wallace Stevens's phrase: what happens when we finally see art or the artist as the "necessary angel"?[25]

Willie appears, like Clov at the end of *Endgame, "dressed to kill"* (p. 61). He is in a new role; he has emerged like some rough beast slouching toward Winnie to be born. Though *"on all fours"* like an animal, he is still dressed like the proper British gentleman: *"top hat, morning coat, striped trousers, etc., white gloves in hand. Very long bushy Battle of Britain moustache"* (p. 61). Willie comes, seemingly, courting his wife, and she greets him—"Well this is an unexpected pleasure!"—as if he were a suitor. If he represents her physical side, the bottom side, as Estragon himself is the feet to Vladimir's head or mind, or Clov is the physical to Hamm's metaphysical, then the dichotomy of the human constitution seems to be erased here, or is on the way to being erased. Conversely, we might think of Willie as the id, as a matrix of desires or of forces beyond our consciousness. If this ascription is useful—though it would oppose the notion that Willie is the doggedly physical half to the would-be imaginative half represented by Winnie—then Willie's emergence in the closing moments suggests the paradox that Winnie's efforts to pass her day through habit and thereby to close off the terror of the imagination now run neck and neck with that deeper source of creativity that she both desires and fears. Hence her ambiguous attitude to Willie when he comes a-courting. At times she seems positive, urging him to feast his eyes on her, enticing him to "live this side now," asking him to make love and "not stand on ceremony," at worst teasing him with the fact that, if he was once potent, now he may need a "hand." Yet she is taken back by his expression, his total silence, the fact that he doesn't hear "cries," the strange way he looks at her, the possibility he has "gone off" his head. The fast-closing union is indeed puzzling. "Is it a kiss you're after, Willie . . . or is it something else?"

I do not think there is a simple answer, a single meaning to the situation here. Winnie's carefuly controlled, ordered world has entered a new stage where the audience does not remain passive, where she must share that stage with something more than an emmet or a couple passing through, where those ambiguous and complex issues that she has successfully ignored by her externalizing "imagination" seem to crystallize in this husband who is both love- and death-bringer, the same old Willie and a new Willie, a creature perhaps invoked by Winnie herself and yet one she cannot fully assimilate. If, initially, Willie represents her bottom half, her lower nature, the anal rather than the cerebral, perhaps now he has been elevated into a figure from Winnie's own imagination, from her inner art that is, until now, perforce a secondary issue in her consciousness. I find the end peculiarly comic, a parody of courting, and at the same time *terrifying*.

The saccharine ending itself does not abate the fear. We hear a surface declaration of love as for the first time Willie says his wife's name; she responds gratefully, of course. Winnie seems in control as, right on schedule, she finds her song sung to a music-box accompaniment. The play itself ends on schedule, with the ringing of the bell and with the newly joined couple looking—romantically, at least on Winnie's part—into each other's eyes. In her version, her vision, she wins, and her name itself—underscored by Willie's last word in the play, the just audible "Win"—takes on the sense of a victory. Like Virginia Woolf, Winnie has had her vision; she has made it through the day, drawn out her audience, succeeded with her heroic, albeit limited art.

Still, the play is pervaded by questions that Winnie does not consider and cannot answer. While this utilitarian art that is a comfort to her serves Winnie's immediate purpose, it may also be a metaphor, by what it excludes no less than what it includes, for the unending, unresolved, unfathomable, unnamable tragic-destructive, ultimately nihilistic underside of existence. In *Happy Days* the playwright seems to show us an art that works, with a successful couple at the end, yet only because of its limitations rather than any larger virtues. The happiest play in Beckett's canon, *Happy Days* also most qualifies the theatrical experience for playwright, actor, and audience. The title may have an ambiguity far deeper than the titles we have considered earlier—*Waiting for Godot* and *Endgame*. It is in *Kapp's Last Tape* and *Play* that this darker element emerges more graphically. In *Come and Go* that darker element is surely the line whispered by the old ladies but unheard by us, unless we choose to fill in—as Winnie will not or cannot—our own internal monologue.

# 4   The Audience Onstage: *Krapp's Last Tape, Play,* and *Come and Go*

*Krapp's Last Tape, Play,* and *Come and Go* are not simply the "other" three plays following those already discussed but are rather important, indeed inevitable steps in Beckett's own experiments with the legitimate theater, the next stage in his inquiry into the theatrical nature of existence, the tension between words and reality, and—most important for the present discussion—the relationship between the play medium and our self-perception.[1] The function of the playwright, the actor (character), and the audience here undergoes a relentless definition and redefinition. These plays also occupy a separate chapter because, beyond the new elements (a single character and a tape recorder, three characters in urns, and even "greater" brevity), the role of the audience is perhaps more significant, at least more obvious than in the three "major" plays discussed so far. Here, in these plays, in the "assemblages" onstage, the audience receives a clearer mirror image of itself.

i

*Krapp's Last Tape*

The play opens in an almost surrealistic mood. It is late at night and in the "*future*." The den, like that in Marlowe's *Faustus,* seems as much an image of the mind as a place for study or seclusion. We see an audience of one, Krapp huddled over his tape recorder, that technological "stage," which is the "other" player of the performance he witnesses and which is, in turn, witnessed by us, the outer audience. The desk faces both us and that onstage audience of one; in a way we have clearly moved beyond the two-character format of *Godot, Endgame,* and *Happy Days,* where one character acted to the "audience" of the other. Yet we have not moved at all: the live audience composed of Krapp listens to himself on tape, at age thirty-nine reflecting on his life a decade before.

The light illuminates only the desk, which becomes, in effect, a micro-cosmic stage, a parody of the legitimate stage in its smallness. And half the characters have been reduced to a recorded voice. The immobile bodies of the earlier plays, the actors confined to the stage, or a wheelchair, or a burial mound, here become a voice without form. When that voice is transformed into a live audience-actor before us, we see only a decrepit old man, a Lear without majesty: purple nose, disordered gray hair, white face, filthy clothes, a labored walk disclosing problems with the liver and bowels—indeed, an actor who degenerates physically before our eyes with each trip backstage for wine and, later, hard liquor. Beside the clowns of *Godot,* the impressive, albeit physically restricted Hamm of *Endgame,* and the happy warrior of *Happy Days,* Krapp—the name seems to tell it all, though I underline the word *seems*—appears to be the next step down.[2]

As Krapp sits with his ear cupped to the tape recorder, the gloom has apparently spread from onstage to offstage. He is us, like us, in the dark, without the benefit of flattering light, doing just what we are doing: not so much waiting as listening.[3] There is no chance of a Godot's coming or not coming; the play has been predetermined, or so it seems, by the contents of the spool of tape that Krapp feverishly seeks. With the degeneration and then downright elimination of the physical, we seem to be on the periphery of the radio plays, in the midst of voices, divorced from any human body, or from much of a body, so to speak. To underscore the loss of the physical, we learn that, along with being hard of hearing, Krapp is *"Very nearsighted (but unspectacled)"* as well (p. 9).

This world is actually smaller than the four or five steps paced out by Krapp as he sets the limits for the stage lights, for as the physical dimension is undercut and then eliminated, we seem to be in a cerebral, inner world. The externals fall away; his actual voice we learn is *"cracked"* (p. 1), and the busy physical work that fills Krapp's opening moments is abandoned once he reacts to the tapes. Soon the den, like the single set of *Endgame,* seems more a symbol of some region of memory than an actual place.[4] We are inside Krapp's head, and his movements, whether about the desk, in terms of it, or backstage, are played out in the arena of the brain, divided as it is among imagination, thought, habit, and the motor areas that are activated in these opening moments.

This is no easy trip from outer to inner. The stage itself insists on being a physical world, certainly initially, and always to some degree; the very tension, the "drama" of the theater is generated by this division between the physical immediacy of the live performance (actors and tangible sets) and the cerebral, otherworldly implications of its heightened language. Matter on stage can be dislocated but it cannot be destroyed, and as much as Krapp can darken his stage, limiting it to his microcosmic desk, he cannot darken it entirely. We approach radio here, but *Krapp's Last Tape* is, properly, not a radio script but one for the legitimate theater.

The banana itself, the "medicine" for his constipation and a pathetically obvious phallic symbol, marks Krapp's decline as a physical being. He both eats and flaunts the fruit, and when even this travesty of the physical begins to wane in its influence, when it "insults" him by nearly tripping him, he pushes it with his foot over the edge into the pit (p. 11). Yet Krapp cannot make it disappear; the gross gesture to the audience only underlines the presence, the indestructibility of the fruit. As in Pirandello's *Henry IV,* the escape into artifice, into the illusion, is not possible. Later Krapp will wisely push the banana skin back into his pocket.

Even more, his drinking accentuates the tug of the physical world against Krapp's own technical-artistic creation. Wine gives way to hard liquor, and with each movement backstage for a drink he loses something of his creative momentum. Curiously, those backstage visits are the closest thing we have in the present play to radio since we only "hear" Krapp's drinking in the popping of corks and the draining of the bottles. The artistic control over the tape recorder is thereby undercut by the demands of objects such as bananas and bottles.[5]

At issue is how to make something literal into something symbolic. The physical, I believe, is here transformed rather than avoided. The search for the proper spool, Krapp's rifling through his desk, gives way to his larger search for his self. The opening of those drawers facing us becomes Krapp's own exposure, for himself no less than for us, the means of revealing his mind, his soul. His "reverse" progenitor here may be Molloy, who spends time "locking the various drawers," closing down or out his life.[6] Spool as a physical object excites Krapp's interest in words, and if his verbal fondling of the word *spool* is self-indulgent, it is still the first step toward a more mature interest in language as the means of finding the self.[7] Krapp moves, then, from objects—the desk, bananas, bottles, tape recorders, woman as merely physical being—to "essences," the search for the self, the creative act, that equipoise between physical dependence and imaginative flight.[8]

Neither abstract thesis nor circus spectacle, the legitimate theater itself is, at its best moments, somewhere in between. There will be other plays where language alone carries us, or, conversely, plays where spectacle determines the limits of the inquiry. Such is not the case here. Krapp both wants and doesn't want to hear the tapes. The inner journey is painful, and his fixation with words, his incompetence in handling the machine, and the frequent trips backstage are evidence of his "avoidance reactions," as the psychologists would say.

ii

Still, the play, Beckett's theater itself, calls for such a journey. Krapp, I believe, liberates himself from language that is divorced from actuality. Beckett's own career is, in the most simple of dichotomies, a movement from novels to the theater, whether it be stage, screen, radio, or television. Appropriately, Krapp's book *Effie* has failed, with only a few copies sold, and those to circulating libraries. The lead character herself, the woman named Effie, will be "reborn" on tape, for though the event in the boat itself is past, it is "revived" in our own witness of a decrepit old man listening and reacting to a recording, itself a reaction to a past event.

The "ledger" (p. 12) is woefully inadequate as a key to meaning, its function confined to the mechanical listing of the subject matter on the tapes: "Mother at rest at last . . . The black ball . . . The dark nurse . . . Slight improvement in bowel condition . . . Memorable equinox . . . Farewell to— . . . love" (p. 13). In a significant gesture Krapp *"sweeps boxes and ledger violently to the ground"* (p. 14), in effect clearing the stage and his mind of literary forms, even of the ledger, this parody of literary form. Offstage lies the physical degradation that has plagued Krapp most of his life; literally on the stage are the paraphernalia of his wasted literary career. What we see, both in spite of and yet complementary to the thematic pessimism, is the "renaissance" of Krapp. In this sense the play is a comedy, not a tragedy, not a gloomy absurdist tract.[9]

In the first live word uttered by Krapp, "Ah!" (p. 12), we confront, I think, not the pessimistic "Ah" uttered by Estragon when Vladimir reminds him that their mission is to wait for Godot. Instead, it has the tone of discovery, literally of finding the desired tape but, in a larger sense, of entering that road leading toward both the discovery and expression of one's self.[10] It is also the "ah" of pleasure, sexual or otherwise, and is at one with the images of creation, most frequent in the play's references to the sea, a persistent creative symbol in Beckett if we recall the sea in *Cascando* or in *Endgame.* It was by the sea, with "great granite rocks the foam flying up in the light of the lighthouse" (p. 21), that Krapp experienced his first moment of revelation, and it was on a boat that Krapp had that sexual encounter which, in his declining years, alone kindles his imagination. Appropriately, the woman, the eternal and literal vessel of creativity, was with him on that boat. There runs throughout the play a host of women, creative and uncreative, but in all cases a reminder of the *anima,* that muse prerequisite for the imaginative process. Indeed, the women referred to here almost serve as scenic dividers: "Mother at rest at last" (p. 13); "Old Miss McGlome [who] always sings at this hour" (p. 15); "Bianca in Kedar Street" (p. 16); the state "or condition of being—or remaining—a widow" (p. 18); the "dark young beauty . . . all white and starch, incomparable bosom, with a big black hooded perambulator" (p. 19); and, at last, the woman in the boat, who, once mentioned (p. 21), supplants all other women.

Sterility is what must be avoided, and Krapp plays on this notion with the word *viduity,* the state of sexually unrealized widowhood. The word, however, is ambiguous and can also refer to an animal, the vidua or weaver bird, or to the black plumage of the male. Thus even widowhood, the sterile condition only one step above that of the old maid Miss McGlome who sings to herself, releases opposite suggestions of creativity (weaving, joining together), suggestions of the procreative nature of art as well as of love. The women in Krapp's life thus stand in a line of growing inducements to creativity.

Interestingly enough, it is the women's eyes that he mentions most often. The motto of *Film*—*"esse est percipi"*—is at one with this woman, the *anima* or spirit, catching his eyes, making him see them, and then making him see himself reflected in them. Ultimately, the women merge with his mother sea, and it is in and by the sea that Krapp has his lasting moments of revelation. In *Cascando* Woburn's embrace of the sea has clear sexual overtones, and yet he fails to follow the narrator's command to use his eyes to look up, with the inner eyes thus replenished. For these eyes, charged with the *anima's* spirit, are the prelude to artistic creation. To imagine the woman Krapp must "close [his] eyes" (p. 15), must look inward. There is here no mention of the eyes of sterile women, namely, of his mother and Miss McGlome, but for the other women, culminating with the girl in the boat, eyes are paramount: first, Bianca the whore, about whom there was "Not much about her, apart from a tribute to her eyes" (p. 16); then, with a "glint of the old eye to come" (p. 18), the "young beauty" in the park who had eyes on Krapp that were like "chrysolite" (p. 19). In this connection, we might think here of the noncreative characters in Beckett, such as Pozzo (who goes blind) and the blind Mr. Rooney, who stands as a sterile counterpart to his wife. There are also characters who, though blind, see with a creative inner eye, such as Hamm, and women, like Winnie, who are all eyes, fashioning a system and a language out of the meager physical things they observe before them. Appropriately, in *Krapp's Last Tape* the girl in the boat has her eyes either shut or, when they open, confined to slits. The heaven's eye, the sun, stands as surrogate, closing her principal eyes and opening the way—"Let me in" is the refrain in this section—for Krapp's imaginative inner eye to function. That eye embraces both his memories of the scene—Beckett's version of moments recollected in tranquillity—and his imaginative use of those memories. When he bends over her to "get them [her eyes] in the shadow," when, in effect, his own act of union and procreation is defined, then her eyes open. "Let me in": he enters another, not just physically but spiritually.

From such union springs an extraordinary declaration, defining the state of equipoise, the conjunction of the physical and the cosmic, and the state beyond language, that eloquent silence we have seen the tramps, Hamm, and Winnie consciously or unconsciously strive to reach:

> We drifted in among the flags and stuck.
> The way they went down, sighing, before the stem!
> *(Pause.)* I lay down across her with my face in her
> breasts and my hand on her. We lay there
> without moving. But under us all moved,
> and moved us, gently, up and down, and
> from side to side. (P. 27)

We are here at the moment of equipoise achieved in Shakespeare's own plays, such as when Florizel in *The Winter's Tale* (4.4.140–43) describes his vision of Perdita as being like the sea, ever moving and yet ever still, that moment when, even as the "earth turns," there are underneath "calm waters." This is the nothingness, that oblivion when otherwise warring factions—sex and vision, the physical and the metaphysical—are suspended. In the words of the narrator of *How It Is:*

> yes or not it's not said I can't see other possibilities pray my prayer to
> sleep again wait for it to descend upon under me calm water at last and in
> peril more than ever since all parries spent that hangs together still.[11]

It is the serenity that Estragon feels when he lies on the ground, staring up at the night sky; or that Hamm struggles toward as he places the old stauncher masklike over his head; or that Winnie achieves when her carefully regulated day ends in a song.

This moment in the boat, in this "little kingdom,"[12] is documented on that part of the tape to which Krapp returns three times. One drifts and yet sticks. The flags are at once alive and yet falling. The bodies join, and the stillness of the two humans is balanced by the movement of the earth, by all that is under them. Even that movement, expressed in the waters that roll under the boat's keel, is performed "gently." It is as if all four movements of the souls in *The Lost Ones* are contained here: constant movement, occasional movement, being stationary, and nonmovement.[13] The frantic actions of the play's opening moment, the destructive action backstage, and the spent life that moves inexorably downward with all that fall are now suspended. As Krapp realized when by the sea, this stillness in the boat is the "dark" he had always resisted but that is "in reality [his] most"—and then the words fail (p. 21). Properly, no word—not *being* or *reality* or *soul* or *heaven*—can be commensurate with the experience. By switching forward in the recording, Krapp manages to juxtapose the two (p. 21). It is a moment of "miracle," and the "fire that set it [Krapp's imagination] alight" is to be distinguished from the fire of the cirrhosis eating away at him. These very motifs of stillness, movement, eyes, lights, coupling, and equipoise are echoed in the extraordinary end to "Imagination Dead Imagine":

> Between their absolute stillness and the convulsive light the contrast is
> striking, in the beginning, for one who still remembers having been
> struck by the contrary. It is clear however, from a thousand little signs
> too long to imagine, that they are not sleeping. Only murmur ah, no
> more, in this silence, and at the same instant for the eye of prey the
> infinitesimal shudder and icy, there is better elsewhere.[14]

## iii

Krapp, unlike Winnie, is engaged in real creation, and not just by means of a hodge-podge of quotes and reactions to physical stimuli. Winnie is robust, if immobile; he is not robust, just dimly mobile, yet proportionately more creative. Krapp moves from the black ball, the symbol of sterility, defecation—an image we later find in *All That Fall*—to the white dog, to a union that is not unlike the temporary peace achieved in Albee's *Zoo Story* between Jerry and the dog.

When Krapp does make a present-tense recording, it is on the surface only a collection of brusque utterances, but just below the surface there is a logic of the most creative order. His imaginative movement, like that of Hamm in his final speech, is dazzling. "Everything there, everything on this old muckball . . ." (p. 24). "Yes" properly initiates the catechism. He calls for Jesus to take his mind off "his homework," and then the "Ah" reappears. Like Lucky's speech, Krapp's play with the language contains an honest insight into his condition, vividly recreates a past event, branches into poetry (his song, "Now the day is over"), and ends with a tremendous outpouring of formed and half-formed images: a body propped up in the dark, a Christmas Eve and its red holly, the sleigh ride on Sunday morning, old loves, and again "Now the day is over." He ends by replaying the original tape, though this time it follows as well as complements a rich verbal, cultural, and personal prelude. The speech marks the culmination of Krapp's development, his finest achievement.[15] The past is not forgotten but rather observed; the present has been elevated from a merely physical reaction to the past; a newly recorded speech blends effortlessly with an earlier recording and with dialogue. As audience we respond anew to the script, just as we do in *Play,* now that a past is recast. Krapp *incorporates* the past, rather than trying to abolish it; he integrates present and past.[16] Earlier dead in a system, in a lost world of harsh recorded memories, the speaker is now alive and eloquently so. Like Winnie he uses songs, yet in place of snatches—as the song exists in its first appearance in the text— "Now the day is over" is completed here. Krapp's mind races over his life, like that of the proverbial drowning man, from decrepit days to the happy times of childhood, "in the dingle of a Christmas Eve, gathering holly, the redberried" (p. 26). The staccato opening conversation, the interruptions, the cynicism are still here as he speaks sarcastically of "All that old misery." Still, even that phrase is counterbalanced by the affirmative "Be again, be again." And yet he cannot conquer time; the process of life, aggravated by time, is downhill from the moment the child leaves the womb—or pops out of the backside, to cite one of the characters' recurrent fetishes.

"Once wasn't enough for you" (p. 27)—the phrase refers to the past encounters with the girl and the present encounter with the sought-after passage on the tape. Krapp takes off the fresh tape, throws it away as if it were an isolated performance, and returns to the machine that tape containing the boat passage. As he interacts with the one certain and affirmative event of his life, the interaction is aesthetically affirmative even if the event itself, an abandonment of love, a separation, is thematically negative. The medium of the theater here relies not on the story itself but on the audience's interaction—Krapp's and ours—with that story. The play is about the union of audience (Krapp, us) and actor (Krapp, Krapp on tape, the tape recorder that bears his voice), and about a thematic union as well, of man and woman, of a man in the present with a man in his past, of the cerebral or imaginative with the physical and time-laden. Krapp's motion in suddenly bending over the machine suggests a coupling at one with the other couplings we have observed: Vladimir and Estragon, Hamm and Clov, Winnie and Willie. Take away the physical counterpart, reverse the classical development of drama by switching from three to two to one character, and yet the need for union remains.

The play is about love, and self-love is a perversion of real love. It is little wonder that Krapp fears being alone; the obsession of Beckett's characters is just that: of not being alone, of being heard, or remaining together even if forming a couple leads to misery. Being alone for Krapp defines the unprofitable time in the winehouse, the one-third of his life spent drinking on public premises, and the aloneness in his den, in the realm of his own mind, until he activates the tape recorder. In the darkness, he confesses, he feels less alone, and we may assume that when the physical reality is blotted out by darkness, the character meets himself, his real but also his other half. Similarly, Hamm in his blindness can dream, can populate his seemingly barren world. By definition the theater demands union, of actors and audience; a play can exist only if it is heard and seen. An audience without the stage mirror is alone, even if a crowd. To see is to affirm existence: *video ergo sum*, to rephrase Descartes. To know oneself is not to be alone, if we define aloneness as that sterile promontory where one loses vision, or confides in things that are only illusions, as in the early movements of the mime in *Act Without Words I*, when the player trusts in the illusory physical aid of the carafe.

The present play starts with Krapp alone, and it seems to end as it began. This is only a half truth. There is one of Beckett's pregnant pauses, and then Krapp's lips move, though no sound issues from them. The sound we hear comes from the tape, and from that special part that ends the reel itself, his earlier narration of the moments in the boat. Time past and time present are merged; it is past midnight now just as it was past midnight years ago, when he was thirty-nine. Krapp is actor and audience listening to his tape, as we are, but now he is also mouthing the words. It is the perfect moment of equipoise: he speaks and yet does not speak. Similarly, Romeo describes Juliet on her balcony as one who speaks and yet says nothing. We have dialogue and a silent actor, and "such silence" that would move us to think the earth "uninhabited" (p. 28). The mechanics almost take over, with Krapp concerned with the proper "citing" of the reel ("Box . . . three, spool . . . five"); but mechanics themselves are elevated by the irony of the situation.

The play ends with this extraordinary union of silent actor and talking contrivance as Krapp on tape and in person speaks of the impossibility of recapturing the best years, and of the fact that an artist's happiness is not the same "chance of happiness" possible when we merely experience rather than create. Then, repeating the sentiments of his early years, yet with those sentiments now elevated by the play's new context, Krapp seemingly denounces what he has just said: "No, I wouldn't want them back." However, the literal meaning of the lines, both in the words and in that moment in time when they were first recorded, must now share the stage with the new symbolic meaning, a meaning defined by the present theatrical context. "Existence" is contrasted with "essence," physical fire with imaginative fire. In this way the dismissal of the earlier years, the preference for the present, for that present moment witnessed by us, is at once cynical yet affirmative. Krapp's achievement as an artist dwarfs his own physical existence. Like Hamm, he is now enclosed in an art world; "having been" turns into "becoming" by means of the repetitive nature of the theater. In a sense, Krapp is immortal, beyond his physical deficiencies. His final action, staring motionless before him as the tape runs on in silence, is a pose, whatever else it is, not of despair but of Buddhist-like serenity. He has achieved the status of an imaginative creation; his name is no longer self-descriptive or even appropriate. As Hamm can say when he has had his vision, "You remain." The short sentence embraces both the notion of art's permanence and the audience's obligation once they set foot outside the theater.

iv

*Play*

The experimental mood of *Krapp's Last Tape* is intensified in *Play.* Here we are confronted with more than just a single mechanical contrivance, that tape recorder elevated to the alter ego of a play's sole character. Rather, *Play* challenges almost every convention of the traditional theater: that actors engage in dialogue with each other, that they be mobile, that they employ facial and bodily movements to complement the dramatic language, that they make entrances and exits, that they do not repeat lines, that they play to the world onstage, that they be seen, that they not stare out at the audience, let alone at a spotlight from behind the audience, and so on. Because of such changes, we approach those very limits where the theater spills over into reality—or at least reality as defined offstage. One of the most advanced of Beckett's plays for the legitimate theater, *Play* is also the closest to what we might call "the reality of the present."[17]

The title itself is manifestly aesthetic, *Play,* even as it is also thematic, *homo ludens.*[18] Curiously, *Play* starts in the most conventional of fashions: the curtain rises. We discover, though, a set more strange than even the ashbins of *Endgame.* Three characters appear in funeral urns, with only their heads protruding, the necks "*held fast in the urn's mouth . . . . [the faces] undeviatingly front . . . so lost to age and aspect as to seem almost a part of the urn*" (p. 45). Nor do the urns match the height of their inhabitants: since those urns are only a yard high, Beckett requires either that traps be used or that the actors kneel. Even the sitting posture is ruled out. If the title is aesthetic, it may also be ironic, for we might wonder how the theater can function under such tremendous inhibitions. With the normal interaction between characters and between characters and audience so circumscribed, perhaps we might have here something more akin to that "public show"[19] of which the Unnamable speaks: as audience, we are voyeurs watching nonactors unconscious of the larger play in progress. Nor is the darkness that is their "fate" when the spotlight avoids them a source of creativity, as it is for Murphy or Hamm. Never particularly articulate, they are even less so when the spot itself dims, and when the light is completely off them they lapse not into pregnant Beckettian silence but rather that nonbeing which Mrs. Rooney decries when she herself is excluded from the dialogue of the passengers waiting for the train.[20]

In a way we are close to radio, as we are in *Krapp's Last Tape:* the tape recorder has metamorphosed into the mechanical urn in which the human voice is divorced from facial movement or physical reactions. The light alone makes them speak, almost as if a giant radio dial gleamed from the audience. Sight and sound blend; it is the light that generates the voices here. We may be in a Nazi interrogation room, as the pitiless spot shines in the faces of the accused, who see the light all too clearly, but not their audience, nor the source of the light (the Godot or playwright behind the scenes), nor even their own bodies. The command issued by the light is inseparable from the title of the play, *Play.* The Bible's "Let there be light" is here monstrously parodied.

We seem, then, to be beyond or, perhaps, below "theater" in the accepted sense of that word. The mood, curiously though, is one of naturalness: the play, as we define play by conventional norms, is an anti-play, a "happening," almost appearing to lack form, a clear starting place. The characters, if we can call them that, simply speak, as if by miracle, with no exposition. They do not step on each other's lines (though there are a few exceptions), and yet, while giving the impression of speaking randomly, they manage to tell the same story, although only if we, as the ultimate audience, piece it together. This is a simple task, however, since the "story" is nothing more than that of a hackneyed love triangle. At times the dialogue itself takes on the naturalness and the irrelevancy (or irreverency) of street talk: the man hiccups in the middle of lines; the mistress refers to a butler, Erskine, though his name contributes nothing to the plot, let alone to the *dramatis personae;* a reference is made to Lipton's Tea, but without explanation; and the action of the man mowing grass is described on several occasions though, try as we may, I do not think we can connect that reported action with the narrations. The story itself is trite, and it is abandoned two-thirds of the way through *Play.*[21]

"Naturalism" here is perhaps not the most accurate word. As in *Godot,* the seemingly random or natural mood of the play coexists with a highly formalized structure that we grasp more surely only when *Play* repeats itself. The setting itself is "somewhere else," and not confined to the present or to conventional notions of time.[22] Perhaps the characters are in Purgatory or some Sartre-like Hell, yet the feeling we get is that everything is happening for the first time, at least on the initial go-around, right on the spot, no matter where that spot is located. Immediacy and distance, familiarity with and yet an assault on those very conventions of the theater which, we have assumed, must be agreed upon if the illusion of the stage is to be maintained—this seemingly confined piece also unravels in its own compex gamut.

What does it mean? That is, can we still have meaning with a violation of established theater practice? If plays normally progress toward a meaning realized at the end, then *Play* violates its own end with repetition. The man confesses his double error in "looking for something" where possibly there is none (p. 61), both when the sun shone (that is, when he was alive) and now when only the spotlight shines (now that he is dead, or is a character in *Play*). Yet the wife, trying to dismiss her situation, trying to take comfort in its meaninglessness, cannot: "If only I could think, There is no sense in this . . . either, none whatsoever. I can't" (p. 56). This is the paradox. As it veers toward reality, toward the simple rendering of the moment, *Play* appears without meaning: the love story is abandoned; clear symbols will not form; and when there is something concrete or consistent, like the mower or the light in the final third, it too dissolves. The balance among the three participants, the symmetry of the structure, the second chance Beckett gives the audience to hear the dialogue and to reexamine the spotlight's function— all these formal aspects invite meaning, call on us to devise an allegory. The title itself embraces mere "play" (something to pass the time) or "play" in the exalted sense of a symbolic composition for the stage.

Time itself, the system by which we impart order and perspective, and therefore meaning to human activity, is both scrupulously observed in the chronology of the love story (in what Mahood would call their "historical existence."[23]) and yet obliterated by the play's reverting to its opening before the ending can be reached. The man's last line, his recognizing that time has been wasted, that "we were not long together" (p. 61), is separated from the jumbled conversation of the women's "One morning as I was sitting" and "I said to him, Give her up," lines that tend to make his observation seem less than final. The man's line stops the spotlight, and therefore stops the play; the line itself is doubly wished for since we have had to repeat the entire play to get it. However, we have heard that same line much earlier, within seconds after the start of the *Play*. The meaning of what is, potentially, the most significant line is therefore obscure since it occurs in two radically different contexts. Besides, the reference to "we" is vague. Does it refer to the characters in their story before *Play* or during *Play*? Or does it also refer to the audience, or the audience in conjunction with the characters?

The line seems poignant, conveying both the brevity of an existence denying the possibility of knowing others, let alone oneself, and the brevity of our conscious life when compared with the eternity of death or the unreal, playlike life after death. The experience of the audience itself can

sometimes contradict the man's observation that "we" were not long together, for I have heard spectators, sophisticated and not so sophisticated,
groan when it becomes obvious that *Play* is repeating itself: do we need to
hear again the trite story, and then again that cryptic dialogue once the
light dims? Beckett, for better or worse, seems a playwright one must *get
through,* but to be asked to get through him and then do it again may be too
demanding—for some. The experience of a Beckett play—the frustration
we share with Vladimir and Estragon, the anticipation of Hamm's own
endgame, the pleasure in Winnie's courage combined with our frustration
with her inanities—seems worth it, but it is essentially an experience, not a
"world" as we would define that state when speaking of the "world of
*Hamlet*" or the "world of *A Midsummer Night's Dream.*" Still, that same experience in *Play* is seemingly ruined by repetition. Perhaps the line is said not
in despair but with relief: we thank the gods that the torture of existence,
like the torture in the interrogation room, is so short, that, abrasive as we
are with each other, we do not need to be abrasive very long.

Given a situation in which characters do not talk to each other, let alone
know of each other's existence, *Play* seems to represent a "failure of communication," to use the current cliché. Perhaps that same failure is a blessing: the souls are not in hell but in bliss—free of mobility, either physical or
social. We see souls tortured by a story and then by a situation that they do
not comprehend; but their thematic discomfort is our aesthetic comfort. In
this paradoxical play, at once "natural" or close to reality because of its
violation of theatrical convention and, at the same time, "unnatural" or
aesthetic because of the gap between its clear metadramatics and equally
unclear meaning, we observe three souls both unlike and like our real
selves. If we equate "real" with what is external, perhaps *Play* simply takes
one step farther that movement from outer to inner, from the world to the
self, that I have been charting since *Godot.*[24]

v

No less startling than *Play*'s dialectic embracing sensitivity to and yet
violation of theatrical conventions is the relation of its onstage audience to
that offstage. In effect, it makes us think about our own role as audience in
the production. As the curtain rises we see an audience of sorts, in urns
rather than chairs, yet clearly facing front in a grim parody of ourselves.
Indeed, if they are not actors by any ordinary definition, perhaps they may
profitably be thought of as an audience. The spotlight comes from us to
them, reversing the normal situation where, before the play, the audience
is illuminated and then cast into darkness with the curtain's rising. Like us,
they are a group of strangers, and their opening dialogue resembles that of
an audience before the curtain rises: many conversations, spoken at once, a
general hubbub rather than the clearly demarcated dialogue we associate

with the theater. Intelligible to the individual speaker, their conversation, as three talk at once, is correspondingly unintelligible to us. Do we not have the mirror image of ourselves?

Our own role as audience highlights this mirror image. In the first half of *Play,* before its own repetition, we ourselves must make the connections among the narrations of the husband, wife, and mistress. Because they do not talk to each other, because each, though obsessed with the same story, still operates on an individual sequence for the narration, they themselves cannot fashion for us a single, consistent narration, as in a conventional play. As for Hippolyta in *A Midsummer Night's Dream,* the stories "grow to something of great constancy" (5.1.26)—but only by our own intervention. We are also asked to make judgments each time we get three versions of the same event: for instance, the husband's returning repentant to his wife. At times only we can resolve breaks in the dialogue, as when the man's "par" is interrupted by W2's "no" and then completed one line later with "—don." (p. 58). They themselves cannot catch, let alone respond to the ironies of the conversations, as when one's account of an incident is contradicted by the unheard and unintentional response of another. Or when one's comments unintentionally establish a new context. W2 expresses her disgust at a man who could go "back to that," but the next line is W1's description of W2 as "pudding face, puffy, spots, blubber mouth, jowls, no neck, dugs you could—" (p. 50). This seemingly endless list of insults is followed by W2's "He went on and on"—and we are tempted, surely, to substitute "She." We become, in effect, coparticipants, artists in a way, taking otherwise formless monologues and, without the speakers' knowing it, making a dialogue, a trinity of conversations that speak to us and are molded into a single narration beyond the intention or comprehension of the individual speakers.

It is as if three individuals, unaware of each other's presence, came separately into an interrogation room, each having been asked to "tell the facts" of a sordid tale involving adultery and betrayal. Actors as pre-curtain audience onstage are now matched with a post-curtain audience of play-wrights working with borrowed material. It is not the story that is unique, as Pirandello confesses in his notes to *Six Characters in Search of an Author*: the story itself is purposely trite. Beckett's concern here, our concern surely, is with the *process* of engaging the audience. We are not passive spectators; our effort, rather than any special quality in the story or the individual narrations, *makes* the play, gives it meaningful narration and form. One of the character's comments before the spotlight might well describe our own reaction to this new orientation to *Play*'s opening half: "I had anticipated something better. More restful" (p. 52). In terms of *Film,* we are E and the three onstage are O, but we are also O, since they give us back, as we have seen, our own self-image.

Still, we will be jolted even from this orientation in the final third of *Play* when the characters switch from narration to a reaction to their condition, particularly to the "new" spotlight, the hellish half-light taking the place of the full-spot. Their worry—"Am I as much as . . . being seen?" (p. 61)—is answered silently by us. We are with the light; both our eyes and the light look on them. As we respond with a silent "yes" to the question about being seen, we acknowledge our creative role as stimulus: we *are* the light, the E of *Film,* and they are now talking to us. Like O with his travels down the street, up the stairway, and into the room, they have consciously avoided us with the narration of the first two-thirds; now they come face to face with the merciless spotlight of our vision, just as O at last looks directly at E. They see us as a hellish half-light, not as the sun, but as some human light. We see ourselves in them; our physical reality matches theirs, for we are fellow participants in a performance, in this *Play.*

Even this "second" orientation is discarded when the play starts again. If the opening two-thirds seems exposition, the same section becomes "process" upon repetition. The trite story is already in our minds; now we can work with greater refinement, looking for clues to character and to the situation in gesture (such as there are), language, and even irrelevancies (the mention of Erskine or the mower or Lipton's Tea) that now can less easily be dismissed. We can watch the horizontal intercourse of the speakers, for if the spotlight is only on one speaker, we now have more firmly imprinted in our memories the surrounding context of the monologues.

With the repetition of the play's final third, our response to the present-tense, experiential (as opposed to narrative) situation is also keener. Repetition is at one here with a purgatorial mood. With a stronger sense of the individuals, thanks to that repetition of their story, we respond more fully to their individual reactions to the light. In an aesthetic sense the repetition enlarges our threshold; with familiarity we take in a larger portion of the process. With repetition, technicalities such as the order of speakers and the relations among the dialogues that may have seemed only half-formed irrelevancies the first time around now take on a more significant, if not clearer role.

The repetition also increases our aesthetic response to the play's title. Life doesn't repeat, but the theater does. In a way, we are present for both the matinee and evening performances. The repetition may seem unnatural, but in point of fact nothing in the theater, even in the conventional Victorian three-acter, is natural. It is all convention reminding us that this is play. Aesthetics merges with thematics. In other ages, the Renaissance particularly, the statement would have been simpler: all the world's a stage and the stage is a little world. If *Play* seems close to reality in the handling of the dialogue and yet, paradoxically, if the unnaturalness of the situation is no less certain, particularly upon repetition, then does *Play* itself comment on the play of life, the very role-playing that Genet would maintain is no less a fact than the role-playing onstage? The extraordinary difference is that whereas the theater confesses its artifice, those living in "real" life act as if an artifice, role-playing, were a reality.[25]

vi

The onstage audience also change radically, though their change is in two steps that, with the repetition, are at once obliterated and then repeated without their consciousness either of a past or of repetition. Of course, the actors behind the characters are aware that the audience now has a new orientation (their third) and, as I have observed from directing *Play,* unconsciously "adjust" the characters with the repetition. Physically and mentally conscious of repeating the lines, actors themselves know that no two performances (within the same play, let alone on successive days) can be identical. In effect, the audience consciously and the actors both consciously and unconsciously make the repetition, like Act 2 of *Godot,* the same and then not the same.

The characters, as we have seen, move from the narration of a love-triangle story to an awareness of their present situation.[26] Their emotions in the first two-thirds are directed to and by memory; in the second third, where the emotions of despair or anger or frustration are no less strong, the presence of the spotlight, underscoring the present-tense nature of the theater in which characters-actors and audience form an ensemble, is itself the stimulus. We move from past to present; they do likewise. If we undergo an orientation to this new type of theater and, particularly, to a theater that asks us to make three adjustments in the course of a performance, they also undergo a similar orientation to the light, to this present.

In a word, they become more *sentient* in the second part, more aware of "this change" (p. 52). Now we are in the inner theater, like that in *Krapp's Last Tape.* They have moved from events that could just as well have been narrated on the street or in a living room to those of the theater itself, as symbolized by its spotlight; and their comments are generated now by the present, by what happens to them rather than what *has* happened. We go from the novel and all past-tense literature (the "old ledger," as Krapp would say) to the living theater. W2 speculates that if the light goes out will she also go out (p. 53), and we can supply an affirmative answer to her question. The theater is not what has been—it is distinguishable from non-dramatic literature and even from film in this regard—but about what is: "Am I as much as . . . being seen?" (p. 61). The key word is as much *being* as *seen.*

Normally the eye sees only the external; but since we are in a theater of the mind, as graphic as that in *Endgame* or *Krapp's Last Tape,* then the characters' eyes focus not on the outside world but rather, like the mind's eye, on their souls. The dichotomy between external and internal becomes as useless as it does in *The Inferno:* Dante is journeying somewhere, but clearly *The Inferno* is as much a state of mind as a state in some infernal geography.

No longer slaves to narration, to the past, to their "historical existence," the characters, even while imprisoned in their urns, are curiously *free.* They *grow* in the second half. W1 wonders about her mental state: is she "unhinged"? What should she utter? Should she weep? If only by questions, the mind is moving about; the intellect struggles, however futilely, to comprehend a situation, instead of focusing on a narration and a self-justification in a story where all the participants were guilty. Like Krapp encouraged by the woman's *anima,* the man now speculates on his state. In his vision, as opposed to his pseudo-factual narration of the first half, he imagines that they could "meet, and sit, now in the one dear old place, now in the other, and sorrow togther, and compare—*(hiccup)* pardon—happy memories" (p. 56). He too is alive with questions: "Am I hiding something? Have I lost?" (p. 57). The otherwise unimaginative W2 is given to metaphor: now, for her life is "like dragging a great roller, on a scorching day. The strain . . . to get it moving, momentum coming" (p. 57). Out of W1's neurosis comes not only questions, albeit shrill, but a vision comparable to the man's: "Perhaps she is sitting somewhere, by the open window, her hands folded in her lap, gazing down out over the olives" (p. 58).

The variety of responses is extraordinary. W1 moves from neurosis to a somewhat serene resignation: "Silence and darkness were all I craved. Well, I get a certain amount of both. They being one, perhaps it is more wickedness to pray for more" (p. 59). No less neurotic or petulant about the past, about the man's rejection of her, W2 is still impressively aware as she questions her new situation. If chained, if in Purgatory, she is still alive and takes a curious pleasure even in the possibility that if she is partially mad, then her altered state will somehow fit the new situation. The man is the most wide-ranging in his associations and in some ways the most circumspect; he moves from an assessment of the change, an acknowledgment that all his life has been "just . . . play," to a hope that all he presently experiences will be "just play" (p. 54), to his imaginary recreation of the woman's new state, to a confrontation with the light (he asks why it doesn't go out), and then to a quiet acceptance. It is marvelous, almost as if Beckett had written two plays: a seeming parody of an adulterous story that we rescue from banality by our increased role as audience, and a "happening" in which the theater serves not as narration of events (in the most restricted sense of the word *narration*) but as stimulus for a new and no less credible situation. That present-tense, internal situation depicted in the last third makes *Play* as exhilarating as *How It Is,* that painful confrontation of our reality couched in poetic prose.

Thus *Play* moves from the external or conventional or narrative or past-oriented (both in terms of story and theater), to the internal or unconventional or experiential or present-oriented (no less in terms of story and theater). Simple, formal, a self-conscious theater, it also establishes a new and complex ensemble among character, actors, and audience.

*Play* is strangely at one with Beckett's other works. The light becomes its Godot, and though there are three characters, it is the interaction between any two that makes the conflict, as in *Godot* and *Endgame.* But *Play* is also like *Happy Days* and *Krapp's Last Tape* in being a play of monologues. And more than all of these it is a play about the theater and, particularly, about our role, both on- and offstage, as defined by the theater and by that reality surrounding it. Like *Come and Go* it is difficult primarily because it is on the frontiers of both life and the stage.

**vii**

*Come and Go*

I take this "dramaticule" as short only in appearance on the printed page, or in its actual playing time.[27] Indeed, after directing this play with both amateur and professional actresses, and before a variety of audiences (students in lecture halls, theater audiences, participants at a conference), I would want to qualify even the comment about the playing time.[28] That time can be lengthened or shortened substantially, depending on the amount of time taken by the many planned pauses, as well as by the opening and closing moments when the three characters, like an audience, sit on the bench confronting the audience on the other side of the stage. Still, perhaps this brief play takes a special familiarity with the playwright to be understood, though I prefer to think otherwise, and my experience with audiences who knew nothing of Beckett tends to confirm this. If the dualities of past and present, audience and actor, theater and reality, narration and experience, and of the relation between the actors on- and offstage are established quickly, even tersely, they are nonetheless there, and I would hope we therefore have sufficient basis to judge this play, as we would any play, on its own grounds. Even more than with *Play*, we are here at the limits of the legitimate theater; consider the brevity, the deceptively simple dialogue, and the fact that the most important lines, defining the condition of the character not on the bench, go unheard beyond the stage itself.[29]

As in *Play* there are three characters, and, with one absent, they work in two's, talking to each other (as was not the case in *Play*), facing us (as was the case in *Play*). In effect, we have at once the picture-frame of *Play*, with an added interaction through dialogue and later through the characters' joining of hands, as well as *Play*'s mirror audience "*facing front,*" those three spectators looking at us with "*hands clasped in laps.*" This is the barest of theaters, no sets and no costumes to speak of, since Beckett calls only for dull floor-length coats, drab hats, and no rings. There is, properly, no "offstage," for when each character in turn leaves the stage she simply steps out of the single spotlight[30] and waits in the darkness until her reentrance.[31] Even the voices are colorless, like those in *Play*, with the one exception of the "O's" that are to be said with some emotion, along with the line immediately following the response to the "news" about the absent character. Only the actors' hands receive some attention: Beckett asks that they be made up "*as visible as possible.*" (We may think ahead to *Act Without Words I*, where at the end the solitary character cups his hands before his face, perhaps in prayer, perhaps suggesting his return to the self after the false inducements of the cruel god tempting him with shade and water, even with a death instrument.)

In a way we are on a playground (Miss Wade's playground is specifically mentioned), and the stage is as bare, as stark as playgrounds generally are. As in *Play,* but more graphically so, Beckett seems to be tearing away at the conventional theater in everything from sets to acting to characterization.[32] We come upon the characters and are with them for a while, and then they go—*Come and Go.*[33] The deceptively casual meeting appears as such only when judged by older notions of plot development, exposition, conflict, and resolution.

There seems to be a clear division here between what I would call thematics and aesthetics, between the past narrative and the present event, a division that the play itself resolves. Thematically, we learn of past events, as in the question "When did we three last meet?" (this is apparently not the first of such meetings). Vi's earlier life is suggested by Ru's reply that there is "little change" in her, and though we cannot know the nature of her illness or the affliction that, we assume, has not been ameliorated, the comments that Flo whispers unheard by us are enough to make Ru "*Appalled*" (one of Beckett's favorite words, as we may recall from *Godot*). We get only the reactions to a long-standing condition: "Does she not realize?" is followed by "God grant not." Besides God, there are references to people and things outside the present play: to Miss Wade's school and playground, to the log on which they once sat, to earlier actions on that log such as holding hands and dreaming, and, more generally, to the "old days," and all the events from that point of time to the present ("Of what came after").

Unlike *Play,* where we serve as audience to connect the narratives, we remain in ignorance here: the dialogue, the events are too sketchy. The characters obviously know the connection between past events and present facts, but they make such connections in whispers that violate the basic rules of stage delivery. As audience to the woman supplying the secret, they are also characters with a background, with information unknown to us. For actors, the trick is to draw on some personal knowledge of tragedy or of some afflicted person so that the emotional reactions on the faces, the sole evidence we receive, are intense.[34] In terms of the past-oriented first half of *Come and Go,* then, our role is reversed from what it was in *Play.* It is not a question of changing orientations, but rather of not having any sure orientation from start to finish.

Yet the intrusive symmetry of the play's structure forces us to face, three times, this narration of the past, of the same elusive facts. In that repetition the characters complete all possible combinations (Vi and Flo, Vi and Ru, Ru and Flo). Such facts *must* be important; the dramaticule cannot be mere entertainment.

Aesthetically, the play is as obvious in its pattern as it is disarming and cryptic in its dialogue. There is even a larger positional pattern. The three sit together; then, for the bulk of the play, one leaves while the remaining two talk about the absent character. At the end all three are together and join hands, with Flo passing the benediction: "I can feel the rings." In effect, the trinary symmetry is even more short-lived, even more come and go. From one perspective the play seems to lose quickly whatever symmetry it has. *Come and Go* appears to be about disruption, though it is bounded front and back by union.

Besides, there is a pattern within the dialogue itself that is repeated three times. One of the two remaining characters calls the other by name; the other responds. There follows a question about the absent character, and then a reply indicating that little has changed in or for her. The two move closer together, thereby setting up the change of positions in the seating arrangement when the talked-about party returns. The woman asked the question replies with a formula. There is first a denial of change, and then an "Oh" when she receives the whispered information from the questioner, information delivered with an "*Appalled*" look on her face. Once she responds with an "Oh," both look at each other, and the questioner puts her finger to her lips. The questioner then ends the brief talk with a wish that God will not give the talked-about party knowledge, this said in response to the other's "Does she not realize?" (or "know" or "been told").

We seem to be on the verge of tragedy, where each victim (all three are so identified at one time or another) knows of the tragedy about to visit or already visiting two others, all the while remaining ignorant of her own. Both the bearer and hearer of her tragic news are, in turn, tortured by the revelation. And for us this lack of information is both frustrating and terrifying, for in the absence of details perhaps we can only imagine the worst.

Complementing this thematic pattern, however, is the play's aesthetic side, the evidence we do receive, our sense of "what's happening" that counterbalances our ignorance of what has happened and has continued up the time of the play. Here, on an aesthetic level, the play is a comedy. The characters lose one of their number only to regain her, and if there are three departures and three dialogues with tragic implications, there are also three unions, albeit unions that dissolve an equal number of times. In these unions the characters, unlike their counterparts in *Play*, are happily aware of each other. They join hands and come together, in a way that must parallel the unions they refer to as having once happened at Miss Wade's. We see a "recreation," within the fiction of the larger play, of a happy memory from the past; the characters are thereby also characters playing actors. This recreation, the memory that is given form, seems to outweigh the tragic implications in the questions about change.

Many spectators have seen the play as dramatizing the pangs of unrequited love, or the fall from youthful hopes to the sterility of old age, from maidenhood on the brink of marriage to spinsterhood. The critic's recreation of the time at Miss Wade's need not be entirely speculative; the three *do* join hands, just as they used to in the "old days."

There is a dichotomy, then, between what is verbally repeated and what is shown. Still, the joining of hands suggests a bridge linking past with present, the tragic-thematic with the comic-aesthetic. The theater as a present-tense dramatic activity seems to "win" here over "nontheater" or over literature defined as nondramatic, past-oriented narrative. The present process of doing, the therapy of the experience for playwright, actor, character, and audience, is to be preferred to the terrors of speculation. Perhaps it can be nothing less, for—again, as Yeats has observed in "Lapis Lazuli"—the poet is always gay. To feel here is "to be," and to think is not to be; it is Descartes confirmed and then denied. In the combined actions of its three characters, possible only when all are present and in a state more dependent on mime than on dialogue, there is a way out of the tragic speculations of the little play's first half. Its title now suggests the flexibility, the effortlessness of art's comic-cosmic dance: come and go and come and go, and so on. Whatever is old, mysterious, tragic, locked into a sterile narration (consider how ineffective are most tales told in Beckett's plays, whether it be Vladimir's song of the dog, Lucky's account of civilization's fall, the set stories of *Endgame,* Winnie's account of Milly, or Krapp's past life) is *revitalized* by what is current, by what is being done.

Miss Wade's log is preserved as the bench. Holding hands on the playground is now metamorphosed into holding hands on the ground of the play, on its "boards," to echo *Godot.* The pattern of tragic questioning and response gives way to the happy, childlike circle formed by the women at the end. In a larger sense, the past-present dichotomy is broken by this merging. The past lives again, and the present action is indebted to precedent. That past is "coming," becoming, and being "actualized"—not just going. Similarly, Lucky's past-tense story of civilization's fall must compete with the present-tense, frantic, circuslike antics of the clowns as they try to stifle him. In a way, Vladimir and Estragon put into violent physical form Lucky's academic discourse. Here in *Come and Go* ideas are dismissed, including conceptions of tragedy; experience, feeling, is celebrated. Hence the benediction to the play is "I can feel the rings." No need for physical rings—and thus Beckett's stage direction that the actresses are not to wear rings. No need for tangible symbols. The characters have worked through the conceptual (the attempt to understand their sad histories that dominates the first half of the play) to the physical (the joining of hands) to the imaginative: rings appear where there are, in reality, no rings. In the Renaissance sense of the artist's task, they have made something out of nothing. When they are together, the three women, going beyond their knowledge of each other's tragedy and acting in blissful ignorance of their own, can *feel* instead of think, can create rings that can be felt if not seen. No need for real rings; pretend ones, the very quintessence of the theater's illusion, will substitute nicely. One cannot lose a pretend ring in the devastating way one loses, all too easily, the tangible things of this earth—including one's youth, or beauty, or sexual ability.

The names themselves seem to support this argument that the play, albeit short, is about the movement from tragedy to comedy, from an ignorant audience to one conversant with what the theater is doing, from excessive thought to expressive joy, from separation to union. Ru suggests "rue" as in "rue the day," and Vi calls up "vie," as in competition, a single "e" serving in both cases. Flo has different implications; her name suggests something organic, a river, a movement rather than a lament or a challenge. If we look at the seating at the start of the play and at the end—a task quite proper if we consider, again, the insistent symmetry of this dramaticule—we notice that in the change from Flo-Vi-Ru to Ru-Vi-Flo, Vi has stayed the same, has not grown, while Ru has gone backward (since going from left to right is the customary direction in Western civilization, in everything from reading to horse racing). Only Flo has moved forward, to our right, and it is Flo who gets the ultimate line.

Besides suggesting the notion of the theater as a unifying force, the word *rings* has what Louis Zukovsky would call "sight, sound, and intellection."[35] We see the rings, in a sense, as the characters join hands in a complicated weaving of their six hands (see Beckett's diagram), and of course we hear the word as well. Beyond this, the term is conceptual: it might refer to the rings or constraints of existence, or to the notion of recurrence, or to memory that persists in the after-effects of sound once the initial stimulus has sounded.

Once aesthetics wins out, then we can happily go beyond language. The play ends in silence, moving from words to actions, to feelings, to silence. Legitimate theater requires dialogue; yet we move beyond that in *Come and Go.* In its comic progression, *Come and Go* seems to anticipate the mimes, *Film,* and the significant camera action of *Eh Joe,* just as *Godot* and *Endgame* suggest a balance in the theater among words, actions, and silence. *Krapp's Last Tape* and *Play* look to the radio plays. All six plays for the legitimate theater, enacting those thematic concerns on which heads that cry in the top of mime have written, both speak to us of and show us directly the delicate, productive company of playwright, actor, and audience.[36]

# 5 Theater of Words: *All That Fall, Embers, Cascando,* and *Words and Music*

There are a host of sounds in *All That Fall* portraying that doomed physical world in which seeing does not result in introspection, a physical world ironically at odds with the medium of radio as Beckett practices it. Indeed, the four radio plays stand in just this relation. In *All That Fall* both human bodies and sounds conflict with nature's sounds and those imaginative "sounds" or words championed by the artist Mrs. Rooney. In the shallow, decaying world of the play the artist, alone and within the internal "world" of her own mind, struggles to achieve insight.[1] In *Embers* this movement from the external to the internal has already been made; we literally hear symbolic sounds coming from the narrator's (Henry's) head. Henry struggles toward aesthetic creation in the midst of a life, now at its embers, that has been one of frustrated physical creation. With *Cascando* and *Words and Music* we move beyond even man's internal world and toward the abstract; in these two later radio plays Beckett, not confined by a physical stage or even by the radio debate of *All That Fall* between the physical-visual and the internal-imaginative, capitalizes on the medium's disembodied characters. In such "theaters" of words and the mind, he presents, through language alone, spoken to each "audience of one"[2] gathered around the set, the abstract portraits of character, actor, artist, and art. We have moved in the four radio plays, then, from the tension generated by an earthly existence wearing away through habit at the internal and the imaginative soul of man, to a pure "inner"-scape. This is all part of a natural progression, both from legitimate theater to radio and within the radio plays themselves. Beckett writes these early plays, I think, not just because he was commissioned to do so, or because he found the medium like the theater. Rather, radio as a distinct medium of words is the next step in his evolution as a playwright.

i

*All That Fall*

The sounds along the road in *All That Fall* ironically suggest the "lingering dissolution" (p. 39) of the physical world, that world primarily of vehicles and their appropriate sounds: the roll and clamor of Christy's dung cart, the bell of Mr. Tyler's bike, Mr. Slocum's car, and, ultimately, Mr. Barrell's train. The sexual innuendos associated with each of these vehicles underscores the limited, pathetic physicality of their sounds and, by implication, of their owners. Sounds are the man here; Mrs. Rooney is both correct and politely incorrect when she reassures Mr. Tyler that his bell is one thing and he another (p. 38): sounds should not be the man, and yet Mr. Tyler is nothing more than a mechanistic, dullish outgrowth of his own inefficient bike. He speaks accurately, albeit unintentionally of himself, of his own faded physicality, when he tells Mrs. Rooney: "My back tire has gone down again. I pumped it hard as iron before I set out. And now I am on the rim" (pp. 39–40). Yet he is not stopped by her sarcastic, "Oh what a shame," a phrase allowing us to take the rim as literal, sexual (the outside of the vagina that Tyler is too old to penetrate), or allegorical (he is a marginal character on the edge of life). Troubles with his bike are at one with impotence: "Now if it were the front I should not so much mind. But the back [Mrs. Rooney's own references to buttocks reiterates a persistent motif in Beckett]. The back! The chain! The oil! The grease! The hub! The brakes! The gear! No! It is too much!" (p. 40). Such innuendos, establishing a noisy physical world antithetical to the sounds in Mrs. Rooney's (and Beckett's) imaginative mind, increase as she nears the station. If that road is Everyman's, it is also an arduous path for the knight-errant, the comic fat woman of the play.[3]

Mrs. Rooney's vision is at variance with the banality, the limited perspective (epitomized in Miss Fitt—the name fits well), the shallow earthiness of the people with whom she interacts. If their world seems dominant, it is also fading, falling. The pun delivers the point: there is some doubt as to whether the mail/male "will . . . hold up" (p. 34). The least of the vehicles, and the one making the least sounds, Christy's cart, has no problems of movement: the last shall be first.[4] As we move upward, however, the problems of mobility increase, from the bike's flat tire, to the car's refusal to start, to the train's lateness.

The vehicles and the people have only their external sounds as a claim to existence, and that existence is frighteningly short-lived as each new sound supplants all previous ones. As opposed to the legitimate theater, a prop or a person in radio cannot continue unheard while we see it. The title marks the physical half of the play. Everything decays and perishes—falls. Mr. Tyler's daughter has lost her "whole bag of tricks" through a hysterectomy. Even if the Rooney's child, Minna, were living, she would be facing menopause, girding her loins for the great change. Mrs. Rooney is no less a part of the very people she transcends; plumper than Winnie, she defines herself as a "great big slop" (p. 37).[5] Objects with their identifying sounds and people with theirs are all decaying. If Mrs. Rooney's entry into Mr. Slocum's car (his name itself puns on impotence) suggests a parody of procreation, that car itself is a death-bringer, running over a mother hen,[6] the vehicle's raucous horn sounding only after the fact. Sexuality, the procreative art by which we defy the fall, redeeming a degenerating race by giving birth to innocent children, itself degenerates to violence and death. Later in the play we hear Mrs. Tully's piercing cries as she is beaten by her husband.

This physical world "climaxes" with the train's arrival: "*Immediately exaggerated station sounds. Falling signals. Bells. Whistles. Crescendo of train whistle approaching. Sound of train rushing through station*" (p. 65). For a time the mail (or male) is indeed "up," and the human voices—nothing more than calls to the passengers: "Dan! . . . Are you all right? . . . Where is he?" (p. 66)—are almost drowned in the "technological" sexuality, the violence of the mechanical noises. Then just as soon as it comes, the train goes, literally extinguished in the collective sounds of the radio play: "*Noise of station emptying. Guard's Whistle. Train departing, receding*" (p. 66). And then a word dear to Beckett: "*Silence.*"[7]

ii

We are ready for the play's second half, that human, isolated, imaginative "symphony" of the Rooneys. We have abandoned the public road, passed through the very image incarnate of externality and brute force, and now we move into the soul, the inner "play" of this strange, outmoded husband and wife. We have been with the Showers and the Cookers, the onlookers, the see-ers who are not thinkers, and now we come to Beckett's bodiless, radio-centered Winnie and Willie.

Occupations, possessions, the world of schedules and order that is Mr. Barrell's—all have been created and then "uncreated" as Mrs. Rooney journeys on the way to her husband. In a brilliant, first-time mastery of radio Beckett capitalizes on the tenuous existence of a medium that is only sound, and a concept of sound that is even less solid than, say, that of concert music, where our physical witness of the actual performance in the auditorium is an experience distinct from a recording. Here in radio the playwright finds a symbol of the potential illusion, the ultimate nothingness of physical existence. The order of descent is from the possibility that we have only the waiting without the certainty of a Godot, to *Play* where we pass time without the injunction to wait, to this present medium in which that verbal and physical play—and the concomitant tension between them—is reduced by half.

It is these physical sounds against which Mrs. Rooney struggles creatively in a way that goes beyond the flesh and its limited procreation. She has, indeed, a certain immunity to those external sounds, for she is so "plunged in sorrow" or, more generally, so developed within herself that she "wouldn't have heard a steam roller go" over her (p. 53). (This discredited claim of the physical, incidentally, may put into perspective the sound of the lawnmower that persists in *Play*'s second half, even when it is firmly established, for us as well as for the three characters, that they exist in some other dimension than the here and now. Both the steamroller and the lawnmower are "rolling" instruments, and, if the characters in *Play* are dead, in the grave, then they may hear the lawnmower, from the physical world above, passing over their heads.)

But there are other sounds in *All That Fall,* natural and symbolic sounds, and there is a silence beyond them. To hear these latter sounds, however, demands a larger consciousness, a sense here of the "play" atmosphere of *All That Fall.* The first step to that larger consciousness is to hold the world at arm's length. Mrs. Rooney, appropriately, is "never tranquil," never fully accepting of the "reality" of the small Irish town; she is "seething out of [her] dirty old pelt, out of [her] skull," and her wish is "to be in atoms, in atoms" (p. 43). Caught in a physical reality—and with her bulk that word *caught* takes on comic dimensions: witness her difficult entry and exit from Mr. Slocum's car—she is also struggling to be free of that very reality.

Interestingly enough, at the start of the play Mrs. Rooney is introduced by sounds of a very different order from those we have just noted. We hear *"Rural sounds. Sheep, bird, cow, cock, severally, then together"* (p. 33).[8] When the BBC proposed machine-made or actual recorded sounds, Beckett asked instead for human approximations. The issue, if I understand it, was not naturalism but "essence," something not fully dependent on physical, let alone auditory realism. The rural sounds lead to a silence and then to the sound of Mrs. Rooney's *"dragging feet."* Within a second we go from nature, both animal and human, to art, with *"Music faint from the house by way,"* the song being "Death and the Maiden," whose melody Mrs. Rooney herself picks up seconds later.[9] This opening gamut of sounds defines her own larger consciousness. Hers is a new state that would absolve her and us from physical dependency and the tragedy implicit in the play's title. She moves, indeed, toward that stillness, that minimal commitment to physical reality that most of the Beckett "heroes" would seek: "stretched out in my comfortable bed," "wasting slowly painlessly away" till at last all physical manifestions would be so minimized "you wouldn't see me under the blankets any more than a board." She drifts on such imaginative wings toward a state where it seems "all the silly unhappiness . . . . had never happened" (p. 51). Nevertheless, her own tears draw her back to the same physical reality she would deny: "What did I do with that handkerchief?" (p. 52).

In the midst of grinding gearboxes, the "ramdam" noise of the road, the aural reminders (which is all radio sound can provide since it cannot supply vision) of the technological age, she stands apart, like the audience, with a greater receptivity to sound, moving beyond the here and now to the truly perceptive, toward the wished-for consummation in silence. The sounds associated with Mrs. Rooney form such a pattern. At one point, for example, we move from the *"Confused noise"* of the Rooneys' descent—*"Panting, stumbling, ejaculations, curses"*—to *"Silence"* to a donkey's bray (an animal at one with yet apart from the procreative world) to silence again (p. 71). An auditory medium by definition, the radio is at one with Mrs. Rooney's own movement away from the visual and physical. She hears what the rest cannot hear—the rural or natural sounds, the symbolic sounds such as the hinny braying—and she sees beyond them: "oh, if you had my eyes . . . you would understand . . . the things they have seen . . . and not looked away" (p. 61). Like Molloy, she can "hear the wind."[10]

But her eyes, her visions are not shared. Whether it be forthcoming retirement, the church, an appointed task, or the certainty (almost) of a train schedule, the other characters, secure in their physical contentment, have looked away, if they have looked at all. Partakers in a universal tragedy where all fall, here in Beckett's revisiting of *The Mirror for Magistrates* the other characters are pathetically unaware of their own. Mr. Tyler speaks of his niece who has lost her whole bag of tricks, yet he is patently blind to his own impotence and sterile humanity. Mrs. Rooney's eyes, again, are at one with nature's and are further to be distinguished from the artificial "nature" of the road or the station. She is like the horse with "her great moist cleg-tormented eyes" and piercing gaze (p. 36). Appropriately, Mrs. Rooney senses a rival in that horse: "Perhaps if I were to move on, down the road, out of her field of vision . . . *(Sound of welt.)* No, no enough! Take her by the snaffle and pull her eyes away from me." Made nervous by a rival, blessed (or cursed) with similarly sad eyes, she also recognizes her own kind and is therefore solicitous, preferring that he be led away gently rather than beaten.

With her soul-mate, Mr. Rooney, she shakes off Yeats's mackerel-crowded seas, shakes off the physical, and finds a stillness where there is "no living soul in sight" and "no one to ask" (p. 75)—a good description of radio and its solitary listener. Out of that stillness now comes a host of symbolic and natural sounds, almost as if she, like Henry in *Embers,* creates the sounds herself, having rejected external sounds beyond her control and inimical to her vision.[11] In effect, at such moments we are in a still, inner world; we have left the roadway. Suddenly we have a series of directions for the radio technician: brief wind, a chirp of birds tired of singing, a cow's moo, followed by sounds of sheep, dogs, hens, with a coda of silence. Murphy refers to sheep as "a miserable-looking lot, dingy, close-cropped and misshapen,"[12] and, indeed, they may be in the "prison of their Arcady."[13] Still, the natural sounds in *All That Fall* seem exotic, *fertile* when contrasted with the death-linked sounds of the road and then of the station. (Miss Fitt, alone with her maker, as if the prophet were prized not as a martyred visionary but as a necrophilic lover, surely epitomizes the dead souls of that public world abandoned at length by the Rooneys). Here, Mrs. Rooney's human voice, that of the presenter, is intertwined with sounds from nature and with the silence waiting on the periphery of human nature itself. Later on the sound of a sheep—an *"Urgent baa"* (p. 80)—cuts across our spectrum, and for a moment Mrs. Rooney takes us to Arcady, and its "pretty little woolly lamb, crying to suck its mother" (p. 81), to a world where "theirs has not changed" (p. 81).

This is her procreative moment, an aesthetic one set against the thematic fall. If hinnies are sterile, they are sterile only in a physical sense. So to

Maddy's question, can hinnies procreate, the answer is: if not in a physical sense, at least in other ways, as generative symbols of sterility, or as vehicles on whose back, so Maddy imagines, Christ himself, son of the Creator, once rode. "That must mean something" (p. 86). Physical procreation, itself marred by time and then erased by death, is set against aesthetic creation, the imaginative act that, while it has no substance (just as radio itself has no substance), defeats time. Art is long, life is short. In the Sonnets, Shakespeare's friend, in marrying and procreating, perpetuates his image through his children, just as Shakespeare confers the immortality of art in describing a friend who, outside of art, cannot escape death's winter that will check his youth's lusty sap. Beckett contrasts the fallacious and the real procreation in *Murphy:* "When not fixed by cupidity, Miss Carridge's imagination was of the feeblest."[14]

Indeed, in the midst of the play's raw sexuality, and the examples of human sterility that are at once glandular, intellectual, and spiritual, Mrs. Rooney stands as a monument to creativity. She would see her world as it is, then refashion it to make sense out of it. For all its pessimism, and despite the surface unattractiveness of its two leading characters, *All That Fall* is a love story about the union of wife and husband in the face of personal and worldly difficulties. Its Adam and Eve make their way home, to paradise, from personal and corporate hells. "Let us hasten home and sit before the fire" (p. 70).

Even from the scant evidence we have, we know that Mr. Rooney is a potential child killer, and the children in the play, such as the Lynch twins, who jeer at the couple and throw stones at them,[15] are mean creatures and therefore hardly inducements to creation. For a second the Rooneys frame the wholesome young boy, Jerry, and it is this same boy who brings them news of another child's death. Mrs. Rooney's own child has died years ago. The other characters are either frigid (Miss Fitt) or impotent (Mr. Tyler) or simply old and beyond caring (Mr. Barrell); and the one other marriage referred to, that of Mrs. Tully, is clearly a disaster. Against such desolation Mrs. Rooney, artistlike, creates a world of words, the only world open to radio—and at least "half" the world open to the dramatic artist in general. The physicality of Beckett's plays, even for the legitimate theater, is always minimal: a single tree in *Godot* that manages to send forth a few unimpressive leaves in the second act; the limited sets of *Endgame, Play,* and, most certainly, *Happy Days.* Against this Mrs. Rooney stands, surely, as creator.

As a creator, she needs others; she cannot bear to be alone, in much the same way that Vladimir, Estragon, Winnie, and Hamm cannot bear to be alone. In the midst of those suggestive sounds, both natural and symbolic, that usher in Mrs. Rooney, we also hear those of the "poor woman" who is all alone "in that ruinous old house" (p. 33). Mrs. Rooney picks up her melody; more than any other character in *All That Fall* she has larger, imaginative sympathies. The fact remains that Mrs. McGlone is like the sparrow in *Happy Days,* a solitary singer, unaware of an audience and therefore consciously pouring forth an unproductive song. The ruinous old house Mrs. Rooney refers to may well be the mind, and it is the artist's function, as well as the source of his suffering (as we will see in *Cascando*), that his public song comes at least as much from inside himself as it does from all that is outside him. It is the microcosmic-macrocosmic principle so graphically illustrated by the mindlike stage set and the "other world" to which Hamm refers in *Endgame*.

Again, radio is the solitary medium. The performer, albeit alive, cannot see and therefore cannot verify his or her audience, and in this medium, when one does not speak, one goes from thematic loneliness to aesthetic nonexistence. Mrs. Rooney is acutely conscious of this fact: "Don't mind me. Don't take any notice of me. I do not exist. The fact is well known" (p. 48). Even when she speaks, when the words come from her heart, she is "all alone . . . once more" (p. 54) when those same words die away. The achievement of *All That Fall* is that while the other characters come and go—the title of Beckett's dramaticule reoccurs—and have their brief existence only in dialogue with Mrs. Rooney, she herself remains, preserved in our memory by her language, by her vision. This is her paradox. She is outside the thoughts and actions and sounds of others, yet she cannot bear total exclusion: the artist needs an audience. Mr. Barrell, solicitously, would take her into the shadows of the waiting room. Conversely, Mrs. Rooney tries to become a public spokesperson when, "*derisively,*" she attempts to speak for those waiting: "Here we are eating our hearts out with anxiety for our loved ones and he calls that a hitch!" (p. 65). Her opposite is Miss Fitt, who delights in being alone with her "Maker" to the degree that she doesn't notice or, more properly, doesn't want to notice Mrs. Rooney.

The eternal dilemma of the wordsmith: at one with the world and yet removed. Appropriately, Mrs. Rooney's symbol in the play seems to be the wind, the sound that calls to mind both the biblical notion of wind as the embodiment of the creating spirit and also Shelley's symbol of the imagination. As Mrs. Rooney moves toward her soul-mate, toward that audience of one, that solitary performer with whom she has received and can receive larger sympathies, the sound of the wind, following on the heels of all the sounds we have observed (mechanical, sexual, physical, natural, symbolic), occurs with greater frequency. That wind comes at the most suggestive, the most climactic times, as when it serves as prelude to the pastoral sounds Mrs. Rooney hears when alone with her husband. Near the end of the play, as the couple laugh together over their predicament, arming their "mind with laughter" as they share a common interest in language, we hear the wind mixed with the sound of rain. Water, the symbol of procreation elsewhere in Beckett as well as in the play we shall soon consider *(Embers)*, unites in this instance with Mrs. Rooney's personal symbol.

Her instrument for such creation, for this countermovement to the universal falling-off in the play, is language. Others use words in a shallow or mechanical sense. Miss Fitt is filled with pieties and the clichés of coreligionists. The attendant characters are given to bad puns, or evasions ("bag of tricks"), or words primarily object-related rather than conceptual.

Mr. Barrell certifies his own prosaic notion of language when to Mrs. Rooney's "Did I understand you to say that the twelve thirty would soon be upon us," he mutters only, "Those were my words" (p. 52). She then plays along with him, by being forcefully precise about the hour; and yet within seconds she leaves Mr. Barrell far behind as she puns on "mail." Mrs. Rooney then defines her state, and her opposition to sounds connoting purely physical objects, as she speaks of her inner sorrow; when Mr. Barrell returns, he only further defines his limited reality: "What is it, Mrs. Rooney, I have my work to do." She then caps his constrictive vocabulary with silence. Once this limited dialogue is over, we hear the sound of the wind, leading to Mrs. Rooney's beautiful monologue in which her subjects are the wind, the rain, and the day as a symbolic measurement for one's life. The monologue itself ends on an intensely personal note as she characterizes her lonely state (p. 53): "I estrange them all. They came towards me, uninvited, bygones bygones full of kindness, anxious to help . . . *(the voice breaks)* . . . genuinely pleased . . . to see me again . . . looking so well . . . *(Handkerchief.)* A few simple words . . . from my heart . . . and I am all alone . . . once more" (pp. 53–54).

Like Winnie and yet on a higher level, Mrs. Rooney struggles with language. Early in the play she tries to incorporate lyrics from songs and poetry: "'Sigh out a something something tale of things, Done long ago and ill done'" (p. 37). Later she abandons such extra-dramatic language for her own poetry. She even tries to join Miss Fitt in her hymn—"the encircling gloo-oom"—but is rebuffed. Again, the language must be her own, and all that she has, for herself and for us as audience, is that language. Like the narrator of *Embers*, like Krapp, she searches for the right word, the right phrase: "Just concentrate on putting one foot before the next or whatever the expression is" (p. 72). This very interest in language is parodied by the bookishness of Mr. Rooney as he speculates on the etymology of *fir* (p. 82), and then joins with Mrs. Rooney in laughing over the possibility that *buff* is at the root of *buffalo* (p. 87). She herself is given to old-fashioned words, in general to quaint Irish expressions (strange in a writer like Beckett who, by writing in French, tried perhaps to clear his own style of Irish expressions and, particularly, of Joyce's influence).

She tries to be understood, to use "none but the simplest words" (p. 35), and yet when the words are delivered there is something "bizarre" in her way of speaking (p. 35). At one point Mr. Rooney accuses his wife of using a "dead language" (p. 80). Again the paradox for the artist: describing the common condition of men and yet hampered by a language that has grown common. The artist needs an audience, but the fine balancing line is between popularity and integrity—though the terms are not mutually exclusive. Shakespeare seems to have maintained that balance throughout a long career; the verdict is not yet in on Beckett, though some have already closed the ledger. I hope that this present study suggests, at the very least, that Beckett is not for a coterie, that his own experiments with such popular and properly public media as radio and, later, television and the cinema give proof of his own attempts to achieve the prerequisite balance for a public artist of merit.

By the end of the play Mrs. Rooney has found her voice. She quotes first from a sermon and then from a doctor, a "lunatic specialist" (p. 83) who diagnosed life, in the form of a young patient whose case he was forced to abandon, as a question of whether we are ever born. In the words of the comic writer Alexander King, "Is there a life after birth?" Malone similarly worries that he "shall never get born and therefore never get dead."[16] Others' words, however, cannot be hers, though they may serve as stimuli. Part of a tradition, the artist also has an obligation to have her own vision. In a beautiful threnody, inspired by the sight of rotting leaves in a ditch, she finally lapses into her own voice: "Yes dear, from last year, and from the year before last, and from the year before that again. . . . There is that lovely laburnum again. Poor thing, it is losing all its tassels. . . . There are the first drops. . . . Golden drizzle. . . . Do not mind me, dear, I am just talking to myself. . . . Can hinnies procreate, I wonder" (p. 85). (I delete here the various directions for sound effects.) Here is a mixture of direct observation, metaphor, rhetorical questions that get to the heart of the play and, by extension, life itself, a definition of the artist—and all interspersed with sounds of the medium, for between the scattered pieces of her dialogue there are directions for silence, rainy wind, and dragging steps. Human sounds are juxtaposed with symbolic natural sounds; dialogue is at once personal and, if Mrs. Rooney is not that removed from us, public as well. Mr. Rooney supplies the coda, ostensibly to the question about hinnies procreating but also by extension, I think, to the threnody: "Say that again" (p. 85).

He is part of Mrs. Rooney; it is her journey to meet him, literally and figuratively, that defines the structure of the play. Because of his blindness Mr. Rooney, like his wife, is not fully part of the visual world. In a sense the Rooneys are variations on the same theme, and, significantly, the day of meeting is Mr. Rooney's birthday, though he didn't hear his wife's birthday greeting when she whispered it to him earlier in the day. The word *birthday* itself echoes ironically against the title, *All That Fall*, suggesting the potential aesthetic renaissance that lies on the other side of the thematic decay otherwise so pervasive.

### iii

Mr. Rooney seems to be his wife's alter ego as he reviews his life, discounting the mechanical and physical details of daily existence, the "thousand unspecifiable sundries," as he yearns, like his wife, for silence, withdrawal, "lying at home in bed" (pp. 77–78). The office routine becomes symbol for him of the inanities of external existence, of leaving one's inner self, of traveling out into the world, the very world that Hamm denounces from his cell-like refuge in *Endgame*.

Yet Mr. Rooney is also petty, addicted to penny-pinching, worrying about the tip given the station boy, calculating the numbers of steps on the station ramp. At times he seems more like a creature of habit, although like his wife he denounces habit. His sounds are those of heavy footsteps, the pounding of his blind-man's stick, and panting. Rather than being creative—his poetry is ultimately only a prose lament—he is reductive. Once they arrive home, it will be Mrs. Rooney, not Mr. Rooney, who will read the novel, *Effie* (Krapp's novel that had failed so miserably with the general public). Above the mundane, sterile level of Miss Fitt or Mr. Barrell, and though mistaken only temporarily for Mr. Tyler and the would-be lovers who meet his wife on the road, Mr. Rooney still lacks his wife's creativity. His are not the pastoral noises, nor the fertile sounds of wind mixed with rain, but rather a transitional sound, the *"Confused noise of their descent. Panting, stumbling, ejaculations, curses. Silence"* (p. 71). The conglomeration here is somewhere between the deadening mechanism of the train pulling into the station and the silence associated with his wife and her transcendent vision.

Mr. Rooney seems, then, like an element fluctuating between his wife and all that she represents, and the townspeople and that limited reality which they encompass. The tension in the play is therefore on three levels: the prosaic one of whether Mrs. Rooney will see her husband; the thematic one of whether Mr. Rooney murdered the child; and the third and greater mystery, one of form rather than substance. Can Mr. Rooney duplicate, as an entity of symbolic sound and dialogue, the increasingly clear aesthetic level of his wife? The structure of the play itself leads to this issue: that first part on the road, followed by the transitional station, followed by the Rooneys' time together.

Like Willie in *Happy Days,* Mr. Rooney threatens either to destroy her (as he may already have done with the boy) or unite with her, love her. The weight here seems to fall on the latter possibility, for after the list of routines, and the petty bickerings over tips and the number of steps, Mr. Rooney moves, near the play's end, toward a vision not unlike Mrs. Rooney's as he dreams "of other roads, in other lands. Of another home" (p. 77). Increasingly he complements her, the way Vladimir and Estragon complement each other and, to a lesser degree, Hamm and Clov, or Winnie and Willie. He sees through her eyes, and she becomes his audience, remaining as silent near the end as she was loquacious at the start. If she needs him—witness the passion she expends in greeting him on time at the station—he also needs her, the way an actor or playwright needs an audience: "You say nothing? *(Pause.)* Say something Maddy. Say you believe me" (p. 82). He also develops the artist's consciousness of delivering dialogue, of performing, to the degree that he often serves as his own audience overhearing himself: "I confess I have it sometimes myself, when I happen to overhear what I am saying" (p. 80).

Initially separated, with Mrs. Rooney isolated by the surrogate husbands on the road, then brought together by a mechanical contrivance, suffering through a series of false starts even as the rest of the characters fade away, together at last, by the end of the play the Rooneys unite, physically and thematically and aesthetically. This is, as we shall see, also the pattern of *Cascando* and, more graphically, of *Words and Music.* Mr. Rooney's lament becomes Mrs. Rooney's threnody. They then can also laugh together over the play on *buff* and *buffalo.*

As they make their way home, the music that introduces Mrs. Rooney at the start of the play returns, along with the procreative sounds of wind and rain. This united couple are now set against the solitary singer: "All alone in that great empty house. She must be a very old woman now" (p. 87). Aesthetic vacancy and physical degradation have been overcome; the positive, romantic element in Beckett, our need for each other, deny it as we may, has been sustained. That "nature" of symbolic sounds, the wind and the rain that now increase in frequency and intensity, witness and thereby ratify the match.

This union is Beckett's way of placing in context the final moments of the play when Jerry comes with news of the boy's death. The evidence is overwhelming: the black ball that Mr. Rooney supposedly has taken from the dead child.[17] We have seen that same black ball referred to in *Krapp's Last Tape,* and its counterpart, the symbol of procreation in the white ball of fur amassed by the emmet in *Endgame.* In one very certain sense Mr. Rooney *has* murdered a child, and the horror of that possibility will not be lost on us. Still, if the pattern of the play, the trinity of "scenes" embracing the journey to, the time spent at, and the journey from the station, is of ultimate importance, then the murder seems almost a comic act, the Death of the Maiden Boy, the ultimate, the most graphic and terrifying renunciation of the physical, even the physical when it is most wholesome and appealing. Aesthetically, the play is not about falling, but rising, about the yeastlike optimism of a birthday. Fat wife and decrepit husband move closer to casting off their flesh, this world. The minister's words, despite the jokes at his expense, are justified by the thematic and aesthetic pattern of the play: "The Lord upholdeth all that fall." Be his vision anarchistic, or absurd, or pessimistic, the artist, as Yeats well knew, is always gay, a visionary singing of the possibility of giving form and thereby meaning to existence. Against the union of this incredible, this seemingly impossible couple, this Adam and Eve making their way back to Eden, stand the ultimate indignities: the physical world, the child-murderer.

Joined with her soul-mate in a way more extensive and promising than that of Winnie and Willie, the artist here finds herself. The flesh is sacrificed and now bodiless, this fact underscored by the medium itself; artist and audience, playwright and actor, are united. We are aesthetically pleased, just as we applaud at the end of *King Lear* rather than merely weep for the death of father and daughter. The play is true to itself. Not propaganda for a theme, it abides by its own pattern; it justifies itself as comedy, even as Beckett in a fit of creative perversity tries to ruin that union by making the lovers so improbable. The message is the medium—to reverse

Marshall McLuhan. For the "shapelessness" of radio, its verbality, its denial of the body—this is the very state achieved by the Rooneys. Killing the child is a thematic counterpart to Beckett's killing off the legitimate theater, an act that, when we consider the increasing brevity of his stage plays, the playwright will repeat later in his career. Art, the medium here, is a road to silence. The role of the artist is to give form to nothingness, to embody it only so that we may see and hear the threat it brings to our external reality. In denying that illusory surface, we only confirm our internal and true self.[18]

**iv**

*Embers*

Beckett's exploration of the medium of radio continues in *Embers,* and the movement from *All That Fall* is comparable to that from *Godot* to *Endgame.* Here in *Embers* separate characters are really one, for all the characters are clearly projections of the artist, of Henry's imagination. He "peoples" his little world in the way a novelist might, and since the medium is radio, there is no need for specific bodies. The artist is alone, with one imaginative world (Ada, the daughter, the music and riding masters) encircling another (the story of Bolton and Holloway).

Despite the central symbolic role of embers (a dying life, a marginal existence, minimal passion), the play opens with the sounds of the sea "*scarcely audible.*"[19] The symbol of artistic creativity is intensely personal here, more so than in *All That Fall,* where it was as much a natural (and hence not fully within Mrs. Rooney's control) as a symbolic sound (an extension of the central figure).[20] In *Embers* Henry controls the sea with his "On's," even as he tries to stifle the sound, this stimulus to creativity, with the sound of horses' hooves and with rocks clashed violently together. The sea would lure him, as it does Woburn in *Cascando,* to destruction, to the inevitable abyss held out by the "prolonged creative effort" (as Hamm says in *Endgame*) that Beckett describes in his study of Proust.

At the start of *Embers* Henry is totally in control of the situation, giving orders (in reality, to the radio technician), presiding over some sort of limbo, a dead-but-not-dead world like that in *Play.* Or it may be that Henry exists in a totally interior world, with his mind representing a "death" *from* the external physical world. To borrow the phrase from *More Pricks Than Kicks,* he may here be "re-enwombing himself."[21] In the words of the play, we are in a "strange place" (p. 95). We may feel with Henry, as the traveler in *How It Is* so aptly phrases it, that there is "only me."[22] Like Hamm, Henry feels a dripping inside his brain, and the converse result of such highly developed, omnipotent self-consciousness is his own external impotence. His marriage is essentially sexless, and the one child of that union a barren creation. Like Hamm and Krapp, Henry is an old man, physically shrunken and introspective.

Furthermore, he is contrasted with the shallow artists of the play, the music master and riding instructor, who are alternately violent and compromising. The music master's method of instruction, his animal grunts juxtaposed with the pupil's outbursts, hints at crude sexual intercourse: "*He hammers note*" (p. 108) as the stage direction has it, and later Henry speaks of hammering out a child. The music master's final outburst, "Eff" (for "fuck"?; and we might recall in *All That Fall* that *Effie* was a novel of adultery), is followed by a highly sensual wail: "*amplified to paroxysm, then suddenly cut off*" (p. 108). This violent interchange leads to Ada's observation that Henry is "silent today."

The range of sounds here suggests the play's larger context: the violent sounds of a past life, "this noise again," as the Unnamable calls it;[23] the sounds of the sea that call Henry to both creation and death; the clearly artificial radio sounds that Henry controls in the opening segments; and the movement toward silence, epitomized in the sterile winter silence of the Bolton-Holloway story.[24] Henry stands, paradoxically, between negative, meaningless noises (such as his clashing stones together) and positive, meaningful silence, between art-less life (or the pseudo-art of music teachers and riding masters) and art-full death, between being an external, public person (the sort of person wished for by his father) and an isolated, private individual (the person he "becomes" in the play once we realize that the cast of characters is imaginary). He wants to talk to someone, and yet he also wants to use talk, or any external noise for that matter, as a means to silence the internal world, as a "white noise" to establish the silence he craves.

Like our divided response to the Opener in *Cascando*, our response to Henry in *Embers* is balanced between the possibilities that what we hear represents either the artist's observations of our world or the inner workings of his own mind. Where and how do externalization and internalization meet? Is the artist seeking or projecting? We know from studies in the psychology of perception that our reality is balanced between what is, as determined by light and time, and what we mentally and emotionally are prepared to see, want to see, or think we see. Radio, as in *All That Fall* and *Embers*, is the perfect medium for expressing this duality. The physical sounds adequately suggest an external universe (the brain, surely, is a physically quiet as well as private place), but the fact that radio is nothing but sound removes it just that much from that physical verification at the heart of the legitimate theater. The present play is as tangible as a coal burning down, an ember, and yet, with a sudden change of words, it can be cosmic, as beyond human comprehension as "Vega in the Lyre very green" (p. 99). We can suddenly move from the verbal "substance" of Holloway's cries, "My dear Bolton, it is now past midnight . . . Please! PLEASE," to "Dead silence then, not a sound, only the fire, all coal, burning down now" (p. 99).[25]

It is indeed a strange world, like and unlike mundane reality. In this sense *Embers* initiates Beckett's "mysteries," plays that, even more that *Endgame,* are clearly taking place within a head. As Beckett's canon grows, he appropriately balances such "mysteries" with plays that—at least on the surface—take place in external, physical time and space, such as the two mimes, *Film, Come and Go,* and *Breath.*

Henry is of that mental world, and is opposed by his father and by Ada. With the *"Violent slam of door"* (p. 102) the father accuses him of wanting to "slam life shut like that," to lock it out. Henry himself may long for the physical and violent life; clashing two stones together, he pronounces "That's life" and then deplores art, represented by the sound of a stone falling far off, as "sucking" (pp. 112–13). But the violent clash is also a fall, a destruction; and the seeming celebration of physical life, this sound without meaning, is also a denunciation. "Sucking" will remind us of Winnie's own notion of being sucked up, of escaping a cruel reality by imaginative vision. Excessive talking is sometimes a sign of neurosis (Ada suggests that Henry see a doctor, Holloway—our first link between the outer and inner story). Or talking can be the necessary activity, however disturbing, of a creative mind.

v

All things are linked. The external world, epitomized by Ada, is prerequisite to Henry's internal world. Symbols, and interior worlds conveyed by symbols, need objective correlatives; an artist cannot use nothingness or silence as their basis. Moving toward the silence of the inner world and to the peace from reality that it promises, the artist progresses on a difficult path to a haven that can never be fully realized, or that can be realized only with great difficulty and with the sacrifice of that seemingly real world which is the point of departure. As it was difficult for Henry and Ada to bear a child, it is difficult for Henry to "bear" the story he must tell, a tale of a doctor called out on a cold night to administer a drug to release a friend from suffering. The story itself becomes, circularly, Henry's own struggle for release, his "semantic succor."[26] He plunges into a sea of creativity only to satisfy the urge, as well as win the right to be silent. Ada, we realize, has drowned at sea.

This paradoxical concept of creativity and destruction, or physical death and aesthetic life, is linked in Beckett's *Proust* with the female:

> And the pleasure he takes with Albertine is intensified by the reaching out of his spirit towards that immaterial reality that she seems to symbolize, Balbec and its sea—"as though the material possession of an object, residence in a town, were the equivalent of spiritual possession." This compound object of desire—a woman and the sea—is simplified of its second element by the habit of the first.[27]

At first Ada is a totally physical being, worried only about Henry's body, about his health, cautioning him not to sit on the cold stones, reminding him to wear his jaggers. She loves the sea: "you wanted the sun on the water for that evening bath you took once too often" (p. 96). It was by the sea where Addie was conceived, but their marriage has also soured Henry on physical procreation.

We have already seen this physicality, this raw human intercourse mocking aesthetic creation, unmasked in the music master's lesson with Addie. Similarly, the riding master may be associated with the same fraudulent art, for as he leads the daughter from trotting to cantering to galloping, she resists his instruction, as she does that of the music master, with a *"wail amplified to paroxysm"* (p. 109). Henry's own self-induced sound of horses' hooves is his way of trying to stifle the sounds of the sea. Normally an image of virility, the horse here curiously suggests the marriage's oxymoron of sterile sexuality.

Yet aesthetic creation will out. On this level, despite the pervasiveness of earthy sterility and death, there is "no question of dying."[28] Not together in life—"We were not long together," as M says in *Play*—Henry brings himself closer to an imaginary Ada, from the dead or from his mind. He first recreates the scene of their solitary love-making, even pointing, with double entendre, to the "hole" where they begat Addie. She suggests, however, the tremendous difference between the actual place as it once existed in time and space and the imaginary place, born of emotions recollected in tranquillity: "When we longed to have it to ourselves there was always someone. Now that it does not matter the place is deserted" (p. 113). The "place," the creation of the radio medium, demands both speakers and listeners. Still, this recollection of the beach stands as that turning point where Ada changes from a dull housewife to a source of inspiration for her husband. Henry's recollections of the love-making, his one physical success, softens his antipathy to the sea: "It's not so bad when you get out on it" (p. 114). He then lightheartedly imagines going into the merchant navy. She in turn launches into a sustained passage of prose that approaches poetry: "It's only on the surface, you know. Underneath all is as quiet as the grave. Not a sound. All day, all night, not a sound" (p. 114). Ada offers here the equivalent of the external-internal dichotomy of which I spoke earlier. She goes on to encourage him: "There is no sense in trying to drown it" (p. 114).

Minutes later she is painting the portrait of Henry's father, in that pose combining contemplation and lethargy that Dante provided Beckett in *The Purgatorio:*

I left soon afterwards and passed him on the road. He did not see me. He was sitting on a rock looking out to sea. I never forgot his posture. And yet it was a common one. You used to have it sometimes. Perhaps just the stillness, as if he had been turned to stone. I could never make it out. (P. 117)

This pose itself is parodied in *Theatre II*:

> He sat doubled in two, his hands on his knees, his legs astraddle, his head
> sunk. For a moment I wondered if he was not vomiting. But on drawing
> nearer I could see he was not merely scrutinizing, between his feet, a
> lump of dogshit. I moved it slightly with the tip of my umbrella and
> observed how his gaze followed the movement and fastened on the ob-
> ject in its new position. This at three o'clock in the afternoon if you
> please![29]

A physical, shallow creature, whom Henry mocks in his opening dialogue,
Ada is here something of an artist, albeit on a low level when compared
with the frustrated artist represented by her husband. She takes an event in
time, physical and dreadfully mortal, and converts it to a statue: "as if he
had been turned to stone." Then she goes on to analyze the portrait's
composition, how attitudes exist in one's mind before they are given form,
the unusual nature of the posture ("the carriage of a head, for example,
bowed when one would have thought it should be lifted" or "a hand suspended in mid air, as if unopened"), the paradox of the father's posture
("no detail you could put your finger on"). At last she offers a metaphor,
albeit a vague one, that inspires her own attempt at portraiture ("just the
great stillness of the whole body, as if all the breath had left it"). Then she
poses a significant question and thereby defines, I believe, her role, or the
role that Henry has given her, that of the *anima* or muse in his inner
drama: "Is this rubbish a help to you, Henry?" (p. 118).

It is not so much the event she narrates but rather the process by which
Henry "recreates" her, moving her from life, from a physical reality where
she was a shallow creature—"The least feather of smoke on the horizon
and you adjusted your dress and became immersed in the Manchester
Guardian" (p. 113)—to a more fully developed soul, a small prototype of
what Henry himself is and, as artist, wants to become. Ada now becomes his
audience: he tells her, "You needn't speak. Just listen" (p. 118).

He offers his story now; he has had a vision. It has been a long time
coming. As audience we have suffered vicariously with Henry, journeying
with him from his autocratic control of radio sounds at the beginning, to
his feeble attempts to tell the Bolton-Holloway story, to his frustrations at
being unable to get the right phrase, let alone finish it, to his diversions by
dialogues with Ada and Addie, and episodes with riding masters and music
teachers. Such diversions, paradoxically, only served to reestablish his
other half, Ada, the muse who has now inspired him. We have gone from
the surface—the sounds of hooves, stones, and shingles near the sea, the
sea itself as a threatening sound, and dialogue with imaginary conver-
sants—to new sounds now below the surface, literally the sound of his own
inner voice in the story-within-a-story. Henry speaks now to himself, with
himself, and to us represented by the silent and, *because* she is silent, nonexistent Ada on the radio "stage." Of course, there is no stage proper in radio,
except the metaphorical stage of the mind.

The Bolton-Holloway story itself is cosmic in its dimensions.[30] There are sounds now recreated only by language and not by the medium's sound effects; that is, we are with the ultimate instrument of sounds, the actor's voice. We hear of, though we do not hear it, the sound of the fire. Henry also tells of the pervasive silence surrounding the midnight meeting of the two old men. All antitheses seem to be present: the fire is still hot, but outside it is bitter cold; fire and snow, sounds and silence. It is clearly a visionary world, like that of Nell in *Endgame* when she imagines going to the bottom of the sea. Henry is surely Bolton, wanting the painkiller, the passport out of life; but he is also Holloway, for as artist he summons whom he will to his mental world, his cerebral stage. As with the story of the boy's death in *All That Fall,* there are mysteries here that seem to clear and then to cloud again: just what does Bolton want, and why, and, beyond that, what happens (since the story itself is cut off)?

Perhaps that story itself, its details, are not so important as the journey to the story, or the parallels between the story and Henry's own life. Both in life and during the play he struggles with Ada to give birth, to amount to something, to combat the negative criticism of both father and wife. Henry also struggles within the play to tell his story; the story itself concerns Bolton's plea to Holloway to administer an injection. The human struggle inside the room is also complemented by that of life outside in the bitter cold and snow.

In some of the most sustained poetry in Beckett, outside of the earlier poems, that struggle becomes universal, the story of all those "poor" who must beg, be it alms from others or meaning from the wallet of existence:

Candle shaking and guttering all over the place, lower now, old arm tired, takes it in the other hand and holds it high again, that's it, that was always it, night and the embers cold, and the glim shaking in your old fist, saying, Please! Please! *(Pause.)* Begging. *(Pause.)* Of the poor. *(Pause.)* Ada! (Pp. 120–21).

Once that story is told Henry faces his own reality: that is, we move from the subterfuge of the story to the storyteller himself, much as Hamm himself substitutes his own story for an abandoned one (that of the father imploring him for bread for his son). The closing moments of *Embers* constitute a direct conversation with the audience. Henry calls out for his wife, his father, and, by way of an expletive, Christ—in that order. Then he caps the Bolton-Holloway story by dissolving it in a wealth of description, all moving toward silence and nothingness: "Holloway covers his face [like Hamm], not a sound, white world, bitter cold, ghastly scene, old men, great trouble, no good" (p. 121). The sounds of boots on shingles and of the sea return. The play ends in a monologue on Henry's present state, as he determines the time, then comments on the meaninglessness of time generally, and on the possible diversions of tomorrow (a plumber at nine). The plumber himself can be taken as metaphor for the "waste" of life. At last he closes in a litany like that of Hemingway's at the end of "A Clean Well-

Lighted Place": "Nothing, all day nothing. *(Pause.)* All day all night nothing *(Pause.)* Not a sound." Punctuation has vanished, along with the customary grammar of subject and verb.

Henry tries to describe the state of death or nothingness, or that theoretical moment when art's story ends. Still, life resumes as we turn off our radio, as we who "remain" (as Hamm says) go about our life. Radio has its own joy, its own demands. As long as we must use words to describe or intone nothing, we have something: the words themselves. A radio emitting no sound might just as well be off—a waste of current and of time. Art rescues itself from that wished-for extinction, for just as Henry reaches for silence, we hear the final sound of the radio play: the *"Sea."* As a principle, the art, the creativity, is inviolate; only the story comes and goes.

**vi**

*Cascando*

There is an inner story in *Cascando,* involving Woburn's reaching the sea, but it lacks the dramatic tension of even the Bolton-Holloway story in *Embers.* Besides, the outer story here is not so much a story as the telling of a story, Voice's struggle to find the most precise words. In point of fact, we are dealing with a radio play even more abstract than *All That Fall* and *Embers.* The issue is the nature of creation, and that issue is most properly enacted through radio, a "conceptual" medium in that its stage sets are all in the listener's mind, its characters fashioned by words, but not in combination with the flesh, as is the case in the legitimate theater, television, or the cinema.

There are really four characters,[31] three of them speaking, and they seem to represent very distinct aspects of the creative performance. Let me establish here a possible allegorical framework for these four: Woburn as the Character, Voice as the Public Side of the Artist and Actor, Opener as the Private Side of the Artist, and Music as the Abstract Principle of Art. Though the divisions are not so neat, of course, as this following analysis would suggest, there are still seven fairly clear sections or stages in the interactions of these four parts. Again, we are dealing in an allegorical fashion with the interaction of concepts, the dimensions of a creative performance, rather than with literary characters. Beckett, in effect, is pushing radio to its limits, away from a parallel relation with the other storytelling arts, those other media for which he has written.

In the first section (pp. 9–12, top) the Opener is calm, removed from any personal involvement in what happens. He protests that he simply opens the play, moving us and the characters from a state of being "dry as dust" (p. 9) to the promised fruition of the month of May. Voice, on the other hand, the Artist as Public Person, struggles to tell the story and, more than that, to finish it. Recasting *Hamlet*'s "To be, or not to be," he can "sleep . . . no more" until he has "finished" his dream, given it form. Like Beckett's other artists, Voice is highly conscious of his mission, interjecting technical notes into the narration, such as commentary on a phrase or the choice of words. We get, in effect, both Woburn's story and the process of storytelling in a single speech: "I resume" and "right the sea . . . left the hills" (pp. 9–10).

With Music, Voice becomes more poetic, progressing from the bare facts of Woburn's leaving his house to portraying the setting itself: "gentle slope . . . boreen . . . giant aspens" (p. 11). Indeed, Voice and Woburn seem very close here, for Woburn's journey is also the journey by which the Artist will be judged, in his own "eyes" and those of the audience: Woburn's reaching the sea is a correlative for Voice's completing his story. That sea, as we have seen in *Embers,* is a source both of creativity and of death, and this dichotomy is underlined here when, as a character, Woburn dies at sea. That death also has echoes of a rebirth. For Voice, his story and, subsequently, his role are completed by Woburn's death; he achieves his wished-for silence only—to use his own words—after he can "say him" (p. 14), giving form to Woburn. Like a projection of the artist, the character Woburn waits at the window, a window to the outside or, perhaps, to the inside, if we recall the dual function of a window as relevant to the position of the viewer.

The voyage is external for the character and internal for the Artist speaking to us; his words go out, "on" as Henry says, so that we may go in. Similarly, the eyes of the woman in the boat would let Krapp in—"Let me in," he cries—and she properly closes them, having little interest in seeing out. The irony of radio is that its "seeing-out," this landscape painted by words and sounds, is an absolute fiction; radio is surely an internal medium. Appropriately, here in *Cascando* the outer (or seemingly outer) landscape is already darkening. As Murphy observes, it is only in the "dark that one can meet."[32] As Voice and Woburn merge, Opener exists only as a functionary here, while Music, the abstract principle of Art, remains constant.

In the second section (pp. 12–13) Opener loses his immunity as in a somewhat neurotic fashion he denies that the story as narrated by Voice and informed by Woburn comes from his head or reflects his own life. In this conservative, anti-autobiographical mood, seeing the artist merely as recorder, as an impartial observer, Opener protests that what we hear is from the outside, that his private person is here irrelevant. Art for him—if we can believe him and if he can convince himself—is just a profession, a "life" on which one lives. However, his position is suspect; he protests too much.[32] Ostensibly, the play was to be about Woburn, not Opener. Opener, though, intrudes, for he must; his public posture enacted through Voice is inseparable from the private side, from Opener. As this internal side emerges, Voice, correspondingly, is quieted, confined to telling the

Woburn story, to filling out details. Quite possibly this trinity of Woburn, Opener, and Voice is a trinity of one. Music meanwhile remains constant, steadfast.

In the third section (pp. 13, bottom-14), Voice resumes his struggle, pulling closer all the time to Woburn even as Woburn himself moves closer to the sea. The impending death might also be a relevation to Woburn, for Voice argues that if Woburn, with his head cast down as if by a "friendly stone,"[33] could only look up, he would see not the paradoxical sea—source of creativity and death—but the stars.[34] Music intervenes at this point *("brief")* to suggest a more constant state, even as Voice stumbles on his own narration ("but no . . . he's"). This comic alternative, the state of starlike silence, and of coldness and nothingness, is then broken by Opener's pressing concern about the popular acceptance of his art. If it all comes from his head, the artist might be dismissed as idiosyncratic. Opener wants Voice to be a public spokesperson, speaking not out of personal feelings but from observations of the real world. Moreover, this new public posture on Opener's part now clashes with the increasingly personal identification Voice makes with Woburn: "this time . . . I'm there . . . Woburn . . . it's him . . . I've seen him . . . I've got him" (p. 13). Literally, Voice must mean that he is succeeding in his portrait and, by extension, telling his own story. Yet "seen" also has the sense of sympathy or empathy, as Voice now fails to disassociate himself from the character (even as Opener would do just that—or try to) Again, Woburn and Voice are essentially thematic; their intertwined stories expose themselves to us as mirror images of men seeking a Godot of nothingness, sleep, completion, death. Opener would be an aesthetic creature, like Music, intense only in the creation of art rather than in any personal identification with the creation. Still, like Molloy with his creations, he will at length have to confess that he has "invented" Woburn only to disguise himself.[35]

By the fourth section (p. 14) Voice is weakening after his creative effort; Music and Opener are now at full strength. Opener seems to have quieted his anxiety by focusing on the nature of art's source; he reverts to his posture in the opening segment and like a conductor directs Music and Voice. Woburn's story itself is reaching its climax. Voice's neurosis now returns as he struggles to complete the story: "sleep . . . no more searching . . . to find him . . . in the dark . . . to see him . . . to say him" (p. 14). As he finishes he stumbles in his vocabulary, even as he becomes more conscious of the process of telling. Opener seems on the verge of a creation for which he is only a presenter or technician. He passes judgment on the interaction of Voice and Music ("Good"), talks generally about the context for artistic creation ("Yes, that's right, the month of May. You know, the reawakening"), and performs his function ("I open").

As Voice and Music draw together in the fifth section (pp. 15–16), Opener defines this union as moving "from one world to another, it's as though they drew together" (p. 15). That is, as the public side of the Artist-Actor approaches his vision, he justifies the art itself (Music), working with it, abiding by its principle that the actual story be inseparable from our experience with it. Art, in Murray Krieger's terms, is at once a *window* (a way of looking out on reality: in this sense, Woburn's death-journey parallels our own) and a *mirror* (a self-enclosed world, whose process, here the struggle for completion, parallels the processes of life itself, our own attempt to see or say our condition to ourselves and to others).[36] The Artist as Public Person (Voice) is defined by his art (Music), just as on a psychological level Voice is represented in Woburn. Between Voice and Music we now have the whole gamut of sounds, words to noise, available to the medium of radio.

Still, this comic union strikes fear in Opener, who cannot shake off the possibility that what he presents is himself: "They said, It's his, it's his voice, it's in his head" (p. 16). He fears that he and Voice are inseparable, that the artist is at once a public and a private person. Clearly art is not just a technique; nor can its principles remain theoretical. Music is not just a state but a performance: we literally hear music. Opener protests this "resemblance" to Voice, let alone to Woburn: how he talks or what he talks about, he insists, cannot define him. He now tosses in confusion, one moment trying to deny that what happens, even the pregnant silences, are his ("mine"), the next moment taking comfort that his critics have been silenced, though mostly out of weariness. Yet he is now afraid to open: he *is* Woburn and Woburn's story, for him, has become too personal. If Woburn is on his way to nothingness, both by thematic death in the sea and aesthetic death when the last word of *Cascando* is spoken, then the death must be Opener's as well. The play is like *All That Fall*, about falling, decline, death; the title itself, *Cascando*, tells us this.

The four characters are merging into one, the order being an initial identification of Voice with Woburn, then Voice with Music (and also with Woburn by definition). Now Opener himself is being drawn in. Voice helps in the union by wondering what is in Woburn's "head" (p. 17) as he journeys to the "vast deep," to nothingness. Since the word *head* has been part of Opener's neurotic litany, the verbal coincidence suggests that the two characters have a single source.

Voice now repeats his promise that a vision of the stars would absolve Woburn of death: "he need only . . . turn over . . . he'd see them . . . shine on him" (p. 17). Woburn, the character, clings to the boat, holding on to life, not seeing death as the release promised by Voice. Ignorant and fearful of death, Woburn is like Opener who considers any identification with his Voice or his character Woburn as death. Music remains constant here, if somewhat muted.

In the sixth section (pp. 17–18, top) Opener's anxieties increase: the "Good" of his critic's judgment give way to "Good God" (p. 17). In a last-ditch effort he tries to initiate another story, one, interestingly enough, not about a one-way journey but about an outing on which one goes only to return. For us, the story recalls Molloy watching the two men, A and C, uncertain if they are leaving or returning home. Still, Opener dismisses the story as "an image, like any other," and makes a last, futile attempt to dismiss his critics ("But I don't answer any more"), taking refuge in his limited role ("I open").

Three of the four (Voice, Music, and Woburn) are having their vision, like Prospero in *The Tempest* as his project gathers to a head, as he staggers under the load of the performance and then is released once his penultimate illusion, the wedding masque, is completed. As the vision culminates in the seventh section (pp. 18–19), Opener suddenly drops his evasions, speaking now "*with Voice and Music*" through a single word ("Good") that Beckett asks be pronounced "*fervently*" (p. 18). Words and Music are together; it is "as though they had joined arms" (p. 18). In the affirmative words of *Malone Dies,* they are moving "On" by hammering out a vision, like Joyce's artist forging visions on the smithy of his own soul.[37] Woburn also joins in (he doesn't "let go"), even as Voice and Music and the sea—the sound is surely implied here—ask him to "come . . . come on . . . come on" (be it to death or aesthetic completion). If it implies a fall, the term *Cascando* is also a musical one, and the structure in this final section is clearly orchestrated, with a perfect synchronization now existing between Words and Music, Voice, and Opener. It is a trio, or, more properly, a quartet.

What Woburn was during his life in that room, what Opener has suffered, real or imagined, at the hands of the public and its critics, Voice's past failure in telling his story, the definition of Music (Art) as influenced by the creations of the past—all this becomes irrelevant here, albeit momentarily, as *Cascando* generates its own vision, its own rules for success. If the play is about the frustrations of the artist, both as a public and as a private person, those frustrations are now lifted: the story is told, and that story supersedes any biographical questions about its source. The process of art, its aesthetics, does not need to remain theoretical; the theory is defined and validated in practice. Music is a participant, not an idea. Woburn himself does not die—as if characters in narrations ever really die—but is encouraged to "come on": to paradise, to aesthetic eternity, to a perfect equipoise between the public and private worlds, to simultaneous being and not being (we will recall the earlier echoes of *Hamlet,* whose Prince dies as an individual only to "live" again as a character in Horatio's narration to Fortinbras). Aesthetic life springs from thematic death. Even the Unnamable rejoices in his self-portrait: "on his belly, singing, I come, I come."[38] In a sense, this seemingly abstract radio play, *Cascando,* is not "about" the process of creation; it *is* a creation. The play's the thing.

## vii

*Words and Music*

The pattern of *Cascando* is repeated in *Words and Music,* with considerable and most interesting variations. *Words and Music* itself is at once simpler and yet more abstract. Croak is the Opener here, a combination Artist as Public and as Private Figure, and he is flanked by Words and Music, the gamut of sounds possible in radio, from noise to language to the abstract physics and mathematics of music itself. Like *Cascando, Words and Music* can be divided, though again a bit arbitrarily, into six sections.

In the first section (pp. 23–24) Music is relatively quiet, a *"humble adsum"* as Beckett characterizes it. Croak is in control, making his appearance after an opening quarrel between his servants. Addressing them by personal name—Words is Joe, Music is Bob—he serves as their conductor here. Croak does present one potentially jarring element: a face in the tower that he has seen while on his way to their meeting (recall the face on the stairway in *Film*).[39] He mentions the experience only briefly and then apparently forgets it. Words, on the other hand, is both quarrelsome, complaining of being cooped up with Music, and bored, as he offers a discourse on Sloth that is nothing but a formula, a string of clichés and generalizations said without conviction or feeling. When even this unconvincing speech finishes, the play seems to lose its energy, as the *"humble"* replies of the servants mix with Croak's neurotic desire that his "comforts" stay "friends."

In the second section (pp. 24–25) the topic is Love, but Words, now conscious of playing a role *("Clears Throat")*, employs the same set speech used for the topic of Sloth. The result is disastrous, and the formula only stresses Words's insincerity. Music, in contrast, moves ahead, providing accompaniment *"worthy of the foregoing, great expression"* (p. 25), all this done to Words's discomfort. In fact, inspired by the seriousness with which he has attacked the subject of love, Music drowns out the words. Chastened somewhat, Words tries again, in part relying on the formula, in part now struggling with new, original phrases. Still, the effect is pathetic—*"prosaic"* in Beckett's stage directions. All this time Croak is in discomfort. His power is slipping; his friends are at once pulling apart and, alternately, trying to unite without his directions.

By the third section (pp. 26–28, top) Words has abandoned the formula. His language is clearer, more organized, indeed too organized, for the discourse on subject three, Age, is almost a parody of the scholar's logic: "Age is . . . age is when . . . old age I mean . . . if that is what my Lord means . . . is when" (p. 26). In Molloy's phrase, his "mania for symmetry [is] too intense."[40] Music continues to lead the way toward some more profitable relationship, providing at first only a *"Long la"* (p. 26), then an *"Improvement of the above,"* then a *"suggestion for the following,"* followed by several "suggestions" and "improvements" (p. 27). Music here is the stimulus, and Words dutifully follows. The antipathy between them is gone. Words even tries to sing, adjusting his lyrics to Music's rhythms; the efforts are feeble, but promising. Croak meanwhile is in even greater discomfort. It is as if the tools of art, the words and music that constitute a song, are running away from the creator. It is Pirandello's inept artist losing not so much characters as the tools of his profession. As befits the greater sense of abstraction in

*Words and Music*, the personality of the artist, be it public or private, is subordinate here to the tools (and their principles of operation) of his craft. *Words and Music* is Beckett's *Art of English Poesie.* Toward the end of this section Music for the first time plays through an entire song.

In section four (pp. 28–29) Words, inspired by Music, now tries a complete poem, "Age is when to a man," the earlier, halting prose snatches now replaced by blank verse. The effect is instant; Croak reacts with "the face" (p. 28). His earlier anguish at the independence of his tools is now magnified; in that epiphany of the face they threaten to reveal to him his true self. The vision *is* in his head,[41] not outside ("on the stairs" or "in the tower"), as Opener protests in *Cascando;* the exposure, the goal of the artist, is also his pain.[42] The one event seemingly peripheral to the play, what Croak has seen before the play proper, is here drawn into *Words and Music* itself. Croak now sees his life in his art, just as Voice increasingly saw himself in Woburn.

Words is now at his most poetic; Music is suggestive and timid. Indeed, Words now threatens to unbalance his role with Music, screaming him down with "Peace!" (p. 29), launching, in section five (pp. 29–30), into an impressive, albeit lengthy prose diatribe. That prose is tightly packed, suggestive, but hardly lyrical; indeed, it almost seems a parody of Beckett's usually spartan efforts: "flare of the black disordered hair as though spread wide on water, the brows knitted in a groove suggesting pain but simply concentration more likely all things considered on some consummate inner process, the eyes of course closed in keeping with this" (p. 30).

Yet the prose passages are significant, even with Music missing. For one thing, Words speaks of eyes formerly closed (the domain of the medium here) and now opened, but eyes also capable of that inner vision we have seen championed in Beckett's other radio plays. The eyes, our eyes, those of the face on the stairs—all are encouraged to look up, just as Voice encouraged Woburn to look up in *Cascando.* The range of references is also wide here, for we are safely beyond the pat formulas and pseudo-philosophies of the earlier sections: from minute descriptions of pinched lips, we move to the galaxy, then to Mira in the Whale at her tenth and greatest magnitude (p. 30). Music responds to this with *"Irrepressible bursts of spreading and subsiding music with vain protestations"* (p. 30) and yet is shouted down by Words. The leader is now a disciple, and not even listened to at that. We have moved from the subservience of the tools, to a preliminary harmony, to a dominance by Words. Croak is far behind, painfully reminded of his pretheatrical life and of the link between life and art when, for him, the face becomes "Lily," a lost love perhaps, some painful memory in his biography that art, with its twin tools of Words and Music, is bringing to the surface.

After a momentary assertion of Music—a *"Triumph and Conclusion"*—followed by a gentler approach by Words, we move in section six (pp. 30–32) to the most intense union of Words and Music, accompanied by Croak's protests and anguish. The creation now has its own identity: the nature or personality of the artist (Croak) and his wants are of secondary importance. The reversal is signaled by the stage direction "*Change to poetic tone. Low*" (p. 31), as Words, led by "*Discreet suggestions*" before and after from Music, launches into poetry: "Then down a little way / Through the trash / Toward where / All dark no begging / No giving no words / No sense no need / Through the scum / Down a little way / To whence one glimpse / Of that wellhead" (p. 32). Words alternately inspires and is inspired by Music. The poem, like the Woburn story, is also about that silence, the state of nothingness that Beckett seeks. As the climax is reached in this wellhead[43] of the poem and in the union of Words and Music, the artist fades away, dropping his club, his footsteps shuffling down the hall.[44]

Art has triumphed; Opener's question about art's source becomes irrelevant here. The play is an aesthetic victory, a comedy, though it may have tragic implications for Croak as the face on the stairway, his Lily, is reincarnated. And there may also be such implications for us, who must respond as real listeners to the poem on death and old age: we cannot rest solely with aesthetic satisfaction. For us the poem is not just a mirror world, as it can be for Words and Music, but a window back on our reality: we "remain."

Then in a comic coda to the piece—and, again, Beckett's organization both here and at the end of *Cascando* is orchestral—Words becomes a bit too familiar with Music, addressing him as Bob, just as Croak had done earlier. That human touch violates the level of abstraction here, not only in the characters but also in the aesthetic satisfaction coming from their creation. After some "*imploring*" from Words, and an apology for the indiscreet personalization, Music begins again, going beyond Words toward the silence which Words also seeks. Then, after a pause, Music, "*with elements already used or well-head alone,*" begins to play, the apology having apparently served its purpose. Words imploringly calls out "Again," and Music, continuing to assert its independence even as it joins Words, repeats "*As before or only very slightly varied.*" There is another pregnant Beckettian pause, and then Words utters the benediction, a "*Deep sigh,*" Word's final utterance that is all words, more meaningful than any single word but also a sound beyond any rational explanation, with its taunting suggestions of sleep and nothingness, perhaps even of death.

We will recall that *Cascando* closes with the sound of the sea. The present play, the most abstract we have, closes with that "*Deep sigh*" from Words. The god of the play, this aesthetic combination of Words and Music, has pronounced it "Good" with a sigh, a sigh that perhaps even suggests the postcoital exhaustion and satisfaction of human lovers, a sound, a sigh, that more than any single word stretches out in silence. As with his efforts in the legitimate theater—and we have seen how Beckett advances the medium from *Godot* to *Endgame* to *Play* to *Come and Go*—Beckett has here taken to its limits a verbal-auditory medium.

# 6 Theater of Sight: *Film, Eh Joe, Act Without Words I* and *II*

In this chapter we move from Beckett's plays for the legitimate theater and radio to the media of cinema and television—and to his two mimes. Since the focus is on what we as audience *see*—there is a single "word" in *Film,* a "Shh"; a mime in *Eh Joe* threatened by a voice off-camera; and a self-evident, physical world in *Act Without Words I* and *II*—this movement itself at once expands and completes the plural term *Theaters* in the title of the present study.

i

## Film

*Film* takes the concept of introspection and makes it actual, *literal,* for *Film* is about what Beckett calls the "searching eye."[1] What we see is actually happening, albeit rehearsed, but then only dimly. The outdoor scenery, particularly, *is* outdoor scenery, chosen from the crumbling neighborhoods of New York City. Bishop Berkeley's motto frames the "play": "Esse est percipi."[2]

And yet even though the initial segment takes place outdoors, the vision called for is ultimately an inner one. *Film* thus works at length against the conception of cinema as being a "documentary" of our real and present world, a "skin-flick," as one of my colleagues has termed it,[3] concerned with the here and now, with what we can *see*. This latter argument holds that one cannot film an abstraction; and yet here Beckett, for better or worse, tries just that. Clearly, O fears inner vision, those private thoughts that make their presence known as he moves symbolically from a public street, to a semiprivate stairway, to the privacy of his own room. Perhaps that room is also the womb, since one of Beckett's notes suggests that it might be his mother's room, "which he has not visited for many years and is now to occupy momentarily, to look after the pets, until she comes out of hospital" (p. 86).[4] Even this "fact" is discounted in the interest of an inner landscape when Beckett informs us that "this has no bearing on the film and need not be elucidated" (p. 86).

The camera may record what it sees, and it may be true that abstractions cannot be filmed. But then everything that is filmed has actually happened, is after the fact; and time itself is surely an abstraction. Besides, the camera is governed by a human hand, directed by a human, and seen by humans with individual perceptions and preoccupations. At once realistic and external, the cinema, I would contend, is no less impressionistic or internal.[5] Cinéastes complain that Beckett, like some minor French New-Wave director, merely plays here with the principles of film, that in charting the same inward voyage found in the novel he violates the sense of the actual that is the cinema's preeminent virtue. I would argue the opposite. In O's journey inward, from the street to the stairway, to the room, Beckett adopts a range for the cinema embracing both the documentary and the psychological, both the "outdoors" and the "indoors." In effect, he spans the two worlds cherished by the Unnamable: "think" (the world) and "rest" (room/womb).[6] The camera itself is elevated from being a mere recorder to the status of a character, for E is at once the camera and also the inner self that O, the outer self, would deny. In effect, E is O inside out.[7] In much the same way Beckett makes the tape recorder in *Krapp's Last Tape* a character, a projection of Krapp at an earlier age and a dialogue partner in his declining years, as well as the muse he invokes for a vision beyond time and mortal love.

Appropriately, E's first sustained contact with O occurs while the latter is asleep, when that outer eye, confined to a material and commonplace world, is inactive. In such a state the setting for the encounter must be that of the unconscious, of dreams. Appropriately, that dream landscape is also a past-tense vision, like that of *Film* itself, for we reexperience there what has already been experienced in a different and sometimes more shallow, sometimes more literal sense during waking hours. In the face of existentialism and perceptual psychology, we know that what *is* is not confined simply to the surface, to the street. Beckett's camera here tries, then, to see the "other" world beneath that surface. To be sure, his "worlds" are often those of streets (for Vladimir and Estragon, and for Winnie) and rooms (for Hamm and for Krapp), but these places, though ostensibly external, seem, after further consideration, to be more likely internal (the mental "space" of *Play,* the verbally created "places" of the radio plays, even the timeless playing arenas of the two mimes). Like *Eh Joe,* with which it has great affinities both thematically and aesthetically, *Film* at its end presents a room being filmed. However, that room is comparatively bare; most of its contents go unnoticed by the camera, and O covers or obscures, as does Joe, pictures, mirrors, and other objects that suggest the surface world or allow for external vision.

This inner quality of *Film* is underscored by the patch over O's eye; he has one eye facing outward, with the other eye forced inward by the obstruction—in effect, the very dichotomy represented by E and O. The seven pictures he examines present this same dichotomy. There is evidence of outer vision: the devouring eyes of the mother holding her child, the dog looking at its master, the little girl looking into her father's face, exploring it with her fingers. The other pictures, though, suggest an inward journey: the child at four with eyes closed in prayer; the young man taking a photograph on graduation day; the man at age thirty, looking forty, with a patch over one eye. The pictures are seen by O, but we see O seeing the pictures through E's perspective. Curiously, E has clear vision, whereas O, the external viewer, looks out through gauze over the camera lens. Beckett's thesis is, surely, that the outer vision is only a fraud, and that the inner is at least as real, albeit more painful.[8]

In calling the external into doubt Beckett grants the internal equal status. "Seeing" becomes an inclusive, rather than an exclusive term. The outer vision is potentially fraudulent (we cannot always trust the mentality of a Watt), but the inner is equally unreal, or at least potentially unreal (we cannot grasp the Knotts of this world). Hamm's handkerchief, the old stauncher that he at length elevates to a symbol of his suffering, metamorphoses in *Film* to the plain handkerchief with which O tries to obscure E's sight. On the stage a prop is both itself and something else. In *Film* the room is literally part of a downtown New York studio, but it is also a mental womb for the purposes of this *Film* or film. The title *Film* is not just an afterthought (as if no other title could occur to such a fertile playwright), nor is it merely literal; it is a permanent "working" title, announcing the film's proper concern.

*Film* is about seeing others and seeing ourselves. As for more advanced characters such as *Murphy*, the issue is "*percipi*" by oneself, not "*percipere*."[9] The couples in the deleted street scenes were all to be "in percipere" and "percipi." In being without facial features for so long, Keaton—O— becomes an Everyman, all of us; in our witness to *Film*, therefore, we are both seeing and being seen. When O's face is finally unveiled in the closing moments, it is too late to separate him from us. We have undergone what the character undergoes, and the process, if not the face, links those watching the screen and the (now) two characters on screen. Appropriately, *Film* begins and ends with an eye. At the start the eye is closed, then begins to open, and is at last completely open to signal the start of our experience with *Film*. At the end the name of the author and "The End" are superimposed over that same eye. We watch the eye, and the eye watches us. We are both O and E, just as Keaton, the character, discovers for himself.

Beckett is thus concerned with what has been called, by other commentators and in other contexts, the "film experience." This sense of an experience, for both audience and character, so overshadows what we might distinguish as the "theme" of O's story that even the motto behind *Film* is dismissed by the author as a "dramatic convenience" (p. 75).

A film needs something on which to hang. One cannot film a nonstory, though Hurwitz in his 1969 film *The Projectionist* tries to do just this. There a movie projectionist rejects his drab life by escaping into a cinema world. As lights in the fictive theater go out, a cartoon flashes on the screen but soon the film breaks. When the fictive audience starts screaming, reacting to the blank wall and the projectionist's ineptitude, the screen becomes smaller. We see a theater and an audience in the movie reacting in the same way as we now do. Conversely, I saw a film years ago in which the camera simply followed around a New Yorker (picked randomly from the phone directory) for twenty-four hours; the audience could, if they had the fortitude, watch all twenty-four hours of film. When its sole figure slept, the camera was there, overhead, recording sleep; it also followed him in the course of breakfast, bowel movements, office routine, his evening. The camera was purposely noninventive, and, as opposed to the almost totally aesthetic focus of the Hurwitz film, this one was almost exclusively thematic. Beckett, however, steers between such extremes; his message is the medium: *Film* is about film is about life is about seeing is about film. We are not playing aesthetic or thematic games here; seeing is not only believing but painful: Beckett speaks of an "anguish of perceivedness" when O violates the "angle of immunity" (pp. 75–76).

Still, the pain is more like birth pains, for once that angle of perceivedness is sustained, the film itself blossoms. The character sees himself and becomes a spectator like us; the camera has had its vision and can now cease its wandering. We move from the back so that we can face O; the camera itself moves from the back to the face. Then Keaton's full face, on which he made his livelihood, comes into its own. In Alan Schneider's words:

> At last came the day we got not only that (dead) goldfish's eye, but those much more vital final close-ups of Buster's countenance in confrontation with itself. It was or could be a terrifying effective last shot, and Buster, finally given his chance not only to let us see his face but to see him act, let loose from deep inside somewhere. When we finally saw it, that face paid off—even if we hadn't known it was Keaton's.[10]

It is this "acute intenseness" that validates the cinema, the painful self-seeing that is a major theme of Beckett's work in four media.

With the tape recorder Krapp *hears* his true self, and one can extend this revelation to the audience of legitimate theater or radio. With *Film,* and the subsequent freeing of the camera, one *sees* his true self; and one can find parallels in the stark visuality of Beckett's characters and stage sets, culminating in those two mimes examined at the end of this chapter. At the end of *Film,* the onscreen viewer sits with his head in his hands, his body a perfect circle, his hands touching his temples, "gently rocking." The pose is not simply one of despair, just as the cynicism sometimes associated with the term *absurdist theater* doesn't even begin to describe Beckett's accomplishments, his own subtle romanticism. The pose is, I think, more one of benediction, the same sense of completeness we get at the end of *Act Without Words I* where, after rejecting the enticements of the world (the carafe, the rope, the razor, etc.), the solitary character doubles up in a fetal position and looks at his own hands. For some, O's pose may resemble that of Murphy in his chair, chained with his seven self-tied scarfs, rocking away in serene contemplation, trying desperately to escape his own physical limitations, trying to get to that "fourth dimension" where time itself is mastered.[11] Here is a retreat to oneself, a denial of the external that, while consciously chosen in the mime, is in *Film* thrust by oneself (E) on oneself (O).

There are no ways to avoid this soul-searching, and Beckett indicates that in the opening shot there is to be only one street, no side streets.[12] Initially O is fleeing, hastening blindly in what Beckett describes as "comic foundered percipitancy" (p. 77), the sort of comic-tragedy opposition that led him to think first of Chaplin, then of Zero Mostel for the role. The field narrows, and in section three the comic action changes from fleeing to a frantic attempt to obscure or remove from the room all objects of perception, be they mirrors or pictures of God or animals or windows. In effect, the generalized and single means of comic avoidance in the opening section is counterbalanced by specific, numerous, increasingly neurotic and thereby personal actions in the final segment. The stairway itself seems like some transitional section, both an ascent for O (to the room of self-perception) as well as a descent, or falling, for the aged flower-lady (deflowered?). She may be the mother that one loses and/or rejects, or the old, "frail" (p. 79) physical self symbolized by her tray of flowers. (O himself tries to avoid symbols, though at length he himself is characterized by the eye and the eye-patch, gateways to his inner world.) In a larger sense the world of *Film* also diminishes, from those initial plans to photograph couples in the street (girls riding bikes, a variety of city types moving in one direction, looking at each other, the couple of "shabby genteel aspect" [p. 77] that O meets), to a single lady on the stairway, to no one but oneself in the room. There is indeed an "unreal" quality (Beckett's word) about the seemingly external world here (p. 76).

The commentary on art and the artist complements this use of the cinema medium. E is surely the eye of the artist,[13] the visual pen of *Film*, whereas O is, initially, the subject, like Woburn. In *Cascando* we will recall that Voice was the artist. The tragic anagram "Wo" (woe) and "burn" (as in hellish pain) may well describe the state of *Film*'s single character. Ultimately the artist is his own subject: O and E must merge. At the end the artist as private person, O, sees himself in the process of creation, E. All other characters are really extraneous to this microcosmic duality, and perhaps this explains Beckett's ease in disposing of the initially proposed crowd scenes. We may also think of Beckett's other lonely but active artists: Krapp, Henry, the speaker in *The Unnamable*. All other art is beside the point, whether it be public "art," such as the newspaper read by the shabby couple, or the ineffective picture of God, or the various parodies of the artist's eye (the eyes of the parrot, fish, monkey, the portfolio, the headrest of the chair, even the photographs).[14] The photographs themselves become more unreal as O progresses from one to seven: natural poses give way to artificial ones (kneeling at prayer with eyes closed), and open figures give way to increasingly obscured ones (the enlisted man at twenty-five, his face covered with an even "bigger" moustache, and at thirty hidden under a hat and overcoat, a patch over his left eye).

All this fraudulent and thereby ineffective art, however, constitutes a step toward the genuine art of *Film,* that movement when what is visual becomes truly cerebral, long after the one word ("Shh") has died away, long after the camera has ceased its frantic odyssey, long after the angle of immunity itself has ceased to be a factor. At the end we are in what Cicero would call a "speaking silence." Given the presence of an acknowledged master of the silent cinema, and in spite of or even because of a script written by a playwright with no previous experience in the film medium, Keaton's pose at the end is one of perfect equipoise, as thematics and aesthetics, object and eye, artist as private person and artist as craftsman converge. It is the pose of Murphy, naked, tied to his rocking chair with scarves, one step toward oblivion, as close to nothingness as Beckett can manage and yet still talk. It is "home" and in the womb, in that same way imagined by Mr. Rooney. As for O, he sits bowed forward, his head in his hands, gently rocking. "Hold it as the rocking dies down" (p. 83).[15]

ii

*Eh Joe*

The television play *Eh Joe* represents Beckett's first venture into that medium. As was the case with *Film,* I think he "exploits," in the most positive sense of that word, the visual and here the verbal nature of a "filmed" medium with the same intensity he showed in the cinema, radio, or, for that matter, the legitimate theater.[16]

*Eh Joe* starts as if it were a silent film, in fact very much like the last section of *Film.* Joe goes through five actions in mime: getting up from the bed, and then opening and closing the window and drawing the curtain; opening and closing the door and then drawing the hanging before the door; doing the same with the door to the cupboard; checking under the bed; and at length sitting on the bed, eyes closed, relaxed, his eyes to open with the woman narrator's first word, "Joe." The focus in this opening section is on the moving object, and Beckett advises *"No need to record room as a whole"* (p. 35). The camera shows Joe full-length, whereas when the voice starts talking it concentrates exclusively on his face, moving three inches closer each time that the woman pauses for a period longer than that between sentences. Joe's actions, surely, are those of *Film*'s O, closing out the external world, attempting to evade detection that, paradoxically, only invites self-examination.

As with the set in the third section of *Film* or the set of *Endgame,* the room here is ultimately Joe's mind. Like the character of "First Love," he is locked out of one room only to find himself in another. In the neurotic words of the Unnamable, "I'm calm, I'm locked up, I'm in something, [and then the inevitable denial] it's not I."[17] In effect, this frantic mime, closing out the external world, only forces the television camera, like that of the cinema, to become an inner rather than an outer device. As in *Film,* Beckett seemingly defies the medium—both in terms of spatial range and immediacy—only to enhance it, for he charts the larger inner space of the soul and thereby redefines what "immediacy" can mean. Even when the "landscape" narrows from Joe's room to his face, that face, like Keaton's, is to show mounting tension. The virtue of a close-up in television is preserved; the camera is at once a technical and a metaphysical device. We are far beyond shallow eyes, such as those of the "green one" whom Joe has seduced and abandoned. We go beneath the "stinking old wrapper" (p. 37) as Beckett uses the medium in a manner reminiscent of its creative stage in this country during the 1950s, when live drama was prevalent, before film set in, before the television industry moved from New York to Hollywood, or before the medium became little more than a purveyor of Hollywood films "made for television." *Eh Joe* is a *live* broadcast. In one sense the camera directs the audience's eye, but then the camera's movements, following Joe about the room and then slowly moving in toward his face, are so simple that we can focus alternately on the entire picture or isolated sections. Our ocular freedom—my point is—is roughly equivalent to that exercised in the legitimate theater. *Eh Joe* is at least as close to that theater as it is to the cinema.

The visual nature of the medium is enhanced by the voice, and that voice is offstage or, more properly, voiced-over. At once low yet distinct, it resembles those in *Play: "remote, little color, absolutely steady rhythm, slightly slower than normal"* (p. 36). Beckett seems to be aiming at something between the voice of a character and that of the impartial, all-knowing artist—a divided voice perhaps closer to Krapp's than anything else. Moreover, since the voice is offstage, then speaking, like vision here, remains an abstraction.[18] Joe is a character who can hear but cannot speak, who can see, to be sure, but whose physical perception is not the issue. We have, in effect, a purer version of that split in *Film* between object and artist, and also a purer merging, since it is clear from the beginning that the voice, like the voices in *Embers,* is inner-directed. We have, finally, a visual-verbal allegory of a monologue, of the self and its solitary world, which is both the final torture and also the refuge for all Beckett's characters.

Only at the climax, as it describes the final moments of the suicide, does the voice change to a barely audible tone, a sign, I would think, that it has become inner to the degree of threatening to go beyond the requirements of conventional art in being something heard only by Joe. Like that demanded by the characters in Pirandello's *Six Characters in Search of an Author,* the performance here, in its movement toward accuracy or refinement, would exclude an audience. Beckett, though, is writing an immediate, live television play, and our identification with Joe cannot be severed. We are looking at and hearing ourselves in a monologue. He hears (but cannot see) himself with that same inner voice that Henry in *Embers* would drown.

The voice speaks to us as much as to Joe; as in *Godot,* where we also wait for the figure who never shows, we are part of the play. For want of anything else, Joe looks at us, just as the eye in *Film* stares at us at the opening and the close. Only the details may be different: we may not have seduced a young girl or bundled "the narrow one" into her Avoca sack, her "fingers fumbling with the big horn buttons" (p. 39). Thus the specifics here give way to a general statement on human imperfection as well as self-satisfaction, and on our search for pleasure or redemption, or both. One might take the title itself and adjust it to "A Joe," with Joe becoming Everyman. The great equalizer is not death but the fact that we each ultimately have and must face ourself.[19] When all voices die, we must hear our own voice as long as consciousness, however dim, persists.

Joe is Everyman, seeing and hearing his true self, the very self we would deny in that external world where other objects and other voices can divert us from such perception. The bastard medium of television is equally personal and catholic. It is also intensely private in that our own home or room is our theater. Beyond radio, television offers vision; beyond *Film,* it offers a more prominent place for dialogue. It is both live and "filmed," or at least "delayed" by the interconnected system of relays from studio to transmitting tower to the television set. If television has degenerated to being the warehouse of old movies, or nothing more than radio commentators reading the news before camera, or a small-scale version of the action movie without the advantages of a large screen and a public audience, still it is not so in Beckett's hands.

The issues in *Eh Joe* are similarly wide, and familiar to those who know the playwright. The world here, both inner or outer, is one of decay; Joe's heart, we are told, might crumble in its dry state if he lies down in the dark. Here is a fallen world, where Joe has sunk from an idyllic past relation with the narrator, to a series of shallow affairs, to prostitutes. Most important, we witness a search for the self, after a lifetime spent running through others, somewhat like the lawnmower that can be heard over the heads of the dead figures in *Play.* Even as the implied or wished-for settings of *Play* (two houses, the Riviera, "our darling Grand Canary," "On the way back by Ash and Snodland") shrink to the bare set and the merciless spotlight, the settings referred to in *Eh Joe* and the "cast of characters" are reduced to what is called in "Text 12" the "poison" inside oneself.[20] Joe's brutality, the displacement of his anger on some "mental thuggee" (p. 37), turns inward; Joe, by the relentless camera and offstage voice, is here impaled on his own bed. Similarly, Henry is both Ada and the object of her sarcasm. Joe is perhaps closest to those characters in Beckett—Pozzo, the Man in *Play,* Henry of *Embers,* O in *Film*—who have avoided the self by frantic activity or dominance over others or by meaningless routines. Perhaps Winnie too, however appealing, should be added to the list. *Eh Joe* is about the reckoning day, and the Voice's rhetorical questions remind him that now, self-locked in a room, having lost all of his public being, he must account.

The play is also about death, about release, a wished-for state that is the comic half or divine comedy to the inferno of any self-searching. This desired end is properly embodied in the story within the story, the tale of suicide that constitutes the Voice's final indictment. Seemingly a figure separate from Joe—he is not the suicide but the instigator—the girl, the *anima,* is at length Joe himself. The present situation is similar to that in *Cascando,* where Woburn also leaves the security of a house for a suicide at sea, lying face down on the beach, as the girl does here, and making a cup in the sand for his face. The paper reports only the fact: " 'On Mary's beads we plead her needs and in the Holy Mass' " (p. 40). Yet the Voice's description of the suicide's final moments, taking Joe and us up to the very edge of death (but, of course, falling a fraction short of it), has the tone not of finality but of serenity, and even of achievement. She lies by that procreative sea which we have heard and seen elsewhere in Beckett, a perfect sacrifice for Joe's love, cupping her face in the sand, making an identification, as it were, between the human and the animate force of nature. Joe's cliché, "Spirit made light" (p. 41), the phony compliment with which he seduced her, now becomes strangely appropriate as the girl, otherwise limited by her physicality ("The green one . . . The narrow one . . . Always pale . . . The pale eyes"), embodies the essence of martyred love. The voice in describing her now drops to a whisper; the only words heard clearly by Joe or by us form a curious combination of the physical and the fanciful: "Imagine," "stone," "Joe, Joe," "lips," "solitaire," "stone," "Eyes," "breasts," "hands," "Imagine," "stones." It is a kind of poetry, cryptic (but then Beckett in *Whoroscope* demonstrates his pleasure in cryptic poetry), suggestive at the level Beckett achieves with his increasingly sparse language.

If *Eh Joe* is about a tragic confrontation, where a Krapp-like figure in his *"late fifties, grey hair, old dressing-gown, carpet-slippers in his room"* (p. 35) must at last see himself as a failure, as burned out, the television play is, at length, an aesthetic comedy, a story of the artist's identification with his art, the coming forth of his story. I refer to the story of the girl, and therefore of Joe, of one who faces death by rushing to it. The Voice is both the *anima* encouraging that story and its instrument, the voice of the artist that at last receives the proper degree of encouragement from Joe as the tension in his face reaches a climax. As with Music in *Cascando,* the Voice is a serene principle of art unaffected by the tortuous theme. That Voice waits, in a sense, for Joe, having already found its own serenity and mission:

> Yes, great love God knows why . . . Even me . . . But I found a better . . .
> As I hope you heard . . . Preferable in all respects . . . Kinder . . . Stronger
> . . . More intelligent . . . Better looking . . . Cleaner . . . Truthful . . .
> Faithful . . . Sane . . . Yes . . . I did all right. (P. 39)

The dialogue is both aesthetic and thematic, defining the state where, facing our silent and solitary self, and the death that is our only reward, we make our final statement on existence. For all of us, artist and spectator, actor and audience, for those who make stories public and those who keep them in their heads, the task is to see ourselves or—using Beckett's peculiar phraseology—"to say" ourselves, to confront ourselves in our individual, idiosyncratic, solitary rooms, to recognize the fact that all fall and decay and, beyond that, to recognize the unending frustration generated by our desire for silence (and nothingness) and our compulsion to speak (and hence violate silence), to go on.

In her penultimate moment the suicide unites with Joe and Joe with her: "Taking Joe with her . . . Light gone . . . *'Joe Joe'* . . . No sound . . . To the *stones* . . . Say it now, no one'll hear you . . . Say 'Joe' parts the *lips . . . Imagine* the hand . . . The *solitaire*" (p. 41). The actress pronounces only the italicized words loud enough for us to hear; as audience we realize that Beckett is taking the play to the edge, but only to the edge, of silence. The actor playing Joe is well enough along in his part, both from rehearsals and from the momentum of the present performance, to grasp the full context of the lines. The Voice reads the script, of course, but says the nonitalicized words mentally or so quietly that they cannot be heard. Actor, actress, artist as O and artist as E, and audience are all one, as we strain to hear or understand a text that is almost annihilated, a story that is painful for both Voice and Joe, a story whose conclusion is physically painful for us as audience striving to hear a voice that is almost indistinct.

Indeed, Joe had earlier admired the woman's elocution, that quality of flint glass in her voice. At this late stage the camera is within inches of Joe's own voice, and since Joe's lips do not move, the effect is almost that of a voice coming from within him. We have the very technique of projection used at the end of *Krapp's Last Tape,* where Krapp's lips move without sounds coming from them, and where, once the final reel starts, Krapp stares motionless, looking out at us, as the tape, his inner voice as it were, delivers a lament uttered years earlier. That tape seems to come from within Krapp in a way analogous, I would argue, to the woman's voice issuing from behind Joe's silent lips.

The larger situation itself is similar to that in the radio plays. Thematically, Joe, like Krapp, is in decline, alone, having lost all human contacts. Aesthetically, both have a vision: Krapp's ability to record an account of his life; Joe's merging of the inner voice with his present state, his recognition that the girl's suicide is his own (both his fault and literally his, in Donne's sense of the bell tolling for thee). He can *say it,* fashioning his story through the girl's; and in saying it to "say Joe," he can talk of himself instead of releasing frustrations on others, on those self-contrived mental thuggees.

In Beckett's mind-body synthesis, voice (soul) and figure (body) are one. The voice speaks though a stilled body; after the opening mime the physical activity is no longer frantic or meaningless. Krapp himself starts his play with numerous actions as he searches for the right tape; yet soon his own voice is the focus, with action itself relegated to sounds offstage.

More than one actor and spectator has suggested that Joe is masturbating—hence his interest in shutting out our prying eyes. Telling him to "squeeze away" (p. 40) on the bed, the woman taunts him with this expression of physical self-love: "Very fair health for a man in your years . . . Just that lump in your bubo" (p. 39).[21] Or: "That's right, Joe, squeeze away . . . Don't lose heart now . . . When you're nearly home" (p. 40). Or: "No one can see you now . . . No one can get at you now . . . Why don't you put out the light?" (p 36). "Watch yourself you don't run short, Joe" (p. 37). "And now this . . . Squeezed down to this . . . How much longer would you say?" (p. 38). "Brain tired squeezing . . . It stops in the end . . . You stop it in the end . . . Imagine if you couldn't" (p. 38). The suggestion here is that the actor is masturbating off-camera since only his face is shown.

On the one hand, then, Joe is abandoned, perhaps reduced to masturbation, an old man with his one remaining pleasure, yet a pleasure that is increasingly hard to perform. Besides, he is taunted in the act by the presence of the woman, or of himself, standing as gaping witness. But the physical act can also be a correlative for the artistic act, the emergence of the story within a story. Like the semen, the story comes from within Joe only to make its way out. The artist's creation thus bears affinity to ejaculation, and we have seen Beckett's artist in *Cascando*, Opener, try to deny that what he produces comes from inside himself. The girl is Joe, and she moves out of his tortured conscience, by way of the narration, to a climactic act by the sea. He dies in her death. Joe similarly brings up himself—he comes. Such physical and aesthetic ejaculations are the prerequisites to serenity and silence, to that wished-for moment when both "*Voice and image* [are] *out*" (p. 41). The story is about release: from life by suicide, from one's obligation by the telling of the story, release from one's conscience by being a witness (Joe as audience, like Krapp) to the story of oneself. For the audience the release parallels the technical release of the medium when the camera merges with the face, avoiding collision, after the ninth move, only by withdrawing both image and voice. The sexual activity that is discreetly not seen is thus productively employed as symbol for artistic endeavor.

The sight and sound of the medium, the audience both on the picture and in the living room, the audience, in effect, both seen and unseen—all move into silence, release. We enter the room only to escape what Beckett calls elsewhere the world's "jargon."[22] The camera, its transmission shut off, goes back to its original position; actors leave the set, and viewers turn at last to the kitchen for a snack, since Beckett allows for no commercial break during *Eh Joe*. Nor could there be any.

### iii

*Act Without Words I*

In the two mimes Beckett literally goes beyond words or sounds—except those sounds which in performance come from the actors' struggles as they are thrown on stage or go through the paces of dressing and undressing. (Such sounds may be a sign either of a primitive or a sophisticated state; the Unnamable's creation Worm can only "murmur,"[23] but in "Text 6" the finest and most profound words are said to be "unnamable words."[24]) However, words and vision are never antithetical in Beckett, never exclusive. Indeed, the two are almost interchangeable since the "essence" of a situation is something that can, in Beckett's works in any medium, be shown or said, or both. Be it the legitimate theater, television, radio, or the cinema, his theater is never "literary" in the way that novels and poetry are.[25]

In these mimes man is stripped of his sounds, deprived of his language, and therefore of any avoidance of self by circumlocution or in the person of mental thuggees. In mime nothing can remain inner or conceptual. Here one cannot instruct the actor to "think" a certain state so as to color the stage dialogue, nor draw on a certain memory so that the resulting intonation will complement verbal imagery. *All* must be shown; the mime has nothing but his body. Beckett's inner state becomes outer here, and, paradoxically, these, his most direct and physical plays, are also his most abstract. The physical here is "verbal" and conceptual enough; otherwise we would be witnessing only gymnastics. This inner cosmos is underscored by the final actions, as the sole character in *Act Without Words I* confronts his own hands, while in *Act Without Words II* one actor returns to the sack as the other kneels alone in prayer. Without words, we also approach that much closer to the state of nothingness and silence so desired in Beckett. At the end of *I* all the props—the carafe, the tree, the cubes—have vanished, and we are left with *King Lear*'s unaccommodated man.

This is also immediate theater; our eyes and minds work in tandem since we cannot choose only to listen to dialogue or, with dialogue in the background, to piece out the play through stage actions. The play either "is" as a whole or is not. The paradox, then, is that mime is at once intensely immediate theater and, since all inner thoughts, emotions, and states are manifest in action, the most purely philosophical. Just as *Waiting for Godot* is both a literal action (for the tramps and for the audience) and a clearly symbolic one (literally, since Godot does not appear), so in the mimes the abstract and the literal are the same.

In *Act Without Words I* there are roughly six sections, stations if you will, through which the sole performer passes from the outer to the inner. We first see him flung across the stage, thrust against his will into a universe he twice tries to escape. Perhaps this is the transit from left to right described in *How It Is*.[26] We witness raw fatalism, the sole character manipulated by some offstage force, yet after two rebuffs the man "thinks better" (p. 125) of further resistance and, in the second section, is rewarded for such mental "evolution" when a tree descends from the flies. Now he is in a period of ease and temptation. There is a circle of shadow as protection from the dazzling light of the desert set, a pair of scissors to trim the nails, and a carafe complete with a label indicating water.

Still, the cruelty of the god persists. The gifts must be won, and in the third section the man struggles in vaudevillian fashion to reach the carafe with the aid of three cubes. Using his intellect, man here becomes a builder, a technician. His efforts are in vain; close to reaching the carafe, he finds it suddenly pulled back up into the flies. Section four offers a variation on three, when the rope that descends so suddenly is used as a lasso. Instead of merely reacting to the god's carrot-and-stick policies, man becomes "inventive" here, in a grisly Beckettian way, fashioning the rope as a suicide instrument, as a hangmen's noose. Yet the "playful" god of the play denies him even this release as the boughs fold against the tree; we observe a replay of the frustrated suicide attempt in *Godot*.

More civilized and imaginative enough to question life and to seek a release, an end to the stage games, man is denied even this alternative, and with section five the "no exit" situation of the opening is repeated. This time, however, only one rebuff from stage right is enough to push man into a reflective mood, and the reflection is followed not by more temptations from off- or above-stage, but by the second option: the scissors as an alternative suicide device. Even this "out" is removed. Having frustrated his creation in his three efforts to escape from the stage, to build his way toward some enjoyment (the carafe), or to leave the world through suicide, the angry god takes away his playthings, the carafe and the tree. The final act, with man on an empty stage, without props, with only himself as a resource, is a statement at once of cynical resignation and of romantic defiance: "He looks at his hands." The impassive face of the actor can convey at once despair—this is all he has left, but then what good are hands without tools or objects of pleasure?—and at the same time a picture of self-reliance, a retreat to the self. That turning inward which is expressed physically is the prerequisite to the inner journey undertaken so hazardously and so often and so triumphantly (with whatever qualifications) in Beckett. We have at length the unaccommodated man, without existential, theological, or linguistic support. Now his unaccommodated stage is bare in a literal way that surpasses the poverty of the formless radio plays, or the minimally accoutered stage plays, or the barren rooms in *Film* and *Eh Joe*.

iv

*Act Without Words II*

Again the set is stark, and we know at once that the landscape is an inner one. The "god" is now present, the goad (Godot?) that twice stirs figure A before he emerges from his sack. Indeed, the enactment of that inner world is itself more graphic here: the characters literally begin in sacks, with one returning there for good.

In *Play* we work as an audience, piecing together the triangle-love story, readjusting our perspective with the repetition of the narration. In the radio plays we cast the sets in our imagination and thereby give them at once a personal and cerebral dimension. In *Godot* and *Endgame* our sense of an inner dimension to the drama conflicts productively with our literal witness of the stage act. The pictorial "realism" of *Film* and *Eh Joe* only raises our suspicion that the rooms are inner wombs. However, if we are an active audience in Beckett's work, no matter what medium he chooses, here in the mimes we are even more so. There are no words; we must supply the silent commentary. The actions are deceptively physical, particularly in *Act Without Words II*, and yet we cannot resist the self-imposed drive toward symbolism and meaning. Since we must "say" to ourselves what the mime means, or can mean, our ears and eyes, the radio and filmic dimensions of the production, are thus engaged. Beckett offers us, in essence, a charade whose answer comes from our participation in the game.

Character A is at once the more slovenly and the more contemplative. Pricked twice by the goad before he emerges from his sack, he seems more inwardly directed: he broods, he prays. In terms of the dichotomy established in Beckett's *Proust*, he is the imaginative man, of this world but only on his own terms. Clearly, A is not addicted to physical reality, and hence the double efforts of the goad to rouse him to action. His affinities among the characters are with Hamm, Vladimir, Winnie, the characters of *Play* in the second section, the elder Krapp, and all those souls troubled by drippings from inside: Mrs. Rooney, Henry, Opener, Joe, O of the final section of *Film*.

B, in contrast, is the more external of the two, though both characters are squeezed together by their pathetic humanity in the face of the goad. With B the goad gains strength by acquiring a wheel and moving farther across the stage. Moreover, it requires only one prick to stir B. This movement across stage, in which the character out of the sack drags his fellow actor still in the sack, might be seen as a parody of the progress of civilization, a linear, mechanical progress that only strengthens the gods (the need for some outer frame of reference) even as it leads man (A) down from a comtemplative inner state to B's more shallow and active outer state. In this view, B is perhaps modern man. Like Pozzo, he consults his watch, is concerned about his physical appearance (his comb), is more precise with the carrot and with his clothes. In *Molloy* he is the man with the map and timetable.[27] Still, like A he must dress and undress; whatever our state or disposition, we are all born naked, wear clothes, die, and have those workaday clothes removed before returning to the grave—from womb to tomb, from sperm to worm. B's notion of place is itself clearer: he looks at his map and his compass. And he is a physical cultist, exercising, attending twice to his teeth and his hair.

Perhaps if we think of A in his first appearance as the past, and B in his single appearance as the present, as that modern man, then with A's second appearance at stage-right we have moved to the future. Is Beckett here optimistic, with A, the contemplative character, getting a second chance?

Or is the pattern of A and then B and then A and then B, *ad infinitum,* best suggested by choosing three appearances rather than two? Or are A and B the same character? After all, they are never seen together, and the figures in the sack are sufficiently indistinct. Or do we overestimate A? He is contemplative, to be sure, but Beckett mocks thinkers in his works, from *Murphy,* to the critics in *Godot,* to the literaray artist in *Krapp's Last Tape.*

Or is A a different figure? When he emerges from the sack a second time, the goad has acquired two wheels; we are witnessing a more complicated, powerful stage prop. Again, it takes two darts in the sack to rouse A. This time he "crawls out of sack, halts, broods, prays" (p. 141). Perhaps the mood is only interrogative on A's part: he prays that things will be better, that the god will be kinder, that he won't have to return to the sack. A seems as full of questions as is the playwright, but his "second life" can only be one of questions since the future cannot form the subject of present-tense drama. One cannot construct a mime out of things that are not yet.

Our own interpretative effort, our making sense of the mime with our silent community, our tendency to detect allegory or symbolism, is itself frustrated. We try to compare *I* and *II.* In the former is there a movement from the primitive to the civilized, from man dependent on the gods to man, once frustrated by them, now dependent only on himself? Is *II* the opposite, a movement from past or primitive man (A on his first appearance) to modern and sophisticated, but shallow man (B)? With A's second appearance do we move still forward, to the unformed man of the future, or to the man of our imaginations? Beckett is not much of a futurist; his goal seems to be getting through and ending the game, or throwing oneself into a state of stasis rather than looking forward to a more positive future. It is what is here and now that matters, *How It Is,* even if "it" be only waiting, or imprisonment, or the end of life, or a purgatory, or our own mind, or the perfection of an artistic moment, or our own pathetic and ugly self, or a story that justifies living, as opposed to not-being or suicide. Just to go on talking or, as here in *II,* praying as the curtain falls may be all we know and all we need to know, not of truth, but of existence, be it true or false, reality or illusion. Perhaps, then, A represents not the future but a regression, with only the promise that at the next performance the play will start again. A is already out of his sack; he has already done his halting, brooding, and praying and now he can get on with it: with the routine involving the carrot and the clothes before he goes back in the sack so that B's turn can come.

Who knows? Our questioning of what A's final appearance means, the possibility that we are over- or under-interpreting the situation, or interpreting it just right even if we are left with a model of indecision or ambiguity—all this may mean that Beckett himself has had his vision. We ourselves are in a stupor, or equipoise; like Murphy before Mr. Endon, we stare ahead—we: playwright, actor, and audience—without certainty, without commitment, sure only that we are staring. The experience is profound in that this is the way it is for us lost ones, waiting at the endgame with no painkiller, at a play, both creating and seeing our creation, in a fallen state, poised between death and life but never realizing one or the other with any certainty. Eh Joe? The curtain mercifully intervenes.

# 7 *Ends and Odds*: At the Frontier of the Stage

In this more recent collection of plays I believe there are major aesthetic concerns not only linking the various pieces of *Ends and Odds* but also placing the collection itself within the larger context of Beckett's work for the theater. These plays for the stage, radio, and television are also the most experimental we have to date. As I mentioned in the preface, the television play . . . *but the clouds* . . . appears in the latest Grove edition of *Ends and Odds* but not in the one I used in the present chapter. Accordingly, I discuss this "addition" in appendix B. The reader will also note that, having been unable to find a suitable "home" for it in earlier chapters, I have taken the liberty to add at the end a little odd or end, Beckett's doubly miniaturized dramaticule, *Breath*.

i

*Not I*

Beckett's *Not I* both includes and reduces to their most basic the visual and verbal dimensions of his theater.[1] The gross mime of the tramps in *Godot* or the abstract mime of *Act Without Words* is reduced to the Auditor's gesture of "*helpless compassion.*" Four times he makes this movement; otherwise he is dead still. Each time the movement is less distinct and, indeed, is scarcely perceptible the third time. He is the audience onstage, our surrogate, all of humanity responding in sympathy to the Mouth as she narrates a tale of both human failure and achievement, a thematic fall and an aesthetic renaissance, set off by two interrogatives ("what?" and "who?") and two exclamations ("no!" and "she!"). He is sexless, in black, concentrating solely on the Mouth, the perfect audience with no bias, with no identity other than that given him by the play; and he is absorbed into the play in direct proportion to the emergence of the Mouth as actor. The Auditor's "neutrality" as well as his weakness may also signal his own growing inability to understand her. We, the "real" audience, may have to assume that responsibility.

As for the voice. Its human support is obscured; we see only a mouth illuminated upstage right, speaking into some invisible microphone.[2] The play is *Words and Music* redone as *Words and Movement*—the quintessential theatrical experience. There is also a purposeful blurring between play and reality, onstage and offstage, for even before the curtain opens the voice begins speaking for roughly ten seconds. The process is reversed when the curtain closes on the Mouth's last audible stage line, "pick it up." The Mouth is further instructed to ad lib dialogue *"as required when curtain fully up and attention sufficient into."* We are witnessing, in effect, the birth of the theater, paralleling the way in which the "tiny little thing" (the girl, the play) goes "out" and "into the world." The aesthetic issue is at one with the thematic one, with the portrait of a buried human life, of all humanity for whom words are either absent or fail to convey the essence of the person, for whom human conversation is stilted or nonexistent. We all are lost ones in the Mouth's narrative. The helpless Auditor defines our state if we fail to listen to and comprehend our own mouths.

The Auditor's four movements serve to divide this story into five sections. In section one (pp. 14–15) the Mouth speaks of an essentially "parentless" birth, the father leaving at conception, the mother at delivery. That life was further unfulfilled because of a vast, missing period extending from the speechless days of infancy to old age (the final discourse in *Words and Music*). In her last days the narrator, now senile, found herself wandering in a field, thoughtlessly picking cowslips to make a ball (and we will recall the white and black balls of *Krapp's Last Tape*, *All That Fall*, *Endgame*, and other plays), on a journey, but to nowhere.[3] Suddenly "all went out." Even the empty, meaningless life of the infant too soon aged dissolved to nothingness. Ironically, this seeming "death" came on an April morning, in the month of rebirth. The narrator speaks here of someone else, "she," *Not I*, but we easily penetrate this disguise. At this point the Auditor shrugs for the first time, in that gesture of helpless compassion, and we reach section two (pp. 15–18).

Now the narrator, or the "she" whose story she relates, finds herself in a new dimension, without apparent body, without any external reality, with only a buzzing in the ears ultimately traced to the brain and with a ray of light, like moonlight, issuing from some unchanging spot. Sound and vision are now abstracted; we are clearly in stasis, the journey arrested when "all went out . . . all that early April morning light." This is the state prerequisite to the real vision that Beckett seeks, though the narrator's first inclination is to assign the state a position on some theological hierarchy: is she in Heaven? or Purgatory? or Hell? or still on earth? Theology tells her that Hell is suffering, yet she feels no pain. Perhaps she has misunderstood suffering as something physical; in point of fact, it may be the absence of what is physical or real, the inability to feel. An extraordinary change now comes over her as she considers acting as a way of validating the suspicion that this is a realm of suffering for which no correlatives exist on earth. She will fake agony, perhaps try to groan—but she cannot. Even a scream seems impossible.

Instead, there is only the silence of a grave (the very silence Joe sought to avoid in the television play). Only the buzzing sound, only the steady light reminds her of her consciousness, despite her physical immobility. We are at the theater distilled, mankind reduced to brain (the source of the buzzing sound) and eyes (receptors for the light). From this state, armed only with an interior noise and a single object for vision, the narrator consciously tries to recount the series of events leading to such altered consciousness. A dim memory of wandering in the field, fixing her eyes on a distant bell (the blending here of eye and ear), is all that will come. Again there is a sympathetic shrug from the Auditor.

In section three (pp. 18–21) things change again. The narrator has passed through consciousness in this life, to the stasis of sudden alteration and diminution, to a new stage where the voice starts to come back. Indeed, in her past life she had been mostly silent, hardly interacting with her fellow humans. Like all of us, she was part of a "Lonely Crowd," to borrow the title from Riesman's sociological study of 1950. Memory returns, and with it she paints the portrait of an isolated life in a supermarket, where even the necessity of conversation when ordering groceries was circumvented by a list:

> just hand in the list . . . with the bag . . . old black shopping bag . . . then stand there waiting . . . any length of time . . . middle of the throng . . . motionless . . . staring into space . . . mouth half open as usual . . . till it was back in her hand . . . the bag back in her hand . . . then pay and go . . . not as much as goodbye. (P. 18)

We are moving out of life into life as reconstructed by art, into that certain, albeit fraudulent world of T. S. Eliot's rose garden. Appropriately in this section the lips start to move, feeling comes back into the head; only the body below the neck remains "unsensed." The word *imagine* is now the most frequent interjection. Ignored, silent, uncommunicative in public life, the narrator as a private individual, as an artist, now goes into a talking fit, her mouth on fire, the words tumbling out of the lips, the speaker unable to stop—like the dancer in *The Red Shoes*. Even the minimal life, this uncommunicative life cannot stop the onward movement of the mind (the state of section two). Once words are possible, then the individual (be she artist or nonartist) can retreat into herself, to the inner world. There his eyes take in the images, feed them to a brain that with an inner voice, the buzzing in the skull, gives words to them, though heard by no one but the artist. Then we advance into the realm of creation, even if that creation be born of nothingness. Now in section three the memories flow: crying as a baby, looking at her moist palms one evening in a place called Croker's Acres. The events are unimportant; there is no logic to them, no plot, but they supply, even at the minimum, stimuli for thought. The artist is here alive, grabbing at straws, at events from past or present to talk about, to keep talking, to stay alive—not to return to life (for what little it was worth) yet, at the same time, not to remain in that unresolved stasis.

For the Mouth the process means recognizing the primacy, the reality of an individual soul in a world that outside one's self is temporal, mortal, artificial, only a play. Such perceptions are increased in the fourth section (pp. 21–22), after the third and weakest shrug from the Auditor. The narrator is becoming her own auditor; and, for our part, we are taking over the Auditor's role. As we draw closer to the narrator, in understanding and sympathy, our surrogate on stage proportionately loses strength. Life now takes the metaphor of a court, where the Mouth as judge, witness, jury, and accused was speechless, or practically speechless—just surviving. We all live on, guilty or not, with nothing in particular to say or conclude about the situation. However, this human tragedy, this absurdist fact of existence, is given form by the narration. Art is our orderly struggle against meaninglessness and disorder. The artist speaks about our nothingness, about that play we foolishly take as reality, an ongoing process of waiting that we try to justify by fashioning Godots who never come. Just before the end of this section, signaled by the Auditor's fourth movement, we catch the first unmistakable glimpse of the narrator as artist: "April morning . . . face in the grass . . . nothing but the larks . . . pick it up there . . . get on with it from there . . . another few . . . try something else . . . think of something else." Here clearly is a mind in the process of creation, conscious of itself the way all of Beckett's artists are: Krapp, Hamm, Pozzo, Mrs. Rooney, Opener.

In the final section (pp. 22–23) the Mouth recalls that this urge to speak was never fully buried. In her lifetime, particularly during the winter months ("A sad tale's best for winter," to echo Shakespeare), she had the Ancient Mariner's urge to stop someone, even in a lavatory, and talk, "start pouring it out . . . steady stream . . . mad stuff" (p. 22). Like Mrs. Rooney's, her narrative had been ignored, misunderstood; she had retreated into herself—until this moment. Here again is Beckett's justification of the theater. It is *now*, happening, obliterating the past, careless of the future, a contractual agreement between actor and auditor, playwright and audience, actor and playwright, actor and character, audience on- and audience offstage. It is pain for the artist to talk, never sure if he is heard or understood. The Mouth begs to stop, but the request goes unanswered. The roar, the light now moving as if in sympathetic activity with this aesthetic renaissance, cannot be stifled; the commitment is irreversible. One must keep on; we have moved from perishable life to imperishable art. The pain is now pleasure.

With this revelation the narrator has escaped from her individual self. She is no longer a substitute (the thinly disguised I) but now has a new role where individuality is subsumed under the aesthetic identity won by the artist. As an artist she achieves an immortality rescuing her and her vision from the vagaries of fate. It is now "she"—this is the hard-won appositive for the narrator—*Not I*, but "she." The Auditor now cannot hide behind those gestures "of helpless compassion," denying that the subject is someone else.[4] In identifying this buried life, this renaissance in which one sees one's self, as Krapp does at the shore when the clashing of the sea suddenly brings his whole wretched existence home to him, the subject becomes us.

We realized that the E is O. The playwright moves from a personal encounter or narration to a universal one. Here is the end of Beckett's art: that it become our reality. No longer Beckett—not I—but us.

The play ends with rejoicing, for God is love, as Winnie insists, and gives us His tender mercies. We are new, made new, revived by this corporate identity, "new every morning." The play can now be repeated, and we can go "back" to life refreshed, since *Not I* concerns the process of our human identification, rather than the specific individual details of that identification. The final command is a simple "pick it up," which I take in two ways: you who remain, the auditors in the auditorium (now that the auditor onstage is silenced), must take the play with you, picking it up and storing it in your memories; and "pick it up," in the musician's sense of "start now." We have moved from physical birth and death to a new life to the essence of art, and away from the frail existence of reality. The play ends with the symbol of fertility, that April morning, and with the Beckettian pose of completeness we have seen in *Cascando* and *Act Without Words I* and *Film:* the face buried in the hands, in the sea, or sand, here in the grass. *Not I*—the title embraces the antitheses, the negative "not" and then the positive "I." It at once defines the singularity of reference for the artist and celebrates his success in moving from the personal to the general.[5]

## ii

*That Time*

Beyond its obvious "character study" of a solitary, white-haired old man hearing and overhearing three sides of his conscience, *That Time* is, I think, a dramatization of a Proustian *Times Remembered*, or at least the Proust that Beckett sees in his early study of that author. Concerned with time, the play also shares Proust's concern with the operations of the creative imagination and the dilemma in the workaday world of the individual blessed, or cursed, with that same imagination.

This dramatization is, surely, internal, for the indistinct inner voices ultimately become "one and the same voice" (p. 28), however "clearly faintly perceptible" the divisions among them should appear. There are more subtle, thematic links between the three voices, for they share common themes of ejection, rejection, aloneness, confusion, and the move toward silence and abstraction. There are also more obvious moments, similar to those in *Play*, where the separate voices employ a similar vocabulary of concern. The word *mother* passes from A to C; C's *marble* becomes B's *stone* (p. 29). The white-haired Chinaman mentioned by B metamorphoses into A's white-haired man, the narrator/narrated. Some especially theatrical words, like *scene*, are passed about, or along, and there are parallel constructions, such as B's "no touching" followed by A's "no getting out" (p. 33).

Beckett would have it both ways: a seemingly external drama, given the stage's physicality and externality in both space and time, exists alongside a "cerebral drama" of thought processes stimulated in the minds of an audience even as they witness the obvious stage metaphor. The "coincidence" of these shared words and concerns and the stage directions themselves that try to balance neatly between the separateness and unity of the three voices suggest that the play is indeed an interior monologue. More than this, the opening stage directions refer to the three voices, or the means of amplifying the voices, as a "threefold source and context," a single starting place as well as a point of return.

We see only the face of the character, an "*Old white face, long flaring white hair as if seen from above outspread*" (p. 28). Is it Godot? Was Godot, all along, merely a projection of Vladimir and Estragon? The Boy had commented, "I think it's [the beard] white, Sir" (p. 59a). At the very least, the present situation, a solitary character onstage listening to voices projected from offstage, bears some parallels with *Not I* and *Eh Joe* and, in a looser sense, with *Krapp's Last Tape, Play* (where we also see only the faces of the three characters), and, in a visual sense, with *Film.* The symmetry of *That Time* is perhaps closest to *Come and Go,* with its own three-part division, signaled by two ten-second silences, paralleling the triadic pattern in the dramaticule of having one character leaving, one character whispering, and one responding with shock. This same three-part division also informs *Film* and *All That Fall.* There is a sense here, too, of musical organization, perhaps that of the sonata, with an exposition, variation, and, to use Beckett's language, refinement of above—not to mention the coda, where A, B, and C have a final "say."

*That Time* begins with statements from the three voices. A is making an imaginative return to his childhood, in particular to a "ruin" at the farthest reaches of the train tracks, where as a child he hid from the world, wrapped in his own imagination.[6] The narrative is a curious blend of specifics (the "grey day," train number eleven) and the generalities or vagaries of a fading memory as the character struggles to recollect his emotions in a state less than tranquil. Perhaps the tracks—no trains travel them anymore—should be taken metaphorically as "trains" or synaptic connections from the sensory perceptions into the mind.

C also tells of a hiding place, "when you went in out of the rain," though C's time apparently follows that of A's narration. The time here is out of joint, faded; and the art not the innocent imagination of a child but the dead art of a Portrait Gallery that functions for C only as refuge, rather than as inspiration for any individual creation. Such "dead" places of art are made fun of in *Murphy* as the Archaic Room of the British Museum, or the Harpy Tomb,[7] places whose records of human activity are as useless as the extravagant numbers with which the narrator of *How It Is* plays.[8] The rain is winter rain, cold and menacing, and not that same water, that matrix of creation, which we have observed elsewhere in Beckett. The seat itself is a cold marble slab. This fact is picked up by B, who recalls sitting "on the stone together in the sun on the stone at the edge of the little wood" (p. 29). His is an abortive love scene, however, with the couple not touching, sitting at opposite ends of the stone, ironically surrounded by yellow wheat and other signs of procreation. We may be hearing the exercise of that discredited voluntary memory.

The prelude completed, the three voices move into the narration of "part one" (pp. 29–31). A is plagued by fading memory as names and other details slip from his mind. The rails themselves are now rusted and totally inoperative. Along with details, concepts themselves fade: "mother" changes to "she." The repetitions betray either an inability to say more about the scene or a neurotic attempt to put in order what few scattered memories and details there remain from childhood. Still, one picture emerges with alarming clarity: that of the child, seated among the nettles, with his picture-book. The "your" is ambiguous: the narrator is talking about the white-haired man, or, if the voices come from the stage character, that "your" is self-reflexive. The single detail, the picture-book, triggers A's most profound vision in this opening section, the child talking to himself, creating "imaginary conversations" among the giant nettles, trying out a variety of voices until he becomes hoarse, a solitary creative voice informing his imagination on a level beyond that of picture books (recall it was Estragon who reduced the Bible to a series of colored pictures). All the while, "they" are out on dark roads or in moonlight looking for him.

B seems plagued by just the opposite problem, a wealth of details that threaten to prohibit any clear, let alone single pattern. We will think, surely, of Krapp and his description of the woman in the punt. Similarly, there is a contrast in B's narration between the abortive love affair itself, so meager that any details of affection slip from his consciousness, and the rush of surrounding details: the symbols of creativity (wheat, blue sky), the stone on which the lovers sit, the associations called to mind. With this wealth of images that "among others floated up" (p. 30) and B's own sensitivity to the "scene" itself, the stage is set, literally, for artistic creation, for the eyes that shut only to allow the inner world to come into focus, for the dissolution of that outer world of frustration, the movement from dependency on a woman to self-reflection. "Scene" soon changes to "whatever scenes," and connections are made to childhood events, perhaps to A's basic picture since the would-be lover's isolation links him with the child for whom "mother" has changed to "she," after which even the pronoun fades from the narration. From this childhood or—before that—the "womb," an amazing picture comes into being: "that old Chinaman long before Christ born with long white hair" (pp. 30–31). B seems to identify the onstage character with some sort of primordial artist, a Godot predating Christ. Once this is accomplished, he ends his first segment by doubting that the woman ever existed, that he was ever loved or tried to love, and finishes with a description that we have seen elsewhere in Beckett, that of artist, alone, trying to fill the space with language, conscious of narrating himself: "just one of those old tales to keep the void from pouring in on top of you the shroud" (p. 31).

As A and B seem to pull closer together, C, stuck in the Portrait Gallery, defines a stultifying art and its context. Childhood, the source of play and creativity, degenerates to sterile pictures of little princes obscured by the dust of ages, the deadening process of time, and the poor janitorial services of a second-rate museum. The attendant, shuffling along in felt slippers, presenting the one threat to the youth or adult for whom the museum is only an alternative to the winter rain, will recall the Croak of *Words and Music* who, overtaken by his creative tools, retreats on those same shuffling slippers. Paradoxically, the sterile museum allows C to make an observation that gets to the core of the problem in *That Time*, namely, that things are "never the same after that never quite the same but that was nothing new" (p. 31).

What to do with, and in, time? The past, for all three voices, is the source of images, the context out of which one creates or, barring that, at least deals with an individual history. But events happen once and are never repeated, and hence the danger is that art becomes only a recorder of the past. If Vladimir and Estragon are stuck in a present, with a corresponding inability to remember or deal with the past, and in a play where the arrival of Godot remains only a possibility, here in *That Time* the narrator or narrators have nothing but the past, or a past that is unique, never the same, never to be repeated, and hence a past that can be lost. The problem is this: how to remember this unique past and, having done this, how to square it with a present that is not the same and yet bears tragic affinities to that past. We return, thus, to the basic issue of Proust.[9]

C's abstraction forms the opening lines of the second section (pp. 31–34). For a few words the character's eyes are open as C intones "never the same but the same as what for God's sake did you ever say I to yourself in your life come on now" (p. 31). C has the most developed tragic sense, and is aware that the stage figure has never asserted himself, has never been anyone. And this cruel revelation is the turning point, the moment of horrible self-truth. For C is an insignificant being, whiling away the time first in the Portrait Gallery and then, in descending order, the Public Library and the Post Office. Indeed, C may suggest Krapp in the present tense, just as B suggests Krapp at thirty, and A Krapp at a much earlier period.

Nevertheless, present and past will merge, for whether reviving the scene at the end of the tracks in reality or though memory, A links past and present. B's own realization that he was alone even when seated with the girl on the stone only reinforces the present loneliness of the narrator, attended by his own voice or voices. All three figures are solitary, though C's isolation seems the most tragic of all. Appropriately, C never mentions mother, but only father. Like the several characters in *Stories and Texts for*

*Nothing* who are exiled, the present three characters are separated from family or lover or, in C's case, an entire society.

All this time A persists in a rather detailed account of childhood, though the memories now extend from the night of exile to the dawn of the next day, that dawn, in effect, signaling the coming of some sort of "truth" (p. 32). The closed station itself crumbles, the "colonnade crumbling away" (p. 33), all these memories culminating, strangely, in the present, with the earliest memory forming the first link with A's present condition as the child on the step is replaced in A's consciousness by the aged, white-haired man on "someone's doorstep" (p. 33).[10] With age the child becomes a public spectacle, that spectacle himself losing all sense of the present, even as the figure of "the child on the stone where none ever came" returns (p. 34). Past is linked with present, and the loss of details admits the first extended abstract statement of the play, one appropriately about indecision and a loss of direction: "not knowing where you were or when you were or what for place might have been uninhabited for all you knew." Here is sustained thinking about a world that may not even exist: no time, no place, no identity even for the speaker—shades of *The Unnamable*!

For B the details of the aborted affair remain clear; indeed, they take on additions such as the dead rat, a perverse and, at the same time, fitting symbol for the ruins of love. The dead rat, either drifting on or caught in the reeds—a parody, perhaps, of Krapp's boat moored on the flags, that still point juxtaposed with the movement of the lovers themselves—triggers a release from the wealth of details, as the physical separation of the lovers is reexpressed as a figure in geometry: "always parallel like on an axle-tree never turned to each other." This leads to the imprecise picture of "just blurs on the fringes of the field," and then to the Dante-like abstractions of "space" and "shades" (p. 33). The lovers, always with "space between," are cold figures, with "no pawing in the manner of flesh and blood" (p. 33). By B's next appearance he has moved even closer to the silence of abstraction, in a way that parallels A's own movement to this abstraction in which past and present are combined. The figures, like those on Keats's urn, are "stock still," their eyes closed, their bodies reduced to the simile of "two knobs on a dumbbell" (p. 34). The "no's" begin to pile on: "no sight of man or beast no sight or sound" (p. 34).

In the final third (pp. 34–37) of *That Time* B starts by sketching anew the details of the love scene, but there is a curiously distant quality about the portraiture: "alone on the end of the stone with the wheat and blue or the towpath alone on the towpath with the ghosts of the mules the drowned rat or bird or whatever it was floating off into the sunset" (p. 34–35). Even these inexact "details" are erased just as quickly with "vanished all vanished" (p. 35). B's narrative is, in a sense, a conscious fiction, or at least B seems conscious of his recreation. The scene, therefore, easily shifts from the field to a beach, with the rat supplanted by a glider, a seemingly irrelevant object like that lawnmower in *Play*. The next time B speaks this glider takes the narrator literally above the beach and beyond the field, as its graceful movements suggest the "great peace" that comes over the lover, stirring the narrator to confess it "hard to believe" he ever "made up that bit till the time came in the end" (p. 36).

A, meanwhile, has so abstracted his own childhood story of exile that the character is referred to now as "the child" (p. 35), as "him" and not "me," the story itself now alive through that same third person sought by the narrator of *Not I*. Again, even this third-person childhood narration slides easily into the present-tense first-person narration of the "scandal huddled there in the sun where it had no warrant" (p. 36), until finally A admits "making it all up on the doorstep as you went along making yourself all up again for the millionth time forgetting it all" (p. 36). More than B, A seems conscious that he is the narrator/narrated; and it is A who, in this section, reintroduces the play's title: "to hide in again till it was night and time to go till that time came" (p. 36).

C seems to be going through the greatest upheavals, as the Post Office, the abode of dead letters, is invaded by the "bustle" of Christmas along the streets, as life outside contrasts with spiritual death within of that solitary character who, looking neither right nor left, finds a vacant seat and drowses away. The Post Office dissolves, in cinematic fashion, to the Library, as literature, Beckett's own point of entry into the world of fiction, is reduced to a "bevy of old ones pouring on the page and not a sound" (p. 37). The most consciously artistic of all three voices—C's, with his forays into museums, portrait galleries, post offices, and libraries—vanishes with the dust, and his state is thereby contrasted with the rain falling outside.

In a coda to the piece, first B speaks, then A, and at last C. B is seen in a posture of self-love, trying like the man in *Eh Joe* to come sexually, but unable to do so, the spent penis displaced by the hollow tree, as inside the window the man's sexual and physical decay—"the great shroud billowing in all over you"—is juxtaposed against the outdoors where even the moonlight "gave up for good" (p. 37). Fully within the fiction of the child's exile, A returns to the "wharf," with a slew of details; but now the child is the man. The "white hair pouring down from under the hat" may refer either to the child's father or the child now grown old. That time, from childhood, now becomes emblematic of all pasts. He has told the story of himself, but now not just about himself. The paradox is preserved. On the one hand, the fictional creation will "always be short" of the reality, yet as the Unnamable knows, "Where I am there is no one but me [it is close enough], who am not" (the fiction is just a fiction).[11] B is the impotent artist, though conscious now of that impotence, no longer demanding or needing love, his desire ablated, as Beckett would say. A is both father and son, the one searching and the one sought. He has the artist's inclusive vision, even if that vision be of lost ones. C's voice lasts the longest as from the dust he sees literally nothing, ending the play in a manner reminiscent of *Come and Go*: "not a sound only what was it said come and gone was that it something like that come and gone come and gone no one come and gone in no time gone in no time." A brief release from tragedy, gone in no time, and therefore a happy one. The character works himself out of enslavement to the present, out of addiction to the physical by a movement to the abstract, out of existence's cruelties born of reflection to the comforts of fiction. Appropriately, the final tableau we see as audience is of a serene character, breathing just audible, with a smile *"toothless for preference."* Time has been conquered by the imagination, but conquered in the sense that the "facts" of the past—sad facts—have been metamorphosed to "sad" fictions of the present experience, and then to our own present experience—as much as that of the listener—with *That Time*.

## iii

*Footfalls*

If *That Time* concerns an aesthetic movement, or triumph if you will, beyond or in spite of time, an attempt to overwhelm thematics or time with aesthetics or narration, *Footfalls* involves the merging of life and art. Not unlike *That Time*, it also represents an attempt to envelop the past in a present-tense narration. In a similar fashion *Come and Go* places a sad and destructive past-tense memory, that time the three women sat on the log at Miss Wade's, within a happy and aesthetic present-tense action, the joining of hands. Still, *Footfalls* more consciously represents a merging, perhaps even a confusion, between life and art, between the "histories" of May and Voice and the stories they tell of mothers and daughters, of old Mrs. Winter and her daughter Amy.

It is a play of tremendous extremes. If narration wins out, indeed if the play itself dissolves and then ends with a narration of new material for a play, *Footfalls* also starts at the most physical level. The stage lights are therefore strongest at the floor, at the Estragon-like level of feet, and proportionately less on the body and "least," in Beckett's words, on the head. We are initially in the realm of Estragon and Clov and Willie, and not that of Vladimir, Hamm, and Winnie. The name May, whatever its implications to the contrary, is ironically given to a woman who, seemingly young, is marked with *"dishevelled grey hair, worn grey wrap hiding feet, trailing,"* a description more appropriate for Krapp or Hamm—perhaps even for Godot.[12] The tremendous movement in the play, made manifest in the change from the physical feet to the invisible second speaker (the source of pure narration), seems generated by the contrasts: M paces in a regular pattern, and V is stationary, yet V initiates the process leading to M's narration. The pacing itself seems a parody, some might even say a literal transcription of habit as defined in the book on Proust; yet the use of memory on the part of both M and V rivals that in *Embers* or, surely, such examples as Hamm's story of the old man begging bread for his son. Even the symmetry of the play, the pacing particularly (for which Beckett even specifies the foot on which the pacing begins and ends), is qualified by

Beckett's insistence that the strip on which M paces be "*a little off centre audience right*" (p. 42). A short play, though not so short as others of Beckett's more recent composition, it is also a wide play, full of opposites, or contradictions.

There are four very distinct sections, signaled by a long pause and the sounding of a chime, fainter with each occasion, that lend a strict order to *Footfalls*. In section one (pp. 42–44) we have little promise of resolution. Even the title, *Footfalls,* sounds like a poor variation of *All That Fall.* In *Mercier and Camier* the characters are "all ears for the footfalls . . . distinguishable from all other footfalls,"[13] and there are similar footfalls in *Watt.*[14] The paradox of silent footfalls is restated in *Fizzles* as the situation "where all the footsteps ever fell can never fare nearer to anywhere nor from anywhere further away."[15] We may be in the realm of thematic tragedy rather than—as I shall propose—aesthetic comedy. From the start there are reminders of other Beckett plays. The whistle of *Act Without Words I* is here the chime, an auditory "breaking" device as opposed to the visual one in *Not I* (that solitary listener who shrugs his shoulders three times) or the ten-second silences of *That Time.* There is a familiar and tense relationship between M and V. Besides the mental and physical dichotomy between the two, V seems closest to Hamm and M to Clov, for M, like Clov, functions as the unwilling servant, straightening the pillow, changing the drawsheet, passing the bedpan, and so on, even going as far as giving V injections (and we will recall not only Hamm's asking for his painkiller but the injection that Bolton demands of Holloway in *Embers*). The very process of waiting, made graphic in M's pacing up and down the stage, will recall the general issue of waiting in *Godot,* or waiting for the train in *All That Fall.*

Two different worlds seem to collide here, epitomized in the hyperconsciousness of M and the initially unconscious state of V. These are the "two shapes" of the play.[16] The father and adopted-son relationship between Hamm and Clov is here the literal mother-daughter relationship between M and V. We are given some fairly specific information about their ages: the mother is eighty-nine or ninety, the daughter, like Mrs. Rooney's Effie, half her age, in her forties. But the "two shapes" also draw closer. V confesses that she hears M even in her deepest sleep, and expresses her anxiety over her daughter's obsession with revolving a mysterious something in her mind: "Will you never have done," followed by what in *Cascando* would be called an addition to the same, "Will you never have done . . . revolving it all." M's "It?" leads into V's closing lines of this first section: "It all. (*Pause.*) In your poor mind. (*Pause.*) It all. (*Pause.*) It all." Separated by age, status, state (stationary or pacing), position in the play itself (questioner or responder), V and M seem curiously linked by this simplistic, perhaps inane exchange. The section had started with an emphasis on the physical, with the light focused on the floor level, with attention given to M's feet pacing back and forth across the stage, and V confined to only a voice "*from dark upstage,*" yet it has since moved to this tantalizing assertion on V's part about M's obsession with revolving something in her "poor mind." The pacing resumes for five seconds only this time, and then the stage is in darkness. The chime sounds fainter, and when the light fades up, signaling a new section of the play, the general stage light is itself diminished.

V dominates section two (pp. 45–46). The M she describes, reinforced by the "real" M who is now discovered facing front at R, "fancies" she is still alone facing the wall. The "narrated" M, reinforced by what we see (but no longer by what we hear onstage once the pacing stops), is now more a creature of mental dimensions. Surely the "old home" described by V is one of those mental room-wombs we have seen elsewhere in Beckett. Other girls at her age went outside,[17] engaged in sports: it is fitting that the sport mentioned is lacrosse, the one in which Beckett excelled as a boy. V is here both describing and watching M, and encouraging us to watch her, even though the "customary" M, the one who paces, is now stilled. As in *Come and Go,* though not so blatantly, we are not given enough facts: what is it M "revolves," and what is "not enough"? On the surface that "not enough" refers to M's insistence that it is not enough to see the feet fall; rather, one must hear them as well, "however faint." M is now given to the auditory rather than the visual. Like Malone she wishes "everything to be heard."[18] According to V, she is something of the historian as well, for her concern is with telling "how it was" (the title of Beckett's *How It Is* perhaps comes to mind). M, in V's narration, has done turnabout: the physical is giving way to the auditory, and the mental to sound waves, and, if you will, thought waves. A quantum leap has been made in this play that, at the start, had established such a tense juxtaposition of the physical (M first) and the cerebral or imaginative (our earliest impression of V).

In section three (pp. 46–48) M's speech builds upon V's in section two; and the heightened artistic consciousness is signaled by May's first word, "sequel" (p. 46), as she resumes her pacing about the stage, but no longer as the essentially physical creature we saw at the start of the play. We are made doubly aware by two false starts in this section that M will be consciously narrating a story of V: first, "A little later, when she quite forgotten, she began to—"; and then, "A little later, when as though she had never been, it never been, she began to walk" (p. 46). M and V seem to be merging since the M of V's previous narration seems old, somewhere farther along the play's announced gamut of forty to ninety; here in section three the V described by M is suspiciously like the M just described by V. Like M, M's V also paces about, though this time the pacing itself, as described by M, is on a mysterious level without sound: "No . . . None at least to be heard" (p. 47). The opposites, the earlier pacing (M) and pausing (V)—parallel to Beckett's dialogue and silence, Vladimir and Estragon, coming and going—now join: we are in a new realm, one of neither white nor black, day nor night. This shift is signaled by the introduction of a new element in M's narration, "the semblance" seen by the narrated V. That semblance itself is clearly juxtaposed between black and white—it is gray— and the description is at once specific and general: "Faint, though by no means invisible, in a certain light. . . . Given the right light. . . . Grey rather than white, a pale shade of grey . . . Tattered. . . . A tangle of tatters. . . . A faint tangle of pale grey tatters . . ." (p. 47). It is almost as if the growing merger of M and V results in this "product," this semblance, a level of the mysterious that can only be reached by such earlier syntheses as that of mother and daughter, stander and pacer, old and semi-old, cerebral and physical. The two halves, so joined, lead to the possibility of someone greater than their sum or, at very least, someone apart—a Godot perhaps, even if it be only a Godot of their own making. Gray, we recall, was the color seen outside by Clov, and gray is, more literally, the median between black and white, the color Beckett often uses to describe that state between speech and silence, between the two impossibilities of dialogue that, like over-tufted grass, chokes on itself and silence that, in being talked about or being conceptualized, is therefore that much more unattainable.

Two stories have now been completed: V's, of a young girl clinging to sound, different from all other young girls, living in self-imposed exile in an old house; and M's, of an old woman encountering a mysterious sem-blance. Once established, the transition from conflict in reality to synthesis in storytelling leads to a dissolution of both the narrated V and the sem-blance—"Watch it pass—*(pause)*—watch her pass"—and then to a careful juxtaposition of artificial light (the candelabrum) and natural light (the moon). Even those two are joined by grammar as the candle's "flames" give way to the moon's "light," with the slender word *their* (also M and V?) linking them: "watch her pass before the candelabrum how its flames, their light . . . like moon through passing . . . rack."

M now moves to the final stage, section four (pp. 47–49), though this time the bell sounds at the close, rather than at its start. Beyond the per-sonal narrations of mother and daughter, beyond V's story of M and M's story of V, we go to a more consciously artificial story, of old Mrs. Winter and her daughter, Amy.[19] The situation here surely parallels the movement in *Embers* from Henry's own personal narration, his troubles with his own wife and daughter, to the Bolton-Holloway story, a story, I might observe, that also served to merge opposite threads, since Henry becomes both the doctor called out on the winter's night and the patient seeking an injection. As was observed, the Bolton-Holloway story itself contains opposites of warm fire and cold outdoors. The dimly self-conscious narration ("Sequel") of M's previous story is enhanced here: "Old Mrs. Winter, whom the reader will remember." M takes pains to cast the story in a strict dialogue form. We have also moved beyond sight to words, returning to the radio plays, returning, in a way, to Beckett's start as a novelist spinning tales of the narrator/narrated. The merging of mother and daughter, of V and M, that we have seen already is now also a figurative merging as M speaks of both a mother and daughter. Yet if we think of M and V as "reality" and of M's present story as fiction, the contrast is immediately suspect, since Amy is an anagram for May, and Mrs. Winter is surely V. If one likes to play with

Beckett's own fascination with the letters M and W, and the more general symbolism of letters, then it may be observed that V is one-half of either M or W.

Actually, the characters, the play's twin narrators, are merging even as the characters in the story, Amy and Mrs. Winter, seem to be separating.[20] An aesthetic merging encases an aesthetic separation; we have simultaneous opposites and parallels in the same form. The revolving in the mind— M's obsession—metamorphoses into Mrs. Winter's obsession with a vision not seen by Amy. M's demand for auditory verification transfers now to an equal insistence by Amy for physical verification. The seeming parallel in the outer and inner stories is at the same time, and again, a contrast: M's mystery is recycled as a "strange thing" (p. 48). We may also suspect that the narrator, May, rejects through Amy the sense of something beyond themselves. Earlier the mother had said, "What do you mean, May, not enough, what can you possibly mean, May, not enough?" (p. 45). Like Hamlet and Gertrude in the Queen's chamber, the former sees more than the latter. This is the source of tension here, though, we must add quickly, it is both an artificial tension (the story within the story) and reflective of an "actual tension," that of the opposing forces established at the start of the play. Even these outer "forces" are no less artificial than those in the story within the story. In point of fact, what is "heard" could be everything from nothing (and that in itself would be proper in Beckett) to sound beyond human understanding (hence the flood of religious references in the closing minutes of the play).

The story within a story, then, seems to establish a division between mother and daughter, just as the story enclosing it has moved toward identification between the formerly opposing figures. Now, though, the first link is established between Amy and Mrs. Winter as the mother insists that she heard the daughter say "Amen": "How could you possibly have said Amen if, as you claim, you were not there?" (p. 48). If the daughter claims to have said or heard nothing, the mother "distinctly" heard the daughter say "Amen." At last, this first link between the inner-story characters leads to the first graphic link between the two stories themselves. The dialogue of Amy and Mrs. Winter sounds like the dialogue of M and V, complete with the mother's complaint "Will you never have done? . . . . Will you never have done . . . revolving it all?"

The union has been made, the final synthesis. We move, paradoxically, in two directions at once: to the union of inner and outer story, or the narrators and the narrated; but also toward the play's absorption in M's fictive world, a fictive world, if you will, doubly and securely encased within a fictive world. *Footfalls* does what the narrator in *Malone Dies* could not do: it removes all traces of the narrator within the story. Yet the play also comes apart, in comic fashion, in the same way, for there is here not so much an absorption in the inner story as there is a parallel. This is the delicate balance achieved by Henry in *Embers,* for the Bolton-Holloway story was at once a new stage in the play and a parallel to Henry's own life. The serenity of that balance here is underscored as the phrase *it all* echoes three times, as the lights fade and the stage goes dark, and as the chime sounds at its faintest. There is a pause for echoes; the light fades to even a little less on the strip. We are going into that greatest dark; "no dark quite like his own dark," as Murphy well knows.[21] May has now vanished, either absorbed completely within the fiction or so complete as the narrator/narrated that her presence becomes irrelevant. In approaching such union we also approach mystery, perhaps the very mystery that Amy/May heard and/or that Mrs. Winter/Voice saw.

iv

*Ghost Trio*

Of the *"Ends"* considered so far, *Ghost Trio* is the most ambitious. This parody of the three-act play treats the formation of a fictive world, that assembling of the materials, both aesthetic and thematic, to establish the theater's illusion of reality. There is also a growing "impurity" as the fairly "neutral" aesthetics of the opening section is fleshed out with thematic elements, culminating in Part III with the appearance of the little boy—shades of *Godot,* or the boy of *Endgame* made flesh. Even this blending of aesthetics and thematics is complicated by the introduction of an adult (F), bearing the potential for tragedy, and by "mysteries" that cannot be resolved: doors that close on their own, corridors that dissolve into geometric figures. *Ghost Trio* is, in a profound sense, a juggling act, encompassing references to almost all of Beckett's earlier work (for the theater, radio, television, and cinema) and yet maintaining its own tightness and integrity as a three-part television "play." It seems to span the difficult thematics of *Godot* (or *Endgame,* for that matter) and the self-conscious aesthetics of *Words and Music* or, to a lesser degree, *Cascando.*

Appropriately, the medium employed here is television—like the legitimate theater, but not quite so "live"; like radio (with offstage voices), but also visual; like *Film,* but with a vastly increased auditory dimension; like the mimes (in F's movements), but also including offstage dialogue that just may come from F's head, even as the female's voice in *Eh Joe* may be the silent actor's interior voice. *Ghost Trio* may be Beckett's most inclusive work so far, as open-ended as *Footfalls* was close-ended and synthetic.

Part I begins with a pervasive neutrality. The voice offstage or, more properly, off-camera is faint, and it announces that it cannot be tuned louder (we shall see this peculiar direction repeated in *Radio I*). Nothing is surprising at first: the chamber itself is said to be "familiar" and the light is "faint" and omnipresent. There is no problem here of intensity. The picture is one without bearings, without handles, either aesthetic or thematic. This neutrality almost threatens to dissolve to nothing as V intones a series of "no's": "No visible source" and "no shadow," and again "no shadow."

Not black or white, the colors themselves are "none," and then we get the qualification "grey," the color that is no color but only a tint between black and white, between all the colors of the spectrum. Gray: the color seen by Clov in *Endgame* and by the engraver described earlier by Hamm. Contributing to this neutrality is the lack of tension between the visual and the verbal, here the camera and V, an aesthetic cooperation to be contrasted with the tension, say, in *Words and Music*.

However, the serene visit by camera and voice to the objects and parts of the room (floor, dust, wall) is disturbed, though ever so slightly, by the introduction of "Door," underscored by V's command to "look again." The door, of course, leads into the room, but it also functions as a "window" to all that is outside. In Part I this metaphoric window will soon change to an actual one. With the first mention of a door, the camera turns to some potentially more stimulating objects, though whether for tragedy or comedy we are not sure: the window, then the pallet.[22] Still, the intrusion is counterbalanced by a return, perhaps we might call it a regression, to the "familiar" door, the now-familiar window and pallet, and the neutral floor and walls.

Just before the end of Part I we catch the first sight of F, the human figure, in a Belacqua-like pose. The change is signaled by the movement from the long-distance A shot to the medium-distance B shot—only later will the close-up C be used. There is also a second element, a suggestive one, the cassette. Is this the source of the voice and hence a parallel to the tape recorder in *Krapp's Last Tape*? Then a third element, shocking perhaps because it enters only in the final moments, less shocking as it forms a trinity with the human figure and the cassette: music.

The choreography completed—the movement from neutrality, to potentially significant elements, to the human figure and his "possessions"[23]—the first section dissolves with a final, long-distance A shot. We have been tempted out of neutrality. For the alert viewer-listener a host of questions emerge. What will be the link between this work and earlier efforts by the playwright? Will the human figure assume a greater role in subsequent parts (we know, of course, that those parts will come because of the promise of the title, *Ghost Trio*)? In a work so self-conscious in its artistry, what will be the balance between art's narration and the emerging thematic concerns? For if silence is aligned with neutrality, then clearly the mood generated by Part I can only be challenged—and challenged further—by speech and sound.

In Part II all shots, except a brief segment from 25 to 28 (and here the comparable section from Part I is repeated, with the camera at position B), are from A, the longest distance. Nevertheless, the sameness, the formality of the camera location is counterbalanced by the considerable "personalization" in this second part, not to mention the quantitative change in the elements of the story itself. V informs us that the solitary figure, "He," is waiting for "her." In this middle section, F, instead of simply reacting as he did in Part I, now moves about, exploring. We can see his face, albeit only for an instant, and are told that his "pose" is "tense." This transitional middle section is thereby alive, with explorations, with increasingly human and thematic elements. If Part I can be accurately labeled "the situation," then Part II is properly the "search." (And we might want to call the final section the "resolution," which, echoing the final chapter of Dr. Johnson's *Rasselas,* is a conclusion in which nothing is concluded.) Neither the furniture, as in Part I, nor the dimensions of the room are here the focus; rather, it is the window and the door, the avenues literal and figurative that take center stage, along with F's interaction with them. We are now more fully into the pattern of *Not I, Eh Joe,* and *That Time,* with F, in moving about the room, becoming the camera, or E, or the physical half of a split personality; and V, the voice, serving as the inner consciousness, or the *anima,* or the cerebral half of that divided personality. Whereas in Part I, V was confined to pointing out features in the room, she now gives both stage directions and reactions to F's explorations: "No one" (p. 58). When F looks in the mirror, as O does in *Film,* it is V who reacts with a *"surprised"* "Ah!" (p. 59).

This change in pace, particularly in the interaction between F and V, figure and voice, is counterbalanced by a regression in stages 25 to 30, when F goes back to *"opening pose, bowed over cassette"* while the camera at B recreates the tableau of Part I showing F in the Belacqua-like position, with close-ups of the head, hands, cassette, with *"face hidden"* and *"Music slightly louder"* (p. 47). Even this regression to the more formal and aesthetic posturing of Part I is suddenly broken by V's repeated announcement that "he will again think he hears her" (p. 60). F goes once more to the door, pushing it fully open this second time. Now he stands *"irresolute,"* and once the door closes "slowly of *itself,"* he returns to that opening pose by the cassette.

Combined here are echoes from Part I, an actual, albeit brief return to the earlier section, and also an increased sense of mystery, not only in the door's miraculous closing but also in F's reaction *("irresolute")* to that door and/or to what is beyond it. Part II grows from Part I, and that growth is at once inevitable and alarming. In Part I the music sounded faintly at position C and died out shortly after B was reached. Here it sounds at A, and it is a *"louder"* music. Then everything stops, and is repeated; or rather V announces "Repeat" as a prelude to the most ambitious section, Part III. Thematics are sharing the stage now, increasingly, with aesthetics.

If Part II represents a leap from the opening segment, then Part III is an *implosion.* V's command to "Repeat" in Part II leads directly to the opening sequence of Part III, a quick cut to F and the door, with music audible. If we take Part I musically as an opening theme, and Part II as its variation, then Part III is the resolution and, at the same time, expansion of that resolution. Much of Part III does repeat Part II though always with a difference. In effect, Part III is a review, but a review with its own integrity.

Now the camera shows the corridor outside the room. Yet this new vista is neutralized by the grayness of the scene, with the emphasis not on the corridor itself but on its rectangular symmetry. Even the precision of the symmetry itself is qualified by the fact that the corridor ends mysteriously "*in darkness.*" Still, despite the qualifications, the play's opening up, this most extensive revelation of a backstage or offstage yet seen in Beckett, is startling, mostly because our level of expectation is so refined, so high. And there are new sounds, such as the "*creak of door.*"

The literal repetitions of Part I in Part II are matched in Part III by a "sense" of Part I, particularly in the shots emphasizing forms: the cassette, for example, is seen as a small gray rectangle against the larger gray rectangle formed by the seat. Aesthetics and heightened thematics seem to be merging here. It is as if three seemingly contrary movements occur at once: an expansion, a contraction (the repetitions from Part II), and a paralleling (Part III's equivalent to the natural aesthetic shots of Part I). There are also two new stimuli: besides the creak of the door, the sound of rain and the "fact" that it is night outside. In addition, some "new" elements are only seemingly so: for example, some of the pictures of earlier parts are repeated, though at a different camera position. We are, surely, in the most inclusive of the three parts; the fact that things are real—that F is a real man—is perhaps less important than that things, real or ghosts or illusions of reality, achieve a larger meaning, even a mystery in Part III's complex pattern of repetition, reversal, and expansion. The camera has achieved a new significance; what it sees—in what order, at what angle, and at what distance—is now "half" the play, revitalizing the otherwise "familiar" (I reintroduce one of the first words in *Ghost Trio*).

All these changes culminate in shot 24, where F, at the head of the pallet and staring into the mirror, sees nothing; more properly, the audience sees no reflection in that mirror. All that exists is a small gray rectangle (with the same dimensions as the cassette) set against the larger rectangle formed by the wall. It is all ghosts, and F is the chief among them. Beckett has, in one sense, pushed to the limit our familiar world, a world of rooms and corridors, of pallets, mirrors, and cassettes, and made it as unfamiliar as if we were in limbo with spirits of the dead. His art has "redone," reconsidered the ordinary, in this productive tension between thematics and aesthetics, between our world and the artistic medium.

We will recall the engraver in *Endgame,* who looked into his art and saw nothing, or the contrasting example in *Film,* when O (object) and E (viewer or artist) were shown simultaneously. Perhaps *Ghost Trio* goes beyond the visually oriented film, that exercise in actual, physical seeing, and at the same time goes beyond the verbally oriented plays. With the visual and verbal so balanced, with sounds here embracing the gamut from doors creaking and rain falling to human voices to music, and with the visual going from familiar things to aesthetic form built upon those familiar things to the dim sight—is it form or content, or both?—at the end of the corridor, Beckett has so balanced contraries that, if not in that world of nonbeing so sought after by his most perceptive and therefore anguished characters, we are at last in the limbo, the world of the just dead, of "forms" that are only the paradoxical forms of ghosts.

My opening observation was that this is Beckett's most inclusive play in *Ends and Odds;* but in those words of the circus barker, "You ain't seen nothing yet!" Suddenly the empty mirror is filled. At 27 we get a close-up of F's face in that mirror, eyes first closed, then opened, the head first bowed but then the top of the head seen in the mirror. The ghost is alive, or at least alive through that process by which art proffers illusions as life. The verbal "Ah" of Part II, when V saw F's face, is balanced here by the actual sight of that face. Furthermore, this parallel with Part II sets off the final and most drastic change in the play. Steps are heard approaching— and then a knock. The door's creak is now a *"Crescendo"* (p. 63). The outside, just hinted at when we saw the dark end of the corridor, now comes rushing in, in the form of a small boy. This is the boy who, the Unnamable knows, "does not often come," one who speaks "for his master," the "bright boy," also so described by Willie in *Happy Days*.[24] Perhaps his appearance represents some maturation on the man's part; we will recall that Knott, with eyes closed and asleep, makes sounds "like the breathing of a child."[25] With him the boy brings, literally, a touch of that fertile water—*"Dressed in black oilskin with hood glistening with rain"*—so often symbolizing creativity as well as death in Beckett. The dead world of the room—dead because it is only personal, dead because it is outside the flux of life itself, dead because it is solely the illusion of the artist—comes into contact with a world of life, in this mysterious mingling of youth and rain. The boy's white face—we will recall the white hands of the three women in *Come and Go*[26]—confronts F's, and then the boy shakes his head *"faintly."* Is that shake positive or negative? Is the boy's promise that Godot will appear a certainty or a put-off? The merging of the interior, dead, aesthetic world and the exterior, alive, thematic world only leads to a new uncertainty. Is the boy's appearance benign or malignant? Is the shake of the head a yes or a no? Similarly, in *Happy Days,* when Willie emerges from his hole at the end, does he plan to kiss or to murder Winnie?

The boy's appearance, which seems like a sudden, albeit unaccountable infusion of reality, is, of course, the ultimate illusion. The familiar room has grown mysterious, interior, and the otherwise innocent boy raises profound questions about what we have just seen. Is the room to be destroyed? Is it a limbo from which F cannot be released, at least not yet? Is the room so fragile that the normal hierarchy, which dictates that men are more significant than boys, is itself reversed? The confined play, bound by its sonata form, and by three camera variations about a small room—all this suddenly explodes.

This final segment ends quickly. The boy departs, slowly blending into the darkness at the corridor's end; the door creaks now in *"Decrescendo"* as the camera moves back to A. And then a change. The camera moves to a close-up of F's head, bowed down over the cassette, in the very position that

Krapp greets us at the beginning of his play. There is a silence—a Beckettian silence—and then F's head lifts; we see it clearly for ten seconds. Then back to position A and fade out. The three-part structure, "in three ratios like a sonata"[27] (opening theme, variation, and resolution), is thrown off by this coda, by the boy's appearance. Order begets disorder, aesthetics leads to thematics, familiarity only conceals mystery. Art, albeit carefully controlled through three distinct camera shots and confined to the familiar, still leads to the unexplainable. This most inclusive of the plays in *Ends and Odds*—with its echoes of *Godot, Endgame, Krapp's Last Tape,* and *Eh Joe*—also makes the most original use of old material. Its inclusiveness extends, therefore, not only to its cross-references to Beckett's earlier work but also to its own ending, raising questions that go unanswered. *Ghost Trio* seems to embrace the two functions of art as practiced in Beckett: an examination of our inner state (the highest achievement of his art) and a voyage without resolution into the world beyond our external reality.

v

*Theater I*

*Theater I*, the first of four "*Odds*" in this collection, is an *Endgame* with a difference. Like Hamm, B is confined to a wheelchair, although he is a bit more mobile (he can propel himself with a pole, albeit with difficulty). In his eagerness to have A's friendship, B seems a little less imperious than his dramatic "predecessor," though it is no less true that Hamm courted Clov, if only to get the painkiller that, ironically, never arrived. A is mobile like Clov, yet also blind like Hamm and more of B's equal than Clov was for Hamm. This latter resemblance between A and Hamm is strengthened when we recall that Clov himself began to imitate Hamm late in that play, though doing so over his master's protests. The parallels with the earlier play may serve as a clue to what is happening here or, more properly, what fails to happen.

The apparent balance between A and B (vision/blindness; mobility/immobility) falls apart because the distribution is both unequal and inconsistent, and this paradox is reflected in the dialogue itself. A asks, "Is it day or night?," but the simple dichotomy is complicated by B's response, "day, if you like" (p. 72). There is something of a prelude here in which the desired union, the merging of complementary forces, is achieved. B wheels onstage, having heard music, and he even speculates that what he hears is some sort of "dream" or "vision." However, it is not a dream but, literally, the music from A's fiddle. This insignificant mystery solved, B tries to "join together" with A. In B's words "the mystery is over," but a second mystery is still possible if they can "join together and live together, till death ensue" (p. 71).

Complicating the union, however, is the contradiction within each character, for each is not so clear-cut as the names A and B would suggest. B seems to be, in one sense, the more physical creature, or at least the half able to see the outside world. A is not only blind but also without a sense of smell—and this latter fact concerns B. At the same time B seems to be the intellectual, asking A at one point if he can "follow my reasoning?" (p. 72), at another point speculating in Beckett's mock-rationalist fashion about the "problem" posed by his inability to do an about-turn in the wheelchair. If he can only go forward, should he go round the world to get home? Even as B sarcastically asks A if his dialogue is too much for his wits, he hopes that A will be able to push him as "far as the corner when I went out of my mind" (p. 73). Like A, B is also in darkness most of the day, or at least for twenty-three out of the twenty-four hours when he sits "in my lair, in my chair, in the dark" (p. 74). If he is the physical half along with being the rational half, it is also true one of his feet has been amputated. B is a mass of contradictions, not only when measured against A but also when matched against his prototypes in earlier Beckett works. He may seem as much like Pozzo as Hamm, dominant, the aggressor, even imitating Pozzo's condescending attempt to mingle with his fellow humans, "with my species" (p. 76), and lamenting the fact that if he loses A he'll "never see anymore again . . . never hear the human voice again." On the other hand, A is not a clear Lucky. Therefore, one possibility is that, given the contradictions in B, not to mention what we might find when we examine A, Beckett may be trying not so much to join the complementary halves of a single being—as he does with Vladimir and Estragon—as to reassemble a single being whose split in personality and physicality has itself not been a clean one.[28]

If anything, A in his need for food seems even more rooted to the physical than B. That food includes everything from tinned food to corned beef to baked beans to a sack of nuts. From B, A needs physical verification, a sense of his surroundings: "Where am I? *(Pause.)* Where was I?" (p. 76). Later he has a curious dialogue with B when B urges him to go. When A refuses, B demands a reason, and that reason is the simple "I can't go without my things." These things—are they objects, or the physical voices that A constantly hears?—are of no "good" to A and yet he cannot go without them. Then he states the paradox: he will either find them in the end, or—after a pause—"leave them forever behind me" (p. 76).

There seems to be a curious link between voices and things, and this leads to the possibility that for all his addiction to food and to physical verification, A's sense of things not only embraces the physical, but also includes voices not fully present and therefore unheard by B. Indeed, of the two A may be more the artist, a foil to B's logician. For A describes himself as "scratching an old jangle to the four winds," the sort of self-deprecating portrait of the artist typical of Beckett. Besides, A is the more solitary, initially denying that he even has had a woman companion. He also has the pessimism of Beckett's artist. To B's "But you must be every day a little more so" (that is, a little more unhappy), A responds violently

that he is "not unhappy enough!" (p. 74). Like some eternal principle, like
the primal artist, A has always been this way, beyond or perhaps below
change: "I was always as I am." A begins the play in the ruins—like the
character in *That Time*—blind, sitting on a folding stool, scraping his fiddle.
His first movement, beyond the fiddle, is to turn his head *"audience right."*
B, at A's second turning right, enters from stage-right, the suggestion here
being that B is the audience for A the artist. Yet once again, any comparisons of qualities between the two are complicated: A may be more like
Hamm than B, and B's sense of logic and order may recall Clov's. A is
perhaps the blind artist of inner vision, singing to a crippled world, the
source of its weakness being precisely its addiction to what is external. The
prelude, where A's playing solved B's mystery, goes in the wrong direction:
the play proper only underscores the incompatibility between this particular artist and this particular audience of one.

A is eager for the night to put an end to his singing and playing: the
commercial dimension of his art, the need for its acceptance by an audience, by B or whomever comes along, is his weak spot. Dora—his mother,
rather than a woman friend?—used to urge him to crawl on all fours with a
cup about his neck, displaying his father's war medals pinned to his rear, a
touch of theater designed not to promote vision but to wring hearts toward
charity. Yet A's fiddle-playing—earlier there was a harp—is for less commercial reasons. Like Henry, he may play to drown out the voices he hears;
like all of Beckett's artists he may try to communicate a vision, an inner one
to be sure, unsold and unacceptable to the public, even the wretched audi-
ence-of-one that greets him in the present day. A, however, seeks neither
commercial nor artistic success, but a stillness, the reward of an evening
and its exterior darkness matching his own inner darkness, his lack of sight,
and his pervasive pessimism.[29] Still, B seeks a union of the two, a friendship
in which their infirmities will be complementary. That same union is frustrated by the tremendous divisions, even as there are tremendous overlap-
pings, between the two characters.

In aesthetic terms we might think of B as the deductive, possibly even
"mechanical" artist, the artist as both observer of the exterior world and its
arranger, putting the scattered observations of his vision into form.[30] Thus
A may be the private side of the artist, one given to feelings (A tells us that
he can "feel" the twilight) rather than deduction, one who hears voices
beyond the normal limits of hearing. We are back to the debate in *Cascando*:
does the artist simply record outside stimuli, or does his vision come from
within? Or do both happen simultaneously, with a balance that is itself
beyond detection or measurement? The two halves may naturally complement each other. In another schema, we may have art as visual (B) and art
as verbal (A), or the combined arts of television (B) and of radio (A), or the
twin dimensions of television and of radio art (the visual existing with the
verbal, even if that visual in radio must be an illusion sustained in the
imaginative mind of the listener).

Whatever the allegorical connections we may choose to make, it is the tensions, rather than any complementarity between A and B, that generate the "life" of the present play. Perhaps "conflict" may be the more accurate word, for despite B's attempts to unite with A, their fledgling relationship degenerates as the play progresses: B fights with A when the latter becomes too excited over a "gift" in the road; they disagree about a woman, about the *anima's* influence; they argue over the significance of the "steps" that A hears, and about their separate states of unhappiness; at one point B strikes A with his pole; they disagree over the significance of "things"; and after a while A proves an embarrassment to B when he insists on resting his head on B's knees.

The irony is that A and B are also complementary; each contains within himself qualities found in the other. Still, they fail as mates in a way that parallels the curious love/hate relationship of Hamm and Clov in *Endgame*. The pattern here is also unlike that in *Endgame* because neither A nor B succeeds on the purely aesthetic level, as does Hamm when he dons his stauncher at the end. Nor is there the balance between the physical and the aesthetic that there is in *Happy Days,* despite the possibility of violence at the end when Willie emerges. The play, befitting the title of the collection, is about "odds," misfits, and misfittings.

The ending is replete with metadramatic imagery. A is alive to sounds, although sounds unheard by B. Ironically in this visual-verbal theater it is the blind A who grasps a dimension of the play beyond B, even as the women in *Come and Go* deliver dialogue unheard by the audience. With A's mention of sounds, B responds with "I can see it." The characters now seem farther apart than ever, yet in "seeing" sounds, B is not still and his movement disturbs A, who now implores him to hear those unheard sounds.

Suddenly B's sight becomes materialistic: he sees the harp on a stool some distance from A. Now the sighted B attacks A, trying to reduce him from harp to fiddle to mouth organ to a solitary voice. The twins are in contention, far beyond the slight argument between Words and Music that was later resolved. Verbal attacks visual as A whirls round and seizes the end of B's pole, wrenching it from his grasp. *"Eh Joe"* becomes B's sardonic "Eh Billy," and instead of the peaceful tableau that closes *Endgame,* or the implied tableau at the end of *Words and Music, Theater I* ends with a vicious taunting of B by A, and with A's drastic action with B's pole.

*Theater I* is the theater coming apart. In this sense it stands as devil's advocate to the movement within aesthetic dimensions that characterized *Footfalls,* or the productive, albeit tense and mysterious union between aesthetics and thematics in the final moment of *Ghost Trio.* It reveals Beckett's familiar pattern, the pairing of partially complementary halves. The delicate balance fails; perhaps it is because the artist is absent, or in the wings, or because the audience is isolated, not asked to participate as they are in *Play* or in *Come and Go.*

*Theater II*

With *Theater II* it would be natural to consider the play along with Pinter's *Birthday Party* for, like Pinter's own *Everyman*, it treats the summing up of a life before death. Perhaps the play may also be seen as a turnabout on *Embers, Words and Music, Krapp's Last Tape*, and *Cascando*, for here the characters, Beckett's familiar A and B, review the author. As such, it is both light-hearted—indeed, parodic—and serious. Like *Ghost Trio, Theater II* also "reviews" the issues and imitates the dramatic structure of a host of Beckett's works in other media. We might think of it as Beckett's version of Yeats's "The Circus Animals' Desertion."

The most direct "clue" that we can take the play as biographical, if not autobiographical, is found in a brief reference buried amidst the large and small details of C's life: "literary aspirations incompletely stifled" (p. 90). By this curiously negative phrase we may infer that C did produce a literary work or works, though not of high quality. Krapp, we recall, is also an artist of very limited success, as is Malone.

Along with this reference there are two other major authorial identifications. After much effort to recall the exact quote from the "Confidences" of C, we learn that he was "morbidly sensitive to the opinions of others," as long as those opinions entered his awareness, whether for pleasure or for pain. C's goal, so informed, was "truth to tell," though the curious phrasing, "truth to tell," leads B to ask where the verb is. The revelation is capped with a serious qualification: "incapable." The process of receiving stimuli from the outside world, whether pleasurable or painful, and then of giving them the form of truth was aborted. The artist is here portrayed not as young man but as failure.

The second direct revelation is that C had a pathological fear of songbirds; we will recall Winnie's distaste for solitary birds singing to themselves and her own pathological need for an audience, even if it be that unpromising audience of one, Willie. Songbirds may suggest the ancient notion of the artist as the solitary singer, penning verses about the mysterious. Surely, this is not Beckett's style, and surely not the portrait of the artist in C's case. Besides, as B adds, C has had throat troubles: his art is of a coarser nature. The irony is that there *is* a songbird in *Theater II*, the male finch who goes on singing after his mate has died. As A comments sardonically: "And to think all that is organic waste! All that splendour!" (p. 100).

There is also a comic portrait of the artist or observer in *Theater II*. B reads the testimony of a Mr. Feckman—a name close to the Feckham mentioned in Lucky's diatribe in *Godot*—who describes seeing C sitting Belacqua-like outside the Post Office (one of the haunts of the character in *That Time*): on one of the bollards hung with chains, doubled in two, hands on his knees, legs astraddle, head sunk—like F in *Ghost Trio*. The initial impression that C was vomiting proved incorrect; rather, he was staring at a lump of dogshit. We will recall the dog in *Krapp's Last Tape* with his black ball—whether plaything or excrement is never certain. When Mr. Feckman moved the lump, C followed it intently, as if it contained the secret of the universe; Feckman in pity then slipped a lottery ticket into C's pocket, a winning ticket as it turned out, and therefore the one positive fact in C's life. "I wonder sometimes if he is still alive," Mr. Feckman concludes (p. 90).

The details now begin to flesh out the portrait. C had an inexhaustible reservoir of sorrow (p. 87), an intellect that remembered only the calamities of history: when plied with drink, he would talk so pessimistically about life that such conversation in his cups inspired a theatrical skit that, we are informed, "went down well." C himself sprang from a family who preserved tears, cherishing sorrow, disdaining joy to the extent that their sorrow seemed like a "corrosive." And all this from Mrs. Darcy-Croker, a person of letters, no less.

The scene has all the earmarks of the clinical examination in *Radio II*, and the light that goes on and off, much to the distraction of the examiners, seems a parody of the penetrating interrogation light in *Play*.[31] Even this light, in this "light" play, degenerates to a match—Portia's affirmative candle superimposed over Macbeth's extinguished light of heaven. There is, I think, a certain difficulty of tone here, for the parody, indeed the mockery of the artist, seems to conflict not with anything in the play proper but with the vestige of a more serious play. *Theater II* also seems to depend on echoes from Beckett's other works. The light recalls and parodies the light in *Play;* the two examiners, superior to the artist, have some parallel to the characters in *Words and Music* who surpass Croak, their creator or director. As in *Embers*, what may be interior voices are made manifest here. The examined life is also the theme of *Cascando*, as is the movement toward death, self-imposed or imposed externally. In their mannerisms A and B are similar to the two characters in *Act Without Words II*, or *Mercier and Camier*. Beyond this, *Theater II* reestablishes the formula of *Eh Joe*, or *That Time*, or *Not I*, with the object of the inquiry silent, reduced to a simple mime (here the movement is even more minimal than the shrugs of the Auditor in *Not I*).

But there is a second story here, an overplot, that threatens to overwhelm the examination of C. Indeed, it may be that C, under the guise of being the examined, is actually examining the examiners; A and B may be on trial without knowing it.[32] For in the course of the play they change from confident detectives to neurotics (certainly in B's case). At the very least, their own desires and frustrations threaten to obscure their mission, in much the same way that Moran loses perspective on his mission to find Molloy, as his own personal tragedy becomes the focus of the search and as he seems to merge with the very character he seeks.

Ironically, A and B begin in complete control of the situation, businesslike, eager for the job to be completed. The stage itself reflects this initial sense of order: the two tables are *"equidistant"* (p. 83) from the wall and the axis of the window, one *"forming symmetry"* with the other. The symmetry, it is true, is thrown off a bit—and we have seen this mischievous asymmetry elsewhere in Beckett—by the fact that one table has a briefcase crammed with documents while the other is bare. Given our minimal levels of expectation, this is significant, or at least disconcerting. Their conversation itself is brusque ("Let him jump"),[33] and the summaries and testimonies of C's life are delivered as if they were routine evidence at a trial: "Work, family, third fatherland, cunt, finances, art and nature," and so on (p. 85). In B's wonderful phrase, the evidence, the details of the case against C, are "tied together like a cathedral" (p. 85). Yet there are also other disconcerting elements, such as the examiners' concern for irrelevancies—"Is that Jupiter we see?"—in the midst of presenting the negative and then the positive aspects of C's biography.

When the business is finished, all is not finished, and it is the introduction of C's own writings, his "Confidences" (p. 91), that drives the play and its examiners beyond these routines or irrelevancies. The light now refuses to "cooperate," and A and B are increasingly absorbed with the mechanics of keeping it lit. As C himself fades from their focus while they are discussing the most intimate details of his life, A and B develop recognizable personalities, much like Estragon and Vladimir. It is not until the play has been in progress for some time that we learn their names, Bertrand (p. 88) and Morvan (p. 92). Now it is B who needs some "animal warmth," though A's chilling "As you like" is hardly encouraging (p. 93). B wants to sit beside A and, after being rebuffed, asks if he can sit opposite him. Even A, though hardly warming to B, wants to "go to bed," to get the job done and be home. B's nerves are on edge and he wishes he were "only twenty years younger" so that he could put "an end to [his] sufferings" (p. 93). Who is on trial here? And could it be that C, like some conductor with his back turned to the two players, is, in reality, directing them?

This countermovement in which the personalities of the investigators take center-stage is itself interrupted by a "*Feeble*" and then a "*Second miaow, louder.*" We may think of similar distractions elsewhere in Beckett: the lawnmower in *Play,* the emmet in *Happy Days,* the flea in *Endgame*—those moments when the character's own carefully narrowed world cannot exclude the world outside, however insignificant it may be. The intrusion, large or small, symbolic or only literal, destroys the internal order; the asymmetrical table with the briefcase was therefore a prelude for what we—along with A and B—are now experiencing. The cat's interruption is itself interrupted by A's digression about the "big fat redhead" (p. 98), one of those "unfortunates" who had been a client in the past. The digression leads to the final and most drastic interruption: the bird's song and the discovery that one of the finches is dead.[34] The bird's song concerns not life but the death of a mate. Or it may be the hen's own final song—a parallel to *Happy Days* when Willie advances on Winnie as she sings the chorus from *The Merry Widow.* The dead bird itself threatens to usurp attention otherwise given to the examiners' discussion about C's own imminent death. The bird dies; there is nothing that can be done on this score. The question is:

can something be done for or to C? Even A threatens to jump out the window when pestered by B about the bird. He then returns both examiners to their mission with the cryptic "How end?" (p. 101).

The play itself ends in mystery—or in possibilities. A strikes a match and inspects C's face, calling B to share his discovery: "Hi! Take a look at this!" But B does not move. A strikes another match, with even more anxiety: "Come on! Quick!" Again B does not move. A's imploring is capped with "Well I'll be," a line that might refer just as easily to his frustration with B as to his surprise at whatever he sees on C's face. Then, with echoes of *Endgame*, A takes out a hankerchief and raises it "*timidly*" to C's face. C's pose before the window itself has potentially significant parallels elsewhere in Beckett. In *Fizzles* the character gazes "before the window" with "all quiet still head in hand listening for a sound."[35] Malone found the window "an umbilicus" and was also, like C, one who studied the stars.[36] In *Theater II*, it should be noted, we "progress" from electric light to candles to matches to starlight. The narrator of "The Expelled" tells us that stars were the "first lights" he knew.[37]

Has C been dead all the time, and is the handkerchief an example of courtesy in covering the dead—a shroud? Or is A wiping off a tear, the otherwise pathetic C at last taking on the dignity of weeping? Or is C, who seemed to have no commitments in his life, here showing sympathy for the dead song-bird, despite his pathology? Why, however, is the handkerchief raised "*timidly*," and by A, the more dispassionate of the two examiners? Or has C been working all the time, directing the scene for two beings who only thought they were in control? Is A timidly wiping the perspiring face of his now-acknowledged master? Is the increasing humanity of the examiners, who otherwise began like calculating machines, now matched by the dim, death's-door humanity of this otherwise Belacqua-like C? Has the decision for this Rosencrantz and Guildenstern already been made for them? Is the play's pattern meant to fall into three parts: the dispassionate review of the evidence, the secondary plot and the distraction from the mission, and at last the revelation that the mission itself was futile? Is this biography of the playwright/artist suddenly on the level of autobiography? Are the controllers—the Pozzos of this world—at length the fools, their mission an irrelevant one?

If the play starts like Pinter's *The Birthday Party*, perhaps it ends more like his *Dumb Waiter*, where the hired assassins themselves assume the role of victim. Perhaps A's difficult "How end?" places the burden ultimately not on himself or his companion, but on the audience. If during his life C failed to communicate, as a person or as an artist, does this last-minute communication, the facial expression that causes A to use his handkerchief, also represent a failure? With A, and also with B, who is farther removed on the stage? With us, even farther removed in the audience? However absurd he was in life, the traitorous first Thane of Cawdor in Shakespeare's *Macbeth* achieved at his death a limited dignity founded on confession and resignation. Perhaps C's end bears a certain parallel. "Nothing in his life /

Became him like the leaving it. He died / As one that had been studied in his death, / To throw away the dearest thing he owned / As 'twere a careless trifle" (1.4.7–11).

**vii**

*Radio I*

*Radio I* is a miniature play in two acts divided by "*Sound of curtains violently drawn, first one, then the other, clatter of heavy rings along the rods*" (p. 110)—a "discovery" if there ever was one. It is also something of a schizophrenic play, with the artist, "He," initially showing a confident public façade and then the neurotic private side of his personality.

In part one "She," clearly the audience, is treated cooly by "He": he has "suffered" her to come since this is his way of meeting his "debts." It is a minimal theater he offers her: no comforts, no heat, no light (with double implications, surely), no adjustments in the volume. And rather cryptic conversation: "SHE (astonished): But he is alone! / HE: Yes. / SHE: All alone? / HE: When one is alone one is all alone" (p. 107).

The two ingredients of his art are Voice and Music, familiar from the early radio play, *Words and Music*. The two are eternal, "without cease," and they can be activated easily with a turn of a dial—radio here serving meta-dramatically for the medium. Even silence is included in this omnipresent art, though it is crudely defined by "He" as a "need" (p. 109). As audience "She" is full of both uncertainties and questions. His art, she finds, is beyond comprehension, and therefore "unthinkable" and "unimaginable." Though she plies "He" with questions, no answers are forthcoming. The public posture of the artist is either so mysterious or so pervaded by an air of confidence that the audience, "She," is made to feel inferior. "He" mean-while seems even less of an Opener and more of a caretaker.

The artist's indifference is challenged only by the woman's repeated observation, "How troubled you look" (p. 106), yet even this fails to pene-trate his resolve. The encounter with the audience ends with one final stab at conversation on her part: "Is that a Turkoman?" (p. 109). We will recall other "mysterious" irrelevancies in *Ends and Odds*. To her question "He" replies rather condescendingly: "To the right, Madam, that's the garbage," and then with "*faint stress*," the "*house* garbage" (p. 109).

With the drawing of the curtains and the signal for the start of the second act, the play changes radically. We hear the artist, alone with his companions, frantically trying to contact a doctor but only reaching his assistant. The character "He" now has a name, Mr. Macgillycuddy, and Macgillycuddy's tone is a combination of impatience and subservience as he tries to bring the "urgent" condition of his Voice and Music to the absent doctor's attention, while his artistic tools continue to grow fainter and—presumably—weaker. The assistant's response is not comforting: "nothing

what? . . . to be done?" (p. 111). And Macgillycuddy is alarmed by the fact
that even though his Voice and Music are "ENDING," they are also coming
"TOGETHER." As in the play *Words and Music,* the tools are assuming a
life and now a relationship of their own. Abandoned already by "She" (the
audience) from the first part, Macgillycuddy is about to be abandoned by
the tools of his craft: "haven't they all left me?"

The dialogue with the assistant is teasingly minimal, especially for radio.
There are references to his Voice and Music being "all alike" (the eternal
principles of aesthetics, perhaps?), to "last what?" (rites?), and to the fact
that their togetherness is marked by a single "breathing." Against a background in which Macgillycuddy's companions are *"together, failing,"* the
doctor's assistant advises "confinement" or rather "two confinements," and
then, after some hesitation, one "breech," all of this accompanied by even
fainter sounds from Voice and Music.[38] The dramaticule now ends, though
whether with hope or despair we are uncertain, since only a *"whisper"* is
called for in Beckett's stage directions, with "He" saying merely "Tomorrow . . . noon. . . ." We will recall a similar line at the end of *Embers,* where
the plumber's coming tomorrow signaled the emptiness of the Bolton-
Holloway relationship.

The play is puzzling; part of that puzzle may come from its own skeletal
content. Nevertheless, if *Radio I* is in a line of descent from *Words and Music*
or even *Cascando,* then it concerns the public and private dimensions of the
artist, and the artist's relationship to the tools of his craft. What is alternately intriguing or frustrating is that such aesthetic allegory is couched in
peculiarly human terms: the attempts by "She" to be cordial, the all-too-
human frustrations of "He," the simple human interaction of a visit or a
phone call.

On a more thematic level the radio play suggests the dichotomy between
onstage and offstage, the performance and the background (the techniques, tools, rehearsals, preparations) for that performance. The su-
premely confident artist is still totally dependent on Voice and Music, and
they are slippery, elastic, highly perishable "beings." The doctor, appealed
to as some sort of show-saving Godot, promises nothing; indeed, he begins
his diagnosis at the most pessimistic level. Beckett, obsessed as much as
most artists, and more, with his relationship to his craft, with the too easily
exhaustible reservoir of his own talents, may comment here on his own
public statements about the futility of art, about its inherent difficulty,
about the silence—the death—that threatens it. If art is a form, and thereby
like those other despised conceptual forms or systems in life, then the form
here perishes once it comes into contact with *Murphy*'s formless dark zone.
Radio seems an especially appropriate medium, for the failure of sound
and the looming silence are the bottom line: there is no visuality, no slapstick as in *Godot,* no physical counterpoint to the wordy hero, as in *Endgame,*
on which to fall back. The audience needs the artist, but the artist also
needs—"It has become a need, Madam"—tools that are all too easily lost, or
that fade with time.

Some critics would prefer to see Beckett's entire career in the theater as a decline from *Godot*, on the assumption that all that could be *said* was said in that first play. Conversely, his movement from the legitimate theater to radio and then to film and television may be seen more positively as an experiment with the different yet related tools of the four media, with the words and music, not to mention the sights, that receive a different emphasis as one moves from *Godot* to *Cascando* to *Eh Joe* to *Film*.

Perception is relative: how much do we see and what are we to do with the objects of our sense? Are the boots in *Godot* proof that the characters existed, at least as far back as Act I? Hearing is also relative: is the voice outside or is it within? Either way there are problems of meaning. Why do artists fail? Or to what degree does the work of art succeed only with the creator? How private and how public can art be? Is *Godot* nothing more than the voiced doubts of its creator? Given Beckett's plurality, or his sense of meaninglessness, what ends do words, bearers of meanings, serve anyway? Is there a relationship between aesthetics and meanings? Does the medium control the message, beyond whatever meanings we, artist and/or audience, assign to the creation? Does art, its aesthetics, have a life of its own, a meaning that is present even before the artist himself approaches his materials or tools? Or is art, the most subtle and creative of forms, for that very reason the most perishable when it contemplates that "dark" zone where there is only the ultimately significant flux that opposes forms, no matter how complex or well-intentioned they may be?

## viii

*Radio II*

In some ways *Radio II* is an expansion of *Radio I*.[39] It raises the same questions but still provides no clear answers, except by its own sometimes complicated example. What does the relationship between the artist and his tools mean? What is the "futility" of art? What is art's goal? And—most especially in the present play—what is the relationship between the artist and his subject matter or—paralleling *Cascando*—the artist and his story?

At the start, A, the Animator, is in charge of the situation, much like "He" of *Radio I*, Croak of *Words and Music*, or Henry of *Embers*. He checks out S, the secretary, like a pilot checking out cockpit controls before a flight, even adding a sexual innuendo: "Good shape?" (p. 16). At the same time he relies on Dick, the silent "actor" in this radio drama, to force dialogue from Fox, his subject, by means of his bull's pizzle. At first hooded, Fox is unfrocked, and polite comments pass between boss and secretary on his "ravishing" face, all of this accompanied by the "*Swish and formidable thud*" of Dick's instrument. Fox then wakes up, and his "radiant" smile raises the issue of whether S should record his physical expressions and body movements—along with the sought-after words: A wavers between "the words alone" and "I don't know, Miss. Depending perhaps."

The play now launches into Fox's examination, though the role of examiner and examined will become confused. That examination begins rather mechanically, with A urging S to skip over the technical and thereby irrelevant matters, although he does have her read the exhortations that draw a fairly clear line as to what should and should not be recorded: one, animal cries are irrelevant; but, two, a literal transcript is a necessity; three, the subject should be fully neutralized. There is a fourth exhortation, yet it remains unstated. The atmosphere is comically clinical here, as if Fox's mental anatomy, which may be revealed by the slightest word, could be educed by the same procedures appropriate for a routine physical exam.

Yesterday's material is rehashed, a little story, apparently told by Fox, about washing a mole and drying him before a fire while a blizzard raged outside. The details are close to those in the Bolton-Holloway story in *Embers,* including a reference to "embers" (p. 118). However, the material produced is unpromising; indeed, the issue of the examination is obscured by A's flirtation with S, as S sheds her overalls and A, barely suppressing his desires, wishes he were "forty years younger" (p. 119). S meanwhile is strangely moved by Fox's exclamation recorded in her notes, "Ah my God my God."

Suddenly Fox speaks; what he says almost seems borrowed from *Krapp's Last Tape.* He tells of a moment by the sea when for the first and only time he felt something of the majesty of existence: "Ah yes, that for sure, live I did, no denying, all stones all sides—" (p. 119). The word "live" is new to Fox's vocabulary and therefore represents a "turn" (to use A's jargon). Fox's "allusion to a life" (allusions "not common" but also "not rare" [p. 119]) is the first time that the subject asserts himself, threatening his master's authority, a situation we have seen several times in Beckett's works for various media. In response to Fox's demands for freedom, for wanting "walls no further," A quickly invokes Dante's *Purgatorio,* holding out the possibility of future change (change in Fox? change in A's investigation?), of "shall be," of the future that A prefers to the past ("I was"). S is no help here: she has not read the *Purgatorio* and only flipped through the *Inferno*—a much more closed world.

Fox is now alive, and A, bending to the pressure, agrees with S, after some disagreement, that kindness might help in eliciting more from the subject. Reacting to this change in policy, Fox bursts forth with a paragraph of sustained prose, speaking of some place, a promontory, where one's gaze is not inhibited, where man's own stature is dwarfed by the immensity of the scene ("little lichens of my little span, living dead in the stones" [p. 121]). The expanse widens: the Coleridge-like "tunnels" going beyond sight, oceans vast, places where "ways end," farewells and endings that also anticipate new journeys. The outburst, like Lucky's in *Godot,* is stifled, this time with a crack from A's ruler. The artist as imaginative "sayer" (Fox) threatens to escape from the artist as clinical-rationalist (A). However, Fox is not quieted as he recounts the seasons, "down in Spring, up in Fall"; A reacts feebly with the critic's "Nicely put!"

Fox persists, and what he now says, almost none of which has been anticipated in his earlier statements, disturbs A. He speaks of a brother, a *doppelganger,* inside him, his "old twin" and the half that he wished to be. That twin holds him back, making demands for food that are impossible to meet without killing Fox himself. Now a little story begins to fashion itself through Fox's testimony. A woman named Maud—we will think perhaps of Tennyson's Maud—proposes that Fox be opened up so that if the twin is still alive he can be breast-fed, a desperate but humane feeding to be contrasted with the scientific "per buccam" or "per rectum" methods mentioned earlier in the laboratory agenda (p. 118). This revelation produces an unanticipated tear in Fox's eye, a "human trait . . . can one say in English" (p. 122). A appears to be the pedant here, drawing a parallel with the angel's tear mentioned in the works of Laurence Sterne, though he can find no parallel for Maud. It is a familiar situation in Beckett: the work, or the character in the work, takes on a life independent of the author, or has a history the surface of which the conscious author A has only tapped. Nevertheless, the story of Maud affects S, for she comments that her own nanny was named Maud, though this information is offered only to assure A that this is the first time Fox has made such a reference.

The story is "unthinkable" or "unimaginable," as the woman in *Radio I* says about the effects of art. A cannot explain it, especially the reference to mother, as if Fox could have no other "parent" than A. S supplies details: Maud is "in milk, what is more, or about to be" (p. 123). And there remains the tear, the "human trait," perhaps that much more startling if Fox has originated as some sort of Frankenstein monster created by A. A, ironically, would claim the twin inside Fox to be the "monster" (p. 123).

Disconcerted, A can only say feebly *("low, with emotion")*, "Can it be we near our goal" (p. 124). The question is: who is determining the goal? The Frankenstein monster threatens, surely, to overwhelm his creator. A reveals his nervousness by trying, a second time, to divert himself by flirting with S, even as he acknowledges that the goal of his inquiry is near. In addition, he berates her for not taking down Fox's words accurately.

Now A is more conciliatory to Fox, *"gently"* asking him to be "reasonable" and acknowledging that "it does not lie entirely with us, we know" (p. 125). The goal seems to be for Fox to say the one thing that will complete him, much as Woburn is urged, pushed, to make his way to the sea so that Voice can "say" and thereby complete him. A is reaching after silence—through Fox, through his creation. There is one "thing" that, if said, can "give you back your darling solitudes," and therefore the more one says the greater the statistical chance of reaching that solitude or silence. The Animator, however, stumbles in his own verbosity as he desperately tries to enhance his image in response to Fox's new posture: "Those micaceous schists, if you knew the effect *(snivel)* they can have on one, in the long run. *(Snivel.)* And your fauna! Those fodient rodents! *(Snivel)* You wouldn't have a handkerchief, Miss, you could lend me" (p. 125). A even confesses that he is unsure of just what they are after as he urges Fox to stop harping on old themes, and asks S to kiss him again for inspiration. The mood is frantic now as Fox howls when touched, with A demanding that S kiss his mouth till "it bleeds! . . . Suck his gullet!" (p. 126). A even admits the possibility of his own error: "Ah . . . perhaps I went too far" (p. 126). S now encourages him to play his role as animator; perhaps animator is a more accurate description for Beckett's present artist.

In some Jungian fashion, the character Fox has existed long before the time of his specific author.[40] Now A and S link Maud with the tear and then with the symbols of life, the milk and the breast. The character Fox seems to have roots not fully or consciously comprehended by the author, and he requires, therefore, an art beyond A's rational clinical efforts.

At last, in a pathetic and comic coda to the encounter, A tries to tack his own story onto these new materials provided by Fox: a story of incest in which Fox has "fecundated" the mother, Maud, with the twin thereby becoming at once Fox's child and brother. All this is said *"very excited"* (p. 127) as A forces S to add the phrase "between two kisses," so that Maud's proposal also becomes dialogue during love-making: " 'Have yourself opened, Maud would say, between two kisses, opened up, it's nothing, I'll give him suck if he's still alive, ah but no, no no' " (p. 128). In effect, A tries a shortcut by inserting his own shallow, conventional words into Fox's difficult, half-formed, but more profound narrative. S meanwhile is breaking under the strain, her pencil, like the artist's tool in *Radio I*, becoming *"Faint."* In addition, she weeps, affected by Fox's story and chafing under having to add to the dialogue as demanded by A.

The radio drama concludes with A's hope that "Tomorrow, who knows, we may be free." We will recall that *Radio I* ended similarly with "He" hoping that by "Tomorrow . . . noon" the doctor might effect a cure for the failing Voice and Music.

*Radio II* seems to be about the interdependence of the artist and his art and material, and in this way is closest to *Cascando*, where Woburn's liberation by the procreative sea of death was clearly connected with the liberation of Words, Opener, and Music. A struggles with his material, material that is put into shape by his efforts, but that also has a history predating him and a future that is not fully within his control. He tries to match his conscious control (his voluntary memory) with the "life" inherent in art and the artistic process (the involuntary memory), yet as "She" observes in *Radio I*—and as the second part of *Radio I* documents—there is an "unthinkable" and "unimaginable" dimension to art that resists such analysis and control.

ix

A Coda on *Breath*

If *Not I* celebrates the emergence of language, of the auditory dimension of the theater, then the play *Breath* elevates the visual.[41] The mime is purified even of humans: all that we see on stage is a pile of rubbish that in Beckett's words is "No verticals, all scattered and lying." Here is our final end, the ashbins overturned, for all that we really are is a handful of dust, some trash that has settled to the stage of life. Visually we witness the birth, life, and death of our humanity, of a civilization, of ourself. Yet nothing is final; the play begins not in darkness but in "minimum light" and ends not in darkness but in the same minimum light.

There are five sections, visual equivalents of the divisions in *Not I:* a five-second opening, with minimum light as we make out the debris littering the stage; a ten-second interval where, initiated by a cry (the birth cry, an "instant of recorded vagitus"[42]), the light goes to maximum; a five-second middle section in silence where, once the "inspiration" following the cry stops (the breath that is to be an amplified recording), we see in maximum light the image of our reality; then a fourth section, with expiration of breath, the lights going to the minimum, ended by a cry (the death cry); and a final five-second section, in silence. Before birth, birth, life, death, the silence of the grave—we have a visual tableau in which, lacking even the minimal humanity found elsewhere in ashbins, wheelchairs, or burial mounds, or in that humanity reduced to voices, man is compressed to cries of birth and death and represented only by his debris. In a way there is nothing ambiguous about the play. The statement is clearer than it has ever been in Beckett: there is a void, we are born, we live, we die, and all that we accomplish is to amass a small amount of rubbish. We are given a mirror image and see only what we are, or what the playwright imagines us to be.

Still, the rise and fall, the "horizontal" cynicism of the occasion, is relieved by the playfulness of the operating aesthetic. Beckett, it will be recalled, originally wrote the piece for the nude-review *Oh Calcutta!*. Fortunately, he turned down—predictably—the producer's suggestion that among the rubbish there be nude bodies. Besides being tasteless, this would have violated the increasing austerity, both in time and scale, allegorization and abstraction, of his dramatic pieces. No, the obviousness of stage techniques here, those mechanical regulations for the production, lend an artificiality to all we see. The breath is to be a recording, as is the cry; the intervals are five or ten seconds, no more and no less; the rubbish is to be as unobtrusive as possible; the symmetry of the presentation is to be obvious. The parody of the theater is to be equally so. A colleague tells me of two friends who traveled 300 miles to London to see the premier performance, expecting that *Breath* would be a full-length play.

*Breath* is Beckett's warning about silence, about our suicidal longing not to be, ultimately about our denial of our humanity. The Beckett heroes— and they are heroes in that they go on, persisting even if they don't understand—are all talkers. Vladimir and Estragon use small talk to wile away the time; Winnie is a torrent of phrases; the characters in *Play* repeat themselves; even O cannot silence himself in E. The radio characters have nothing but their dialogue, and, as Mrs. Rooney argues, without words we lose a sense, as do others, of our existence. In this perspective *Breath* is deliberately shallow, a warning that human life, always on the edge of meaning-lessness, is unredeemed unless we "say it." We win our right to death, to silence, even to being, by speaking to someone else, to an audience, at the very least to ourself. The narrator in *Not I* can't stop talking, and because of her pain the play ends positively, set to repeat the cycle from negativity to affirmation at the next performance.

*Breath* is a trifle that speaks to us by its own sacrifice. The Unnamable himself gives our span of life but five minutes "to be born, grow, languish, and die."[43] For those conversant with Beckett's dramatic productions, this may represent the unthinkable step, away from that balance between sight and sound, between fullness and suggestiveness, a play that violates the larger balance between the radio dramas and the mimes, between the elo-quently verbal stage plays and the eloquently visual *Film*. For those coming to the play for the first time, it seems to mock and thereby challenge the great plays of the medium. However, by showing what drama can become, what civilization is without communication, without the human voice and the complementary voice of the artist, *Breath* only points to what *should* be said, offstage and onstage, so that we may know ourselves, so that we may, in Beckett's phrase, say ourselves.

# 8  Beckett's Black Holes: Some Further Thoughts

i

From the open road of *Godot* to the room/womb of *A Piece of Monologue*, Beckett's world moves inexorably toward some inner space: *Godot*'s own seeming outdoors is only a ruse; and in this latest monologue (along with its companion pieces discussed at greater length in the appendix) the "black beyond" of the Speaker's "ghost room" is the true destination of Beckett's theaters. With no ultimate correlative in what passes as everyday reality, his is a world that can only be imagined. Like a black hole in space, Beckett's world is there but not "there" by any definitive measurements known to conventional physical science. A friend who has done some of the major research on black holes and found his existing vocabulary inadequate to define the phenomenon once justified his teaming up with a poet in these terms:

> My work as a physicist has always been with what "is," and so, for me, the dilemma in investigating black holes was how to speak of them in scientific language, or the only language I thought I had, geared as it is to what exists. How to describe this phenomenon whose invisibility, whose non-existence—if you will—stems precisely from the fact that mass is so concentrated that light, instead of reflecting what is there, is itself absorbed into that mass. And, of course, without light we cannot see, and seeing is both believing and therefore confirmation of what exists. My solution was to team up with a poet.

When I asked him why a poet, his reply was the simple:

> Well, you know, poets spend all their lives developing a vocabulary to describe what is beyond sight, mysterious—what is not "there" in the normal sense of the word. After all, a metaphor is an equivalent for something which, without the metaphor, could not be perceived—or at least not perceived as clearly.

I would suggest that the third zone, as described in *Murphy*, that arena of constantly moving forms with no correlatives in the real world, is Beckett's black hole. The issue for Beckett becomes how to "say" it with language and with the theater of the real world. His challenge, like that of my friend the physicist, is to find a more adequate vocabulary—a proper medium.

Black holes are still unknown, one of the final frontiers of science and science fiction. They bear a double-edged promise of both death and a new, altered life. Beckett's plays or Murphy's third zone entertain similar paradoxes, and may allow us to glimpse another world, always there, and not unrelated to our own, indeed an extension of our own that would perhaps dwarf all our previous conceptions of reality.[1] Beckett's trajectory spirals outward and inward, yet does not return. His work absorbs and concentrates itself, as does the mass of the black hole. As audience, we move from the roads, train stations, city streets, to the self, to the inner world. Nevertheless, this inner world is integral to a change of state, an inward consummation of our "normal" world. For Beckett was there all the time. The high roads thus lead nowhere in Beckett, as he centers his inquiry on man.[2]

Winnie in *Happy Days* tries to avoid the trajectory, opting for habit and its limited happiness. We do not fault her for this: the journey into the self is surely terrifying. A more substantial artist, Mrs. Rooney, is unafraid, but the cost of the final, imaginative symphony of the Rooneys as they make their way home is the death of a child, the killing off of the conventional world and of the theater as conventionally understood. Beckett first rejects the ordinary world and then embraces that world with a larger definition reached only after a perilous and brave journey through the black hole of the imagination. The process leads to a liberating moment of equipoise, when a character, while still in the ordinary, albeit rejected world, is aware of the inner world of himself that at once complements, challenges, and ultimately absorbs and compresses what he has previously taken as reality.

Such moments of equipoise are many in Beckett. For Winnie it is the future when "no further pains are possible," when she is caught between the heat of the day "when flesh melts at so many degrees" and the cold of the night when the "moon has so many hundred hours" (p. 18). For Hamm it is his final line, as he discards the trappings even of his self-centered world, throwing the gaff to the audience, placing the old stauncher over his head, leaving the challenge of living to those who "remain." Krapp's own intimation of that momentary equipoise occurs first at the sea's edge, when an entire life spent trying to deny the "dark" in himself is suddenly exposed, this prelude itself followed by his replaying that portion of the tape where he describes at once the perfect stillness of the lovers and the converse movement of the waters beneath as he floated in a punt, taking the final embrace of a soon-to-be-aborted love affair. Even Vladimir and Estragon achieve a modest victory when Vladimir's "pull on your trousers" holds the contradictory notions of pulling on one's pants or lifting them up, as the clowns themselves are equipoised between mobility and immobility.

## ii

The theater itself possesses this same equipoise. Literally "of" this world, with tangible sets and live actors, live in a way that literature itself cannot duplicate, the theater is also clearly "not of" this world: reality is compressed into an illusion of itself; nothing on stage is literal, and the language employed, while rooted in the immediate experience sustained by actor and audience, has a reference, a destination that is initiated by but not confined to the present. In a larger sense, words themselves are at once illusions, ultimately nothing.

Beckett has said of *That Time* that the play rests "on the very edge of what is possible in the theater,"[3] and the first thing we might infer here is that the play is too wordy: that given the almost still figure onstage bombarded by stereophonic sounds from the three offstage voices, we have something more akin to a dramatic reading, a Browning-like monologue delivered before an audience, rather than a play balancing the visual and the verbal. John Knowlson, however, cites a revealing holograph note from the playwright: "To the objection visual component too small, out of all proportion with aural, answer: make it smaller on the principle that less is more."[4] Is this not the very principle, compression and absorption, behind the black holes? The argument that sees Beckett as too verbal, or even too cerebral—the assumption being that verbosity is the first stage of an addiction leading to the cerebral—could apply, seemingly with greater logic, to the bodiless radio plays, or even to *A Piece of Monologue,* where a reductive judgment would be that we have in essence a radio play disguised as legitimate theater: there is, after all, minimal stage action and only one-and-half props, a *"standard lamp"* and only half a bed *("Just visible extreme right, same level, white foot of pallet bed").* But given the philosophic conflict that informs Beckett—a rejection of the external world and an attempt to "say" or picture onstage an internal world—it follows that in Beckett's theaters words themselves are the perfect "objective correlative." Again, I use that term in the affirmative but also paradoxical way that Eliot does when he defines the artist's task as giving form, temporary existence, to "mysteries" (of the mind, of the larger forces governing humanity) by taking words that have objective referents in the physical world and then pressing them into artistic service as signifiers for those mysteries which, without such artistic use of language, could not be known but rather only inarticulately felt.[5] If we narrowly define the physical-visual stage in terms of props, sets, and stage action, then, properly, "less is more" in Beckett, for the "almost" absence of the physical is perfectly in accord with Beckett's own discounting of the physical world, that seemingly substantial world championed by the Mr. Tylers, Mr. Slocums, and Mr. Barrells with their own pathetic objects: bikes (that work improperly), cars (that have trouble starting and then, once started, run over mother hens), and trains (that are late-arriving instruments of death).

The paradox of both words and the theater itself, then, may explain why the judgment that Beckett is too wordy or cerebral is misdirected. He makes an honest use of the physical stage, whether it be the minimal stage sets suggesting a shrunken world, the world left us after Hiroshima, or the more opulent physical world implied and then dissolved in the radio plays.

Given his own increasing concern with space, time, and physical movement, with that "choreography" of the play as meticulously documented by Ruby Cohn in her chapter "Beckett Directs" in *Just Play: Beckett's Theater*,[6] his is *preeminently* theater, in the most basic and the best sense of that word, a medium itself equiposed between the audience's eyes and ears.

Again, it is little wonder that both playwright and his characters are obsessed with words, and—what is more—obsessed metadramatically with them. One thinks immediately of Vladimir playing with *calm,* or of Mrs. Rooney struggling to use nothing but the simplest words with the people she meets, even as she is characterized by her husband, albeit fondly, as one given to a "dead language," or of Krapp playing with a series of words ("spool," "viduity," and so on). Not only are the radio plays all words, but with *Cascando* and then again with *Words and Music,* words themselves are personified. *Words and Music* itself ends with a sound, that "deep sigh" from Words produced by breath itself, the initiator of all speech. Otherwise a silent film, *Film* (which Beckett revealingly subtitles a "Film Script"), has a single sound, the "Shhh" uttered by the couple of "shabby gentility" that O meets on the street. As with the two mimes, here in the absence of words we as audience must supply the verbal commentary no less silently from our seats.

A common observation among those who describe Beckett and his plays is that in speaking about the desire for silence, the playwright avoids silence: as long as we talk about falling into the abyss, abandoning a discredited external world, we delay the final step, however wished-for it may be. At the end of his torrent of words the Unnamable concludes: "I can't go on," only to follow that negative with the positive, "I'll go on" (p. 414). That inner, silent state, the "Life in the Box,"[7] is Beckett's own frontier. We can come close to wordlessness in Beckett, but still we cannot abandon words. *Eh Joe* ends with the off-camera voice pronouncing only selected words loud enough for us to hear, but however peaceful she may be now that she has found a "greater" love, she cannot *not* speak. *Breath* demonstrates what happens when we do not speak, as it spans the gamut of human speech, initiated by the opening "vagitus" cry and closing with "expiration," when breath itself escapes from the dead body of the stage world. In this sense, sounds in Beckett are also semi-words; they are never mechanical, never random, never without the very meanings we would attribute to their richer relatives, words themselves. For those characters most involved with language, sounds bear no less meaning than actual words; this is surely true both for Mrs. Rooney, attuned as she is to the sounds of Arcady, and for Henry in *Embers.*

In the radio plays the audience supplies the physical correlative for the words, the stage set that can only be implied by the medium. Yet such involvement is not confined to the radio plays, for words are used in *Godot* to describe a god who is not physically present, and the most significant factor in Hamm's life, the boy who threatens to upstage the god, is described in radio fashion by Clov. Thus we fill out the seemingly meager visual tableaux of the legitimate theater plays, add unspoken commentary to the mimes, or join the words coming from offstage or off-camera with what we see in the television plays. We confront first the full figure of Joe closing out the external world from his room/womb and then, with successive camera moves, see less of the room and more of Joe until his own face usurps the screen and the words seem to come from his brain, though not his lips. Through this forced union of our mind's eye and the medium at hand we see the very world that is Beckett's impossible goal: that macrocosm, the internal world, inside that seeming microcosm, man himself.

### iii

Beckett's theater is both reflective and concentrated, for he uses the medium, the theater that most seems to mirror the external world, to explore an internal world that has had no correlatives. "What frustration!" as Malone or the Unnamable might say. But for Beckett, as well as for Fox in *Radio II,* who uses words in the same profound, albeit paradoxical sense, it cannot be otherwise. Little wonder that the Animator, an artist of meager, mechanical abilities, not only cannot understand Fox but feels compelled to alter his text so that it will be more "acceptable"—but to him, not to us.

Our experience of a play, *any play,* is a *process,* a sequence of dynamic, not static mirrors. The play becomes that static mirror only upon reflection after performance. Beckett's theaters pretend to be nothing more than process; his play has more in it of "be" than "mean." Our experience, whether as actor or audience, is temporal, sequential; our knowledge of the outcome or even of the meaning is a separate thing from the ongoing witness of a performance. A process does not explain but, at its best, can only duplicate or imitate, offering a constantly changing mirror for the otherwise unfathomable process of life itself. The radical Beckett may now seem very, very conservative; the unconventional becomes the conventional.

The continuum of his titles seems to address this very process: one is waiting for Godot but the wait is without end (many commentators have pointed out that a more literal translation would be "While Waiting for Godot"); *Endgame* does not disclose its final move, since Hamm is stilled at the close but not dead; *Happy Days* anticipates the next performance when, as if nothing had happened, Winnie will start anew, embedded this time not to her neck, as she is at the end of Act 2, but to her waist; *Play* would replay ad infinitum if the playwright had not called a merciful halt to the interrogation light; a fall is quite properly an ending, but the title *All That Fall* implies that even this ending continues from generation to generation; the dying coals of *Embers* are neither fire nor ash, life or death, but rather a processional state between the two. The theater ends only to start anew the next performance: Ionesco's stage directions at the close of *The Bald So-*

*prano* imply that with the next performance the Smiths and Joneses can start fresh by exchanging roles; Horatio promises to tell Fortinbras and the courtiers he assembles the very story we have just witnessed. And while we have a promise that Iago will be executed, he does not die within the confines of *Othello;* thus we may speculate that he represents a principle of evil, perhaps Coleridge's "motiveless malignancy," as eternal as is Desdemona's goodness, which Othello ratifies with his suicide, his own self-inflicted "ending." Process will inevitably fail to be compatible with the goal of the intellectual who assumes that intellection itself can resolve all. It is no surprise, therefore, that the pseudo-intellectual New Yorkers who answered the ad to see *Waiting for Godot* could no more bear the play than the tourists earlier at the Coconut Grove Playhouse.

The theater itself leads naturally to mystery, if only because mystery stands at loggerheads with resolution. One astute scholar-director has observed that the "open end-signs" of the theater practiced at the high level of a Shakespeare and a Beckett are antithetical to our notion of closure.[8] There are, accordingly, mysteries at the end of *Ghost Trio* that remain just that. Is the boy's shake of the head to be taken positively or negatively? is he himself benign or malignant? is the room to be destroyed? is it a limbo from which F cannot be released? at least not yet? Even a single, physical gesture begets such irresolution, such puzzlement: what is the tear in C's eye meant to signify in the closing moments of *Theater II*? and what precisely does A ask B to "take a look at"? Lear's own "Look there," as he bends over the dead body of his beloved Cordelia, is more a question than a statement: at what, precisely, are the onlookers, onstage and off, supposed to look?[9] Is Lear deluded? hopelessly insane? does he rather call attention to the image and hence "meaning" of Cordelia? does he have a vision of ecstasy, as A. C. Bradley has argued? or is he sanely and sadly announcing only the literal fact that she is dead and can "come no more"? The world reflected in Beckett is an internal one, but the ambiguity seems no less than if the world mirrored were in the public domain. Each involves a process caught in the form, rather than in content. Because process is nothing substantial, it engenders mysteries. The engraver in *Endgame* sees nothing in his art, and Beckett has argued that the playwright's impossible task is to write about nothing—as if it were something.[10]

The charge brought by the Puritans against the theater in Shakespeare's day was not just that it was immoral but also that the playwright, in emulating God's role, was a blasphemer trying to create *ex nihilo.*[11] To make something out of nothing. Yet we cannot bear nothing; we must impart order to process itself lest process be indistinguishable from or even lead to chaos. The theater, more than any other art form, seems to be something. Yet the play itself ultimately dissolves into process, that sequential order between its chronological parts contained in turn within the larger sequential order of successive performances: on Tuesday it comes and then goes, and then comes and goes again on Wednesday. Characters caught in the past, like Hamm's Nagg and Nell, alone get "closure" in the savage sense of closed ashbins—"Screw down the lids," Hamm instructs Clov (p. 24). For those for whom life is a process leading to a definite goal, like Pozzo, stage life can be cruel indeed. Winnie wants order, has a goal, the singing of her song, but she is also aware, however dimly, of a larger mystery that her ordered day cannot obscure: there is a revolver in her bag that mysteriously floats to the top, despite its weight. The migraines that Winnie suffers announce that she cannot live life through her closed system without discomfort.

iv

One ends as one begins, and my first observation in the *Godot* chapter was that, whatever else it is or is not, and whatever we "make" of Beckett's first professionally staged play, the play itself is a happening, a present collaboration among those waiting: be it the playwright himself who has confessed that if Godot had "come" for him, if he could "say" him, he could end his own waiting by not having to write the play; or Vladimir and Estragon who wait onstage; or the audience for whom the nonappearance of a divinity is no less a factor. This sense of the theater as a present-tense happening is eloquently captured by Knowlson in his comments on *Not I*. He suggests that the experience being observed by the audience, the Mouth spewing forth her story after a lifetime of silence, is "virtually synonymous with ᴛhe experience being narrated," and, further, that the "mind of the spectator outside the play, seeking to understand and explain what is going on, also has its echo within the drama in the form of the rational mind of Mouth, struggling to make sense of what is happening to it."[12]

This sense of a present-tense and parallel collaboration between actor and audience is at one with the pervasive, self-reflective, theatrical metaphors in Beckett, reminding us that both sides have roles in the production. Accordingly, Hamm's story—the past that has crippled him physically and visually, the parents with whom his relation has soured, the unwilling servant threatening revolt from the master—is supplanted at the end by Hamm's own conscious playing, the theatrics of his final speech as he literally asserts his role. Disclosing himself as the archetypal figure of tragedy, the sufferer with his bloody stauncher, and thereby echoing his progenitors, Hamlet and Lear, he is now self-enclosed in his newly-minted inner theater, its dimensions marked by the stauncher as he at once distinguishes himself from and challenges the audience: "You . . . remain." One-half of the theatrical equation has been completed, "Finished," or "nearly finished" (p. 1), because the other half, the audience, has yet to leave its seats, to leave that "stage" now defined as encompassing the entire auditorium. The baton or, more properly, Hamm's gaff has been passed. Our role in this larger production can only await resolution—or the illusion of one.[13] Krapp's own metadramatic achievement, as he "lipsyncs" words recorded from his past even as he metamorphoses the fire burning within him, the cirrhosis, to a fire akin to the inspiration of the muse, supplants his equally sad history, the life of artistic failure, wasted by that third of each day spent drinking in public houses.

Whether his theme be read as comic or tragic, romantic or absurdist, Beckett's theater comes into its own, justifying itself by its own enactment and allowing its central characters, conscious of their artistry, of their ability to impart form to a sad or meaningless world, to achieve victory. This very renaissance distinguishes them from their earlier selves or from those other characters swallowed up by life precisely because they lack the perspective afforded by this double-edged sword of the imagination. The reward for such terrifying perception, for violating the otherwise safe angle of "perceivedness," is knowing the difference between those who truly see—"oh, if you had my eyes" (p. 61), as Mrs. Rooney says to her unseeing fellow-waiters and travelers—and those who do not, those who, like Mr. Slocum, can only gaze incomprehensibly "through the windscreen, into the void" (p. 47), content as he might be in an ignorance that is to him unknown and therefore no impediment to his personal, albeit limited happiness.

In such abstract radio plays as *Cascando* and *Words and Music* this victory is even more pronounced: it is ultimately the process of telling Woburn's story through Voice, aided by Opener and Music, that is the goal or Godot of *Cascando*. In *Words and Music* the tools of art seize the power at the end, as Croak shuffles off, rejected, his own story—be it discourses on selected topics or his past with the mysterious Lily—being of no consequence. In her most recent book on Beckett, Ruby Cohn stresses Beckett's own movement toward aesthetics, form, both as playwright and as director.[14] John Knowlson reaches a similar conclusion when he argues that in Beckett's latest work for the legitimate theater and for television, movement and form, the aesthetic choreography of the play, "appear . . . as intimations (though necessarily imperfect ones) of a state of grace, harmony, economy and beauty akin to that discovered by Kleist's speaker in the movement of the marionette and glimpsed perhaps most clearly by Beckett in music itself."[15] Knowlson's phrase "though necessarily imperfect ones" is an apt one, since for Beckett aesthetics makes a parabolic curve and rejoins thematics. Hence the final tableau of *Act Without Words I*, when the solitary figure cups his face in his hand, suggests a theatrical turning to itself, as all the accoutrements of a god-ordained world are removed and the actor is left with his sole self, even as it offers an image of the modern, existential man for whom a priori systems conferring meaning prove unacceptable. If the Animator's inability to fathom Fox's own prose in *Radio II* can be taken metadramatically as the split between the artist (here a fairly mechanical artist, one doubtless given to voluntary, as opposed to involuntary memory) and his material, the same moment is also an image of our own human split between consciousness and the unconscious, the very split Murphy tries both comically and tragically to repair.

Only two of Beckett's plays, *Godot* and *Happy Days*, have the act divisions of the conventional theater. However, Beckett's own method of dividing the plays into "acts" seems no less insistent: an Auditor's carefully timed shrugs of helpless compassion in *Not I;* the use of a story within the story in *Embers, Cascando, Words and Music,* and *Footfalls;* repetitions of and, at the same time, variations on earlier sections in *Act Without Words I* and *II, That Time,* and *Ghost Trio;* recurrent sounds or noises, such as W's "More" in *Rockaby* and the Listener's "knock" in *Ohio Impromptu;* even the intrusion of the medium itself, such as the nine camera angles in *Eh Joe.* Beckett substitutes other devices that even more starkly underscore the "acts" of the play unfolding before us. These graphic divisions, again, call attention to process itself, to the successive stages in the play's own evolution. "Thematics" as narrowly defined (what the play purports to mean, as a reflection of personalities and issues outside the theater) gives way to "aesthetics," for Beckett's theater turns to itself as the ultimate metaphor. By such processive acts or movements the play signals its own intentions: it is a happening, increasingly absorbed in its own form, even as its trajectory turns back on that very world to which the spectator himself must return.[16]

Given this theater turning to itself, it is inevitable that the three ingredients for any production—artist, actor, and audience—should be prominent in Beckett's work. Hardly artists of the first order, though Estragon does confess to having once been a poet, Vladimir and Estragon turn playwright in the play's second act, building on the play-within-the-play, that "history" of events in Act 1, even imitating Pozzo and Lucky from the night before and thereby adding a "Player Lucky" and a "Player Pozzo" to the characters we have seen and will see again. By the later plays, this portrait of the artist is less subtle. In *Radio I* we see a single artist split between his confident public self (the "He" interviewed by "She") and a neurotic private self (Mr. Macgillycuddy—now so named—on the phone, concerned about the health of his Voice and Music). The play's second half thus enacts Beckett's oft-quoted description of the artist who, once he turns from an illusory public world to the no less illusory world of the self, realizes that he has "nothing with which to express, no power to express," even as he has "the obligation to express."[17] He cannot go on; he must go on—the very paradox confronting Mr. Macgillycuddy: "Tomorrow . . . noon . . ." (p. 112).

The artist in Beckett is also actor and audience: the existential dualism, that nauseous split between doer and thinker, self and other, is recast in the inseparable "roles" of actor and audience as they cleave to the playwright, their source or *primum mobile.* Krapp plays audience onstage to his self of years before, revisiting through his voice—the voice of the very actor we see before us—both the portrait of an artist who has failed as well as that mixed bag of scenes constituting an actor's performance. I call him an "actor" since Krapp, using the tape recorder to bridge that split between man as actor-doer and observer-audience, portrays himself as a man cast from his mother, seeking mothers through a series of surrogates, finding temporary happiness with a single woman, the lady in the punt, and then ruining his life through drink. However, Krapp as audience and actor at length merges with Krapp as artist when he first tries to create a new tape and then, recombining the roles of playwright and actor, uses the words of an old tape to complement the mime with which he ends his play. In *Breath* and *Come and Go* we ourselves must take on a creative role, since the playwright purposely denies us dialogue in *Breath* and a chance to hear the most significant line in *Come and Go*.

The theater is the vehicle for revelation, for seeing into and saying Beckett's black holes. Beckett's goal, "to let Being into art,"[18] is often likened to a dream voyage. In his sleep Hamm can see woods through which, despite his impediments, he could "run" and "make love." At the climax of *Film* O falls asleep in his Murphy-like rocking chair and there dreams. On waking, he sees E for the first time, thereby violating the angle of immunity, yet in that violation finding the self that has dogged him on the street and along the stairwell. Given to habit, followers rather than leaders, and only dimly creative, Vladimir and Estragon fear sleep—and its ensuing dreams. But no measurements from the real world offstage, no account of the time spent before Act 1 or between *Godot*'s own two acts, will account for the dreamlike, unresolved stage world in which they wait.[19]

The creative principle, the stimulus for this liberating dream vision, is often a woman, such as the various women in Krapp's life who culminate in the lover in the punt, or Henry's own Ada. O's moment of vision occurs, properly, in his mother's room, and that mother may have materialized earlier in the aged flower-lady on the stairs. While the tools of his craft overwhelm Croak in *Words and Music*, he still has a vision, prompted by the growing union of his artistic tools, of Lily's face on the stairs. The operations of the involuntary memory, aroused by the woman or *anima*, an intuitive female principle, radically invade the rational, schematic, public, shallow male principle, epitomized in the loveless Pozzo, the reductive Willie, or in Henry before he softens his own ego with a productive memory of Ada. Similarly, in Shakespeare the woman is often the source of vision or liberation, or freedom from potential tragedy—Portia, Hippolyta, Cordelia, Desdemona, Hermione, and Paulina.

When this liberating, involuntary memory works, it breaks the seeming reality of the outside world and penetrates deeply, through those three zones to our own inner world. The movement itself is sudden, spontaneous, both terrifying and pleasurable, a variation and a reversal of the Joycean epiphany, one in which the connection is not between the perceiver and the world—as when Corley in Joyce's "Two Gallants" holds to the street light's glare the golden coin given him by the prostitute—but rather between the perceiver and himself. Joyce, in Beckett's equation, is involved with the public world; his "secretary" with that private sphere, with Being.[20] In *Footfalls*, the two operative words to describe such vision are M's "revolving in her mind" and V's "semblance."

Hence, the medium itself becomes a "character" in Beckett, indeed the chief participant in this process. The stage plays stress the act of creation, whether it be an actor warming to his part, or struggling with that same part, or the coequal warming or struggling of the audience. Even as radio disembodies the physical theater, it forces the listener, himself personified in *Ohio Impromptu,* to establish a physical, albeit imaginary theatrical correlative. The supposed real life caught by the camera in *Film* is, at its core, only an illusion: the camera is not random, and in *Film* the task of metamorphosing the literal and squalid street, stairwell, and room into symbolic places is shared equally by artist and viewer, by E and O, by Beckett and his audience who frame their surrogates on screen. The mimes speak to us because our mind, its repository of words otherwise dammed up like that of the Mouth in *Not I,* refuses to be silent, as each of us provides, instead, a private, idiosyncratic "commentary" to this art form that only *seems* to deprive us of the words of the legitimate theater. The television plays themselves recall the "golden days" of the medium in our country, where the advantages of the cinema's camera were combined with the immediacy—of *live* television—characterizing the legitimate stage. The medium, in Beckett, is never a mere vehicle, no more so than the audience is. In Beckett the *message is the medium,* even to the degree that the medium threatens to achieve a life, a personality of its own.

Beckett's theaters thus become the "hero" in worlds otherwise populated by little people, by clowns, failures, the maimed, the impotent, the neurotic, the absurd, the comic and the tragic. The issue is not to determine what we are. In the absence of a secure divinity or even a clear humanistic ethic that could survive what we did at Hiroshima or in the Holocaust, Beckett has little confidence, it seems, in preexisting schemes defining what is "good" in man. The issue surely is not even what we can become, for that would imply a clear goal, or Godot ratifying our earthly pilgrimage. Rather, the issue simply is to see ourselves, to say ourselves, to be, and to be conscious of our being. We may not be able to change, given the eternality of process, nor even to "mean something," given the absence of a divinity or a single, larger plan for our existence. But we can be ready, as when Hamlet says that the "readiness is all," or Edgar, comforting Gloucester, sees the "ripeness" as all. The theater allows us to see in process and through its imitation or illusion what is otherwise infinite, beyond our comprehension; and yet it can only duplicate through a reverse mirror image the life that seethes about us—magnificently, disastrously, beautifully, obscenely. Still, the theater offers us practice in being ready, ripe, alert, prepared mentally and emotionally for that life. Its pleasure, the *dulce* that the Renaissance commentators combined with *utile* in speaking of the high purpose of art, is at one with the serenity found by the individual who can know without necessarily being able to change, who can rejoice or suffer and still know that comedy or tragedy are themselves not constants. In a joyous sense, the theater is the best preparation we have for any future, and—at length—for death itself. Hamlet speaks to this larger purpose informing the theater, most surely one informing Beckett's theaters, when he concludes just seconds before the duel with Laertes:

If it be now, 'tis not to come; if it be not to come, it will be now; if it be not now, yet it will come—the readiness is all. (5.2.220–222)

Beckett's theaters embody this state of readiness, and their concern is man himself, as both microcosm and macrocosm. For all the tantalizing theological overtones in Beckett, his theater is of this world, *secular,* showing us men and women moving through this little O, this earth. Man is Beckett's focus, not his institutions, not those metaphors built on the assumption that the external world is substantial. Nothing is outside man; all is within. Hence his dismissal of politics, as that word echoes its Greek root in *polis,* or the city of man. "We are alone. We cannot know [the world outside us] and we cannot be known"[21]—but we can know ourselves. That knowledge is often painful, terrifying, but to say ourselves is a step away from the abyss, a nod in the direction of comedy rather than tragedy. It is Beckett's "Gaiety transfiguring all that dread."[22] At length we internalize his plays, refashion them on our own inner stage, and then become the final "text" of his performance.[23]

Without art we have only tragedy, grain upon grain, life that gives birth straddling a grave, a brief passage through a happy banquet room before we, like that solitary bird in the medieval legend, are driven into the storm again, a moment by the fire such as Bolton has while the storm rages outside. Beckett's theaters, I believe, are similarly affirmative, however gray the landscape pictured there. If there is only a solitary tree in *Waiting for Godot,* there *is* a tree nevertheless.

In "Lapis Lazuli" Yeats imagines two Chinese, carved in stone, making their way toward some little house halfway up a mountain, and accompanied by a "third" man carrying a musical instrument. As the three men look down on all the tragic scene below, they look with eyes wrinkled by time and by the tragedies of time, and yet their eyes, albeit wrinkled, are also "gay." Yeats himself may be that third man joining his two fictive creatures on stone. My own involuntary memory likes to imagine that a second Irishman joins the small company at that half-way house. As he looks down on the Vladimirs and Estragons, the Krapps, the Unnamables of his own stage worlds, his own eyes, deep within that athletic, craggy, weathered face, are similarly gay. Beckett's gamut is ultimately comic.

# Appendix A
# Music, Mathematics, and the Rhythms of Beckett's Theaters: *Rockaby, Ohio Impromptu,* and *A Piece of Monologue*

In her account of Beckett's production of *Waiting for Godot* for the Schiller Theater in 1975, Ruby Cohn calls attention to both the "scattered symmetries" and the larger "binary rhythms" that subsume the numerous pairings in the play: Vladimir and Estragon, Pozzo and Lucky, the hat and the shoes, the turnip and the carrot, horizontal country road and vertical tree, and so on.[1] The same binary rhythms, I believe, inform the three recent plays examined here. Their stories as well as the issues raised seem of less consequence than the insistent dualities of the plays, the mathematical balance, the choreography or what I call "the Rhythms of Beckett's Theaters." George Steiner's argument that, for our age, mathematics and music are fast becoming the dominant mode of communication seems appropriate here.[2] The word, the staple of the traditional theater, has become so fragmented in meaning, so jaded, so idiosyncratic as our twentieth-century relativism empties the universe of gods, that we now require both the immediacy of the physical, indeed the sensual "language" of mathematics and music as well as their symmetry that, in its own way, supplants that hierarchical symmetry of a Godot-ordained cosmos.

i

*Rockaby* both asserts and then deconstructs these binary rhythms. Conversely, the implied dualism in the pairing of construction and destruction is itself the play's dominant rhythm, its own source of movement or dynamics, as the apparent dualisms—W/V; past/present; window/window opposite; perceiver/ perceived; onstage presence/offstage voice; even the "going to"/"and fro" of the rocking chair itself—give way to singularity as W drops the attempt to confirm existence through "another like herself" staring at her through the open blinds of a window opposite her own. After pairing herself with a dead woman, the mother whom she described at length in section three, she takes a cynical solace in herself, her sole self, indeed

206

losing even this consciousness of self as she becomes the third person or other who orders the self to "rock her off" and to "fuck life."

Those twentieth-century attempts to find oneself through the encounter group where we learn to "relate," to empathize with and through others, are here patently a charade. *"Her recorded voice,"* the entry for V under the play's own brief *dramatis personae,* at once celebrates the special effects of the modern electronic theater that can enact the split between self and other, even as it exposes the fraudulence of the stage illusion itself: the audience at the Center for Theater Research in Buffalo who saw Billie Whitelaw onstage surely did not think that the offstage voice belonged to a second actress.

Still, framed by the concept of self (W) and other (V), the play's apparent dualism is underscored by Beckett's own "tampering with" the medium: the onstage actor confined to a single word, *More,* almost in defiance of the legitimate theater, listening to her voice from offstage. The single medium thus bifurcates, and, as with *Krapp's Last Tape,* we have a piece for the legitimate theater that has much in common with radio, and, as with *That Time,* an actor who is more akin to a mime. W herself is similarly divided. On the one hand, her face is "expressionless," lit only when the "subdued spot" focuses on it when "still or at mid-rock." An alternate lighting plan would have the spot constant on the face, albeit subdued, with this constant light contrasted with the successive fades of the larger spot that includes the chair as well. Either lighting plan for the face becomes irrelevant at the end, however, when the "head slowly sinks, comes to rest" and the spot fades. In effect, the lighting is the unconventional stage lighting of *Come and Go.* On the other hand, the nondescript actress is not entirely so: that same "expressionless" face is highlighted by "huge eyes," and her "white hands," similar to the ladies' hands in *Come and Go,* grasp the armrests. If W loses identity in failing to find another, or by merging into the character of her own mother, just as M and V merge and then remerge in *Footfalls,* she also seems physically unique: the costume calls for a "black lacy high-necked evening gown," with "jet sequins" that glitter during the rocking, and—most wonderful of all—an "incongruous frivolous head-dress set with extravagant trimmings to catch light when rocking." Her "attitude" is to be "completely still" with the only movement being a slow incline of the head once the spot on the chair fades out, and this seems to oppose the superficial glitter of the costume, with its suggestion that W is dressed for some formal, perhaps even playful occasion ("incongruous frivolous head-dress").

With its minimal set or props, and otherwise overwhelmed by language from some invisible mouth, the play ironically appears to elevate the physical over the verbal, for the language itself functions in ways other than denotative. There is a story, certainly: the mother, like W, sat silently at the window, hoping to see another face in the window across the street, but, despairing of this, at last went "down the steep stair," sitting there in a rocker "till her end came." Yet in a very specific way the mother's story is irrelevant, since the play ignores such history by its present enactment of W's decision, announced in the very first lines, not to continue reenacting her mother's search for another. We see, therefore, the endgame, not its full reenactment. Past gives way to present; even the play's own sense of time—the stages in which W, like her mother, searches, despairs, and re-treats—is an illusion: the opening line, not the closing lines, is "till in the end / the day came / in the end came / close of a long / when she said / to herself / whom else / time she stopped / *time she stopped* going to and fro" (p. 9). The decision has already been made, and the recorded voice thus tells a story—of either mother or daughter—that is at variance with what the play itself shows.

Words and music (the "going to and fro" of the chair) are themselves at variance. If we take the binary rhythms of the words as significant ("all eyes / all sides / high and low / for another / till in the end / close of a long day / to herself"), as a verbal rhythm complementing both the physical movement of the rocking chair and the contrastive binaries of the physical stage itself (lighting, costume, "Attitude," even the chair with its "rounded inward curving arms to suggest embrace"), then language here is more physical than denotative, more significant in its rhythms than in its meanings.

In rejecting Shroder's suggestion that at the end Clov recover Hamm with the sheet so that the *Endgame*'s own end would mirror its beginning, Beckett told the German actor (I use here Ruby Cohn's translation): "Between the beginning and the end lies the small difference that lies precisely between beginning and end."[3] Between the beginning and the end of *Rockaby* lies a similar difference. There are really two "stories"—I use the word in a tentative sense, given the comments above about words as signifiers and words as mathematical-musical rhythms—and thus even here the play's duality reasserts itself, thematically as well as aesthetically. The mother, we are told, went "off her head" as even her minimal life sitting before the window facing the street was reduced to that of a solitary figure with "famished eyes" rocking in a room with its blinds down, that room itself reached by means of a "steep stair." Then one day, no, one "night" as V corrects herself, the mother died. The daughter's life, of course, parallels her mother's, but since the third-person narrative appears more an attempt to deny the real "I" of the story, W herself, and since W is already at the end of that story, in that very room to which the mother herself retreated, then thematics dissolve into the present-tense happening onstage: we watch the creation of a second story, its antecedents (the mother's history, or W's) being of little consequence. Indeed, the mother may be nothing more than a convenient fiction, an attempt by the stage's single persona, one split into body and voice, to deflect a painful experience from herself, to pass it off as another's. The line "time she went right down / was her own other" (p. 19) sounds too close to "was her own mother." Hence the "small difference," I believe, is between the ending of this irrelevant, possibly fraudulent history and the actual ending we as audience witness. Beckett instructs V to reduce her voice—"voice gradually softer"—near the phrase "saying to herself" in the play's closing moment. With a single "no" followed by "done with that," W dismisses the charade, the pretended dualism in which she has paralleled her mother's life with her own. The mother is or has been no more present than the mother in *Film,* whose room O uses or, more preperly, returns to: we will recall that Beckett himself dismisses these facts as of "no bearing" (p. 86).

The single character, however bifurcated, thus struggles with that most pervasive human dilemma as Beckett perceives it: to be alone, to be known by none, and yet to feel compelled to say it, to establish a connection with another, to be seen and to be heard by another. The mother is the illusory face behind the other window. More literally, we as audience are also that face, but unlike the mother, we are not fictions. We both see W and hear her through V, with our two senses forced to combine onstage vision with backstage sounds. But just as the senses of hearing and seeing combine as the single agent through which we apprehend the play, all the time the two characters (mother/daughter; W/V) were one. We have hints of this not only in the similarity of the costumes—V tells us that the mother also wore her "best black"—but in those moments at the end of each of the four sections when W and V speak a phrase *"Together":* "time she stopped," "living soul," and "rock her off." The stage holds only one living soul, witnessed, ratified by us also, functioning collectively as a single audience. The tragedy of W's pretended mother, one of aloneness and alienation, is supplanted by the "comedy" in which her story, the endgame, is seen and heard. W completes her mission: to say and to be observed. Her pose at the end is serene. Raw life itself, the world without art, outside the theater, that world eternally mediating between the private and the public, one's self and others, is told to "fuck off," as the character hugs the single stage prop, the rocker, "saying to the rocker / rock her off / stop her eyes/fuck life/ stop her eyes"—and at last: "rock her off / rock her off" (to sleep, to sore labor's bath, to the close of the day's anguish). The "small difference" lies between the implied (or past) story and the actual (or present) one we observe.

Despite the narrator's cynicism, then, there is "another creature there / somewhere there / behind the pane / another living soul" (p. 16): the audience. W's increasingly reduced demands—"another like herself, / a little like"; "another living soul / one other living soul"; "a blind up like hers / a little like"; "let down the blind"—are met and met again in the form of the theater and its audience, an audience not of one but of many. The pun on "pane" ("behind the pane"), like the pun on "blind," itself plays on the tragedy that would otherwise be W's without us, without the theater whose own equation begins with the apparent dualism or separation or actor and audience.

The four sections of *Rockaby* move us toward this aesthetic comedy, this resolution in the final tableau of the serene figure, its head bowed, the rocking stilled, a situation that reminds us, as it reminded Murphy, of the "end" of all rocking chairs: to rock us off to sleep, out of a troubled world and into an inner composure. What else could justify such an otherwise unstable chair? this "parody" of chairs normally designed to seat one firmly?

Thus history gives way to the present, dualism to singularity in that present, tragedy to comedy. The symmetry of the binary rhythms is abandoned, and Beckett himself scatters irritants that will work against such symmetry: the rocker is "*slightly off center audience left,*" and, as we have seen, the demands for another person are reduced from "another like herself" to "let down the blind." The process itself supplants the seeming stasis generated by dualism and the contradictory rhythms it includes: the play is not *Godot* ending with the frustrating juxtaposition of "let's go" and "*They do not move.*" The tragic story, an old maid rocking away, repeating her mother's own tragic story, gives way to the finding of self, and the consequent abandonment of the search for another. In W we also find our other and hence our self, in this strange figure whose otherwise inconsequential story we cannot dismiss, any more than we can Winnie's in *Happy Days.* As in *Come and Go* there are no rings here to bind us, yet at the end there *is* a union, however intangible. The daisy-chain pattern of holding hands in the earlier dramaticule is here W's embrace by the rocking chair; again, Beckett specifies that the chair should have "inward curving arms to suggest embrace." W finds herself after having tried, like Mouth in *Not I,* to deny the self by speaking of another. As the spot fades, we as audience are the face she has sought.

ii

Even more consciously than *Rockaby, Ohio Impromptu* plays on the seeming antitheses of dualism and singularity, and hence the appropriateness of the "*Impromptu*" in its title. A set piece, completely arranged ahead of time, this dramaticule gives the illusion of being an impromptu play in the tensions established before R's first words, "Little is left to tell. In a last—." (Even this line is replayed when, responding to L's first knock, R repeats "Little is left to tell" before progressing to the next sentence sequence, "In a last attempt. . . .") During the ten seconds between the light's fade up and R's turning the page—the last page, Beckett is careful to tell us—we observe dualism arrayed against singularity: two characters, L and R, both their positions onstage and their names (Listener and Reader) paralleling the pairing of onstage (L) and off-stage audiences, sitting in two "*plain armless white deal chairs,*" yet surrounding on that table a single book and, curiously, a single "*Black wide-brimmed hat at center.*" Like Krapp's tape recorder or the bench in *Come and Go,* the onstage area itself is divided between the small area actually illuminated and the "*Rest of stage in darkness.*" One character speaks and one is confined to knocks, but the two are dressed identically: "*Long black coat. Long white hair.*" Each props a bowed head in the right hand, while resting the left hand on the table. The audience receives conflicting signals, twos and ones; *Ohio Impromptu* will play on this situation.

The story itself reflects this tension between duality and singularity. R tells L of a man who moves away from his friend, from a place "where they had been so long together," to a "single room on the far bank," with a single window—no less—from which he could see the "down-stream extremity of the Isle of Swans" (p. 28). Now alone, he cuts a solitary figure, pacing the islet alone in a black coat—the first clue that narrator and narrated are both separate and the same—topped with an "old world Latin Quarter hat" (p. 29), perhaps the very black wide-brimmed hat we see on the table. However, this movement away from a union—friends, lovers, man as self and other, actor and the audience formed by the friend, just as L is properly audience to the actor R—only sets new dualities in motion: the isolated figure observes how in its "joyous eddies" the receding stream is divided into "two arms" that "conflowed and flowed united on" (p. 29). Besides, the character's single state is itself short-lived, for in the midst of his anguish at being alone, where his "old terror of night" revisits him and "fearful symptoms" return with double force, he is visited by a man, sent by his abandoned friend, whose mission is "to comfort" him. A new union is now formed, one of reader and listener, as on successive nights, both irregularly and yet always at the same hour, the man revisits the formerly isolated character, reading to him from the "same volume" and then disappearing without a word. In effect, a past-tense union begets its own dissolution that, in turn, begets a new union in which the visitor is surrogate for the abandoned friend. One night the visitor brings word that there is "no need to go to him again, even were it in your power" (p. 33), and then, violating his normal schedule of irregular visits but regular arrivals (at the "same hour"), he stays with the character. R describes both as buried in silence, in what Beckett calls "profounds of mind," set against a gray background, one without life or features: no dawn to be seen through the single window, no sounds of reawakening from the street below (p. 34). The two characters, this Woburn of *Ohio Impromptu* and his visitor, seem like statues or halves of a single tableau as they "sat on as though turned to stone." This tableau of the inner story is then enacted in the outer story as R and L *"simultaneously"* lower their right hands to the table, raise their heads, and look at each other *"Unblinking. Expressionless"* (p. 35). The final tableau of the outer story is held for ten seconds and then fades.

*Ohio Impromptu* takes up a story that may remind us of the superficial "plot" of *Cascando:* the aborted relationship, the attempt by the central character to find relief in isolation, the undoing of that state by an ambassador from the "dear face," followed by a severing of the link with the abandoned friend, this very severing allowing for a new union in the inner story that is then enacted by the final tableau of L and R in the outer story. At length, however, thematics fade as "the sad tale [itself is] a last time told" (p. 34), thereby giving way to aesthetics: this confrontation of the three

Listeners (of the inner story, L, and us) and three Readers (of the inner story, R, and the actor playing R). Even the earlier realistic details—Isle of Swans, the Latin Quarter, the receding stream, the suggestion of a biography in the character's "great error"—are dissolved with "Nothing is left to tell" (p. 34). The possible allusion to the line from Shakespeare's *The Winter's Tale* ("A sad tale's best for winter" [2.1.25]) in "The sad tale a last time told" (and there is no "sound of reawakening" outside, no sound of spring) seems to locate the play in the consciousness of the storyteller. Then, too, the play literally ends not with the inner story but with the tableau formed by R and L, silent, expressionless, now beyond both story-telling and listening. What we make of the inner story cannot be the entire play. The title itself, *Ohio Impromptu*, calls attention not to a story but to original auspices of production (the Drake Union, Stadium 2 Theater, at Ohio State University, May 9, 1981), even as it underscores the present-tense, "momentary" nature of Beckett's theater.

In the 1960s Harold Pinter habitually sent each of his plays in manuscript to Beckett before anyone else was allowed to see them; he has also acted in Beckett's *Radio II*. In a 1954 letter to a friend he recognizes Beckett's diminished thematics and the corresponding, indeed overwhelming sense of the theater:

> The farther he goes the more good it does me. I don't want philosophies, tracts, dogmas, creeds, ways out, truths, answers, *nothing from the bargain basement.* . . . he's not leading me up any garden, he's not slipping me any wink, he's not flogging me a remedy or a path or a revelation or a basinful of breadcrumbs, he's not selling me anything I don't want to buy. . . . He brings forth a body of beauty. His work is beautiful.[4]

The "beautiful" in *Ohio Impromptu* may be at one with these two movements: one, the rhythms of dualities and singularities, a Beckettian mathematical addition and subtraction; the other, a linear process from thematics to metadramatics. If the movement in *Rockaby* is from duality to singularity, the movement here is from thematic isolation (or singularity) to an aesthetic union. We participate in this movement by coming to the play, joining with others to form an audience, and joining with the actors to collaborate in the theater's own illusion. The Listener onstage both enacts and thereby reminds us of our own significant role in the equation. When the play's central character tries to break a union, he only exposes himself to terrors and fearful symptoms, so terrible, in fact, that when Reader makes reference to the more elaborate account of the disease as "described at length page forty paragraph four" (p. 31), he is "checked" by Listener's hand, the first of only two such uses of that hand otherwise employed in knocking on the table.

Those knocks themselves seem to function as a way both of underscoring important passages—"Little is left to tell," "Then turn and his slow steps retrace," "Seen the dear face"—and of driving the story along by providing a sort of physical recharging, a goad, for the Reader. The play drives on to its conclusion, its final "saying" that, paradoxically, is those wordless fifteen seconds after the book has been closed. If, initially, Reader seems dominant and Listener passive, we realize that both dissolve into fictions. Philosophically, the two, though apparently separate, may be the self and other of the existentialist, but if this is so, that dualism itself is only a convenient fiction to be absolved by the quiet union in the final tableau as "*Simultaneously they lower their right hands to the table. . . .*" In point of fact, there has been no separation, no breaking of the union: the dear face is at length not abandoned but rather incorporated in that two-as-one final tableau. Not ultimately bound by the conventional story theater—as, for example, I have argued Lucky and Pozzo are—and thereby responsible only to itself and to the present moment and auspices of performance, the play is a comedy presenting in its closing moments a single, "composite" character—hence the single hat, the duplicate poses, the identical appearances—who has found himself, who flees himself only to return. The play thus abandons external geography for the inner world, the "Profounds of mind," a dark zone, like the dark third zone of *Murphy*, "Of mindlessness. Whither no light can reach. No sound" (p. 34).

Like an elegy, the play works us out of grief, and beyond separation. Beckett's theaters, in all four media, show us, rather than tell us, what the theater does when it turns to itself, how it is an experience no less valid or valuable than any experiences offstage, even as it is also a window to the world outside the playhouse. In this sense, *Ohio Impromptu* is a vignette about separation, about loss, about the terrors of isolation, and about the comfort of companionship, just as *Krapp's Last Tape* offers a dark portrait of life misspent, and just as *Waiting for Godot* imitates our own search in life for meaning, or even for ways to pass the time. Thus, *Ohio Impromptu* underscores the theater's essential *comedy*, its ability to give both perspective and resolution to the frayed, unresolved anxieties in life. It is about the pleasures inherent in a good book or, more properly, a good play. Not absolving us of tragedy, it can still contain it, and this is, to be sure, no small accomplishment.

### iii

Like *Come and Go*, *A Piece of Monologue* has two distinct parts. Indeed, its first half echoes the attempt in *Come and Go* to come to terms with a sad history. The Speaker's second lighting of the lamp (p. 74) announces both the second half and an extraordinary change as the play moves from past to present, from the voluntary to the most sustained exercise of the involuntary memory in the Beckett canon.

The first half is literally mired in the past. Like the Mouth of *Not I*, the Speaker traces his history from birth, through the days of cradle and crib, to the "first fiasco" in nursing, to the present. We see an old man with "*White hair, white nightgown, white socks*" isolated in a room defined by a lamp two meters to the left, its white globe *"faintly lit,"* and a pallet bed to his right—shades of *Ghost Trio*—also white, and *"Just visible."* We are in Joe's bedroom, or that of Malone—and at the end of the game. The Speaker exercises his voluntary memory on the remains of family portraits once pinned to the walls, now "down one after another" and "torn to shreds and scattered" (p. 71). The drawing pins that do remain hold up a few shreds as reminders of the past. Outside the room life abounds in the "new needles turning green" (p. 70); inside, a decrepit old man struggles with memories, kindling his imagination by lighting the wall with a lamp by means of a fairly elaborate ceremony: first finding in the dark the loose matches in his right-hand pocket; then striking one on his buttocks, the way his father taught him; removing and setting down the milk-white globe; then striking a second match when the first expires; taking off the lamp's chimney, striking a third match when the second expires, and lighting the wick; putting back the chimney, this followed by the death of the third match— the routine ending with his putting back the globe and turning the wick low. This routine complete, he turns to the east wall—Beckett is insistent on that direction, and we might associate the east with life and light—yet his actions, however methodical and detailed, are futile: the pictures of his family or loved ones never materialize; the routine itself must therefore be repeated and repeated; and, to add to the confusion, there is a second light, a "faint light in room," whose source the Speaker cannot detect and that, much to his irritation, mocks his feeble attempts to activate his imagination. The entire routine is not only futile but painful: memories of his mother and father smiling on their wedding day only serve to remind him that he is "alone," "forgotten. All gone so long" (p. 72). Beneath the bed the thousand shreds of the pictures are sullied by dust and spiders. As section one ends the portrait of the Speaker darkens: he stands "stock still staring out. Into black vast. Nothing there. Nothing stirring. That he can see. Hear" (p. 73). His will to move is sapped; the light, like that in *Theater II,* expires again (p. 74).

When he repeats the lamp-lighting routine, the play changes radically. The several steps in lighting the lamp are now compressed into four short sentences, and the monologue moves from the straightforward narration of the first section to a highly conscious account of the process of narration. The movement duplicates that in *Play,* from the first-half recitation of the adulterous story to the three characters' concerns, after the dimming of interrogation light, with their present state. The speaker now describes the scene as a stage designer might: the gown and socks are white "to take faint light" (p. 74), as is the hair and the foot of the pallet. As the Speaker stares at the wall—this time he faces west, with its implications of death or ending—there is a "slow fade up of a faint form," though it is not yet identified.

The third lighting of the globe is couched in a way suggesting that the Speaker both acts and sees himself in the process of acting; this is the realm of the narrator/narrated. He observes his own "faint hand" holding aloft the milk-white globe. As the chimney is removed, the Speaker imagines the two hands and chimney "in light of spill" as the spill is applied to the wick. When the chimney is put back on, the hand with the spill disappears and then a second hand also disappears. He now imagines the chimney "alone in gloom." A hand reappears with the globe as the globe is put back on and the wick turned low; we now see a "pale globe alone in the gloom," even as the brass bedrail catches the renewed light.

The Speaker is an incipient artist here, drawing his own portrait, reflecting on movement rather than merely moving. The routine is seen as just that. The opening mechanical instructions for lighting the globe—"the way his father taught him" (p. 71)—imply a learned response from the distant past, but they are now adjusted to form an imaginative picture. His inability earlier to dismiss the mysterious faint light—"Whence unknown. None from window. No. Next to none. No such thing as none" (pp. 70–71)—is transformed into the revelation that the "starless moonless heaven" is its source, that the light "dies on to dawn . . . [but] never dies" (p. 74).

This time he sees something as he stares into the dark: the dark itself "slowly parts again" and there is a "grey light" (p. 75). The involuntary memory now focuses that "faint form" into the portrait of a funeral: rain pelting, umbrellas round a grave, all this "seen from above," with black canopies and a black ditch beneath, and rain "bubbling in the black mud" (p. 75). These images give way to a complete, imaginative inner picture, one that cannot be pinned on a wall and therefore cannot be subject to time and decay, nor to the dust and spiders beneath the bed. We thus move from a mechanical art, that of home photography, to imaginative creation, the funeral as recreated in the mind, its image thrown upon the west-facing wall to distinguish it from the east wall that now holds only the sad remains of family portraits. The movement here is analogous to that in *Film* when O progresses from the seven photographs to the imaginative seeing of himself as he confronts E fully for the first time.

With this change from past to present, from voluntary to involuntary memory, from thematics to aesthetics, the Speaker suddenly becomes conscious of his own voice, as does Mouth in *Not I*. If the monologue opens with a cruel linking of birth and death ("Birth was the death of him") and a dismissal of words themselves ("Words are few. Dying too"), it now celebrates the birth of language. The will to move that had been crushed is now reactivated: there is a faint cry in his ear, and the mouth is now agape. A hiss of breath closes the lips, and the Speaker feels the "soft touch of lip on lip" (p. 75) as a cry issues from him. The physical action is like the birth process itself, as the first word "gathers in his mouth" and as the lips, which had been closed with the hiss, are now parted and the tongue is thrust between them. The actor's instrument, indeed that mouth which is currently delivering the monologue, takes center stage. The lamp (as a source of voluntary memory) and the bed (as either a grave or a mockery of a place once given to love and procreation) now fade from the Speaker's self-announced focus, as the play luxuriates on the mouth now poised to speak, and as the Speaker, no longer confronted with a void, stares beyond "through rift in dark to other dark" (p. 77). We ourselves are poised for receiving an imaginative creation, a *Times Remembered* or revisiting of the past that, like Krapp's as he lipsyncs the recorded tape otherwise consigned to chronicling his ill-spent life, will rekindle the present with the past, obliterating in its wake distinctions made by that cruel agent time.

The Speaker himself can now confront the source of his anguish. He has tried to avoid this moment, tried to "move on to other matters" (p. 76); now he acknowledges there "never were other matters. Never two matters" (p. 79). As he races through the lamplighting routine a final time, the routine itself is compressed to "Spill. Hands. Lamp" (p. 78). Then the "frame" of the funeral reappears, but this time with a new detail: a "coffin on its way." Like Donne in his rhetorical questioning of for whom the bell tolls, the Speaker acknowledges that the imaginative picture, that coffin now on its way, prefigures his own death: "Loved one . . . he all but said loved one on his way" (p. 78). Suddenly, as with Croak's vision of Lily on the stairs in *Words and Music,* the focus is sharpened: the coffin takes a specific loved one on "Her" way. Coming to terms through his own imaginative recreation of the past, abandoning mechanical reproductions, he has *had his vision,* in Virginia Woolf's sense of that phrase.[5] "Thirty seconds" is literally a cue to the stagehand to dim the lamplight, for it will now be supplanted by the "faint diffuse light," a mysterious light beyond rational human control that has earlier alternately terrified and puzzled the Speaker.

Now in this monologue full of repetitions and variations, we suddenly get new material, as we do in the final third of *Ghost Trio.* First, the Speaker sees himself as he repeats the directions for costume and make-up that earlier had existed outside the play proper: "White hair catching light. White gown. White socks. White foot of pallet edge of frame stage left. Once white." The terrifying past is now dissolved into mere "ghosts," and that word reverberates with "Ghost light. Ghost nights. Ghost rooms. Ghost graves. Ghost . . . he all but said ghost loved ones" (p. 79). In point of fact, the monologue now acknowledges itself: art is "ghosts" in this sense of being fictive, insubstantial. This aesthetic birth encapsulates the "one matter" (p. 79) of the story: "The dead and gone." Art becomes our way of saying and coping with death. Not alive, mere words, words, words, it is itself the perfect correlative for that undiscovered and insubstantial country from whose bourne no traveler returns.

As *A Piece of Monologue* ends, the "word," we are told, "begone." The monologue is about to end, its words going and soon to be gone; words, having done their work, can now go, can give way to vision. The human light, the lamplight, is going. In effect, the physical (light) and verbal (words) dimensions of the legitimate theater are now about to go, the play having finished or the Speaker having worked his way through an enervating history to a creative account of and encounter with the ultimate subject: "The dead and gone" (p. 79). The mechanical light, the "*standard lamp*" as Beckett calls it in the stage directions, dies, but not the "other." I take that reference to "other" (or "the unaccountable. From nowhere. On all sides nowhere") to be the larger, mysterious, more significant involuntary light of the memory: here the Speaker's ability to form his own vision, to escape art linked to the actual. There were no pictures of the funeral on that wall, only portraits of the once living. It is the passage from life to death, not social poses, that must be the concern not only of Beckett's Speaker as he approaches death but of us all. For the Speaker the globe is "alone gone." Now this fact is of no concern to him; we alone notice the lamp dim, though, ironically, he himself has given the cue for that dimming: "Thirty seconds." The Speaker is staring beyond, his vision complete; he has won victory by confronting imaginatively what he had otherwise avoided. As when Hamm had his vision, we, the audience—all those who are still living or, conversely, who cannot claim the immunity of a life circumscribed by art—we "remain."

iv

What distinguishes these three latest Beckett plays is a certain healthy balance between thematics and aesthetics, for the process of art here clearly becomes a way of understanding or containing the real tragedies of life, whether it be one's inability to find another kindred soul *(Rockaby)* or the fear of being alone *(Ohio Impromptu)* or the fear of dying *A Piece of Monologue).* Such themes are converted from issues of philosophy or theology or sociology into subjects for art that through the surrogates onstage (the daughter in the rocking chair, the Listener, and here the Speaker) enables us both to understand and, within the "frame" of the play, to contain them. Death itself is not absolved or eradicated; but death is subsumed as a subject for art, as an entry into its mirror world. In that fact there is a certain comfort; appropriately, the visitor in *Ohio Impromptu,* who may be aligned with the Reader or actor, has come to bring "comfort." The play does for us what life cannot: however absolutely tragic death or loneliness or isolation may be offstage, each is the conveyance for a comic, meta-dramatic victory onstage. Within the play, the Speaker can face the otherwise "Unaccountable," as can his audience.

These three latest plays have sometimes received a less than positive critical reception, the judgment so invoked insisting on newness, an ever-rising curve in the playwright's development.[6] But Beckett seems to cling to the verities, both in terms of subject and what he sees as the function of art. From this second perspective, *Rockaby, Ohio Impromptu,* and *A Piece of Monologue* are welcomed to the canon precisely because they say again what needs to be said.

# Appendix B
## . . . *but the clouds* . . .

Winnie quotes numerous authors, Hamm's "Our revels now are ended" echoes Prospero's own lines, while Dante is a pervasive influence in Beckett. Still, a single work, Yeats's extraordinary poem "The Tower," informs Beckett's television play . . . *but the clouds* . . . to a degree unequaled in the playwright's canon.[1] Reading the poem elucidates more than a title or W's (the woman's) own cryptic lines, for there are deliberate parallels between the two works.[2]

### i

Yeats poses the problem: the poet's physical powers are failing, "decrepit age" tied to him "as to a dog's tail," yet his imagination has never been more "excited, passionate, fantastical." How can he pursue poetry, however, if his roots in the physical world are diminished? More specifically, if his "ear and eye" are now in decline, how can he exercise his creative powers in seeing and then seeing beyond the world of the flesh? Perhaps he should retreat to the abstractions of philosophy, choosing "Plato and Plotinus for a friend"?

Pacing along the battlements of the tower, he sends his "imagination forth," because it does not depend on "day's declining beam," on physical ability alone (20–21). Memory itself will provide the field of vision, and such memory now spews forth a host of figures, artists of lesser or greater degree: the aristocratic Mrs. French, epitomized in the opulence of her "silver candlestick" and "dark mahogany," whose grandeur inspired a serving man to clip "an insolent farmer's ears" with garden shears (25–32); the peasant girl passing farmers who are drunk at a country fair and driving them to madness with her song, however much they may have confused the "brightness of the moon" (her song) with their own "prosaic light of day" (41–48); and the blind poet who composed that song and thereby finds an ancestor in Homer (49–56). Most of all, Yeats remembers his own creation, Hanrahan, whose physical and poetic abilities were one, a man who could "plunge" into the "labyrinth of another's being" (110–12). Given his physical state, can the poet now create from memory? Or, as Yeats phrases it, "Does imagination dwell the most/Upon a woman won or woman lost?"

218

(113–14). As he defines both the poetic process and the influence of poetry, Yeats answers affirmatively that rhetorical question first posed.

The aged poet is more secure in his craft. That he cannot engage in life to the same degree as other men is now seen as a sign of his uniqueness. As opposed to the farmers who misread the girl's song in terms of their own limited mentality, the poet, Yeats in the twilight of his career, perforce identifies with the dark, with the swan that "must fix his eye/Upon a fading gleam" and there in the "glittering stream" sing "his song" (140–45). Invoking and then refashioning Bishop Berkeley—even as Beckett himself had qualified Berkeley's notion of an all-seeing God or Godot ratifying mankind on this earth—Yeats extends his argument: through memory, the creative man establishes his own "Translunar Paradise" (156), fashioning a world the way a daw fashions her nest by dropping "twigs layer upon layer" (168), establishing a fictive world, born of memory, that embraces the "whole" "lock, stock, and barrel," even life and death themselves (148–50). Albeit incapacitated by his "sedentary trade" (180), the poet can identify with "young upstanding men/Climbing the mountainside" and can leave them both his "faith and pride" (173–75).

Some critics see the poem's final stanza as bittersweet, an affirmation that still holds a trace, or more, of anguish at old age:

> Now shall I make my soul,
> Compelling it to study
> In a learned school
> Till the wreck of body,
> Slow decay of blood,
> Testy delirium
> Or dull decrepitude
> Or what worse evil come—
> The death of friends, or death
> Of every brilliant eye
> That made a catch in the breath—
> Seem but the clouds of the sky
> When horizon fades,
> Or a bird's sleepy cry
> Among the deepening shades.

Is Yeats divided here, sincere or insincere, resolved or not resolved? I would argue that the two final images, the clouds and the bird's sleepy cry, set as they are against backgrounds of a fading horizon and deepening shades, provide that resolution. Physical decay is neither ignored nor dismissed lightly; it announces the death of friends and, conversely, prevents Yeats from responding passionately to the "brilliant eye[s]" of his youth. However, the compensation for such loss is an enhancement of vision. Old age forces him to turn to memory, and that memory in turn provides an image for his new perspective on loss (dulled, distant, like clouds in the sky, and no clearer, no keener than the cry of an invisible, sleepy bird) even as it anchors such vision in objects (as opposed to Platonic abstractions) of the physical world. The poet is like the clouds of the sky, with normal men and yet apart; he is like the bird singing to man, able to drive him mad precisely because his voice is not obvious (its cry is "sleepy") and because he finds his origins not in the daylight reality of lesser artists (all those, excluding Hanrahan, who used art for more practical purposes) but in the "deepening shades" of a "Mighty Memory" (86).

ii

The setting of Beckett's television play suggests the diminished physical arena, or the constricted powers of old age. Shadows surround all sides of the five-millimeter diameter that constitutes the stage, and the maximum light is concentrated in the circle's center, with only a "gradual lightening from dark periphery." In Beckett's stage directions, the shadows themselves are described as "deep," and perhaps like the oppressive shadows encircling the narrow bench in *Come and Go,* or the shadows into which Krapp moves once he leaves the desk stage center. Indeed, the gamut of life itself—the external world ("1. West, roads."), the world of the individual ("3. East, closet."), and the world of the mind ("2. North, sanctum.")—is clustered around the circle, though it is only implied. In parallel fashion, the medium here, television, is also constricted; as opposed to the mobile cameras of *Eh Joe* and *Ghost Trio,* we have here one stationary camera and only three possible shots: a near shot of M from behind, "bowed over invisible table," against a "dark ground"; a close-up of the woman's face "reduced as far as possible to eyes and mouth"; and a long shot of the set empty or with MI. Perhaps the set resembles the interior of a church, with the altar (sanctum) to the north, the congregation (or audience) taking the position behind the camera to the south, and the choir stalls arrayed on the east and west, perpendicular to the altar. Perhaps we see a service for the dead, or a summing up of one's life before the altar—the situation as depicted in *Theater II.*

The play itself has four distinct sections, comparable to the three sections and that coda (lines 181–95) in Yeats's poem. Within that structure the play deals with the same issues of artistic creation in old age and creation itself.

Section one (numbers 1–19) is at once a lament for the past, for those times—"always night"—when the woman appeared, and the invocation necessary for her appearance so desired by M. The mood is clearly past tense: "When I thought of her it was always night. I came in—" and "When she appeared it was always night." The contemplative M, seated at the invisible table, opens the play by recalling W's earlier appearances, confusing her appearance with his own, and thereby raising the possibility that the woman is not a separate being but rather an image of his own creative imagination, his own mind, like the women in *Embers, Eh Joe,* and *Ghost Trio.* She appears only after M has left the roads and changed into his robe and skullcap (located in the closet to the east side), after he, in effect, has abandoned the "break of day" and "brought night home," even as Yeats makes a distinction between the day's literal reality and his own night of creativity. M gives way to MI, who then demonstrates through actual stage movements (he enters from the west, goes to the closet, changes clothes, returns to center stage, and then enters the sanctum to the north) the past appearance as described by M. As in *Come and Go*, the effort to "say" the past dissolves into a present enactment of that past (or "Shall we hold hands in the old way?" as Vi would say). Stage 18 offers an uninterrupted rehearsal, a dress rehearsal, of the four actions prerequisite to the woman's appearance, and as M disappears in the north shadow, the voice pronounces the first section closed: "Right."

Section two (numbers 20–26) concentrates on M's life in the sanctum, in the realm of his mind. V now plays a larger role, informing us that there in the dark M would "beg" her to appear, that such begging came from long-standing "use and wont," that the begging was always silent ("a begging of the mind"), and that either she appeared or failed to appear (at which point he "wearied, and ceased"). V then speculates about what would be his state if she never appeared: his alternatives would be to busy himself with "something else, or with nothing" or to wait for the break of day when he could shed robe and skullcap and "issue forth again."

Surely V, through M, is rephrasing in Beckett's own fashion the dilemma Yeats presents. Experience in the real world (the "roads") provides the grounds for artistic vision, but such experience in itself does not guarantee creation. The bridge between life outside the circle and that creative life inside the sanctum is a delicate one: at stage 22 we get our first brief glimpse ("2 seconds") of W. Now, half the short play is completed, and we have yet to hear the woman. If M is a sedentary character, like the aged Yeats, the issue is this: can memory alone, can prior experience serve as a sufficient stimulus for vision and the language with which it is conveyed? Stage 25 repeats stage 18 as MI goes through the motions preceding W's appearance (leaving one's room, traveling the roads of life), thereby completing the other half of the circle (returning to one's room from those roads, shedding the clothes of the daylight world, and clothing oneself in robe and skullcap). Again, the section closes with V pronouncing a single "Right."

Section three (numbers 27–52, to the opening word "Right") returns us to the sedentary M of the play's opening. Now, in a pseudo-logical (or lightly mathematical) style he introduces the variant possibilities for the woman's appearing. He can "distinguish three cases." One, she appeared and then disappeared "in the same breath" (almost total frustration, aggravated by a tantalizingly brief second appearance, the woman's own *Come and Go*); two, she lingered before disappearing (here M is able to flesh out her otherwise brief portrait with the line "With those unseeing eyes I so begged then alive to look at me"). With this second possibility thus raised, W's appearance expands from two to five seconds. The third possibility is the most fertile; she not only appears and lingers, but utters, albeit *"inaudi-*

*bly,"* the lines from Yeats: ". . . clouds . . . but the clouds . . . of the sky." M's voice joins hers *("murmuring, synchronous with lips")* in "but the clouds." (We will recall a similar direction at the end of *Eh Joe* when only the italicized words spoken by the woman are audible to us.)

W is the muse, the mysterious source of creativity that is hard to invoke and even harder to sustain. M's progress from the roads to his room to the sanctum of his mind thus represents the gamut of activity experienced by the artist as he himself moves from participation in the real world to his own artistic refashioning of that experience so that life becomes both existence and essence. The meager line from W itself demonstrates at once the difficulty and the achievement of such creation, the artist's uniqueness and hence isolation in a world otherwise given to less fragile, more tangible occupations. In a sense, both poem and play are about "how it happens," about the anxiety of creation, and also about its joy, for this time the rehearsal (stage 42) not only repeats the full circle of stages 18 and 25 but leads to intermixed shots of M and W and the combined speaking (audible and inaudible) of artist and muse. As V implores her to "speak" to him (stage 50), the next stage (51) dissolves to the stationary shot of M; the implication here is that she speaks inside his head and that M's V and W (like M and V in *Footfalls*) are part of the same equation.

Stage 52 opens with V's "Right," the benediction, in effect, following the successful rehearsal that led to the miniature performance contained in 50–51. M had told us earlier that he begs her to appear in his mind; accordingly, when W speaks, she speaks without audible words. It is the artist, M, who then transfers those sounds to the public. In terms of *Cascando*, MI is Opener and M is Voice, the public and private dimensions of the artist, though the duality is ultimately blurred once we realize that the public artist (on the roads) is inseparable from the private side (the sanctum, or M at the "invisible stool bowed over invisible table"), art itself, even Beckett's art, being a compromise between the artist's vision of what is outside him and his filtering of that externality through his own imagination.

After the benediction "Right," we learn that M has not given us all the "cases": there is one more, "by far the commonest, in the proportion say of nine hundred and ninety-nine to one, or nine hundred and ninety-eight to two," when vision proves impossible, when the bridge between the roads and the sanctum breaks and W does not appear. If this is the case, if poetic inspiration fails, then the only alternative—short of suicide, short of acknowledging the absolute futility of the artist's task, that "suffering"[3] akin to failure—is to busy oneself with "something else, more . . . rewarding." The voice struggles for an example, and produces "cube roots" or "nothing" or "that MINE" (in the sense of tangible things to be excavated, or one's self without the obligation to express that self or sanctum to others). But Beckett's V here, like Yeats's poet in "The Tower," cannot live with these alternatives, with a goal other than that of creation. For such alternatives lead only to—said with a pause—"the back roads," roles given more to habit than imagination, the world of solid achievement, and rewards. As we know from Beckett's *Proust,* such habits have little to do with man's inner reality, his sanctum or spirit.

Yeats's difficulty with his role as artist stems both from old age and from his hesitation in committing himself to an endeavor that by definition is lonely, of and not of the ordinary world, difficult as the mountain itself is difficult to climb for those upstanding men he admires. Beckett's M— surely Beckett himself—concentrates more on the conditions of artistic creation, its complicated set of requirements: experience on the road, retreating to one's self, interacting with the principles of art here embodied in the woman, trying to effect a balance between the eye (both inner and outer) and the ear (both inner and outer). In Yeats the poem itself, or the poet through the poem, delivers the persona from the initial dilemma: the final images of far-off clouds and a sleepy bird singing in darkening shades stand as correlatives both for the poet's tragedy (his removal from the world of the fair, from political life as broadly defined) and his accomplishment as he speaks of the poet's life through two symbols from that same everyday world.

In the coda to Beckett's television play—stages 53 to 60—the play delivers us from that unwanted fourth case. First, in mime MI emerges from the sanctum, exits to this closet, and, after removing his inner clothes (robe and skullcap) and donning his outer clothes (great coat and hat), reemerges and then disappears "in west shadow." Does he enter the road in despair (case four) or in hope (cases one to three, with three being the preferred state)? V pronounces "Right," that word associated before with completion yet now ambiguous: it may simply be a stage direction, since the road is literally stage right.

Suddenly the play delivers its vision: there is a dissolve to M, then to W, and then we hear the voice of the artist (V without W's voice, or V and W now at one) as we see a 5-second shot of the woman's eyes and mouth—that is, the visual and verbal dimensions of Beckett's theaters, whatever the medium. We hear again the lines from "The Tower," but this time the poem, even as the play itself is doing, completes itself: ". . . but the clouds of the sky . . . when the horizon fades . . . or a bird's sleepy cry . . . among the deepening shades. . . ." One last shot of M is seen, and then a fade into darkness. Like Keats's "Beauty," the play is both its own excuse for being and, therefore, justification for the creative act of performance. The play has fulfilled case three, the union of playwright and muse, public and private artist, thereby establishing that delicate balance between the two worlds, even as it champions that inner world without which the external world would be only meaningless, random. Redoing Bishop Berkeley, even as Yeats himself suggested, Beckett creates here a "superhuman / Mirror-resembling dream" (164–65).[4]

# Notes and Pertinent Sources

## PREFACE    Beckett's Aesthetics: Theories and Practice

1. *The Unnamable*, p. 410. All references to Beckett's works are to the Grove Press editions (see n. 63 of this chapter); and the text for quotations from Shakespeare is *The Complete Signet Classic Shakespeare*, gen. ed. Sylvan Barnet (New York: Harcourt Brace Jovanovich, Inc., 1972).

2. *The Unnamable*, p. 294.

3. *transition* 21 (1932): 148. For commentary on Beckett's own criticism, see John Fletcher, "Samuel Beckett as Critic," *The Listener* 74 (1965): 862–63; and J. Mitchell Morse, "The Ideal Core of the Onion: Samuel Beckett's Criticism," *French Review* 38 (1965): 23–29.

4. Deirdre Bair, *Samuel Beckett: A Biography* (New York and London: Harcourt Brace Jovanovich, 1978).

5. *Proust*, p. 64.

6. Frederick J. Hoffman, *Samuel Beckett: The Language of Self* (New York: Dutton, 1964).

7. "Dante . . . Bruno. Vico . . Joyce," in *Our Examination round his Factification for Incamination of Work in Progress* (Paris: Shakespeare and Co., 1929), pp. 3–22.

8. I take this list of Beckett's philosophic influences from John Pilling's excellent review in *Samuel Beckett* (London, Henley, and Boston: Routledge and Kegan Paul, 1976), pp. 110–31. For a good discussion of Beckett's debt to Schopenhauer, J. D. O'Hara, "Where There's a Will There's A Way Out: Beckett and Schopenhauer," *College Literature* 8 (1981): 249–70. O'Hara suggests that Beckett humanizes the will, giving it a consciousness that Schopenhauer denies, even as he takes from that will the freedom assigned by Schopenhauer.

9. *Stories and Texts for Nothing*, "Text 12," p. 135. For Beckett's debt to existentialism see Edith Kern, *Existential Thought and Fictional Technique: Kierkegaard, Sartre, and Beckett* (New Haven, Conn.: Yale University Press, 1970), pp. 162–240. Kern, for example, speaks of the character's dilemma in Beckett as the "essential isolation and the incommunicability of his most crucial experience" (p. 184).

10. *Proust*, p. 11.

11. "Fingal," *More Pricks than Kicks*, p. 29.

12. Lawrence Harvey offers the most comprehensive account of Beckett's critical positions in *Samuel Beckett: Poet and Critic* (Princeton, N.J.: Princeton University Press, 1970). See also Harvey's "Art and the Existential in *En attendant Godot*," *PMLA* 75 (1960): 137–46; and "Samuel Beckett on Life, Art, and Criticism," *Modern Language Notes* 80 (1965): 545–62.

13. "Imagination Dead Imagine," *First Love and Other Stories*, p. 66.

14. "La Peinture des van Veldes, ou: le monde et le pantulon," *Cahiers d'Art* 20, 21 (1945–46): 349–54, 356. And comments by Pilling, *Samuel Beckett*, p. 19.

15. *The Lost Ones*, p. 42.

16. *Stories and Texts for Nothing*, "Text 13," p. 138.

17. *Proust*, p. 9.

18. Ibid., p. 49.

19. Ibid., p. 16.

20. Harvey, *Samuel Beckett*, p. 435.

21. *transition* 16, 17 (June, 1929): 268–71. See Robinson Bradbury, "A Way with Words: Paradox, Silence, and Samuel Beckett," *Cambridge Quarterly* 5 (1971): 249–64.

22. *Stories and Texts for Nothing*, "Text 11," p. 131.

224

23. *Murphy*, pp. 111–13.

24. Ibid., p. 250.

25. *Stories and Texts for Nothing*, "Text 13," p. 112.

26. *Malone Dies*, p. 189.

27. *The Unnamable*, p. 351.

28. *Malone Dies*, p. 192.

29. *Watt*, p. 254.

30. Harvey, *Poet and Critic*, p. 423.

31. *Watt*, p. 77.

32. *The Unnamable*, p. 352.

33. Harvey, *Poet and Critic*, p. 430.

34. Pilling, *Samuel Beckett*, p. 128.

35. "Three Dialogues with George Duthuit," in Martin Esslin, ed., *Samuel Beckett: A Collection of Critical Essays* (Englewood Cliffs, N.J.: Prentice-Hall, 1965), p. 21. And Livio Dobrey, "Samuel Beckett's Irreducible," *Southern Review* 6 (1973): 205–21, where he argues that the "Three Dialogues" accurately describe Beckett's own work, and his concept of silence existing below the Cartesian *cogito*.

36. "Dialogues," in Esslin, *Critical Essays*, p. 17.

37. *Stories and Texts for Nothing*, "Text 5," p. 99.

38. *Proust*, p. 19. See, also, John Pilling, "Beckett's *Proust*," *Journal of Beckett Studies* 1 (1976): 8–29.

39. *Proust*, p. 20.

40. "The Expelled," *Stories and Texts for Nothing*, p. 9.

41. *Proust*, p. 55.

42. Ibid., p. 56.

43. Ibid., p. 59.

44. "Dante . . . Bruno. Vico . . Joyce," pp. 3–22.

45. "Dieppe 3," *Poems in English*, p. 59.

46. *Molloy*, p. 65.

47. *How It Is*, p. 73.

48. *Proust*, p. 8.

49. "Three Dialogues," in Esslin, *Critical Essays*, p. 17.

50. *The Unnamable*, p. 363.

51. "Poetry is Vertical," *transition* 21 (1932): 148.

52. *The Lost Ones*, p. 60.

53. *Molloy*, p. 64.

54. *How It Is*, p. 146.

55. These remarks about *Antony and Cleopatra* are taken from the preface to my *When the Theater Turns to Itself: The Aesthetic Metaphor in Shakespeare* (Lewisburg, Pa.: Bucknell University Press, 1981), pp. 9–10.

56. For this notion of the critic as audience member, I am indebted to Morris Weitz, *Hamlet and the Philosophy of Literary Criticism* (Chicago: University of Chicago Press, 1964).

57. "Dante . . . Bruno. Vico . . Joyce," p. 13; and see comments by Pilling, *Samuel Beckett*, p. 14. Maurice Valency speaks of Beckett as being like Pirandello, though "more poignant" in his pervasive theatrical metaphor, in his *The End of the World: An Introduction to Contemporary Drama* (New York: Oxford University Press, 1980), pp. 388–418, quotation on p. 417.

58. The comments on *Godot* are from my preface to *When the Theater Turns to Itself*, pp. 20–22.

59. See my "Florida and Beckett: *Waiting for Godot* and *Come and Go*," *Vision* 1 (1979): 122–129.

60. Ruby Cohn comments on *Eleutheria* in *Just Play: Beckett's Theater* (Princeton, N.J.: Princeton University Press, 1980), pp. 163–72. Also, Richard L. Admussen, "Samuel Beckett's Unpublished Writing," *Journal of Beckett Studies* 1 (1976): 66–74. Clas Zilliacus in *Beckett and Broadcasting* (Abo, Finland: Abo Akademi, 1976) also discusses efforts to translate *All That Fall* and *Embers* to the stage in "The Plays Out of Their Element" (pp. 169–82). Recently Beckett

has given Frederick Neumann permission to perform his fiction piece *Company;* Ruby Cohn suggests that this signals "fiction *and* drama as a new concentrate," in her "Beckett's Theater Resonance," *Beckett Humanistic Perspectives,* ed. Morris Beja, S. E. Gontarski, and Pierre Astier (Columbus: Ohio State University Press, 1983), p. 13. See too in that same volume the fine article on *Company* by Enoch Brater, "The *Company* Beckett Keeps: The Shape of Memory and One Fabulist's Decay of Lying," pp. 157–71.

61. "The Calmative," *Stories and Texts for Nothing,* p. 28. In "Beckett and His Interpreters" Martin Esslin suggests three general areas that critics might explore: Beckett's erudition, the structural principles of the works themselves, and the impact of the work upon the critic (the critic's personal "translation" of a playwright who invites just such translation). *Meditations: Essays on Brecht, Beckett, and the Media* (Baton Rouge: Louisiana State University Press, 1980), pp. 75–92.

62. In the notes that follow and in the text itself, I make use, of course, of a great many of those scholars and critics who have commented on Beckett. However, it seems appropriate at this point to call attention to some important works that were on my desk at all times but that are referred to infrequently or not at all in the notes themselves. Indeed, some of the entries below had, for me, a pervasive general influence even though I make no specific or consistent reference to them.

(1) Lionel Abel, *Metatheatre: A New View of Dramatic Form* (New York: Hill and Wang, 1963).

(2) Alfred Alvarez, *Samuel Beckett* (New York: Viking, 1973).

(3) Herbert Blau, "Meanwhile, Follow the Bright Angels," *Tulane Drama Review* 5 (1960): 89–101.

(4) Herbert Blau, *The Impossible Theatre: A Manifesto* (New York: Macmillan, 1964).

(5) Frederick Busi, *The Transformation of Godot* (Lexington: University Press of Kentucky, 1980).

(6) John Calder, ed., *Beckett at 60* (London: Calder and Boyars, 1967).

(7) Richard Coe, *Samuel Beckett* (New York: Grove Press, 1964).

(8) Ruby Cohn, *Samuel Beckett: A Collection of Criticism* (New York: McGraw-Hill, 1975).

(9) Ramona Cormier and Janis L. Pallister, *Waiting for Death: The Philosophical Significance of Beckett's "En attendent Godot"* (University, Ala: University of Alabama Press, 1979).

(10) Guy Croussy, *Samuel Beckett* (Paris: Hachette, 1971).

(11) Francis Doherty, *Samuel Beckett* (London: Hutchinson, 1971).

(12) Tom Driver, "Beckett by the Madeleine," *Columbia University Forum* 4 (1961): 21–25.

(13) Colin Duckworth, *Angels of Darkness* (London: Allen and Unwin, 1972).

(14) Martin Esslin, *Samuel Beckett: A Collection of Critical Essays* (Englewood Cliffs, N.J.: Prentice-Hall, 1965).

(15) Martin Esslin, *The Theater of the Absurd* (New York: Doubleday and Co., 1961).

(16) Martin Esslin, "Voices, Patterns, Voices: Samuel Beckett's Later Plays," *Gambit* 7 (1976): 93–99.

(17) Raymond Federman, *Journey to Chaos: Samuel Beckett's Early Fiction* (Berkeley: University of California Press, 1965).

(18) Raymond Federman and John Fletcher, *Samuel Beckett, His Works and His Critics: An Essay in Bibliography* (Berkeley and Los Angeles: University of California Press, 1970).

(19) Beryl S. Fletcher, John Fletcher, Barry Smith, and Walter Bachem, *A Student's Guide to the Plays of Samuel Beckett* (London and Boston: Faber and Faber, 1978).

(20) John Fletcher, *Samuel Beckett's Art* (New York: Barnes and Noble, 1967).

(21) John Fletcher and John Spurling, *Beckett: A Study of His Plays* (New York: Hill and Wang, 1972).

(22) David I. Grossvogel, *The Blasphemers: The Theatre of Brecht, Ionesco, Beckett, Genet* (Ithaca, N.Y.: Cornell University Press, 1965).

(23) Ihab Hassan, *The Literature of Silence* (New York: Alfred A. Knopf, 1967).

(24) Ronald Hayman, *Samuel Beckett* (London: Heinemann, 1970).

(25) David Hesla, *The Shape of Chaos: An Interpretation of the Art of Samuel Beckett* (Minneapolis: University of Minnesota Press, 1972).

(26) Josephine Jacobsen and William R. Mueller, *The Testament of Samuel Beckett* (London: Faber and Faber, 1966).

(27) Ludovic Janvier, *Pour Samuel Beckett* (Paris: Les Editions de Minuit, 1966).

(28) Ludovic Janvier, *Samuel Beckett: par lui-meme* (Paris: Editions du Seuil, 1969).

(29) Sighle Kennedy, *Murphy's Bed* (Lewisburg, Pa.: Bucknell University Press, 1971).

(30) James Knowlson, *Light and Darkness in the Theatre of Samuel Beckett* (London: Turret Books, 1972).

(31) Jean-Jacques Mayoux, "Beckett and Expressionism," *Modern Drama* 9 (1966): 238–41.

(32) Jean-Jacques Mayoux, "The Theatre of Samuel Beckett," *Perspective* 11 (1959): 142–55.

(33) Vivian Mercier, *Beckett/Beckett* (New York: Oxford University Press, 1977).

(34) Vivian Mercier, *The Irish Comic Tradition* (Oxford: Clarendon Press, 1962).

(35) Patrick Murray, *The Tragic Comedian: A Study of Samuel Beckett* (Cork, Ireland: Mercier, 1970).

(36) Jean Ominus, *Beckett* (Paris, Bruges: Desclée de Brouvier, 1968).

(37) Leonard C. Pronko, *Avant-Garde: The Experimental Theatre in France* (Berkeley: University of California Press, 1962).

(38) Alec Reid, *All I Can Manage, More Than I Could: An Approach to the Plays of Samuel Beckett* (Chester Springs, Pa.: Dufour Editions, 1968).

(39) Konrad Schoell, *Das Theater Samuel Becketts* (Munich: Fink, 1970).

(40) Nathan A. Scott, *Samuel Beckett* (New York: Hillary House Publishers Library, 1965).

(41) Israel Shenker, "Moody Man of Letters," *New York Times*, May 6, 1956, sec. 2, p. 1.

(42) Alan Simpson, *Beckett and Behan and a Theater in Dublin* (London: Routledge and Kegan Paul, 1962).

(43) James T. Tanner and J. Don Vann, *Samuel Beckett: A Checklist of Criticism* (Kent, Ohio: Kent State University Press, 1969).

(44) William York Tindall, *Samuel Beckett*, Columbia Essays on Modern Writers 4 (New York: Columbia University Press, 1964).

(45) Eugene Webb, *The Dark Dove: The Sacred and Secular in Modern Literature* (Seattle: University of Washington Press, 1975).

(46) George E. Wellwarth, *The Theater of Protest and Paradox: Developments in the Avant-Garde Drama* (New York: New York University Press, 1964).

(47) Robert N. Wilson, "Samuel Beckett: The Social Psychology of Emptiness," *The Writer as Social Seer* (Chapel Hill: University of North Carolina Press, 1979), pp. 134–44.

63. I have used the following texts for Beckett:

*Cascando and Other Short Dramatic Pieces* (New York: Grove Press, 1967). *(Cascando, Words and Music, Eh Joe, Play, Come and Go,* and *Film).*
*Company* (New York: Grove Press, 1981).
*Endgame* (New York: Grove Press, 1958).
*Ends and Odds* (New York: Grove Press, 1977). *(Not I, That Time, Footfalls, Ghost Trio, Theatre I, Theatre II, Radio I, Radio II).* Note: the 1981 edition adds *. . . but the clouds. . . .*
*Film* (New York: Grove Press, 1969).
*First Love and Other Stories* (New York: Grove Press, 1974). ("First Love," "From an Abandoned Work," "Enough," "Imagination Dead Imagine," "Ping," *Not I, Breath).*
*Fizzles* (New York: Grove Press, 1976).
*Happy Days* (New York: Grove Press, 1961).
*How It Is* (New York: Grove Press, 1964).
*Krapp's Last Tape and Other Dramatic Pieces* (New York: Grove Press, 1960). *(Krapp's Last Tape, All That Fall, Embers, Act Without Words I, Act Without Words II).*

*The Lost Ones* (New York: Grove Press, 1972).
*Mercier and Camier* (New York: Grove Press, 1975).
*More Pricks Than Kicks* (New York: Grove Press, 1972).
*Murphy* (New York: Grove Press, 1957).
*Poems in English* (New York: Grove Press, 1961).
*Proust* (New York: Grove Press, 1970).
*Rockaby and Other Short Pieces* (New York: Grove Press, 1981). *(Rockaby, Ohio Impromptu, A Piece of Monologue)*.
*Stories and Texts for Nothing* (New York: Grove Press, 1967). ("The Expelled," "The Calmative," "The End," "Texts for Nothing 1–13").
*Three Novels by Samuel Beckett* (New York: Grove Press, 1965). *(Molloy, Malone Dies, The Unnamable)*.
*Waiting for Godot* (New York: Grove Press, 1954).
*Watt* (New York: Grove Press, 1959).

64. Ruby Cohn, *Just Play: Beckett's Theater* (Princeton, N.J.: Princeton University Press, 1980); and James Knowlson and John Pilling, *Frescoes of the Skull: The Later Prose and Drama of Samuel Beckett* (New York: Grove Press, 1980).

65. *Malone Dies*, p. 182.


## CHAPTER 1.  *Waiting for Godot*: The Art of Playing

1. See, for example, the variety of critical responses to *Godot* in Ruby Cohn's edition, *Casebook on "Waiting for Godot"* (New York: Grove Press, 1965), and Ruby Cohn, "Beckett's German *Godot*," *Journal of Beckett Studies* 1 (1976): 41–49. I should also mention at the outset a fine book on the play by Bert O. States: *The Shape of Paradox: An Essay on "Waiting for Godot"* (Berkeley: University of California Press, 1978). States's approach is, for want of a better word, "philosophical" to my theatrical, but we see very much the same play. He speaks of Beckett's ideas as lurking under the surface action, the trivial riding upon the profound, and the corresponding "freedom of inference" (p. 25) that the play encourages. Especially revealing are the discussions of "generic time and place" in the play, the "mythic poetry" (p. 44) of Lucky's speech, the intersection of fortune and accident (in the chapter on "The Fool of Time," pp. 61–72), Estragon's and Vladimir's being forced into time without content and thus into "a diversionary routine which is the last refuge of the dying ego" (p. 81), and the gap between expectation (the future) and the memory (the past), between logic and those moments when "the unforeseen suddenly erupts" (p. 114).

2. For a detailed account of "Happenings," Albert Poland and Bruce Mailman, eds.; *The Off, Off Broadway Book: The Plays, People, Theatre* (Indianapolis, Ind.: Bobbs-Merrill, 1972). And for the work of a specific artist see *Joseph Beuys: Life and Works*, ed. Götz Adriani, Winifred Konnertz, and Karin Thomas (Woodbury, N.J.: Barron's Educational Series, 1979). Charles Peake places Beckett within and without the conventions of the theater in "*Waiting for Godot* and the Conventions of the Drama," *Prompt* 4 (1964): 19–23.

3. Mircea Eliade, *Cosmos and History: The Myth of the Eternal Return* (New York: Harper Torchbooks, 1960). On the meaning of time in Beckett see Jeffrey G. Sobosan, "Time and Absurdity in Samuel Beckett," *Thought* 49 (1974): 187–95; and Robert M. Torrance, "Modes of Being and Time in the World of *Godot*," *Modern Language Quarterly* 28 (1967): 77–95.

4. Richard Scheckner distinguishes two rhythms in the play: one of the play and the other of the stage. Pozzo is worried about time, Gogo and Didi about place; and in the play, time and space constitute "discontinuous coordinates." To battle this discontinuity, the characters rely on habits, memory, and games. Yet even when the Godot-game is over, the theater-game keeps the actors in their places: they cannot move. Richard Scheckner, "There's Lots of Time in *Godot*," *Modern Drama* 9 (1966): 268–76.

5. *Stories and Texts for Nothing*, "Text 8," p. 112.

6. For a good account of the challenges in directing the play, Walter D. Asmus, "Beckett Directs *Godot*," *Theater Quarterly* 5 (1975): 19–26.

7. "The Expelled," *Stories and Texts for Nothing*, p. 16; and *The Unnamable*, p. 295.

8. *Mercier and Camier*, p. 13. For comments on "time consciousness" (p. 474) and the "temporal discontinuity and spatial separation," Thomas Postlewait, "Self-performing Voices: Mind, Memory and Time in Beckett's Drama," *Twentieth Century Literature* 24 (1978): 473–91.

9. For a survey of the sometimes amazing identifications given to Pozzo and Lucky see Melvin J. Friedman, "Critic!," *Modern Drama* 8 (1966): 403–8. Could Pozzo be Joyce and Lucky Beckett? For a detailed and most impressive account of the relationship between Beckett and Joyce, I refer to Barbara Reich Gluck, *Beckett and Joyce: Friendship and Fiction* (Lewisburg, Pa.: Bucknell University Press, 1978).

10. See Alain Robbe-Grillet, "Samuel Beckett, or Presence on the Stage," in *Snapshots Towards a New Novel* (New York: Grove Press, 1966), pp. 111–25.

11. The pioneering article on *Godot*'s structure is, surely, Edith Kern's "Drama Stripped for Inaction: Beckett's *Godot*," *Yale French Studies* 14 (1954–55): 41–47.

12. *The Unnamable*, p. 314.

13. For an account of the first prison production of *Godot* see "1. The Play's the Thing," "2. "Memos of a First-Nighter," "3. San Francisco Group Leaves S. Q. Audience Waiting for Godot," *San Quentin News* 28 (Nov. 28, 1957): 1, 3. A more detailed account of my own experience performing this play in Florida's state prisons is found in "Florida and Beckett: *Waiting for Godot* and *Come and Go*," *Vision* 1 (1979): 122–29.

14. There is a fine chapter on *Watt* in Raymond Federman, *Journey to Chaos: Samuel Beckett's Early Fiction* (Berkeley and Los Angeles: University of California Press, 1965); and Jacqueline Hoefer, "*Watt*," *Perspectives* 11 (1959): 166–82.

15. *Watt*, p. 254.

16. "Fizzle 5," p. 39; *Watt*, pp. 136–38, where Watt examines three frogs lying in a ditch and croaking—contrapuntally.

17. I describe this production, and its metadramatic implications, in some greater detail in "When the Theater Turns to Itself," *New Literary History* 2 (1971): 407–17.

18. *Happy Days*, p. 31. I have not focused on *Godot* from a Christian, or generally theological perspective. But see Richard Coe, "God and Samuel Beckett," *Meanjin* 24 (1965): 66–85; Bernard Dukore, "Gogo, Didi, and the Absent Godot," *Drama Survey* 1 (1962): 301–7. More directly, Ronald Gray, "*Waiting for Godot*: A Christian Interpretation," *The Listener* 57 (Jan. 24, 1957): 160–61; also Kenneth Hamilton, "Negative Salvation in Samuel Beckett," *Queen's Quarterly* 69 (1962): 102–11. On this issue of a Christian interpretation of Beckett, Kristin Morrison adopts, I think, a circumspect view in "Neglected Biblical Allusions in Beckett's Plays: 'Mother Pegg' Once More," in *Samuel Beckett Humanistic Perspectives*, ed. Morris Beja et al. (Columbus: Ohio State University Press, 1983), pp. 91–98. She finds the Bible "a subtle yet significant presence" (p. 97).

19. See Sartre's preface to *The Maids and Deathwatch*, trans. Bernard Fechtman (New York: Grove Press, 1962).

20. A fine article on the relationship between structure and meaning is Konrad Schoell's "The Chain and the Circle: A Structural Comparison of *Waiting for Godot* and *Endgame*," *Modern Drama* 11 (1968): 48–53. For "underplot" see *Endgame*, p. 78.

21. It is illustrative to place Beckett's conception of plot against, say, Aristotle's in his *Poetics*, where plot, the "structure of the incidents" (p. 23) as Aristotle terms it, is the most significant element in the drama's illusion. Walter Jackson Bate, besides furnishing the relevant passages from Aristotle's *Poetics*, offers a fine analysis of the criticism itself in *Criticism: the Major Texts* (New York: Harcourt, Brace and World, Inc., 1952). Ronald Hayman remarks on Beckett's relation to drama past and present (and future) in "*Godot* and After" and "Beckett and Before," *Theatre and Anti-theatre: New Movements Since Beckett* (New York: Oxford University Press, 1979), pp. 1–16, 17–47.

22. *Mercier and Camier*, p. 77.

23. Again, my "When the Theater Turns to Itself," pp. 407–17.

24. Ruby Cohn effectively places Beckett's "absurdity" within the context of other thinkers and playwrights in "The Absurdly Absurd: Avatars of *Godot*," *Comparative Literature Studies* 2 (1965): 233–40.

25. Still, for some critics, the play can be reduced to basics: see, for example, C. Chadwick, "*Waiting for Godot*: A Logical Approach," *Symposium* 14 (1960): 252–57.

26. If *Godot* lacks a single meaning, perhaps it has several "meanings" existing at once in what Norman Rabkin has called a "complementarious" situation: *Shakespeare and the Common Understanding* (New York: The Free Press, 1967).

27. In this regard see Ted L. Estes, "Dimensions of Play in the Literature of Samuel Beckett," *Arizona Quarterly* 33 (1977): 5–25. Estes focuses on *Godot* and *Play*.

28. Bernard Dukore presents a parallel view in "Controversy: A Non-Interpretation of *Godot*," *Drama Survey* 3 (1963): 117–19.

29. In "Dramatic Language in Samuel Beckett," *Calcutta Review* 2 (1970): 73–83, Chaitanya argues that in *Godot* there is a separation of speaking and action, a lack of purpose in the play's speeches that negates any dramatic conflict.

30. Curtis M. Brooks offers a more theological orientation for *Godot* in "The Mythic Pattern in *Waiting for Godot*," *Modern Drama* 9 (1966): 292–99. The tree, the center of the mythical world, symbolizes the renewal of life, but the play, divided between sacred and profane time, offers only repetition without renewal.

31. *The Lost Ones*, p. 8.

32. Gabor Mihalyi provides a somewhat optimistic reading, seeing the play as a tragicomedy, as a negation of negation. To represent an alienated world, the artist needs an alienated form. But Beckett cannot acquiesce in that final negation because genuine art itself is incapable of negation: "Beckett's *Godot* and the Myth of Alienation," *Modern Drama* 9 (1966): 277–82. For a less qualified and therefore even more optimistic view see Dan O. Via's introduction and commentary in *Samuel Beckett's "Waiting for Godot"* (New York: Seabury Press, 1968).

33. In "The Anti-Aesthetics of *Waiting for Godot*," *Centennial Review* 16 (1972): 69–81, Stephen M. Halloran distinguishes between traditional aesthetics (which contends that the work of art contemplates life with disinterest) and Beckett's own anti-aesthetics, his literalness. Vladimir and Estragon, in this view, cannot evade life through language or conceptualization. They are more conscious than we are, closer to the literal bone, and therefore cannot interpret a play that is, for them, only literal. We, on the other hand, must become critics, must assume the burden of interpretation. On the theatrical language of the play, Kathleen George, *Rhythm in Drama* (Pittsburgh, Pa.: Pittsburgh University Press, 1980), pp. 42–48 especially.

34. See Jerome Atkins, "A Note on the Structure of Lucky's Speech," *Modern Drama* 9 (1966): 309; Edith Kern remarks on Lucky's speech in "Beckett's Modernity and Medieval Affinities," *Beckett Humanistic Perspectives*, pp. 31–34. She comments that the play's title itself is "one of the half-serious, half-playful bilingual combinations so often encountered in medieval French literature" (p. 34).

35. Here again is that nihilistic "blessed pus of reason" of which the Unnamable speaks. *The Unnamable*, p. 353.

36. See Ruby Cohn, "Outward Bound Soliloquies," *Journal of Modern Literature* 6 (1977): 17–46, where she investigates ways in which characters, through soliloquy, talk directly and, as in this instance, metadramatically to the audience.

37. *How It Is*, p. 122.

38. In this regard, one finds most salutary the book by John Fletcher and John Spurling, *Beckett: A Study of His Plays* (New York: Hill and Wang, 1972), with its account of productions, theater anecdotes, and its general concern for the playwright's theatrical "history."

39. George Barnard concentrates on the play's "psychological and purely human aspects" (p. xi), finding a split between the "inner-self" and the "pseudo-self," and thus reading *Godot* as a drama of the "split mind" where, for example, Pozzo represents sensations and Lucky thought (p. 100). *Samuel Beckett: A New Approach* (London: J. M. Dent and Sons, Ltd., 1970).

40. Hugh Kenner, *Samuel Beckett: A Critical Study* (Berkeley and Los Angeles: University of California Press, 1968), pp. 159–60.

41. Mark J. Sachner holds that in the trilogy each narrator seizes actual experiences and refines them into literary experiences, so that living itself increasingly becomes an artistic game. Still, there is also an increasing inability to distinguish fact from fiction, and the artistic consciousness is thus a double-edged tool: "The Artist as Fiction: An Aesthetics of Failure in Samuel Beckett's Trilogy," *Midwest Quarterly* 18 (1977): 144–55.

42. In "On Poesy or Art," in Bate's edition of *Criticism: the Major Texts*, p. 23.

43. See Ruby Cohn, "Play and Player in the Plays of Samuel Beckett," *Yale French Studies* 29 (1962): 43–48; and Robert Hollander, "Literary Consciousness and the Consciousness of Literature," *Saturday Review* 83 (1975): 115–27.

44. This is a prop with a considerable history in Beckett. Consider the "brown boots" caked with "mud" or the "single boot" in *Malone Dies*, pp. 272, 197.

45. *The Complete Poems of Emily Jane Brontë*, ed. C. W. Hatfield (New York: Columbia University Press, 1941), "Remembrance."

46. We may be seeing a primary man "split in two" (*Murphy*, p. 109).

47. This metadramatic approach is brilliantly employed in James Calderwood's *Shakespearean Metadrama* (Minneapolis: University of Minnesota Press, 1971); and earlier, and in a more informal fashion, in Anne Barton (née Righter), *Shakespeare and the Idea of the Play* (Baltimore, Md.: Penguin Books, 1967).

48. Scheckner shows how the "us" of the first act changes to "me" in the second, in "There's Lots of Time in *Godot*," pp. 268–76.

49. On this aspect of the play, Edith Kern, "Beckett as Homo Ludens," *Journal of Modern Literature* 6 (1977): 47–68.

50. Even a pain in the neck can be "irrefragable proof of animation" (*The Unnamable*, p. 353), though such animation is not necessarily meaning.

51. In this regard, my own assessment of the play's ultimately comic stance parallels Ruby Cohn's argument, from a different perspective, first in *Samuel Beckett: The Comic Gamut* (New Brunswick, N.J.: Rutgers University Press, 1962) and then refined in *Back to Beckett* (Princeton, N.J.: Princeton University Press, 1973). On the play's consciousness of the theater see June Schlueter, *Metafictional Characters in Modern Drama* (New York: Columbia University Press, 1979), pp. 53–69. She sees the characters as "participants in theater . . . having nothing to show" (p. 55), forced to play theatrical games in a world where "man's alternative to absurdity is action" (p. 62).

52. For me, the world Pozzo envisions and then recreates in his Act 2 "fall" strikes the same tone of pessimism discussed by Michael Robinson in his study, *Beckett: The Long Sonata of the Dead* (London: Hart-Davis, 1969).

53. In a sense the tramps are like the past-less, concept-less and therefore "option-full" heroes that my colleague William R. Robinson finds generated by the medium of the cinema: see "The Movies, Too, Will Make You Free," *Man and the Movies* (Baton Rouge, La.: Louisiana State University Press, 1967), pp. 112–36. Enoch Brater comments on "The 'Absurd' Actor in the Theater of Samuel Beckett," *Educational Theatre Journal* 27 (1975): 197–207. Brater argues that in Beckett Camus's absurd figure confronts on stage a level of absurdity not imagined before. In *Not I* a "literal absurdity" is created simply by the speech-less actor (the Auditor) standing there.

54. For example, James Eliopulos, *Samuel Beckett's Dramatic Language* (The Hague, Paris: Mouton, 1975).

55. See Thomas Barbour, "Beckett and Ionesco," *Hudson Review* 11 (1958): 271–77.

56. Though they did not make their way into the actual notes above, I found the following studies of *Godot* especially helpful:

(1) Jerome Ashmore, "Philosophical Aspects of *Godot*," *Symposium* 16 (1962): 296–304.

(2) Jeremy Beckett, "*Waiting for Godot*," *Meanjin* 15 (1956): 216–18.

(3) Frederick Busi, *The Transformations of Godot* (Lexington: University Press of Kentucky, 1980).

(4) Harry L. Butler, "Balzac and Godeau, Beckett and Godot: A Curious Parallel," *Romance Notes* 3 (1962): 13–17.

(5) Robert Champigny, "Interpretation de *En attendant Godot*," *PMLA* 75 (1960): 329–31.

(6) Ramona Cormier and Janis L. Pallister, *Waiting for Death: The Philosophical Significance of Beckett's "En attendant Godot"* (University, Ala.: University of Alabama Press, 1979).

(7) Colin Duckworth, ed., *En attendant Godot* (London: George C. Harrap and Co., 1966).

(8) A. J. Leventhal, "Mr. Beckett's *En attendant Godot*," *Dublin Magazine* 30 (1954): 11–16.

(9) Jerald Savory, "Samuel Beckett's *Waiting for Godot*," *Explicator* 35 (1976): 9–10.

## CHAPTER 2.    *Endgame*: The Playwright Completes Himself

1. *Malone Dies*, p. 180; *The Unnamable*, p. 346.

2. *Stories and Texts for Nothing*, "Text 2," p. 82.

3. As the narrator of "Fizzle 8" observes, "For to end yet again skull alone in the dark" (p. 55).

4. And this is the state described and sought by *The Unnamable*, p. 373.

5. "Eunug I," *Poems in English*, p. 23.

6. In "A Note on Perception and Communication in Beckett's *Endgame*," *Modern Drama* 4 (1961): 20–22, Allan Brick shows how in dialogue Hamm and Clov become a subject and an object for each other's need to communicate. In this play of divided selves, with the warring halves defined as "hate" and "need," there is no "introspection" or "extrospection" in the common meanings of those two words. For a somewhat different view of the characters' communication, not to mention the playwright's, see Charles R. Lyons, "Beckett's *Endgame*: An Anti-Myth of Creation," *Modern Drama* 7 (1964): 204–9. In J. P. Little's comparison of Beckett and Ionesco, Beckett's characters are seen as in exile from their true selves, their original sin that of being born. "Form and the Void: Beckett's *Fin de partie* and Ionesco's *Les Chaises*," *French Studies* 32 (1978): 46–54.

7. Ruby Cohn, "Play and Player in the Plays of Samuel Beckett," *Yale French Studies* 29 (1962): 43–48.

8. Anthony Easthope, "Hamm, Clov, and Dramatic Method in *Endgame*," *Modern Drama* 10 (1968): 424–33.

9. Hugh Kenner, *Samuel Beckett: A Critical Study* (Berkeley and Los Angeles: University of California Press, 1968), pp. 159–60. Helene Keyssar, commenting on a production of the play in 1975 at Amherst, calls the set a "boat" (p. 236). "Theatre Games, Language Games and *Endgame*," *Theater Journal* 31 (1979): 221–38.

10. Ethel F. Cornwell and Laura Barge, "The Beckett Hero," *PMLA* 92 (1977): 1006–8. B. S. Hammond, in "Beckett and Pinter: Towards a Grammar of the Absurd," *Journal of Beckett Studies* 4 (Spring 1979): 35–42, speaks of how the characters "often try words out for size, put on words as one would put on a new pair of shoes" (p. 38).

11. John Fletcher, "Actor and Play in Beckett's Theater," *Modern Drama* 9 (1966): 242–50.

12. *Stories and Texts for Nothing*, "Text I," p. 75.

13. I am, of course, talking about the way *Endgame* "works" metadramatically, about Beckett's aesthetic "strategy." For an excellent article on the same topic, but from a different approach, Richard M. Eastman, "The Strategy of Samuel Beckett's *Endgame*," *Modern Drama* 2 (1959): 36–44. And see the analysis of talking in *Endgame* by Dina Scherzer, "Beckett's *Endgame*, or What Talk Can Do," *Modern Drama* 22 (1978): 291–303, where, using J. L. Austin's *How to Do Things with Words*, she speaks of doing with talk, playing with talk, talk on talk, and talk on and in language.

14. In *Watt* the old servant leaving Knott's house also appears "dressed for the road" (*Watt*, p. 39), though in leaving Knott, rather than Hamm—God, rather than the artist—he has only a stick in hand, and no bag or bowler.

15. In "The Comic Apocalypse of King Hamm," *Modern Drama* 9 (1966): 310–18, John J.

Sheedy finds a fusion of the comic and the apocalyptic in the play. As in Babylon, one can only finish what is already finished: that is, there can be only destruction, not integration (p. 311). Hamm is the Master-King, trying not to exercise the power to end the world, for that would be to ratify the power that created the world in the beginning. Abandoned by his creations—Clov, Nagg, and Nell—he sees his world as a game; and as his family falls from him, only his own inner reality is left. Hamm, in effect, is the "something" that is taking its "course." As God, Hamm "must demand as well as suffer the denials of his last creation before he can claim his proper non-existence" (p. 318). The play echoes the negative questions raised by Hiroshima and by the Holocaust.

16. Again, Richard Scheckner's comments on the relationship between time and place in "There's Lots of Time in *Godot*," *Modern Drama* 9 (1966): 268–76.

17. Hans-Peter Hasselbach offers a parallel analysis of the Hamm/Clov conflict in "Samuel Beckett's *Endgame:* A Structural Analysis," *Modern Drama* 19 (1976): 25–34.

18. "*King Lear* and *Endgame*" in Jan Kott's *Shakespeare Our Contemporary* (Garden City, N.J.: Doubleday, 1964), pp. 87–124.

19. P. Merivale, "*Endgame* and the Dialogue of King and Fool in the Monarchical Metadrama," *Modern Drama* 21 (1978): 121–36. Paul Lawley offers an excellent analysis of the play in "Symbolic Structure and Creative Obligation in *Endgame*," *Journal of Beckett Studies* 5 (Autumn 1979): 45–68. Lawley contrasts the mythic past and the gray present, the nature (before) and the nonnature (now), and defines language as all we have and yet as a servant that can in turn master us. Particularly revealing is his description of the father in Hamm's story: "The vassal is nothing less than a personification of Hamm's own impulse to survive" (p. 63). Hamm can neither delight in nor reject his own creative impulse.

20. For some interesting and varied comments on the place of Nagg and Nell in the evolution of the play, Ruby Cohn, "Earlier Endgames," *Modern Drama* 21 (1978): 109–19, and her "The Beginnings of *Endgame*," *Modern Drama* 9 (1966): 319–23; also, *Materialien Deutsche zu Becketts "Endspiel"* (Frankfurt am Main: Edition Suhrkamp Verlag, 1968).

21. For a most detailed interpretation of the play, Franzi Maierhofer, *Samuel Beckett, "Endspiel": Interpretation* (Munich: Oldenbourg, 1977).

22. On silences in Beckett, and elsewhere, Ihab Hassan, *The Literature of Silence* (New York: Alfred A. Knopf, 1967).

23. As in *Malone Dies*, the cupboard containing one's possessions and probably the painkiller to which Molloy refers (p. 102) is never opened (*Malone Dies*, p. 184).

24. *The Unnamable*, p. 414.

25. See Richard Lee Francis, "Beckett's Metaphysical Tragicomedy," *Modern Drama* 8 (1965): 259–67.

26. For a religious interpretation of such pessimistic visions, Thomas D. Essele, "The Apocalypse of Beckett's *Endgame*," *Cross Currents* 26 (19): 11–32

27. *Malone Dies*, p. 221.

28. Again, for Beckett's relationship with Joyce see Barbara Reich Gluck, *Beckett and Joyce: Friendship and Fiction* (Lewisburg, Pa.: Bucknell University Press, 1978).

29. Jack E. Frisch argues that the play is, in reality, not one of space but of language, and therefore even smaller than the single stage set would indicate. "*Endgame*: A Play as Poem," *Drama Survey* 3 (1963): 257–63.

30. I. A. Richards, *Principles of Literary Criticism* (New York: Harcourt, Brace, and World, 1950), p. 246.

31. We have known this boy before: in "The Calmative" he is holding a goat by the hand, offering the narrator a sweet (*Stories and Texts for Nothing*, p. 33).

32. See the chapter on *The Tempest* (pp. 192–211) in my *When the Theater Turns to Itself: The Aesthetic Metaphor in Shakespeare* (Lewisburg, Pa: Bucknell University Press, 1981).

33. Gerald Weales makes a convincing argument for the characters' being conveyed primarily by the language of *Endgame*, rather than by plot, action, or even set. "The Language of *Endgame*," *Tulane Drama Review* 6 (1962): 107–17. Indeed, Weales argues that the language is so subtle, so central to characterization, that the play, to be understood, needs more than a single hearing.

34. I have focused on the heroic aspects of Hamm as artist, but for a different perspective on Hamm as a tragic figure see David H. Lowenkron, "A Case for 'The Tragicall Historie of Hamm,'" *Arizona Quarterly* 30 (1974): 217–28. James Acheson, "Chess with the Audience: Samuel Beckett's *Endgame*," *Critical Quarterly* 22 (Summer 1980): 33–45, defines the audience as the black piece, Beckett as the white in a chess game that the playwright, as our omniscient opponent, always wins, even as he invites us to try on various critical approaches, none of them adequate to explain the world of the play. June Schlueter, *Metafictional Characters in Modern Drama* (New York: Columbia University Press, 1979), concentrates on the play's theatrical language, arguing that here "self is role" and that "the world of the shelter is created completely by play" (p. 68).

35. There is a similar concern for temperature and for the general physical climate in *The Lost Ones* (pp. 16–17).

36. *The Unnamable*, p. 360.

37. *Malone Dies*, p. 197.

38. I think that Kenner's remarks on these final moments in *Endgame* are especially insightful. *Samuel Beckett: A Critical Study* (New York: Grove Press, 1961), pp. 160–65.

39. Again see Essele, "The Apocalypse of Beckett's *Endgame*," pp. 11–32.

40. The issue of paradoxical statements and of dramatic contradictions in Beckett is considered by Rolf Breuer, *Die Kunst der Paradoxie: Sinnsuche und Scheitern bei Samuel Beckett* (Munich: Fink, 1976). Richard Keller calls the organizing principle of the play a comic "series of inversions and negations" (p. 511). "Dialectical Laughter: A Study of *Endgame*," *Modern Drama* 25 (1982): 505–13.

41. In "Fizzle 8" Beckett speaks of a "Place of remains where once used to gleam in the dark on and off used to glimmer a remain," of a "skull alone in the dark," and of "Remains of the days of the lights of day never light so faint as theirs so pale" (p. 55). Indeed, the opening section of "Fizzle 8" repeats much of the language of *Endgame*'s end.

42. Like that of *The Unnamable* (p. 379): "Can it be they are resolved at last to seize me by the horns. Looks like it. In that case tableau any minute. Oyez, oyez, I was like them, before being like me. . . ." For Robert Wilcher, Hamm and Clov are caught in Anouilh's trap without hope, their situation being inevitable and therefore tragic. "The Museum of Tragedy: *Endgame* and *Rosencrantz and Guildenstern Are Dead*," *Journal of Beckett Studies* 4 (Spring 1979): 43–54.

## CHAPTER 3.   *Happy Days*: Creation in Spite of Habit

1. Ruby Cohn also finds the character not absolutely pathetic but possessed of a certain comic spirit, in *Samuel Beckett: The Comic Gamut* (New Brunswick, N.J.: Rutgers University Press, 1962), pp. 257–59. Also, Horace Gregory, "Beckett's Dying Gladiators," *Commonwealth* 65 (1956): 88–92.

2. Again, see James Eliopulos, *Samuel Beckett's Dramatic Language* (The Hague, Paris: Mouton, 1975). And the comments on the dead language of Beckett's plays, particularly that of *Happy Days* and *Krapp's Last Tape*, in Andrew K. Kennedy's *Six Dramatists in Search of a Language: Studies in Dramatic Language* (Cambridge: At the University Press, 1975), pp. 130–64.

3. We will recall her namesake in "Fingal" (*More Pricks Than Kicks*).

4. *The Lost Ones*, p. 57.

5. See Laura Barge, "'Coloured Images' in the 'Black' Dark: Samuel Beckett's Latest Fiction," *PMLA* 92 (1977): 273–84.

6. For a list of the literary references made by Winnie see Ruby Cohn, *The Comic Gamut*, pp. 253–59. Also, James Knowlson, "Beckett's 'Bits of Pipe,'" in *Beckett Humanistic Perspectives*, ed. Morris Beja et al. (Columbus: Ohio State University Press, 1983), pp. 16–25, with comments on "ensign crimson" on p. 19. Knowlson concludes that the literary citations in *Happy Days* serve "to invoke the active imagination of the spectator, liberating it rather than imprisoning it with the shackles of reference" (p. 24). And Anthony S. Brennan, "Winnie's Golden Treasury: The Use of Quotation in *Happy Days*," *Arizona Quarterly* 25 (1979): 205–27.

7. *The Unnamable,* p. 376.

8. Perhaps this is the parasol taken from Lady McCann in *Watt* (p. 31); and it is mentioned in *Mercier and Camier* (p. 29).

9. But for a more pessimistic, and perhaps "standard" reading, David J. Alpaugh, "Negative Definition in Samuel Beckett's *Happy Days," Twentieth Century Literature* 11 (1966): 202–10.

10. A reading closer to the present one is that of Michael Beausang, "Myth and Tragi-Comedy in Beckett's *Happy Days," Mosaic* 5 (19): 59–77.

11. See Ethel Cornwell and Laura Barge, "The Beckett Hero," *PMLA* 92 (1977): 1006–8.

12. For Winnie as artist, Hannah Case Copeland, *Art and the Artist in the Works of Samuel Beckett* (The Hague: Mouton, 1975), especially pp. 127, 196–98.

13. See the chapters *"The Taming of the Shrew:* Induction to the Theater" (pp. 31–53) and *"A Midsummer Night's Dream:* the Celebration of Art" (pp. 79–103) in my *When the Theater Turns to Itself* (Lewisburg, Pa.: Bucknell University Press, 1981).

14. For the detailed analysis of this theme, Michael Robinson, *The Long Sonata of the Dead* (London: Hart-Davis, 1969).

15. *Proust,* pp. 28–29.

16. See Simon Trussler, *"Happy Days:* Two Productions and a Text," *Prompt* 4 (1964): 23–25; Volker Canaris, ed., *Das letzte Band. Regiebuch der Berliner Inszenierung Herausgegeben* (Frankfurt am Main: Suhrkamp, 1970).

17. A balanced assessment of the relationship between author and character can be found, I believe, in Richard Eastman, "Samuel Beckett and *Happy Days," Modern Drama* 6 (1964): 417–24. Eastman speaks of the play as being a "charged vacuum" (p. 422), as a heroic attempt (with great qualifications) on Winnie's part, as well as Beckett's, to provide minimal meaning for an empty world. *Happy Days,* in Eastman's view, is therefore more than a recapitulation of old themes. Willie's appearance at the end—the ambiguity of which Eastman will not resolve—represents a triumph of sorts, and a triumph that Winnie herself takes gracefully but also stoically.

18. "The Expelled," *Stories and Texts for Nothing,* p. 13.

19. *The Unnamable,* p. 325.

20. *How It Is,* p. 103.

21. The narrator of "The End" comments: "Most of the time I looked up at the sky, but without focussing it, for why focus it? Most of the time it was a mixture of white, blue and grey, and then at evening all the evening colours. I felt it weighing softly on my face, I rubbed my face against it, one cheek after the other, turning my head from side to side" (p. 64).

22. George Barnard in *Samuel Beckett: A New Approach* (London: J. M. Dent and Sons, Ltd., 1970) analyzes Winnie as a "pseudo-personality," as someone never achieving genuine relationships, as one deduced that she is happy. The relationship with Willie is therefore one of cruelty, not of love (pp. 120–24).

23. See Ruby Cohn, "Play and Player in the Plays of Samuel Beckett," *Yale French Studies* 29 (1962): 43–48.

24. On this topic, Edith Kern, "Beckett and the Spirit of the Commedia dell' Arte," *Modern Drama* 9 (1966): 260–67. I call attention also to "Review: *Happy Days* Directed by Samuel Beckett. Royal Court Theatre, London, June, 1979," by James Knowlson, *Journal of Beckett Studies* 5 (Autumn 1979): 141–43.

25. Wallace Stevens, *The Necessary Angel: Essays on Reality and the Imagination* (New York: Random House, 1965), p. 22.

## CHAPTER 4.   The Audience Onstage
### *Krapp's Last Tape, Play,* and *Come and Go*

1. Jules Aaron provides a good account of *Krapp's Last Tape,* in the context of earlier and later Beckett's plays, *"Krapp's Last Tape, Not I, Happy Days,* and *Act Without Words I," Educational Theatre Journal* 25 (1973): 102–4. Also see James Knowlson's edition of *Samuel Beckett: Krapp's Last Tape,* Theatre Workbook 1 (London: Brutus Books, 1980), where the bulk of the essays are concerned with production.

2. Defecation is one of Beckett's obsessions, or fetishes (in the anthropologist's sense of charging an ordinary something with larger meaning). The "act" has a long history. Otto in "What a Misfortune" *(More Pricks Than Kicks)* makes a living selling "toilet requisites" and "necessaries" (p. 117). We will also recall Murphy's wish to have his ashes flushed down a toilet—appropriately in the Abbey Theater. In *The Unnamable* there is speculation that the final breath released from the body comes through the anus (p. 342). And when we are born, our first experience with the world is a "taste of shit" *(Molloy,* p. 16).

3. Krapp may be finding himself or fleeing himself: Ethel F. Cornwell, "Samuel Beckett: The Flight from Self," *PMLA* 88 (1973): 41–51.

4. For a good account of the staging of this play, Martin Esslin, *"Not I/Krapp's Last Tape,"* *Plays and Players* 20 (1973): 39–41.

5. Bananas and booze are here Krapp's two "props" for the external world; in the words of Malone: "Laxatives? Sedatives? I forget. To turn to them for calm and merely obtain a diarrhoea, my, that would be annoying." *(Malone Dies,* p. 255).

6. *Molloy,* p. 125.

7. In "From an Abandoned Work," *First Love and Other Stories,* the phrase is "words have been my only loves, not many" (p. 48).

8. For a converse view of Krapp's lack of progress, Sandra Gilbert, "All the Dead Voices: A Study of *Krapp's Last Tape,*" *Drama Survey* 6 (1968): 244–57. SueEllen Campbell, in "Krapp's Last Tape and Critical Theory," *Comparative Drama* 12 (1978): 187–99, finds Krapp, at the end, accepting his past. The play's meaning is to be found "at the intersection of change and stability, diachrony and synchrony" (p. 198).

9. In this light, Bernard F. Dukore, *"Krapp's Last Tape* as Tragicomedy," *Modern Drama* 15 (1972): 351–54.

10. Krapp's "search," as I have called it, has also been dismissed as shallow, the play itself as portraying gloom without relief. For example, Robert Brustein, "Krapp and a Little Clap-trap," *New Republic* 143 (Feb. 22, 1960): 21–22. For a sober assessment of what I have seen as Beckett's "romantic" hero, see Robert Langbaum, "Beckett: The Self at Zero," *Georgia Review* 30 (1976): 884–905. For the genesis of the play, James Knowlson, *"Krapp's Last Tape:* the Evolution of a Play, 1958–75," *Journal of Beckett Studies* 1 (1976): 50–65.

11. *How It Is,* pp. 17, 44.

12. "The End," *Stories and Texts for Nothing,* p. 70.

13. *The Lost Ones,* pp. 13–14.

14. "Imagination Dead Imagine," *First Love and Other Stories,* p. 66.

15. It is "the monologue" *(How It Is,* p. 79): "did he think just enough to speak enough to hear not even comma a mouth an ear sly old pair glued together take away the rest put them in a jar there to end if it has an end the monologue."

16. One of the best articles on this play, an article that balances thematics and aesthetics, is Arthur Oberg's *"Krapp's Last Tape* and the Proustian Vision," *Modern Drama* 9 (1966): 333–38.

17. See Richard L. Admussen, "The Manuscripts of Beckett's *Play,*" *Modern Drama* 16 (1973): 23–27; Sgoshana Avigail, "Beckett's *Play:* the Circular Line of Existence," *Modern Drama* 18 (1975): 251–58; and Renée Riese Hubert, "Beckett's Play between Poetry and Performance," *Modern Drama* 9 (1966): 339–46.

18. Again, Edith Kern's "Beckett as Homo Ludens," *Journal of Modern Literature* 6 (1977): 47–68. In "'What's It Meant to Mean?': An Approach to Beckett's Theater," *Critical Quarterly* 18 (Summer 1976): 9–37, Robert Wilcher comments on the audience's involvement in *Play* and Beckett's challenge to us to interpret (pp. 30–32). And in "Beckett's Plays and the Photographic Vision," *Georgia Review* 34 (1980): 801–12, William J. Free finds *Play* a "model of psychoanalytic experience and its quest for a case history" (pp. 808–9). In Beckett the characters' "existence depends on nothing more than our consciousness of them on their stages" (p. 811).

19. *The Unnamable,* p. 381.

20. See *Murphy,* p. 26, and the hero's addiction to "the dark."

21. For a solid analysis, focusing on structure (all-important, perhaps overwhelmingly im-

portant in *Play*) and thematics, Bernard Dukore, "Beckett's Play, *Play*," *Educational Theatre Journal* (1965): 19–23.

22. And Rosemary Pountney, "Samuel Beckett's Interest in Form: Structural Patterning in *Play*," *Modern Drama* 19 (1976): 234–44.

23. This is their first-half account of what is for Mahood one's "historical existence" (*The Unnamable*, p. 319).

24. It reverses the normal and wasteful movement of the "dreary ooze of your being into doing," with physical existence here taking the form of a tawdry love triangle (*Murphy*, p. 37).

25. See the mixed review by Charles Marowitz, *"Play," Encore* 11 (1964): 48–52.

26. Separate, at odds, they are also united by the historical triangle, by the current interrogation—like the five people waiting for Murphy, all clearly defined individuals, yet all the same in their common "need" of the offstage Murphy (p. 202). Robert Mayberry in "A Theatre of Discord: Some Plays of Beckett, Albee, and Pinter," *Kansas Quarterly* 12 (Summer 1980): 7–16, contrasts the liberating potential of language in *Play* and the inviolable authority of the spotlight (pp. 7–8).

27. See James Knowlson, "Good Heavens [a review of the stages of *Come and Go*]," *Gambit* 7 (1976): 101–5; and Breon Mitchell, "Art in Microcosm: The Manuscript Stages in Beckett's *Come and Go*," *Modern Drama* 19 (1976): 245–60.

28. I describe my own experiences with this play in "Florida and Beckett: *Waiting for Godot* and *Come and Go*," *Vision* 1 (1979): 122–29.

29. For a detailed account of the play, "Samuel Beckett: *Come and Go*," by Horst Priessnitz, in Horst Oppel, ed., *Das Englische Drama der Gegenwart: Interpretationem* (Berlin: Schmidt, 1976).

30. Like the matron in "Yellow" (*More Pricks Than Kicks*) who "simply disappeared" (p. 168), "the woman was there one moment and gone the next. It was extraordinary."

31. The stage, like that in *The Lost Ones*, is "suitably lit from above" (p. 29).

32. Even the bench itself is minimal; when three occupy it, it disappears. We may think of the bench in "The End," *Stories and Texts for Nothing*, beside a river seemingly "flowing in the wrong direction" (p. 51); or in "First Love," *First Love and Other Shorts*, of the bench on which the lovers meet, located behind a mound of solid earth (shades of *Happy Days!*).

33. A phrase echoing throughout Beckett. Watt and Erskine, new and old butler, balance each other, for as one comes the other goes. In "Text 4," *Stories and Texts for Nothing*, the narrator mentions "he who somehow comes and goes" (p. 93).

34. At the same time, all three, because they are incomplete and not portrayed directly, seem like "puppets," Beckett's word to dismiss everyone but the central character of *Murphy* (p. 122).

35. Louis Zukofsky, *A Test of Poetry* (London: Routledge and Kegan Paul, 1952), p. vii. A most provocative article on the play is Hersh Zeifman's *"Come and Go:* A Criticule," in *Beckett Humanistic Perspectives*, ed. Morris Beja et al. (Columbus: Ohio State University Press, 1983): 137–44. Zeifman points out that since Flo is the only character holding two left hands, it is right she have the final line about rings. Zeifman traces the Shakespearean echoes: the three ladies and *Macbeth*'s three witches, and the theme of human destiny (p. 139); the flower names—Flo(wer), Ru(e), and Vi(olet)—from Ophelia's flowers in *Hamlet*, and the association of the women, therefore, with "both natural phenomenon (flowers) and death" (pp. 140–41); and the theme from *King Lear*'s line "Men must endure / Their going hence, even as their coming hither" (p. 142). Zeifman's reading is a more pessimistic one than mine: for him the play enacts how we shuffle about, coming and going, but going nowhere, until our death is sealed by destiny. He also points out the most complete text of the play to be found in *Modern Drama* 19 (1970): 257–60.

36. See also Gay McAuley, "Samuel Beckett's *Come and Go*," *Educational Theatre Journal* 18 (1966): 439–42, and Christopher Ricks, [comments on *Come and Go*], *The Listener* 78 (Aug. 3, 1967): 148.

CHAPTER 5.   Theater of Words
*All That Fall, Embers, Cascando,* and *Words and Music*

1. The book that is indispensable in providing information about the production of Beckett's work for both radio and television is Clas Zilliacus's excellent *Beckett and Broadcasting* (Abo, Finland: Abo Akademi, 1976). In "Beckett, The Camera, and Jack MacGowran," *Myth and Reality in Irish Literature,* ed. Joseph Ronsley (Waterloo, Ontario: Wilfried Laurier University Press, 1977), Alex Reid calls Beckett "an explorer" when it comes to media such as radio and television. Beckett is so versatile because he is aware of "other men's professional paraphernalia" (pp. 219–21).

2. Years ago Arthur Godfrey—the radio and television personality of the 1940s and 1950s—said that in radio the performer must remember that he or she speaks not to a theater audience (in the sense of a crowd gathered for a performance) but, more likely, to an audience of one stationed near the set, and that this fact should influence everything from the psychological mind-set of the performer to the actual delivery of the lines. In effect, in Godfrey's view radio is a one-way conversation between performer and the solitary listener, with miles separating them.

3. For a more detailed account of the structure of *All That Fall,* David J. Alpaugh, "The Symbolic Structure of Samuel Beckett's *All That Fall,*" *Modern Drama* 9 (1966): 324–32. On language in this play as at once something inherently deceptive and yet also a tool for affirming life, albeit comically, Gregory A. Schirmer, "The Irish Connection: Ambiguity of Language in *All That Fall,*" *College Literature* 8 (1981): 283–91. Schirmer makes an especially nice link between Mrs. Rooney and Christy (p. 290).

4. In "The End," *Stories and Texts for Nothing,* the various forms of transportation of *All That Fall* are greatly simplified: a single ass carries the narrator to the protective cave by the sea.

5. In *Mercier and Camier* there is a "big fat woman writhing feebly on the ground" (p. 33).

6. Called a "verminous hen" in "Enueg I," *Poems in English,* p. 24.

7. For a focus on the play's doomed "society," Francis Doherty, "Samuel Beckett's *All That Fall,* or 'All the Oppressions,'" *Recherches Anglaises et Americaines* 5 (1972): 80–84.

8. It is the classico-romantic scene from "Love and Lethe" in *More Pricks Than Kicks.*

9. The private and therefore uncreative Jacques Moran appropriately hates the Elsner sisters for their music (*Molloy* p. 105).

10. *Molloy,* p. 198.

11. See Louise O. Cleveland, "Trials in the Soundscape: The Radio Plays of Samuel Beckett," *Modern Drama* 11 (1968): 267–82.

12. *Murphy,* p. 99.

13. *Stories and Texts for Nothing,* "Text 9," p. 120.

14. *Murphy,* p. 148.

15. From "Yellow" *(More Pricks Than Kicks):* "So now his course was clear. He would arm his mind with laughter, laughter is not quite the word but it will have to serve, at every point, then he would admit the idea and blow it to pieces. Smears, as after a gorge of blackberries, of hilarity, which is not quite the word either, would be adhering to his lips as he stepped smartly, *ohne Haste aber ohne Rast,* into the torture-chamber" (p. 164).

16. *Malone Dies,* p. 225.

17. The Unnamable would use a ball (or a box) to "limit" Worm's reality (p. 3).

18. Also, W. S. Eddelman, "Design Notes for *All That Fall,*" *Drama at Calgary* 2, no. 1 (1967): 47; L.B.F., "'All That Fall' by Samuel Beckett Has a Concert Reading," *New York Times,* October 8, 1957, p. 41; and Charles Christy Hampton, "Staging *All That Fall,*" *Drama at Calgary* 2, no. 1 (1967): 37–41, and *"All That Fall;* Productions II and III; Final Report," *Drama at Calgary* 2, no. 4 (1968): 37–41. For a negative reading of the play, where "what goes up must come down and what goes down will likely stay down" (p. 90), Daniel E. Van Tassel, "Rise and Fall in Beckett's *All That Fall,*" *Éire-Ireland* 14 (Winter 1979): 83–90.

19. See David J. Alpaugh, "Embers of the Sea: Beckettian Intimations of Mortality," *Modern Drama* 16 (1973): 317–28.

20. The sea is, at best, a paradoxical symbol in Beckett. The landscape of *Mercier and Camier*

is "without seas" (p. 7); and the narrator of "The End," *Stories and Texts for Nothing*, "couldn't bear the sea" (p. 60). The Unnamable describes a "far calm sea dying" (p. 9). But Molloy's sight is "better at the seaside" (p. 75), and even for the Unnamable the water can both "kiss" and be "dead" (p. 392). Paul Lawley comments on the sea as a covering, a reenwombment (p. 27) in "*Embers:* An Interpretation," *Journal of Beckett Studies* 6 (1980): 9–36. Ada's image of the father is that of "a resignation which combines in its physical manifestation the solidity Henry craves with the impending loss of consciousness he fears" (p. 35). Lawley makes an especially telling connection between Ada and Dad, Addie and Daddie. As father, Henry has an obligation to create; his is "the obligation of the imperfect consciousness" (p. 35), "the tenacious but futile struggle of a consciousness for survival and towards identity amidst both outer and inner flux" (p. 36).

21. "A Wet Night," *More Pricks Than Kicks*, p. 60.

22. We may feel with Henry, as we do with the traveler in *How It Is*, that it is "only me" (p. 146): "only me yes alone yes with my voice yes my murmur yes when the panting stops yes all that holds yes panting yes worse and worse no answer. . . ."

23. *The Unnamable*, p. 308.

24. See Clas Zilliacus, "Samuel Beckett's *Embers*: A Matter of Fundamental Sounds," *Modern Drama* 13 (19): 216–25.

25. This is the silence "almost unbroken" so prized in the trilogy (*The Unnamable*, p. 295): "That I am not stone deaf is shown by the sounds that reach me. For though the silence here is almost unbroken, it is not completely so. I remember the first sound heard in this place, I have often heard it since. For I am obliged to assign a beginning to my residence here, if only for the sake of clarity."

26. *Watt*, p. 83.

27. *Proust*, pp. 33–34.

28. *How It Is*, p. 9.

29. See *Theater II* (*Ends and Odds*), p. 89.

30. A winter night is described in "Text 12," *Stories and Texts for Nothing*, p. 133: "It's a winter night, where I was, where I'm going, remembered, imagined, no matter, believing in me, believing it's me, no, no need, so long as the others are there, where, in the world of the others, of the long moral ways, under the sky, with a voice, no, no need . . . but . . . to make possible a deeper birth, a deeper death, or resurrection in and out of this murmur of memory and dream." See also Hersh Zeifman, "Religious Imagery in the Plays of Samuel Beckett," in Ruby Cohn's edition, *Samuel Beckett: A Collection of Criticism* (New York: McGraw-Hill, 1975), pp. 85–94.

31. In a similar fashion there are four Molloys (p. 115): "He that inhabited me, my carica-ture of same, Gaber's and the man of flesh and blood somewhere awaiting me." *Cascando, Words and Music*, and *Radio I* use music as a "character," and have scores written expressly for them. On this topic, Clas Zilliacus, *Beckett and Broadcasting*; and also Marcel Mihalovici, "Ma Collaboration avec Samuel Beckett," *Adam* (1970): 65–67, and 337–39. Other works use re-corded music, such as *Ghost Trio* (the "Largo" of Beethoven's *Fifth Piano Trio* ["The Ghost"]); and music plays a significant role in the "dialogue" of the other plays ("Now the day is over" in *Krapp's Last Tape* or the song "Death and the Maiden" in *All That Fall*).

32. *Murphy*, p. 234.

33. "The Calmative," *Stories and Texts for Nothing*, p. 45.

34. Echoes of the end of Dante's *Inferno* ("and see the stars again" in "Text 9," *Stories and Texts for Nothing*, p. 121).

35. *Molloy*, p. 112.

36. Murray Krieger, *A Window to Criticism: Shakespeare's Sonnets and Modern Poetics* (Prince-ton, N.J.: Princeton University Press, 1964).

37. *Malone Dies*, p. 280.

38. *The Unnamable*, p. 371.

39. Or the "notable face" in "Ding-Dong," *More Pricks Than Kicks*, p. 44; or "my mother's face" in *How It Is* (p. 15).

40. *Molloy*, p. 85.

41. Along with the narrator of *Fizzles*, and Opener, he tries to deny any personal involve-

ment, or that the story comes from his "head" (p. 27).

42. In the words of the Unnamable: "This story is no good, I'm beginning almost to believe it" (p. 330).

43. A word close to the Unnamable's "dayspring" of our being (p. 400).

44. Described earlier in "Text 8," *Stories and Texts for Nothing,* as "old feet [that] shuffle on." (p. 115). In "Audio-visual Beckett," *Journal of Beckett Studies* 1 (1976): 85–88, Katharine J. Worth contrasts the "distinctly austere, even monastic" music in *Words and Music* with the "flamboyance of words" (p. 87).

## CHAPTER 6.    Theater of Sight
### *Film, Eh Joe,* and *Act Without Words I* and *II*

1. *The Lost Ones,* pp. 7–8: "Consequence of this light for the searching eye. Consequences for the eye which having ceased to search is fastened to the ground or raised to the distant ceiling where can none be."

2. See Raymond Federman, *"Film," Film Quarterly* 20 (1966–67): 46–51.

3. W. R. Robinson, "The Imagination of Skin: Some Observations on the Movies as Strip-tease," *The Film Journal* 2 (1975): 44–53.

4. We will recall Molloy's "mother's room" (p. 7), or the room in which Malone "continue[s] to fit" (p. 235): "No matter, what matters is that in spite of my stories I continue to fit in this room, let us call it a room, that's all that matters, and I need not worry, I'll fit in it as long as needs be."

5. I argue this point at greater length in "A Cinema for Shakespeare," *Literature/Film Quarterly* 4 (1976): 176–86.

6. *The Unnamable,* p. 335.

7. Ruth Perlmutter offers a fine study in "Beckett's *Film* and Beckett and Film," *Journal of Modern Literature* 6 (1977): 83–94. And Sylvie D. Henning, "Samuel Beckett's *Film* and *La Dernière Bande:* Intratextual and Intertextual Doubles," *Symposium* 35 (1981): 131–53. Contrasting mediate and immediate knowledge (p. 139), she comments that neither voluntary nor involuntary memory in *Film* "can ever really unite the various doubles of the self" (p. 146).

8. See Vincent J. Murphy, "Being and Perception in Beckett's *Film,*" *Modern Drama* 18 (1975): 43–48.

9. *Murphy,* p. 246: "the absence (to abuse a nice distinction) not of *percipere* but of *percipi*" (from the Mr. Endon episode).

10. *Film,* by Samuel Beckett, with an essay "On Directing *Film,*" by Alan Schneider (New York: Grove Press, 1969), p. 88. Stanley E. Gontarski, in *"Film and Formal Integrity," Beckett Humanistic Perspectives,* ed. Morris Beja et al. (Columbus: Ohio State University Press, 1983), pp. 129–36, discusses first the film's genesis, pointing out, for example, that in earlier stages there was to be more than one word (the present "Shh"). He then finds *Film* imperfect, a "string of unsolved problems," that would be corrected in the "single room" plays, such as *Eh Joe, Ghost Trio,* and . . . *but the clouds.* . . .

11. *Murphy,* p. 181.

12. See Raymond Federman, "Samuel Beckett's *Film* on the Agony of Perceivedness," *James Joyce Quarterly* 8 (1971): 363–71.

13. And Enoch Brater, "The Thinking Eye in Beckett's *Film,*" *Modern Language Quarterly* (1975): 166–76.

14. Or at least no photograph or painting so profound as that in Erskine's room in *Watt* (p. 128): "The only other object of note in Erskine's room was a picture, hanging on the wall, from a nail. A circle, obviously described by a compass, and broken at its lowest point, occupied the middle foreground, of this picture. Was it receding?"

15. Also, Richard F. Dietrich, "Beckett's Goad: From Stage to Film," *Literature/Film Quarterly* 4 (1976): 83–89, and Charles C. Hampton, "Samuel Beckett's *Film,*" *Modern Drama* 11 (1958): 299–305.

16. There has not been much separate commentary on *Eh Joe;* but see Robert Brustein, [*Eh Joe*], *New Republic* 142 (Feb. 22, 1960): 21; *New Republic* 150 (Feb. 1, 1964): 30.

17. In "First Love," *First Love and Other Shorts*, the narrator tells us: "One day, on my return from stool, I found my room locked and my belongings in a heap before the door" (p. 14); *The Unnamable*, p. 405.

18. There is "a voice without a [visible] mouth" in "Text 13," *Stories and Texts for Nothing*, p. 137.

19. He seems to have a cell-mate in Molloy: "A fine rain was falling and I took off my hat to give my skull the benefit of it, my skull all cracked and furrowed and on fire, on fire" (p. 61).

20. *Stories and Texts for Nothing*, "Text 12," p. 134.

21. The phrase also occurs in *The Unnamable* as "Squeeze, squeeze" (p. 310).

22. *The Unnamable*, p. 326; and "And now this noise again" (*The Unnamable*, p. 308).

23. *The Unnamable*, p. 337. I cite here the extensive analysis of the mime by Cesare Segre, "The Function of Language in Samuel Beckett's *Acte sans paroles [I]*," in *Structures and Time: Narration, Poetry, Models*, trans. John Meddemmen (Chicago: University of Chicago Press, 1979), pp. 225–44.

24. *Stories, and Texts for Nothing*, "Text 6," p. 105.

25. And see Jules Aaron, "*Krapp's Last Tape, Not I, Happy Days,* and *Act Without Words I*," *Educational Theater Journal* 25 (1973): 102–4. In "Samuel Beckett's Art Criticism," *Contemporary Literature* 21 (1980): 331–48, John P. Harrington observes that the limits of language are revealed when applied to the nonverbal arts. In Beckett the power of language is that of incantation rather than signification.

26. *How It Is*, p. 125. And Stanley E. Gontarski, "Birth Astride a Grave: Samuel Beckett's *Act Without Words I*," *Journal of Beckett Studies* 1 (1976): 37–40. He finds the character an "image of rebellion" (p. 40), and though here a "superior force defeats the inferior" (p. 38), man is born in his refusal to act.

27. *Molloy*, p. 124.

## Chapter 7.   *Ends and Odds*: At the Frontier of the Stage

1. There are several excellent studies of *Not I* by Enoch Brater: "Noah, *Not I*, and Beckett's 'Incomprehensibly Sublime,'" *Comparative Drama* 8 (1974): 254–63; "The 'Absurd' Actor in the Theater of Samuel Beckett," *Educational Theatre Journal* 27 (1975): 197–207; and "The 'I' in Beckett's *Not I*," *Twentieth Century Literature* 20 (1974): 182–200. And Martin Esslin, "*Not I/ Krapp's Last Tape*," *Plays and Players* 20 (1973): 39–41. On this issue of Beckett approaching the frontiers of the stage, Larry W. Riggs observes that "esthetic awareness" requires the "suspension of belief in the conventional categories of theatrical, literary, and personal experience" (p. 689): "Esthetic Judgment and the Comedy of Culture in Molière, Flaubert, and Beckett," *French Review* 54 (1981): 680–89.

2. That organ, the mouth, has a rich heritage in Beckett. *In Malone Dies* Christ is prefigured in the mouth of Sucky Moll in the shape of a crucifixlike tooth (p. 264). A Voice without a mouth is described in "Text 13," *Stories and Texts for Nothing*, p. 137. Predictably, the Unnamable doesn't "feel" a mouth on himself (p. 382) but professes, rather, that some inner mouth tells him what to say. In "The Orphic Mouth in *Not I*," *Journal of Beckett Studies* 6 (1980): 73–80, Katherine Kelly speaks of the Mouth as "human and not inhuman" (p. 77), as one trying to silence herself through language and thereby "turning Orpheus' skill against himself" (p. 80). In this reading the Mouth joins Beckett's company of "lunatics" (p. 80). Rosemary Pountney tells of how she mastered the long part by breaking it into "sense paragraphs": "On Acting Mouth in *Not I*," *Journal of Beckett Studies* 1 (1976): 81–85.

3. This situation has echoes elsewhere in Beckett. There is a "meadow" in "The Calmative" (*Stories and Texts for Nothing*, p. 30), and one of the scholarly errors cited in *Murphy* is the confusion of Wordsworth's "lovely 'fields of sleep' with 'fields of sheep'" (p. 100). In "Enueg I," *Poems in English*, a "field on the left went up in a sudden blaze" (p. 23); the narrator of *How It Is* longs for "grass flower of the field" (p. 78).

4. The voice in "Text 4," *Stories and Texts for Nothing*, has a similar conflict with "He": "He would like it to be my fault that he has no story, of course he has no story, that's no reason for

trying to foist one on me" (p. 92). This entire story seems to have numerous parallels with *Not I*.

5. In "Being and Non-Being in Samuel Beckett's *Not I*," *Modern Drama* 19 (1976): 35–46, Hersh Zeifman describes the Mouth as one seeking salvation (p. 38), sifting through a life, as do the three characters in *Play*, to find a key. But the conclusion must be that the Mouth will never cease searching and therefore will never materialize. The circular reasoning of the play, then, is: if she isn't the one suffering, then she doesn't have to face the knowledge that there is nothing to tell. On the genesis of the play, Stanley E. Gontarski, "Beckett's Voice Crying in the Wilderness, from 'Kilcool' to *Not I*," *Publications of the Bibliographical Society of America* 74 (1980): 27–47. Gontarski observes that in the final version the themes of rejection, isolation, and the absence of love were made more universal.

6. Like the station in ruins in "Text 7," *Stories and Texts for Nothing*, p. 110, and at the "end of the line" in *Watt*, p. 244.

7. *Murphy*, p. 84.

8. *How It Is*, pp. 112–21.

9. For a short and most sensible account of the relationship between Beckett's critical premises and his art, J. Mitchell Morse, "The Ideal Core of the Onion: Samuel Beckett's Criticism," *French Review* 38 (1964): 23–29. See Walter D. Asmus, trans. Helen Watanable, "Rehearsal Notes for the German Premier of Beckett's *That Time* and *Footfalls* at the Schiller-Theater Werkstatt, Berlin (Directed by Beckett)," *Journal of Beckett Studies* 2 (1977): 82–95. Asmus points out the pun in "sequel" (seek-well). Enoch Brater calls the play an experiment in "fragmentation" and notes Shakespeare's Sonnet 73 ("That time of year thou mayest in me behold") as one of its sources (pp. 75–76) in "Fragment and Beckett's Form in *That Time* and *Footfalls*," *Journal of Beckett Studies* 2 (1977): 70–81. Antoni Libera finds Beckett concerned with ways in which "one can talk away the emptiness that is always lurking inside one" (p. 88), and sees the smile at the end as a "resigned recognition that emptiness will ultimately overwhelm the character, his consent and capitulation to it" (p. 89). "Structure and Pattern in *That Time*," as adapted by John Pilling from the translation of Aniela Korzeniowska, *Journal of Beckett Studies* 6 (1980): 81–89. In " 'Making Yourself All Up Again': The Composition of Samuel Beckett's *That Time*," *Modern Drama* 23 (1980): 112–20, Stanley E. Gontarski detects a movement from "hostility" among the three fragments to a "harmonious relationship" (p. 117). In *The Irish Drama of Europe from Yeats to Beckett* (Atlantic Highlands, N.J.: Humanities Press, 1978), Katharine Worth describes the end as "a triumphant 'weaving' of a life, an achievement" (p. 264). I note her "Review Article: Beckett's Fine Shades [:] *Play, That Time*, and *Footfalls*," *Journal of Beckett Studies* 1 (1976): 75–88.

10. In *Murphy* the park rangers similarly cry, "*All out. All out. All out.*" (p. 281).

11. *The Unnamable*, p. 355.

12. There is a May/Maia mentioned in *Malone Dies* (p. 234), and Watt speaks of a "third person" named Anne/Mary (p. 51) and then of "May's spinster daughter Ann" (p. 101).

13. *Mercier and Camier*, p. 104.

14. *Watt*, p. 37.

15. "Fizzle 8," p. 60.

16. *The Unnamable*, p. 296. And Enoch Brater, "A Footnote to *Footfalls:* Footsteps of Infinity on Beckett's Narrow Space," *Comparative Drama* 12 (Spring 1978): 35–41. He finds the play challenging the audience's power of perception, and comments on the paradox of "its own completion and continuity," "its own uneasy presentness" (p. 40). Martin Esslin speaks of the play in "A Theatre of Stasis—Beckett's Late Plays," in *Meditations: Essays on Brecht, Beckett, and the Media* (Baton Rouge: Louisiana State University Press, 1980), pp. 117–25, including remarks on *Not I* and *That Time*, both "monodramas" (p. 119).

17. In effect, May reverses the situation in "The Expelled," *Stories and Texts for Nothing*, which opens with the narrator being sent out of the house (p. 9).

18. Like the Unnamable she wishes everything to be heard: "And at the same time I am obliged to speak. I shall never be silent. Never" (p. 291).

19. There is a Mrs. Winter in "Dante and the Lobster," *More Pricks Than Kicks*, p. 20; or, more accurately, there is a suggestive confusion among the house of his aunt, the aunt's name,

and the season in which Belacqua visited the old woman.

20. Aesthetically, we are moving into what the Unnamable would call a "safe place"—with "no way in, no way out." Though he adds that this place is "not like Eden" (p. 348).

21. *Murphy*, p. 91.

22. There is a parallel in *Malone Dies:* "just wide enough to contain you" (p. 241); and Knott makes a complete circle of his pallet (the boundaries being the head and feet) once a year (p. 207).

23. In *Malone Dies* (p. 246): "Quick quick my possessions."

24. *The Unnamable*, pp. 299, 310, 376.

25. *Watt*, p. 146.

26. Perhaps a look of "self-immersed indifference to the contingencies of the contingent world" (*Murphy*, p. 168).

27. "Sanies I" *(Poem in English)*, p. 30.

28. Like Fellini, Beckett is fascinated with beggars and with the physically impaired. The character in "The End," *Stories and Texts for Nothing*, begs at some "sunny corner" (p. 63); and there is a blind paralytic at the corner of Fleet Street in "Ding-Dong," *More Pricks Than Kicks*, p. 39, or later a "mysterious pedlar" (p. 44). This physical impairment affects the narrator himself in "Text 8," *Stories and Texts for Nothing:* "But that other who is me, blind and deaf and mute, because of whom I'm here, in this black silence, helpless to move or accept this voice as mine . . ." (p. 113). The ultimate example of afflictions, excluding the Unnamable, must be Sam in *Watt*: paralyzed "waist up," "knees down" (p. 107).

29. See Steven J. Rosen, *Beckett and the Pessimistic Tradition* (New Brunswick, N.J.: Rutgers University Press, 1977).

30. In his concern about the possibility of a straight line of movement leading him help-lessly around the world, he mocks the intellectual geography championed by the Unnamable: "beyond the equator you would start turning inwards again" (p. 317).

31. Molloy could settle for a "dim lamp" (p. 108); he mentions it again (p. 144).

32. Camier is said to be a "Private Investigator" with a "Soul of Discretion" (p. 54), though we never see him overtly practice his trade; and Gaber has the examiner's official notebook in *Malone Dies*.

33. There is also speculation in *Mercier and Camier* about throwing oneself "out of the window" (p. 28; repeated p. 46).

34. The bird is referred to as a "vile parrot" in "Text 11," *Stories and Texts for Nothing*, p. 108.

35. See "Fizzle 6" (p. 44) and "Fizzle 7" (p. 51).

36. *Malone Dies*, p. 223, p. 184.

37. "The Expelled," *Stories and Texts for Nothing*, p. 22.

38. Like the song thrush in *Molloy*, theirs seems to be "sadly dying" (p. 93).

39. Martin Esslin offers some perceptive comments on this recent piece in "Beckett's Rough for Radio," *Journal of Modern Literature* 6 (1977): 95–103. Or see Esslin's "Samuel Beckett and the Art of Broadcasting" in *Meditations*, pp. 125–54.

40. I might note here that some years ago Sheldon Isenberg, my colleague in the Religion Department, and I gave a graduate course on "Beckett and Ritualism." To read *Waiting for Godot* in the context, say, of Eliade's works is stimulating. I suspect the anthropological ap-proach, especially with the emphasis on ritualism, would be a profitable one for understand-ing these latest plays, especially the still puzzling *Radio II*. I also call attention to the comments on motifs in Beckett by Thomas J. Taylor, "That Again: A Motif Approach to the Beckett Canon," *Journal of Beckett Studies* 6 (1980): 107–10.

41. See John Calder, *"Breath," Cahiers de la Compagnie Madeleine Renaud-Jean Louis Barrault* 93 (1976): 5–7.

42. A word first mentioned in *Murphy* (p. 23).

43. *The Unnamable*, p. 362. In "Theatre Diary," *Journal of Beckett Studies* 4 (Spring 1979), Ronald Hayman observes that the best possible perspective on current London theater is "Beckettian" (p. 66), that we can judge what the theater does or fails to do—presently he finds it "without an avant-garde"—by using Beckett's experiments as a yardstick.

## CHAPTER 8.    Beckett's Black Holes: Some Further Thoughts

1. I have discussed the Shakespearean parallel to the larger reality in "The Celebration of Art: *A Midsummer Night's Dream*," *When the Theater Turns to Itself: The Aesthetic Metaphor in Shakespeare* (Lewisburg, Pa.: Bucknell University Press, 1981), pp. 79–103.

2. Alfred Harbage uses this phrase in *As They Like It: A Study of Shakespeare's Moral Artistry* (New York: Harper, 1961), p. 40.

3. See James Knowlson and John Pilling, *Frescoes of the Skull: The Later Prose and Drama of Samuel Beckett* (New York: Grove Press, 1980), p. 219.

4. Cited by Knowlson from Reading University Library Ms 1639, *Frescoes of the Skull*, p. 219.

5. T. S. Eliot, "Hamlet and His Problems," *Selected Essays: 1917–1932* (New York: Harcourt, Brace and Company, 1932), p. 125.

6. Ruby Cohn, *Just Play: Beckett's Theater* (Princeton, N.J.: Princeton University Press, 1980), pp. 230–79.

7. Hugh Kenner uses this phrase in *Samuel Beckett: A Critical Study* (Berkeley and Los Angeles: University of California Press, 1968), p. 133.

8. Bernard Beckerman, "End-signs in Drama," lecture given March 6, 1981, fifth annual Comparative Drama Conference, University of Florida.

9. Consider Marvin Rosenberg's account of the various ways this final scene has been played, *The Masks of King Lear* (Berkeley and Los Angeles: University of California Press, 1972), pp. 318–21; and Terence Hawkes's argument that Cordelia "speaks" in this scene, "That Shakespeherean Rag," in *Shakespeare's "More Than Words Can Witness": Essays on Visual and Nonverbal Enactment in the Plays*, ed. Sidney Homan (Lewisburg, Pa.: Bucknell University Press, 1980), pp. 69–70.

10. "Three Dialogues with George Duthuit," *Samuel Beckett: A Collection of Critical Essays*, ed. Martin Esslin (Englewood Cliffs, N.J.: Prentice-Hall, 1965), p. 17.

11. Barry Adams offers a good account of this controversy in "The Audiences of *The Spanish Tragedy*," *Journal of English and Germanic Philology* 68 (1969): 221–36.

12. Knowlson, *Frescoes of the Skull*, p. 205.

13. At the end of Genet's *The Balcony* Irma says to the audience onstage and—surely—offstage as well: "I'm going to prepare my costumes and studios for tomorrow. . . . You must now go home, where everything—you can be quite sure—will be even falser than here. . . . you must go now. You'll leave by the right, through the alley . . ." (New York: Grove Press, 1958).

14. Cohn, *Just Play*, especially pp. 189–279.

15. Knowlson, *Frescoes of the Skull*, p. 283.

16. See the distinction between art as mirror and window in Murray Krieger, *A Window to Criticism: Shakespeare's Sonnets and Modern Poetics* (Princeton, N.J.: Princeton University Press, 1964).

17. See "Three Dialogues," ed. Esslin, p. 17.

18. Lawrence Harvey, *Samuel Beckett: Poet and Critic* (Princeton, N.J.: Princeton University Press, 1970), p. 435.

19. This notion of the theater as a dream is the concern of two fine studies: Jackson Cope, *The Theater and the Dream: From Metaphor to Form in Renaissance Drama* (Baltimore, Md.: Johns Hopkins University Press, 1973); and Marjorie Garber, *Dream in Shakespeare: From Metaphor to Metamorphosis* (New Haven, Conn.: Yale University Press, 1974).

20. There is a discussion by Barbara Reich Gluck on the difference between the public Joyce and the private Beckett in *Beckett and Joyce: Friendship and Fiction* (Lewisburg, Pa.: Bucknell University Press, 1973), pp. 105–22. In "Samuel Beckett: The Dialectics of Hope and Despair," *College Literature* 8 (1981): 227–48, Michael Mundhenk finds Beckett the private artist, in contrast, say, to the "public" Joyce, and thereby concerned with alienation from artistic means, from the artistic product, from the self, and from one's fellowman. Yet in this literature of self-consciousness, pervaded by a self-critical nature, Beckett goes on (p. 239).

21. Beckett, *Proust*, p. 49.

22. *The Variorum Edition of the Poems of W. B. Yeats*, ed. Peter Allt and Russell K. Alspach (New York: The Macmillan Company, 1957). For more on Beckett and Yeats I refer to essays

in Kathleen McGrory and John Unterecker, eds., *Yeats, Joyce, and Beckett: New Light on Three Modern Irish Writers* (Lewisburg, Pa.: Bucknell University Press, 1976).

23. The point made by Marshall McLuhan, "Roles, Masks, and Performances," *New Literary History* 2 (1971): 221. I have also found particularly touching the comments in "Extracts from an Unscripted Interview with Billie Whitelaw," by James Knowlson, *Journal of Beckett Studies* 3 (1978): 85–90. Whitelaw sees her friend and director as a positive man.

## APPENDIX A.    Music, Mathematics, and the Rhythms of Beckett's Theaters *Rockaby, Ohio Impromptu,* and *A Piece of Monologue*

1. Ruby Cohn, *Just Play: Beckett's Theater* (Princeton, N.J.: Princeton University Press, 1980), p. 263.

2. George Steiner, *Language and Silence: Essays on Language, Literature, and the Inhuman* (New York: Atheneum, 1970), see especially pp. 13–14, 24–25, 30.

3. Ruby Cohn, *Just Play*, p. 243. Also, Enoch Brater, "Light, Sound, Movement, and Action in Beckett's *Rockaby,*" *Modern Drama* 25 (1982): 342–48. Brater finds that the "voice and protagonist finally become one" (343), that here "a poem comes to (stage) life" (p. 345). In this "steady accumulation of expository facts" (p. 346), the drama is born out of the present conflict between what we hear and see, between the recorded and then the live voice. The woman "becomes the image created by her own inner voice," and in this work where "technology wears a human face," we have an image if not of tragedy, then at least "of dramatic poetry" (p. 348).

4. Quoted by Lawrence Graver and Raymond Federman in *Samuel Beckett: The Critical Heritage* (London, Henley, and Boston: Routledge and Kegan Paul, 1979), p. 12. I am indebted to the article by Pierre Astier, "Beckett's *Ohio Impromptu:* A View from the Isle of Swans," *Modern Drama* 25 (1982): 331–41. After talking about the play's ten-month composition, Astier quotes a monologue by Beckett, listed below, in which he expresses anxiety about going to the Ohio. Astier then suggests that Beckett translated this self-dialogue into the present play. Particularly illuminating are his comments about how the play itself "provided through its very achievement the relief for which Beckett had been longing" (p. 335), and his tracing the place names to their origins in Paris, particularly the original and now considerably changed Isle of Swans. Astier contrasts the city's left bank (the Old World) and its right bank, (the New World with its Avenue du Président Kennedy), and weaves this contrast into Beckett's own movement from Europe to America for the Festival. *Ohio Impromptu* treats, at length, the issues of relief and freedom; Astier further makes an especially telling link between this late play and Beckett's *Eleutheria.*

In "Qu'est-ce qui arrive? Some Structural Comparisons of Beckett's Plays and Noh," *Beckett Humanistic Perspectives,* ed. Morris Beja et al. (Columbus: Ohio State University Press, 1983), pp. 99–106, Yasunari Takahashi observes that in the play's own "profounds of mind" the "'someone'" coming out of that "'sacred country'" is "'the other' and one's deepest self; that 'country' is at once 'unknown' and half-remembered" (p. 106). This same collection also reprints "*Ohio Impromptu* Holograph, Typescript, and Production Script," pp. 189–207. In the "Verso of Leaf 1" (pp. 191–92) we have the monologue by Beckett, brilliantly analyzed by Astier above, where the playwright asks, "What am I to say?"; is told, "Do not overstay your leave . . . if you do not wish it to be extended"; and, when asked to be himself both "before" and "after," asks, "Not during?"

5. The last line in Virginia Woolf's *To the Lighthouse* (New York: Harcourt Brace and World, 1955) is "I have had my vision." For Kristin Morrison in "The Rip Word in *A Piece of Monologue,*" *Modern Drama* 25 (1982): 349–54, the ripword, the word the speaker longs for and that lays bare the play, is *begone*. After a survey of the play's "plot," she connects the lamp with that mentioned in *Othello:* "If I quench thee, thou flaming minister" (5.2.8). The Speaker here slowly entertains the thought that the death preoccupying him may be his own and thus his "attempts at distraction do not work" (p. 352). Our only real subject is death, and "Words, speech, expression are thus a kind of parturition" (p. 353). In *The Dark Dove: The Sacred and*

*Secular in Modern Literature* (Seattle: University of Washington Press, 1975), Eugene Webb comments that for Nietzsche, Ibsen, Wallace Stevens, and Beckett, reality (the outside) threatens to destroy the only self with which they seem able or willing to identify, "the self that is a tissue of illusions" (p. 74). Speaking of *A Piece of Monologue* in "Beckett's Theater Resonance" in *Beckett Humanistic Perspectives*, cited above, Ruby Cohn finds that "what began as narration appears here to be performed" (p. 12), that we witness "Beckett's view of life *theatrically imaged*" (p. 13).

6. For example, Michael Wood's "Comedy of Ignorance," *New York Review* 28 (April 30, 1981): 49–52.

## APPENDIX B.    *. . . but the clouds . . .*

1. The text for Yeats is *The Variorum Edition of the Poems of W. B. Yeats*, ed. Peter Allt and Russell K. Alspach (New York: The Macmillan Company, 1957).

2. There is, of course, an extensive literature on Yeats's "The Tower." I found particularly useful: Richard Ellmann, "The Art of Yeats: Affirmative Capability," *Kenyon Review* 15 (1953): 364–66; James H. O'Brien, "Yeats' Dark Night of Self and *The Tower*," *Bucknell Review* 15 (1967): 10–25; Donald A. Stauffer, "The Reading of a Lyric Poem," *Kenyon Review* 11 (1949): 434–35; Sarah Youngblood, "A Reading of 'The Tower,'" *Twentieth Century Literature* 5 (1959): 74–84; Marjorie Perloff, "'The Tradition of Myself': The Autobiographical Mode of Yeats," *Journal of Modern Literature* 4 (1975): 560–73; and Daniel Hoffman, *Barbarous Knowledge: Myth in the Poetry of Yeats, Graves, and Muir* (New York: Oxford University Press, 1967), pp. 62–83. Both Ellmann and Hoffmann suggest the influence of Berkeley on Yeats. I am also indebted here to my colleague Brandon Kershner, whose reading of the last stanza is more divided than my own. He sees the poem as working dialectically, alternately affirming and rejecting the two roles: "(1) imagination, the subjective, the poetic, the abstract, the Platonic (lunar); and (2) pride, activity, arrogance, the daily, concrete (solar), the objective." At the end Yeats is "attempting to rise above the dichotomy."

3. *Proust,* p. 16.

4. *. . . but the clouds . . .* was first shown on BBC's "The Living Arts" along with *Not I* and *Ghost Trio* in a program that Beckett himself titled "Shades." There was a conscious degree of distortion in the sound track, which contrasted with the clear, silent, memory image. The production itself received some harsh reviews. Richard North in *The Listener* (April 21, 1977) said both television plays "brought on the yawns," and Dennis Porter in *The Sunday Times* (April 24, 1977) asked: "Is this the art which is the response to the despair and pity of our age, or is it made of a kind of deliberate futility which helped such desecrations of the spirit, such filth of ideologues come into being?" Obviously, I am miles apart from these readings. But see Beryl S. Fletcher, John Fletcher, et al., *A Student's Guide to the Plays of Samuel Beckett* (London and Boston: Faber and Faber, 1978), p. 210. In "'The Lively Arts': Three Plays by Samuel Beckett on BBC2, 17 April 1977," *Journal of Beckett Studies* 2 (1977): 117–22, John Calder observes that . . . *but the clouds* . . . is close to *That Time*, that M is "immersed in guilt towards a missed opportunity . . . a regretted course of action" (p. 120).

Also see Martha Fehsenfeld, "Beckett's Late Work: An Appraisal," *Modern Drama* 25 (1982): 355–62. Particularly intriguing are her comments on Beckett's latest work, *Quad*, a mime for four players, involving colored lights, the sounds of footsteps, percussion instruments, and no text. *Quad* was composed for the Stuttgart Preparatory Ballet School and produced there in June 1981. After suggesting echoes in other works—*Footfalls, Ghost Trio, . . . but the clouds . . .*, and the mimes—she offers a detailed report on just what *Quad* involves, along with some wonderful comments by Beckett's cameraman, Jim Lewis. The players are, properly, mimes, not dancers, wearing floor-length gowns, and cowls, holding themselves in the same position Billie Whitelaw used in *Footfalls*, their bodies bent forward as if resisting a cold wind. The instruments themselves are outside the square, with each player occupying one of the corners, and moving from darkness into the light, and then to a dark area in the center that all seem to want to avoid. The players move in relation to each other and yet seem unaware of the others. For each the "only cessation perhaps lurks in the black center that is to be avoided at any cost, even at the risk of perpetual movement" (p. 361). Near the end of the fascinating account Fehsenfeld observes that Beckett increasingly seems to be exploring the relation between literature and the visual arts, that he is distilling (not reducing) his work "to shadows of what *is* and is *to come*" in "a continuing beginning towards transparency" (p. 361).

# Index

(Note: a single list of Beckett's works is provided on pages 22–28, note 63.)